The Cambridge Companion to Eighteenth-Century Poetry analyzes major premises, preoccupations, and practices of English poets writing from 1700 to the 1790s. These specially commissioned essays avoid familiar categories and single-author approaches to look at the century afresh. Chapters consider such large poetic themes as nature, the city, political passions, the relation of death to desire and dreams, appeals to an imagined future, and the meanings of "sensibility." Other chapters explore historical developments such as the connection between poetic couplets and conversation, the conditions of publication, changing theories of poetry and imagination, growing numbers of women poets and readers, the rise of a self-consciously national tradition, and the place of lyric poetry in thought and practice. The essays are well supported by supplementary material including a chronology of the period and detailed guides to further reading. Altogether the volume provides an invaluable resource for scholars and students.

THE CAMBRIDGE COMPANION TO
EIGHTEENTH-CENTURY POETRY

CAMBRIDGE COMPANIONS TO LITERATURE

CAMBRIDGE COMPANIONS TO CULTURE

THE CAMBRIDGE
COMPANION TO
EIGHTEENTH-
CENTURY POETRY

EDITED BY
JOHN SITTER
Emory University

CAMBRIDGE
UNIVERSITY PRESS

PUBLISHED BY THE PRESS SYNDICATE OF THE UNIVERSITY OF CAMBRIDGE
The Pitt Building, Trumpington Street, Cambridge, United Kingdom

CAMBRIDGE UNIVERSITY PRESS
The Edinburgh Building, Cambridge CB2 2RU, UK
40 West 20th Street, New York, NY 10011-4211, USA
10 Stamford Road, Oakleigh, VIC 3166, Australia
Ruiz de Alarcón 13, 28014 Madrid, Spain
Dock House, The Waterfront, Cape Town 8001, South Africa

http://www.cambridge.org

First published 2001

Printed in the United Kingdom at the University Press, Cambridge

Typeface Adobe Sabon 10/13pt   *System* QuarkXpress®   [SE]

A catalogue record for this book is available from the British Library

Library of Congress Cataloguing in Publication data

The Cambridge companion to eighteenth-century poetry / edited by John Sitter.
p.   cm. – (Cambridge companions to literature)
Includes bibliographical references and index.
ISBN 0 521 65090 9 (hardback)   ISBN 0 521 65885 3 (paperback)
1. English poetry – 18th century – History and criticism.   I. Sitter, John E.   II. Series.

PR551.C27   2001
821'.509 – dc21   00-063059

ISBN 0 521 65090 9 hardback
ISBN 0 521 65885 3 paperback

CONTENTS

CONTENTS

ILLUSTRATIONS

NOTES ON CONTRIBUTORS

BARBARA M. BENEDICT is Professor and Chair of English at Trinity College, Hartford, Connecticut. As well as essays on eighteenth-century popular culture, literature, Jane Austen, and book history, she has published *Framing Feeling: Sentiment and Style in English Prose Fiction, 1745–1800* (1994) and *Making the Modern Reader: Cultural Mediation in Early Modern Literary Anthologies* (1996). Her book *Curiosity: a Cultural History of Early Modern Inquiry* will be published in 2001.

RALPH COHEN is William R. Kenan, Jr., Professor of English at the University of Virginia. He is the author of *The Unfolding of "The Seasons"* (1970), the editor of numerous books on eighteenth-century literature, criticism, and literary theory, and the founder and editor of *New Literary History*.

DAVID FAIRER is Professor of Eighteenth-Century English Literature at the University of Leeds. He is the author of *Pope's Imagination* (1984), *The Poetry of Alexander Pope* (1989), the editor of *Pope: New Contexts* (1990) and *The Correspondence of Thomas Warton* (1995), and the co-editor of *Eighteenth-Century Poetry: an Annotated Anthology* (1999).

TIM FULFORD is a Professor of English at Nottingham Trent University. His books include *Coleridge's Figurative Language* (1991), *Landscape, Liberty and Authority* (1996), and *Romanticism and Masculinity* (1999). With Peter J. Kitson, he co-edited *Romanticism and Colonialism* (1998).

CHRISTINE GERRARD is a Fellow and Tutor in English at Lady Margaret Hall, Oxford. She is the author of *The Patriot Opposition to Walpole: Politics, Poetry, and National Myth, 1725–1742* (1994) and co-editor of *Eighteenth-Century Poetry: Annotated Anthology* (1999).

BREAN S. HAMMOND is Professor of English at the University of Nottingham. He is the author of several books and articles on eighteenth-century subjects, including *Gulliver's Travels* (1988) and, most recently, *Professional Imaginative Writing in England, 1670–1740* (1997).

J. PAUL HUNTER is Professor of English and Humanities and Director of the Franke Institute for the Humanities at the University of Chicago. He has written books on Defoe, *The Reluctant Pilgrim* (1966), on Fielding, *Occasional Form* (1975), and *Before Novels: the Cultural Contexts of Eighteenth-Century English Fiction* (1990). He is working on a cultural history of the Anglophone couplet.

CLAUDIA THOMAS KAIROFF is Professor of English and Associate Dean of the College at Wake Forest University. She is the author of *Alexander Pope and His Eighteenth-Century Women Readers* (1994) and co-editor, with Catherine Ingrassia, of *"More Solid Learning": New Perspectives on Alexander Pope's "Dunciad"* (2000).

JENNIFER KEITH is an Assistant Professor at the University of North Carolina at Greensboro. Her publications include essays on Finch, Pope, Thomson, and Blake. She is completing a book on representation and the feminine in British poetry from Katherine Philips to Charlotte Smith.

DAVID B. MORRIS is a writer and lives in New Mexico. He is the author of *The Religious Sublime* (1972), *Alexander Pope: the Genius of Sense* (1984), *The Culture of Pain* (1991), *Earth Warrior* (1995), and *Illness and Culture in the Postmodern Age* (1999). He serves as Adjunct Professor of Medicine at the University of New Mexico.

JOHN SITTER, Charles Howard Candler Professor of English at Emory University in Atlanta, is the author of *The Poetry of Pope's "Dunciad"* (1971), *Literary Loneliness in Mid-Eighteenth-Century England* (1982), *Arguments of Augustan Wit* (1991) and editor of *The Eighteenth-Century Poets*, two volumes of the *Dictionary of Literary Biography*.

PATRICIA MEYER SPACKS is Edgar F. Shannon Professor of English at the University of Virginia. Her books include *The Poetry of Vision* (1967), *The Female Imagination* (1975), *Imagining a Self* (1976), *The Adolescent Idea* (1981), *Gossip* (1985), *Desire and Truth: Functions of Plot in Eighteenth-Century Novels* (1990), and *Boredom: the Literary History of a State of Mind* (1995).

1700   Death of John Dryden; Sir Richard Blackmore, *A Satire upon Wit*; William Congreve, *The Way of the World*; John Dryden, *Fables Ancient and Modern*; John Pomfret, "The Choice"

1701   Act of Settlement establishes Hanoverian succession; War of Spanish Succession begins; John Dennis, *The Advancement and Reformation of Modern Poetry*; John Philips, *The Splendid Shilling*

1702   Death of William III (8 March); Coronation of Queen Anne (23 April); Edward Bysshe, *The Art of English Poetry*

1703   Daniel Defoe pilloried and jailed for political pamphleteering; Mary Chudleigh, *Poems on Several Occasions*

1704   Marlborough defeats French at Battle of Blenheim; Dennis, *The Grounds of Criticism in Poetry*; Sir Isaac Newton, *Optics*; Jonathan Swift, *Tale of a Tub*, *Battel of the Books*

1705   Joseph Addison, *The Campaign*; Bernard Mandeville, *The Grumbling Hive, or Knaves Turned Honest*

1706   Sarah Fye Egerton, *Poems on Several Occasions*; Isaac Watts, *Horae Lyricae*

1707   Act of Union unites Scotland and England into Great Britain; Sir Charles Sedley, *The Poetical Works*

1708   William King, *The Art of Cookery*; John Philips, *Cyder*

1709   The Copyright Act; Act for the Encouragement of Learning; George Berkeley, *New Theory of Vision*; Anne Finch, Countess of Winchilsea, "The Spleen"; Alexander Pope, *Pastorals*; Matthew Prior, *Poems on Several Occasions*; Swift, "Baucis and Philemon"; Richard Steele, *The Tatler* begins (published until 1711)

1710   New Tory ministry under Robert Harley (later Earl of Oxford) and Henry St John (later Viscount Bolingbroke) makes peace abroad despite internal rivalries – lasts until death of Queen Anne in August 1714; John Dunton, *Athenianism, or the New Projects*; Swift, "A Description of a City Shower"

1711   Joseph Addison and Richard Steele, *The Spectator* begins (runs until 1712 and resumes for eighty numbers in 1714); Pope, *An Essay on Criticism*; Shaftesbury, *Characteristicks*; Swift, *Miscellanies in Prose and Verse*

1712   Blackmore, *Creation*; John Ozell, translation of Boileau, *Works*; Pope, *The Rape of the Lock* (two-canto version), *Messiah*

1713   Treaty of Utrecht ends War of Spanish Succession; Swift made dean of St. Patrick's Cathedral, Dublin; Addison, *Cato*; Berkeley, *Three Dialogues of Hylas and Philonous*; Finch, *Miscellany Poems on Several Occasions*; John Gay, *Rural Sports*; Thomas Parnell, *An Essay on the Different Styles of Poetry*; Pope, *Windsor-Forest*

1714   Death of Queen Anne (1 August); Coronation of George I (20 October); Scriblerus Club meets regularly in Dr. Arbuthnot's quarters at St. James Palace; Gay, *The Fan*, *The Shepherd's Week*; Mandeville, *The Fable of the Bees*; Pope, *The Rape of the Lock* (five-canto expansion); Nicholas Rowe, *The Tragedy of Jane Shore*

1715   Jacobite Rebellion in support of "James III" (the Old Pretender); Nicholas Rowe becomes Poet Laureate; Sir Samuel Garth, *Claremont*; John Hughes's translation of Spenser, *The Works*; Pope's translation of *The Iliad of Homer*

1716   Gay, *Trivia, or the Art of Walking the Streets of London*; Lady Mary Wortley Montagu, *Town Eclogues*, *Court Poems*

1717   Giles Jacob, *The Rape of the Smock*; Parnell's translation of *Homer's Battle of the Frogs and Mice*; Pope, *The Works* (includes *Eloisa to Abelard*)

1718   Laurence Eusden becomes Poet Laureate; Susanna Centlivre, *A Bold Stroke for a Wife*; Charles Gildon, *Complete Art of Poetry*; Matthew Prior, *Poems on Several Occasions*

1719   Daniel Defoe, *Robinson Crusoe*

1720   "South Sea Bubble" collapses; Gay, *Poems on Several Occasions*

1721   Robert Walpole comes to power

1722   Defoe, *Moll Flanders*; Parnell, *Poems on Several Occasions*

1723   Jane Barker, *A Patchwork Screen for the Ladies*

1724   Swift publishes *Drapier's Letters*

1725   Francis Hutcheson, *An Inquiry into the Original of our Ideas of Beauty and Virtue*; Pope's translation of *The Odyssey of Homer* and edition of *The Works of Shakespeare*; Young, *The Universal Passion*

1726   John Dyer, "Grongar Hill"; Swift, *Gulliver's Travels*, *Cadenus and Vanessa*; James Thomson, *Winter*

1727   Death of George I (11 June); Coronation of George II (11 October); Gay, *Fables* (first series); Pope, *Peri Bathous, or Of the Art of Sinking* in *Poetry*; Swift, Pope, et al., *Miscellanies in Prose and Verse*; Thomson, *A Poem Sacred to the Memory of Sir Isaac Newton*

1728 Gay, *The Beggar's Opera*; William Law, *A Serious Call to a Devout and Holy Life*; Pope, *The Dunciad* (in three books); Richard Savage, *The Bastard*

1729 Pope, *The Dunciad Variorum*; Swift, *A Modest Proposal*; Thomson, *Britannia*

1730 Colley Cibber becomes Poet Laureate; Stephen Duck, *Poems on Several Subjects*; Thomson, *The Seasons*

1731 *Gentleman's Magazine* begins (runs until 1914); George Lillo, *The London Merchant*; Pope, *An Epistle to Burlington*

1732 Richard Bentley's edition of Milton's *Paradise Lost*; George Granville, Lord Landsdowne, *Genuine Works in Verse and Prose*; William Hogarth, *A Harlot's Progress*; William King, *The Toast*; Swift, "The Lady's Dressing Room"

1733 Bolingbroke, *Dissertation Upon Parties*; Hogarth, *A Rake's Progress*; Lady Mary Wortley Montagu and Lord Hervey, *Verses Addressed to the Imitator of Horace*; Pope, *An Essay on Man, An Epistle to Bathurst*; Swift, *On Poetry: A Rhapsody*

1734 Pope, *An Epistle to Cobham*

1735 Pope, *An Epistle to Dr. Arbuthnot, An Epistle to a Lady, The Works*; Thomson, *Liberty*

1736 Swift, "The Legion Club"

1737 Stage Licensing Act; Elizabeth Cooper, *The Muses Library: Or, A Series of English Poetry*; William Shenstone, *Poems upon Various Occasions*; John and Charles Wesley, *A Collection of Psalms and Hymns*

1738 Bolingbroke, *Patriot King*; Samuel Johnson, *London*

1739 David Hume, *A Treatise of Human Nature*; Swift, *Verses on the Death of Dr. Swift*

1740 War of Austrian Succession; Dyer, *The Ruins of Rome*; Samuel Richardson, *Pamela*; Horace Walpole, *An Epistle from Florence*

1741 Henry Fielding, *Shamela*; Handel, *Messiah*; Hume, *Essays, Moral and Political*

1742 Fall of Walpole; William Collins, *Persian Eclogues*; Fielding, *Joseph Andrews*; Pope, *The New Dunciad* (Book IV); Edward Young, *The Complaint, or Night Thoughts on Life, Death, and Immortality* (to 1745)

1743 Robert Blair, *The Grave*; Pope, *The Dunciad in Four Books*

1744 Death of Alexander Pope; Formal declaration of war with France; Mark Akenside, *The Pleasures of Imagination*; Sarah Fielding, *The*

1784   Death of Samuel Johnson; Charlotte Smith, *Elegiac Sonnets*

1785   Cowper, *The Task*; Thomas Reid, *Essays on the Intellectual Powers of Man*

1786   Robert Burns, *Poems, Chiefly in the Scottish Dialect*

1787   Mary Wollstonecraft, *Thoughts on the Education of Daughters*

1789   French Revolution begins; William Blake, *Songs of Innocence*

1790   Burke, *Reflections on the Revolution in France*

1791   James Boswell, *Life of Samuel Johnson*; Thomas Paine, *The Rights of Man*

1792   Wollstonecraft, *A Vindication of the Rights of Woman*

1794   Blake, *Songs of Innocence and Experience*; William Godwin, *Caleb Williams*

1798   Godwin, *Enquiry concerning Political Justice*; Thomas Malthus, *An Essay on the Principle of Population*; William Wordsworth and Samuel Taylor Coleridge, *Lyrical Ballads*

I

JOHN SITTER

Introduction: the future of eighteenth-century poetry

Because accounts of eighteenth-century English poetry so commonly stress either its supposed preoccupation with the past or its immersion in the topical present, it may help to begin by speaking of its future. Many of the period's poets did write with a "neo-classical" eye on the classical past, especially Latin models, as indeed did most Renaissance writers. Similarly, many seem to have considered the pressure of present political events one of poetry's larger concerns, as several of the chapters in this book testify, and thus wrote often on timely subjects. But perhaps more distinctive of the eighteenth century poets than their sense of the past and appetite for news – traits which we partly share – is their tendency to look toward the future.

In our time the future has long since absconded from poetry, moving into the precincts of science fiction, and even there frequently shrouded in dystopian dread. It is difficult to imagine serious poets today invoking posterity, making predictions, or addressing a citizenry of the future. Precisely because we seem to have lost the future as a dimension of meaning in so much of our discourse and perhaps in poetry especially, the temporal expansiveness of eighteenth-century poetry can be alien and salutary. Salutary not because it is always optimistic about the future – many of its most powerful glimpses of futurity are darkened – but because it assumes a larger theater of human action and significance. Most immediately, an appeal to the future makes a claim that one's moment is of moment. More profoundly, it assumes that there will *be* a human future, whose inhabitants might understand the claimants and find their words and deeds interesting.

Early-eighteenth-century writers were sometimes capable of making such claims while simultaneously regarding them ironically. Joseph Addison, for example, celebrates military victories over the French in *The Campaign* (1705) with the earnest hope that his poem "may tell posterity the tale." But Addison also tells the still current joke about the man who balks when asked to contribute to the good of future generations, complaining "We are always doing something for posterity, but I would fain see posterity do something for us" (*Spectator* 583). Jonathan Swift's greatest poem, *Verses on the Death of Dr. Swift*, seems addressed in large part to posterity, but the same Swift had earlier observed "how free the present age is in laying taxes on the next. *Future ages shall talk of this: This shall be famous to all posterity*. Whereas, their time and thoughts will be taken up about present things, as ours are now."[1]

We might begin with a distinction between poems (or parts of poems) *about* the future and *for* the future, although the distinction often blurs. Into the first category fall most poems of praise and optimism, panegyrics on the present, predicting the importance of current events or at least the promising direction of the current of events. Thus Pope's *Windsor-Forest* (1713) proceeds from the recent accession of Queen Anne – "And Peace and Plenty tell, a STUART reigns" – to the imminent signing of the Treaty of Utrecht (ending the divisive War of Spanish Succession on terms profitable for England) and on to the prediction of British imperial greatness. Speaking through the voice of Father Thames, Pope imagines Britain as the "World's great Oracle in Times to come" (line 382). Such optimism often begins but does not end only in nationalism:

> Oh stretch thy Reign, fair *Peace!* from Shore to Shore,
> Till Conquest cease, and Slav'ry be no more:
> Till the freed *Indians* in their native Groves
> Reap their own Fruits, and woo their Sable Loves . . .
>
> (lines 407–10)

Predictions of British dominance usually assume British benevolence. John Dyer, in *The Fleece* (1757), is less subtle than Pope, wholly convinced that Britain "ne'er breaks / Her solemn compacts, in the lust of rule," and confident that the woolen trade will enrich shepherds as well as traders:

> Ye too rejoice, ye swains;
> Increasing commerce shall reward your cares.
> A day will come, if not too deep we drink
> The cup which luxury on careless wealth,
> Pernicious gift, bestows . . .
>
> (IV, lines 661–62, 669–73)

But by the mid century some poets had begun to feel that empire's wealth was already compromising the conquerors' future. In "The Revenge of America" (1755), for example, Joseph Warton has the spirit of the South American Indians envision "all Europe's children curst / With lucre's universal thirst."[2]

Optimistic predictions are less common than warnings and in general less successful poetically, although William Collins manages a vaguer, more palatable political hopefulness in the two most political of his *Odes on Several Descriptive and Allegoric Subjects* (1746). The "Ode to Mercy" prophesies that "Thou, Thou shalt rule our Queen, and share our Monarch's Throne!", while at the close of the "Ode to Liberty"

> Our Youths, enamour'd of the Fair,
> Play with the Tangles of her Hair,
> Till in one loud applauding Sound,
> The Nations shout to Her around,
> O how supremely art thou blest,
> Thou, Lady, thou shalt rule the West!

It is probably not accidental that Collins's better poems (such as "Ode to Evening" and "Ode on the Poetical Character") are agnostic or anxious regarding the future, although just why darker prophecies tend to brighten poetry is not an easy question. In any case, most of the more impressive accounts of the future envision darker days ahead, even – as in the famous ending of Pope's *Dunciad* – an imminent "universal Darkness" that "buries all."

Whether *The Dunciad* is seriously intended *for* the future or muses *about* the future as a way of shaming the present has often divided readers who regard it as arguably Pope's greatest work or as the expense of poetic spirit in a waste of topicality. The question need not be so divisive, since there is no reason the poem might not be pointed in both directions, or why either direction necessarily makes for better poetry. Clearly many poems have endured that were not explicitly addressed to the future, and even more clearly the presumption that posterity will be interested may prove absurd. But it is striking how many major and minor eighteenth-century poems do at least partly attempt to speak beyond the immediate audience to an indeterminate future readership. In Pope, as we shall see, the gesture is so frequent as to be nearly a signature; but other writers, satiric and non-satiric, also appeal to future judges.

Thomas Gray as well as Swift writes a poem, *Elegy Written in a Country Churchyard* (1751), in which the undervalued poet is memorialized for later ages. *Verses on the Death of Dr. Swift* is Swift's complexly comic attempt to create his own elegy and eulogy in poetry and, especially through its numerous footnotes, to leave the "true history" of the times for posterity. Swift's notes, unfortunately cut in many modern reprints, are an essential part of the work and aim to right the record as well as identify individuals. When Swift's putatively "impartial" spokesperson sketches him in lines such as these,

> "In exile with a steady heart,
> He spent his life's declining part . . .
> His friendship still to few confin'd
> Were always of the middling kind . . ."
>
> (lines 431–32, 435–36)

each couplet is footnoted. Swift annotates "exile" with this account of his appointment to the deanship of Dublin's St. Patrick's Cathedral: "In Ireland, which he had reason to call a place of exile; to which country nothing could have driven him, but the Queen's death, who had determined to fix him in England, in spite of the Duchess of Somerset, &c." The second couplet points to an explanation that "In Ireland the Dean was not acquainted with one single Lord Spiritual or Temporal. He only conversed with private gentlemen of the clergy or laity, and but a small number of either." Information like this would have been of some rhetorical force for Swift's contemporaries but seems written as well for an imaginary time capsule.

Charles Churchill's less familiar satire, *The Farewell* (1764), exemplifies an interesting mixture of prediction, warning, petition, and curse. Speaking as alienated patriot, Churchill wonders (lines 339–68) whether in "some not distant year" a "damned aristocracy," looking "on freedom with an evil eye" will seek to "divide the people and the throne" and eventually "destroy them both." Churchill's satire is not only omnidirectional but anticipatory:

> Should there be found such men in after-times,
> May Heav'n in mercy to our grievous crimes
> Allot some milder vengeance, nor to them,
> And to their rage this wretched land condemn.

Such appeals to "after-times" are a way of criticizing present-times, of course, and frequently on two counts. First, a "vision" of the future may work to show the danger or degradation of a current condition. Thus at the close of Oliver Goldsmith's *The Deserted Village* (1770), the poet not only sees the effects of the current depopulation of the countryside but foresees its results:

> Even now, methinks, as pondering here I stand,
> I see the rural virtues leave the land . . .
> Downward they move, a melancholy band,
> Pass from the shore, and darken all the strand.
> Contented toil, and hospitable care,
> And kind connubial tenderness are there . . .
> And thou, sweet Poetry, thou loveliest maid . . .
>
> (lines 399–400, 403–6, 409–10)

While many, such as Samuel Johnson, dissented from Goldsmith's conviction that urbanization and "luxury" would ruin the country, even Johnson was ready to predict the impermanence of commercial structures, contributing one of the closing lines of the poem, warning "That trade's proud empire hastes to swift decay."

A second way in which an appeal to the future may criticize the present is by announcing that the poet cannot safely or fruitfully tell all the truth here and now. "Publish the present Age," Pope declares, "but where my Text / Is Vice too high, reserve it for the next" (*The First Satire of the Second Book of Horace*, lines 59–60). Those words were published in 1733; five years later, Pope appended a note to the two poems in dialogue now called *Epilogue to the Satires* that, like many of Swift's notes, seems wholly directed to future readers, although hardly so: "This was the last poem of the kind printed by our author, with a resolution to publish no more; but to enter thus, in the most plain and solemn manner he could, a sort of PROTEST against that insuperable corruption and depravity of manners, which he had been so unhappy as to live to see . . . Ridicule was become as unsafe as it was ineffectual." Indeed, all of the first dialogue seems transformed into a sort of letter to posterity by the poet's closing turn from present vice to eventual vindication: "Yet may this Verse (if such a Verse remain) / Show there was one who held it in disdain."

Readers of Pope generally associate his invocation of the future with a growing pessimism that culminates in the poetic apocalypse of *The Dunciad*, a gloom in which neither

> *public Flame*, nor *private*, dares to shine;
> Nor *human* Spark is left, nor Glimpse *divine*!
> Lo! thy dread Empire, CHAOS! is restor'd;
> Light dies before thy uncreating word;
> Thy hand, great Anarch! lets the curtain fall;
> And Universal Darkness buries All.

The long road leading from the "Great *Anna*" who takes tea and counsel at Hampton Court in *The Rape of the Lock* (first published in 1712) to the "great Anarch" of *The Dunciad* (completed in 1743) does wend through much political disillusionment on the part of Pope and his friends. But it also maps some strong imaginative continuity, for Pope's use of the future connects nearly all the poetic genres he attempted. In fact, a closing prediction or petition concerning the future of the subject at hand is Pope's most characteristic way of concluding a poem, from the start of his career to the end. We have already looked at the prophetic close of *Windsor-Forest*. *The Rape of the Lock* ends with the declaration, gallant but genuinely predictive, that Belinda and her hair will be immortalized by the poem: "This *Lock*, the Muse shall consecrate to Fame, / And mid'st the Stars inscribe *Belinda's* Name!"

Lesser known early poems also end with predictions. *The Messiah* (1712) is an explicitly prophetic poem, an account in Virgil's manner of Isaiah "Rapt into future Times" (line 7) as he foretells the birth of Christ. The *Epistle to Mr. Jervas* (1716) ends with a declaration that Jervas's portraits of the Countess of Bridgewater "shall warm a future age," even lasting "a thousand years," and that "soft *Belinda*'s blush" – Jervas painted Pope's comic heroine – "shall . . . forever glow." Pope's tragic heroine, Eloisa, closes her dramatic struggle by predicting that "some future Bard shall join / In sad similitude of griefs to mine" (*Eloisa to Abelard*, lines 359–60), a forecast from the twelfth century of Pope's situation in 1717. In the same year the speaker of the "Elegy to the Memory of an Unfortunate Lady" looks forward to his own death: "Ev'n he, whose soul now melts in mournful lays, / Shall shortly want the gen'rous tear he pays" (lines 77–78). *Shall* is the operative word in all of these endings. The complimentary epistle "To Mr. Addison, Occasioned by his Dialogues on Medals" (1720) imagines a time when English commemorative coins will, like those of Rome, enshrine national heroes: "Then future ages with delight shall see / How Plato's, Bacon's, Newton's looks agree" (lines 59–60).

By the time Pope wrote his great ethical and satiric poems in the 1730s, the turn toward the future was deeply characteristic. Not only the dark cultural prophecies of the end of his career (the *Epilogue to the Satires* and final *Dunciad*) but works such as *An Essay on Man* and most of the *Epistles to Several Persons* (1731–35) end with disclosures of what *shall* follow. When a "future age" recognizes the true worth of Henry St. John, Viscount Bolingbroke (still in political disgrace when Pope addressed *An Essay on Man* to him), the descendants of his enemies "shall blush" for their ancestors while the poem itself "shall . . . / Pursue the triumph, and partake the gale" of Bolingbroke's resuscitation. The respective addressees of the *Epistle to Burlington* and the *Epistle to Cobham* shall "proceed" (imminently) to revive the nation's architecture and die (distantly) while praying for its political salvation. Martha Blount, to whom the *Epistle to a Lady* is addressed, has no "Tyrant" of a husband in her life but does have, "the world shall know it, / . . . Sense, Good-humour, and Poet." Even in his modernization of the fourth satire of John Donne, Pope manages to invoke posterity. Pope turns Donne's immediate wish that the author not be ignored or prosecuted for his rough heterodoxy – "yet some wise man shall, / I hope, esteeme my writs Canonicall" – into a more remote appeal: "However, what's now *Apocrapha*, my Wit, / In time to come, may pass for *Holy Writ*."

William Cowper, a poet for whom Holy Writ was a terrifying text, gives us an interesting perspective from near the end of the century on the poetic use of the future. Often convinced that the Final Judgment could not be far off, "in these, the world's last doting years" (*Charity*, line 604), Cowper finds the role of poetic prophet attractive – and fraught. In the long conversational poem *Table Talk* (1781) Cowper sees a corrupted England probably doomed to lose its grandeur – "Ninevah, Babylon, and ancient Rome, / Speak to the present times, and times to come" – and its freedom, as tyranny "Gives liberty the last, the mortal shock; / Slips the slave's collar on, and snaps the lock" (lines 432–33, 476–77). At this point, the interlocutor breaks in to ask whether the now "lofty" poet pretends to "prophesy" as well as "preach." Cowper gives a complex answer. On the one hand, he claims a vatic role for the poet, reminding readers that "in a Roman mouth, the graceful name / Of prophet and of poet was the same" (that is, *vates*) and that the inspired poetic mind is far-seeing:

> when remote futurity is brought
> Before the keen inquiry of her thought,
> A terrible sagacity informs
> The poet's heart; he looks to distant storms;
> He hears the thunder ere the tempest low'rs;
> And, arm'd with strength surpassing human pow'rs,
> Seizes events as yet unknown to man
> And darts his soul into the dawning plan.

Yet Cowper then insists that his own poetry lacks such prescience and abruptly disavows the role he has just described so energetically: "But no prophetic fires to me belong; / I play with syllables, and sport in song" (lines 479, 492–99, 504–05).

A similar ambivalence regarding visionary poetry dominates the end of *The Task*, the blank verse poem of over 5,000 lines that Cowper began in the fall of 1783 as a playful assignment (a friend suggested he celebrate the invention of the sofa, the ostensible subject of book 1) and published in 1785 after having brought much of earth and heaven into view. Toward the end of the poem's sixth and final book, Cowper warms to the subject of the Second Coming and then checks his flight:

> Sweet is the harp of prophesy. Too sweet
> Not to be wrong'd by a mere mortal touch;
> Nor can the wonders it records be sung
> To meaner music, and not suffer loss.   (VI, lines 747–50)

This time, Cowper forges ahead, if not with the "terrible sagacity" described in *Table Talk*, with conviction.

> But when a poet, or when one like me,
> Happy to rove among poetic flow'rs
> Though poor in skill to rear them, lights at last

On some fair theme, some theme divinely fair,
Such is the impulse and the spur he feels
To give it praise proportion'd to its worth,
That not t'attempt it, arduous as he deems
The labor, were a task more arduous still.   (VI, lines 751–58)

Yet the future now available to Cowper's imagination is not political or cultural but heavenly, as he turns in most of the remaining 250 lines to contemplate apocalyptic harmony. It would take William Blake, in the 1790s and after, to try to bring the tasks of political and spiritual prophecy together in poetry.

Whatever eighteenth-century poetry imagined of the future, its actual relation to posterity has been problematic for much of the past two centuries. Since the rise of Romanticism, prevailing literary premises and habits have predisposed many readers to underestimate the poetic richness of many eighteenth-century works. It is common for poetry of the period to wear its imagistic and metaphoric complexity lightly, so to speak, downplaying rather than advertising its potential intricacies. When Samuel Johnson describes the Persian hero Xerxes retreating in ignominy and a "skiff" after his defeat by the Greeks at Salamis, one of the few details given is the lone boat's "encumbered oar" (*Vanity of Human Wishes*, lines 248–49). It is possible to read the poem many times before grasping the imaginative horror of a boat rowing through and over the bodies of the dead.

Such miniature dramas are waiting to be *produced* by active readers, much as the script of a play is brought to life by imaginative interpretation, and the full realization of these effects often requires a readiness to go beneath the placid surfaces of eighteenth-century urbanity. When Swift writes, in *Verses on the Death of Dr. Swift*, that "Her end when Emulation misses / She turns to Envy, Stings and Hisses" (lines 35–36) it is left to the alert reader to see as well as hear, to see the images as well as hear the jaunty epigram. If we take only one or the other – only the round jest or the flickering personification of Emulation contracting into Envy – something deeply characteristic of the period will be lost: its intuition of playfulness as part of poetic behavior. "For he is a mixture of gravity and waggery," Christopher Smart wrote in praising his cat Jeoffry in the astonishing *Jubilate Agno* (1758–63), adding shortly after, "For he is good to think on, if a man would express himself neatly." The expressive ideals of poets in the Romantic tradition – which is to say most poets of the nineteenth and twentieth centuries – have tended to value "gravity" *or* "waggery" alternately rather than the mixture Smart found so arresting. Thus, modern readers may find it difficult to grasp simultaneously the satiric ridicule and imaginative wonder of a poem such as Pope's *Rape of the Lock*, or to understand that the same poet could see a single event with pathos and irreverence at the same time. When two farm laborers who were about to be married were killed during a sudden lightning storm Pope wrote two sentimental and somewhat heroic epitaphs for them. He also wrote, more privately, this couplet with a punning reference to venereal disease:

> Here lye two poor Lovers, who had the mishap
> Tho very chaste people, to die of a Clap.[3]

To one sort of sensibility such doubleness is ethical duplicity, and we still hear its irritation in some critical writing on Pope. A more fruitful approach recognizes psychic alternation as humanly interesting and hesitates to overestimate – or oversimplify – "sincerity" as a poetic virtue. This is not to say that eighteenth-century poets themselves were indifferent to sincere expression; Samuel Johnson's impatience with Milton's *Lycidas*, for example, and with much of the poetry of the witty "Metaphysical" poetry from Donne to Cowley was a complaint against inauthentic emotion. But it may be that the vantage point of postmodernism, which tends to regard the boundaries both of the self and the "poetic" as unfixed, permeable, and always artificial, now allows us a more open engagement with the multi-voiced poetry of the eighteenth century.

The following chapters, accordingly, presuppose little except that it is time to seek fresh approaches to the range of English poetry written between about 1700 and 1790, that the relation between past achievement and future readers is now to be negotiated anew. The past always requires introduction and explanation, but its more demanding requirements are imagination and empathy. We have tried, while providing helpful backgrounds and frameworks for understanding eighteenth-century poetry, to keep in view the potential excitement of both recognition and resistance. In literary as in other kinds of meaningful travel, the challenge is to be at once ready to recognize kinship and appreciate the alien. If we sense no similarity we soon long for home; if we grasp no strangeness we might as well not have set out.

NOTES

1 *The Prose Works of Jonathan Swift*, ed. Herbert Davis et al., 14 vols. (Oxford: Blackwell, 1939–68), I, 243.
2 Joseph Warton's "The Revenge of America" appeared in 1755 in volume IV of the important miscellany (anthology) edited by Robert Dodsley, *A Collection of Poems*; it is also available in John Wooll, *Biographical Memoirs of the late Rev Joseph Warton* (1806), p. 158.
3 Pope's several versions are available in the one-volume Twickenham Edition, *The Poems of Alexander Pope*, ed. John Butt (New Haven: Yale University Press, 1963, rev. 1973), pp. 462–63.

2

J. PAUL HUNTER

Couplets and conversation

Writing and talking were closer in the early eighteenth century than they are today – and so were poetry and prose. A variety of institutions, but especially the urban coffee houses which hosted continuous conversation about public events and issues, encouraged the blurring of social distinctions we take for granted: between public and private, for example, or between the working and leisure classes, and especially between conversation and written texts. Texts – whether newspapers, pamphlets about current events, or printed books – were quoted extensively and became the basis for much of the public conversation, and (in turn) conversation and its colloquial and dialogic habits often migrated into print. It is not that the oral/written distinction had no meaning, but the two modes were mixed so regularly in daily practice that oral conversation took on many of the stylistic habits associated with formal writing, and the written word often was conversational in tone and habit. Poetry, where tradition set strong metrical and formal expectations, often found the cadences of conversation appealing as a vocal counter-measure.

It's not that poetry then was an oral form – more that poetry was self-conscious in its remembrance that it had oral roots and that the poetry/prose distinction was not a rigid one.[1] But besides similarities of manner, poetry shared a lot of the matter of prose: that is, the subject matter for poetry was not circumscribed in the way it has tended to be over the past two centuries, so that poetry then was written about virtually anything – ordinary life and topics of daily interest as well as large conceptual issues of philosophical, theological, social, or national interest. There were poems about farming, fishing, cooking, walking the streets of London, storms, fashions, insults, drunkenness, trade practices, cats, and geography, as well as about historical events, the national debt, class distinctions, colonization, religious beliefs, standards of morality, gender expectations, slavery, philosophical principles, private feelings, and sexual behavior. No subject was too small or too grand for poets to tackle, and readers regularly talked in public places about their reading. Conversation was a form of public utterance, almost of publication; often texts were created *from* conversation, and texts and talk easily followed from one another. Anyone might participate in the ongoing text-into-talk discussions, although in practice these conversations were far more likely to occur in London than in the country, in "polite" society rather than among the working classes or servants, and among men rather than women.

What poems would an early-eighteenth-century reader be reading, and how were they related to the conversations of the moment? One way to begin to think about these issues is to look at books of poetry published at the turn of the century. The 1690s had seen the increasingly systematic publication of collections (usually called "miscellanies") that were topical, thematic, or ideological in focus – John Dryden's four miscellanies, for example (soon to be followed in the same mode by other major poets who collected kindred spirits), and the nearly thirty volumes of *Poems on Affairs of State* that resurrected the political issues of the previous generation. And of course volumes of poems by individual poets were continually appearing, especially the remembered poets of the previous generation who seemed to represent the rise of an "English" or "British" tradition. Milton, for example, who had died a full generation before, was repeatedly reprinted, as were such other well-known seventeenth-century poets as Herrick, Cowley, Rochester, Behn, Dryden, and (especially) Waller. Newer, younger poets were also beginning to be known. Matthew Prior, Daniel Defoe, Jonathan Swift, William Congreve, and Richard Blackmore already had established, or begun to establish, reputations, and soon others would do so: Mary, Lady Chudleigh; Joseph Addison; Anne Finch, Countess of Winchelsea; Elizabeth Singer; Sarah Egerton; Thomas Parnell. Mostly, new poets became known by being printed in miscellanies of some kind, but sometimes short collections of a new poet's work would appear (as with Egerton in 1703).[2] Those who sought a reputation typically published ambitious individual poems, usually about some current event or controversy: a war, the succession of a new monarch, the union with Scotland, the death of a prominent public figure, the signing of a peace treaty.

A knowing reader of 1710, especially someone who frequented the London coffee houses and kept up with literary talk, might know of a very young poet who was already being talked about because of his extraordinary talent – a protégé of older writers such as Wycherley, Walsh, and Congreve. He was just twenty-two years old and badly deformed physically because of a teenage injury and subsequent bout with tuberculosis of the bone, but he was handsome of face, graceful in manner, and verbally talented to the point of genius. Already many saw him as the future hope of English poetry, and already he had undertaken the kinds of tasks expected of far older and more mature talents – the writing, for example, of an ambitious treatise (in the manner of Horace) on the nature of poetry. He was Alexander Pope, and he was destined to be known as the craftsman who brought the couplet – already the dominant form of English poetry for more than a century – to its most finished state of formal perfection and at the same time popularized its accessible conversational ease.

Before discussing particular poetic practices, however, I want to suggest more fully the historical adjustments that need to be made to engage eighteenth-century poems fully. For all its supposedly "universal" qualities, poetry often does not translate easily from one culture to another, and present-day readers sometimes find the poetry of earlier ages intimidating. The "history problem" is not so much that words and grammar have changed (although usage does evolve in silent and sometimes surprising ways), or even that historical events and customs recede in collective memory and sometimes need footnotes to become intelligible to later readers. More important is the fact that poetry itself is conceived differently in different times and places: it has different purposes, tries for different effects, imagines its cultural place in different ways, represents experience differently, and even looks and sounds different. Every age and every culture see things in their own way; they make distinctive social and literary assumptions and have their own topical and tonal habits and practices. Poetry in the eighteenth century is, for example, far more "public" than we are used to, more critical or satirical in stance and tone, and often more argumentative than lyrical or celebratory. Poets felt themselves to be participating in the public sphere, not just commenting on it; they expected active readers who would respond to their formulations of policies, ideas, and opinions. Readers of poetry represented a strong and diverse cross-section of the population, not just small coterie groups interested in aesthetics and fine writing. Poetry was issue-dominated, highly rhetorical, and centered on present-day happenings

Take for example a poem by Pope *(An Epistle from Mr. Pope, to Dr. Arbuthnot)* that opens this way:

> Shut, shut the door, good *John*! fatigu'd I said,
> Tye up the knocker, say I'm sick, I'm dead,
> The Dog-star rages! nay, 'tis past a doubt,
> All *Bedlam*, or *Parnassus*, is let out:
> Fire in each eye, and Papers in each hand,
> They rave, recite, and madden round the land.
> What Walls can guard me, or what Shades can hide?

They pierce my Thickets, thro' my Grot they glide,
By land, by water, they renew the charge,
They stop the Chariot, and they board the Barge.
No place is sacred, not the Church is free,
Ev'n *Sunday* shines no *Sabbath-day* to me:
Then from the *Mint* walks forth the Man of Ryme,
Happy! to catch me, just at Dinner-time.   (lines 1–14)

There's a lot here to figure out from an eighteenth-century point of view before we can begin to appreciate the issues that affect us today. Who is the "good John" addressed by the speaker of the poem? Where is this door that shields the private poet from the public figure, and what does the speaker need protection from? Why does the door-answerer need to make up social lies to turn the seekers away? Who are the "they" who seek to intrude, and why are they described as both invasive and insane? What kind of personal situation would justify so exasperated and explosive (if rather exaggerated and comic) an opening set of lines? Why is this personal frustration a public issue?[3] The poem is immediate, present-centered, and urgent; the speaker feels besieged because of his poetry and his social position, and the poem quickly goes on to describe authorial rivalries and the prominent place of writing in contemporary London. The poem starts by assuming that readers already know something about – may even have been talking among themselves about – the contemporary world of writing and rivalry, and the poet moves swiftly from description to argument: that most writers these days are dependent, competitive, obsequious, and a public nuisance. To come to grips with the poem even on an elementary topic level, a modern reader needs a quick tutorial in a variety of historical issues and assumptions.

Three kinds of barriers stand between us and the poems that delighted and ignited readers of the eighteenth century. One involves the functions expected of poetry, its place in the social fabric, and the way readers use it in their everyday lives; the second depends on the subject matter of poems, which then was less predictable, less constricted, and more comprehensive than it is in our time; the third results from the formal aspects of poetry – the way poems look on the page and sound to the ear, matters very different when rhyme and meter determine the basis of lineation and the way words show themselves visually.

Poetry in our time is largely an acquired – and certainly a minority – taste, and poets are not now considered public figures, however esteemed they may be as artists or "public intellectuals." But it has not always been so. Poets may never have been as influential or as threatening to the social and political order as Plato feared when he proposed to ban them from his Republic, but there have been times and places in history when poetry was central to the vitality of a culture – when poets were taken seriously as cultural spokes-people and when they were widely enough read to have a significant impact on public opinion. Poets in these times often mingled with the great and powerful, and sometimes they were consulted on matters of public policy or cultural implication. It would be easy to exaggerate, looking back from the contrasting assumptions in our own time, how influential poets may have actually been – how much practical impact they actually had on the wider public. But their *symbolic* place in society was sufficiently recognized that their poems achieved wide attention; responsible, alert, and public-minded people were expected to read widely in the poetry of the time. Poetry then was not confined to a selected group of themes, tones, and topics and not marginalized as discourse. Rather, it was considered a standard means of public communication, and poems (like political pamphlets, religious and philosophical treatises, and newspapers and periodicals) were often the basis for public discussion.

One such time was the early eighteenth century. Not *every*one read poetry of course; not everyone read at all. Just over half of the British population then was literate; more men could read than women, but female literacy was rising fast; and young women, especially those who lived in London and other population centers, were by the end of the century almost as likely to read as their male counterparts.[4] Literacy was still governed heavily by class, but this too was changing, as reading became pragmatically important for growing numbers of people, especially in the rising commercial classes and for those in any class who were dependent on trade. What people read varied widely, but nearly everyone who was capable of extensive reading – that is, all those who could do more than just read a few words under necessity or duress – regularly read at least some poetry as a matter of course. They virtually had to, if they meant to talk knowledgeably about public matters and if they wished their conversation to be taken seriously, because much of the relevant writing about major issues was in verse. Prose might be sufficient for minor moments of history, but larger cultural issues and matters of long-term perspective almost demanded verse. And most of those issues were imbedded in present events so that in effect poetry reviewed the current and the passing on its way to larger questions and judgments.

The fact of wide reading about public issues, in both poetry and prose and across a fairly broad and expanding social spectrum, marked European culture generally in the early eighteenth century. What was then developing was the modern "public sphere" (in which an informed citizenry becomes more widely active in discussing and, ultimately, deciding issues of public concern). The concept of a public sphere and its rise concurrent with European nationalisms and urban culture, as developed by Jürgen Habermas and expanded by others, may only partly explain the development of modernism, but it helps us to understand the power of print and its role in developing both an audience and a working model for participatory government. And the public prominence of poetry is important to the audience/activist axis because of what was at the time a certain fluidity between writing and orality, texts and talk.

From a modern point of view – when reading blends less easily into ordinary conversation – perhaps the most surprising eighteenth-century cultural practice involving poetry was the widespread two-way interaction between the written and the oral. The closeness of oral exchange to the traditions and texts of writing – the way texts flowed into talk and then (often) back into texts again – was in part a function of the developing public sphere, but behind it was both the hunger for authority that the print world testifies to and a long tradition of conversation as a ratiocinative and discursive (rather than just ceremonial) practice. We know less than we would like about the world of talk in pre-print times, and we have to beware of a tendency in just about any time to idealize the ages before it; it is not necessarily true, for example, that ages more dependent on oral memory were more skilled at oral discourse than when print began to fill more of the memory function. Still, the very idealization of the conversation of previous ages – and the attempt to recreate in an age of print a new version of the conversational ideals of an earlier oral age – means that the eighteenth century held very high standards for conversation, expecting a planning, ordering, and perhaps even artistic sense about it that is very different from our modern expectations. One index of the relationship between written and oral is the sheer number of treatises (in both prose and poetry) written in dialogue form – writing that pretends to be oral because it imitates the give-and-take of social conversation. Another index is the simple extension of written discourse into social talk – in which the points of written texts of all kinds are extended into polite (and some not so polite) conversation. This conversation took place in a variety of settings public and private – country houses, village gatherings, pleasure gardens, on stagecoaches – but the most important institutional location was in the ubiquitous urban coffee houses, sometimes called "penny universities" because the price of a dish of coffee provided hours of sociality and talk.

Coffee houses became quite suddenly *the* place to see and be seen in late seventeenth-century England, especially in London; and the conversation in coffee houses was quickly legendary.[5] Those who had (or felt they had) a stake in public affairs – politicians, merchants, investors, men of letters, projectors and planners of all kinds of schemes, clergymen, and those in growing professions such as medicine and law – all frequented coffee houses, often on a daily basis; and the sense (or illusion) was that news and policy were not only talked about but actually generated there. A kind of polite and urbanely ambitious urban society developed around coffee houses (the *Spectator* papers capture the spirit and tone of the phenomenon very well),[6] and individual houses resembled private clubs, for many had a regular clientele and developed a distinctive character, tone, and perspective. Some groups gathered to discuss poetry, others for economic or political interests; some were partisan and committed to particular lines or ideologies, others were more topic- or debate-centered. All were very conscious of current events, fashion, and the present as the focus for any intellectual issue.[7]

Available libations included tea and chocolate (which were also new rages created by trade with faraway places) and often wine or beer and ale, but coffee itself was the social lubricant of choice, especially appropriate for the stimulant society represented by coffee-house habits and habitués. Coffee houses provide, among their many historical contributions, a striking example of the importance of conversation and the continuity between text and talk. The daily and weekly papers started the gossip of the day – and then produced the material for the next day's news – and newly printed treatises, plays, poems, and publications of all sort provided the basis or starting point for much of the conversation. Often printed materials (especially periodicals) were available within the coffee houses themselves, which also served as mini-libraries and contemporary archives. The world of conversation presumed a nation of readers.

Poems in any age can be about many things – everything really that human beings think about or respond to. But in practice, the subject matter of poetry is heavily influenced by cultural expectations in any given time and place, and poets tend to put their most sustained work into the issues that contemporary readers are most apt to want to read about. Thus in our time the focus of poetry tends to be on private experience and personal emotions. Modern readers, conditioned by Romantic alienation from the public sphere and by twentieth-century practice that radically privatized feelings, tend to think of poetry as more for our hearts than our heads. We seldom look to poems as sources of facts, or for an analysis of ideas, or to watch an argument unfold. And the emotions we seek in poetry are likely to be the softer and more delicate ones rather than more harsh and bitter ones – love not hate, kindness not anger or resentment, understanding and gentleness not conflict or retribution, support not criticism. Poems may surprise us by dealing with more brutal realities than we bargain for, but today we associate poetry mainly with things that we want to feel more deeply about and appreciate more fully, not with attitudes or emotions we wish to purge or forget. Our expectations for poetry tend heavily toward the private, the personal, the emotional, and the lyrical, while eighteenth- century expectations tended toward the public, the social, the discursive, and the argumentative.

Eighteenth-century poetry can be emotional and lyrical too, and you can catch almost any eighteenth-century poet in moments that anticipate – or at least parallel – our tastes and assumptions. But the public role of the poet as spokesperson and analyst for the culture meant that "larger," more far-reaching, more impersonal, and more public topics of discussion usually drove their poetic choices. It is not that individual experience is ignored; the poetry is full of particulars, and often poets do recount their own subjectivity in quite intimate ways, but the focus tends to be on the social – societal – implications of all events and experiences rather than on their purely individual or personal outcomes.[8] Pope, for instance, whose career is in many ways typical, used poetry to argue his politics, his ideas about social interaction, his sense of the place of poetry in public life, and his convictions about the place of human beings in the cosmos. They were *his* ideas, of course, not generic positions, and the expression can be very personal, but the focus is on implications in a social world of shared experiences and predicaments. His most ambitious poem, *An Essay on Man*, tries to explain very complex theological and philosophical ideas in common language: where do human beings fit into the larger order of the universe? Why is there evil in the world, and how is its existence tied to questions of choice and free will? How can the idea of evil be reconciled to the notion of a good and benevolent divine maker? What are the implications of the human predicament for everyday behavior and aspirations? Actually this long poem (1,304 lines) was intended to be part of a longer poem still, a poem that would deal with applied ethical issues as well and provide a popular justification for a Judeo-Christian system of thought, belief, and action – quite an agenda for a single poem.[9] Pope's other poems similarly illustrate eighteenth-century directions, taste, habit, and expectation. *The Rape of the Lock*, for example (which was perhaps Pope's most successful youthful poem), was based on a quite private episode – the stealthy snipping of a lock of a young woman's hair by a male suitor. Pope might not have felt free to turn such a moment into a public poem except that the incident provoked an intense feud (Montague–Capulet style) between the families involved and was widely talked about, and he wrote the poem in part to reconcile the families and restore a communal sense among his friends. But the poem became something much larger: an account of social relationships of the time, a review of the battle of the sexes, a discussion of gender roles and contemporary behavior more generally, a survey of elegant habits in the leisure class and an examination of luxurious tastes and desires, and a representation of modern conversation. The poem was written for rhetorical purposes far larger than personal and family feelings – though the understanding of those feelings and how they operated within a particular social context was crucial to the larger moves. Similarly, *Windsor-Forest* and *An Essay on Criticism* showed the young Pope concerned with issues his contemporaries were thinking and talking about. The first celebrates the Peace of Utrecht which (temporarily) quieted the long-standing conflict between England and France, but in doing so manages also to examine ideas about land and landscape, maritime power and trading practices, the history of war and hunting, and the implications of compromise and peace. The second lays out the principles of both writing and reading and offers a direction to contemporary poetry by reviewing ancient and modern ideas about the relationship between poetry and the nature of things (on the one hand) and poetry's effect on society, on the other. Even *Eloisa to Abelard*, his youthful and highly emotional poem about a passionate love affair between a priest and a nun, illustrates the interests and tendencies of the time, for Pope's way of exploring deep personal feelings involves writing about a well-known historical episode and articulating it, through the thoughts and words of Eloisa herself, in terms that contemporaries could talk about and debate. Throughout the poem, we are deeply conscious of being observers of Eloisa, voyeurs reading or overhearing her thoughts as she writes them in a "private" letter to her lover. One may suspect (correctly) that Pope was exploring some of his own feelings about inappropriate or frustrated passions in writing the poem at all, but his way of writing about such issues was filtered through public concerns and public interpretation. The private thought and individual observation needed to be considered relative to larger social and cultural expectations, as suggested by the following account of a morning scene in contemporary London. This poem by Jonathan Swift represents a far cry from traditional love poems about the dawn.

> Now hardly here and there a hackney coach
> Appearing, showed the ruddy morn's approach.
> Now Betty from her master's bed has flown,
> And softly stole to discompose her own.
> The slipshod prentice from his master's door
> Had pared the dirt, and sprinkled round the floor.
> Now Moll had whirled her mop with dexterous airs,
> Prepared to scrub the entry and the stairs.
> The youth with broomy stumps began to trace
> The kennel-edge, where wheels had worn the place.
> The smallcoal man was heard with cadence deep;
> Till drowned in shriller notes of chimney-sweep.
> Duns at his Lordship's gate began to meet;

And Brickdust Moll had screamed through half a street.
The turnkey now his flock returning sees,
Duly let out a-nights to steal for fees.
The watchful bailiffs take their silent stands;
And schoolboys lag with satchel in their hands.

Poetry in our time both looks and sounds quite different from eighteenth-century poetry, again because we assume different modes and conventions as well as functions and topics. Modern poetry looks less formal on the page. It is less likely to be arranged in symmetrical rectangles (stanzas) or other repeated shapes, and more likely to have variable line-lengths; it is apt to give a somewhat scattered sense of placement and present an apparent fragmentation of arrangement and meaning. Similarly, patterns of repetition in sound (when they exist) are apt to be less obvious and call less attention to themselves. Modern poetry is not formless or patternless, but it calls little attention to its shapes and patterns of repetition, and as readers we have come not to expect (or like) conscious and visible kinds of echo or reflection. We are in fact often rather suspicious of such devices, thinking them at best ostentatious, at worst mechanical and cute.

Take rhyme for example. Many modern readers are annoyed by rhyme; we find it hard to take seriously such conscious repetitions – or partial repetitions – of sound. We tend to find sound echoes monotonous and predictable – just about the opposite of what they were for earlier poets and audiences – and therefore somewhat conventional and perhaps sentimental in their effects and implications; the most familiar examples to us are in bad greeting cards or sentimental verse that uses expected rhyme as its only rhetorical trick. Either that or it seems ironic or comic, witty in linking together things that don't belong together. Satiric skits, musical revues, and parodic verses often use the sound equivalents of caricature – and produce effects very like those of social or political cartoons – as a way of linking things ludicrously. (Musical comedian Tom Lehrer, for example, rhymes "Ave Maria" with "Gee, it's good to see ya.") Such comic linkages that depend on inappropriate parallels descend at some distance from traditional rhyming practices which *test* whether words with similar sounds belong together – they ask whether sound-alikes are mean-alikes – but the instant comedy they produce gives away the fact that their conclusion is firm: we already know there is no appropriate comparison to be made.

Eighteenth-century poems on the other hand call a certain positive attention to formal features – conscious patterns and often ostentatious repetitions of visual or aural devices. Rhyme is a staple of eighteenth-century verse, linking particular words and syntactic arrangements so as to call special attention to word and phrase connections and sometimes implying a kinship poets might not dare assert directly. Satirists were, for example, fond of rhyming "kings" with "things" and "rule" with "fool."[10] Moreover, the visual reflects the aural (spelling usually reflects sound repetition) and provides a guide to voice and ear: the eye matches similarities of sight and points to pairings. Arrangement on the page becomes a set of directions related to meaning and response; the emphasis is on seeing the poem as a conscious work of art that employs words and syntax toward a progressive, cumulative, reflective end. Poems, arranged in stanzas or paragraph blocks, *look* as if they move consciously from one more or less symmetrical shape to another toward some kind of end result, and that is in fact what they mean to do. Even the way the lines end – with a conscious stopping at the end of a certain number of syllables – suggests visually the way the poem structures meaning; often the line-ends involve pauses (indicated by commas, periods, or other punctuation), and the punctuation provides not only a vocal guide to where and how long to pause[11] but an indication that clauses and sentences are proceeding rationally, cumulatively, and progressively toward some end. Visually we are watching an argument in progress.

And if the poem we are reading is a typical eighteenth-century poem it is probably in couplets – that is, in pairs of lines rhymed with each other but not physically (and visually) set off from each other in discrete two-line units. Rather, the spatial divisions are likely to involve paragraphs (as in prose) that are somewhat irregular in length, so that visually on a page there are something like stanzas (often with a line of space in between), but they are not of equal length, as stanzas usually are. The irregular blocks suggest the uneven progress of prose or conversation, an irregularity of pace within the symmetry. Spatially, the poem suggests parallels and repetitions and echoes but not the kind of exact symmetry of shape that suggests replication, mathematical precision, or a smooth and logical procedure. And the echoes or links of sound are matters both of similarity and difference, precise regulators of reference and meaning and not just decorative add-ons.

The eighteenth century's strong preference for couplets – a preference over both unrhymed lines and over more elaborately rhymed stanzas – is sometimes described as a puzzling self-imposed limitation that cramped the style of poets and constricted the effects they could produce.[12] But poets themselves (and their eighteenth-century readers) were highly conscious of the couplet's advantages. For one thing, as the expected, almost obligatory mode for serious poetry, the couplet signaled ambition and seriousness, indicated the express intention of engaging in extended argumentative discourse, and promised the basis for systematic consideration of important issues. When (unusually) poets write very short poems in couplets (as when, for example, they create a single couplet as the entire poem), they call special attention to the pithy, truncated, witty, and epigrammatic quality they are trying for in that specific instance – rather than the sustained, cumulative development of argument normally expected when couplets are used as the building blocks of long poems. John Gay, for example, proposed this for his own epitaph:

> Life is a jest, and all things show it;
> I thought so once, but now I know it.

The full wit of the couplet involves readers imagining themselves as visitors to a graveyard, hovering over the inscribed stone that is holding down Gay's decaying body, comparing then and now; but the effect begins from the brevity and shrunken mortality of the lines themselves. What kind of argument is this? the lines ask. And the answer is that cleverness and verbal dexterity – highly prized in the eighteenth century but also highly distrusted – have substituted here for argument. This is wit, not discourse. The couplet – because of its habits of concision, balance, and pointedness – can be very effective in short bursts like Gay's epitaph, and poets often showed off their wit in single couplets or a few strung together for quick comic or surprise effect; but mainly the couplet was used for longer poems where the building-block possibilities of two-line units – their gathering, ruminative, cumulative functions – were more evident. The couplet won its dominance in the age because it was considered the single most appropriate poetic mode for dealing with problems and issues of serious public import; it constituted the language not only of public ceremony but of sustained discourse.[13] Its habits of brevity and conciseness – the art of focusing quickly on the crucial issues and terms – created its cumulative usefulness for argument and debate.

Most eighteenth-century couplets are constructed in "pentameter" – that is, in lines of five poetic feet or stressed syllables[14] – and most follow a fundamentally iambic rhythm (alternating unaccented and accented syllables, with the rhyme falling on the final accented syllable): "Go, perjured youth, and court what nymph you please, / Your passion now is but a dull disease" (Egerton, "To Philaster," lines 1–2). "Well then, the promised Hour is come at last, / The present Age of Wit obscures the Past" (Dryden, "To Congreve," lines 1–2).

Couplets in iambic pentameter have traditionally been called "heroic" couplets because their potential stateliness and gravity became associated during the seventeenth century with epic or heroic verse; their dignified tone and ability to sustain step-by-step paragraph development increasingly meant that not only epic or historical or narrative poems used pentameter couplets but also almost all long poems and many poems of medium or even shorter length, though the term "heroic" has persisted as the popular quick-reference term for pentameter couplets generally. But both longer and shorter couplets (that is, of more or less than five feet) were also widely employed, pairing lines as short as a single foot or as long as six or seven feet. Tetrameter (or octosyllabic) couplets were especially popular for lighter verse (Samuel Butler had used them to great burlesque effect in the seventeenth century, and Swift exploited their comic possibilities ruthlessly), but they could also show a lot of satiric tooth, as in "To the Ladies" by Mary, Lady Chudleigh.

> Wife and servant are the same,
> But only differ in the name:
> For when that fatal knot is tied,
> Which nothing, nothing can divide,
> When she the word *Obey* has said,
> And man by law supreme has made,
> Then all that's kind is laid aside,
> And nothing left but state and pride.
> Fierce as an eastern prince he grows,
> And all his innate rigour shows:
> Then but to look, to laugh, or speak,
> Will the nuptial contract break.
> Like mutes, she signs alone must make,
> And never any freedom take,
> But still be governed by a nod,
> And fear her husband as her god:
> Him still must serve, him still obey,
> And nothing act, and nothing say,
> But what her haughty lord thinks fit,
> Who, with the power, has all the wit.
> Then shun, oh! shun that wretched state,
> And all the fawning flatterers hate.
> Value yourselves, and men despise:
> You must be proud, if you'll be wise.

Competing forms of verse were available, many of them even more rhyme-intense than couplets, and although a variety of them were used for this and that, none achieved anything like the popularity of couplets. Most common for short poems were quatrains (four-line stanzas) of some kind or other, usually cross-rhymed (that is, the lines are rhymed not consecutively as in couplets but rather in alternating lines); the abab rhyme is perhaps the commonest. Quatrains and other fairly short stanzas (tercets, quintains, sextains, etc.) are frequently the marks of leisure and play – they are almost off-duty signs – and ordinarily the subjects treated in these forms are informal, domestic, teasing, local, and personal, though the poems themselves are not necessarily unambitious.

Another major category of forms involves "odes" – serious and demanding poems of middle length, often with high claims about philosophical abstractions, states of mind, human ponderings generally, and cultural mysteries and darknesses. Odes tended to be meditational or reflective in focus, and they showed the poet more alone or in reverie than more typical public poems. Odes had had a powerful vogue in the middle of the seventeenth century and flourished again a century later. Most odes claimed to emulate either Horace or Pindar (and thus claimed classical roots); both their structure and verse form tended to be intricate and elaborate. When they claimed to follow Horace, stanzas were even in length and rhyme pattern (but with intense rhymes that called a lot of attention to their conscious artistry); when they claimed to be Pindaric, the stanzas were long (sometimes more than twenty lines long) and often maintained only a partial symmetry with each other (that is, lengths and rhyme patterns varied from stanza to stanza). Individual stanzas might contain wildly varied line lengths, with some lines as short as two or four syllables and others so long that the line could not be fully expressed on a normal printed page. The dignity of such ambitious poems (and the individualized independence of the poets who created them) was often asserted and championed, and they provided a kind of minor counter-tradition to public poems, but only in the later half of the century (when poetry tastes generally were beginning to shift more toward the meditative, the solitary, and the private) did they pose a real alternative for most poets.[15] Poets regularly experimented with the form and subject matter of the ode, but most felt far more comfortable with the expectations of the couplet. One measure of the powerful domination of the couplet is the tendency of all long-stanza forms to slip into (whatever their basic rhyme scheme) consecutively rhymed lines that, while they cannot strictly speaking be called couplets, are based on the same principle of consecutive-line rhyme rather than cross rhyme: a typical Pindaric stanza has more consecutively rhymed lines than cross rhymes.

The only serious competitor to the couplet in long, ambitious, public poems – whether epics, historical poems, occasional poems, georgics, panegyrical poems, celebrations, advices, or satires – was blank verse. Milton had famously attacked the whole idea of rhyme in a prefatory note added to later editions of *Paradise Lost*; he was not the first to despise rhyme nor the last, and in fact lively debates about rhyme erupted during the entire two-century dominance of the couplet. Like the pentameter couplet, blank verse was used mainly in ambitious long poems with public implications and appeared less often in shorter and less ambitious works. Milton remained a very popular poet throughout the eighteenth century and he had admirers and imitators of all kinds, but his desire to rid his culture of its "barbaric" (his word) preference for rhyme was dramatically unrealized. Blank verse was never in those years more than a minority taste, and (oddly enough) blank-verse lines almost always seem more formal and less conversational than couplets.

By definition, poetry is more planned and calculated than "ordinary" language. Good couplet poems – like poems of any other kind – are hard to write, requiring both technical skill that can be learned and talent that cannot, and they purposely take on a kind of "artificial" quality to set them apart from more casual formulations of language. There is ultimately nothing "natural" about rhyme as such, and for eighteenth-century readers (as well as for us) it calls attention to itself and to the words that it links through sounds. Many other conscious rhetorical devices and strategies – antithesis, chiasmus, syllepsis, and zeugma, for example – also help create a sense of crafted finish and formality so that poems on the page do not look at all offhand, random, or casual. And yet these poems also claim informality, ease, and ready accessibility, as if readers can approach them in a way similar to prose, make ready sense of them, and only intuit their art.

Couplets often seem "conversational," a lot like talk even though they are punctuated by rhyme and other consciously devised intricacies. Contemporaries could read them gracefully, without pausing to puzzle consciously over their strategic craft, and modern readers – once they get by the initial strangeness of rhyme, rhythm, and rhetoric and become used to the standard habits – can let them trip off the tongue just as easily. In fact, once we get used to the satisfying harmony of couplets it often becomes necessary to slow down, consciously note the implied and oblique as well as syntactic connections, and sort out meanings and implications that are a lot more complex than they look and sound. How can the aims of poetry be so "formal" on the one hand and so colloquial and informal on the other?

The short answer is that couplets never try to deny that they are artful, calculated, rhetorical, and "artificial" even when they strive to be smooth, accessible, colloquial, and conversational. They don't try to emulate talk *exactly* – just provide a tone and simplicity of vocabulary and syntax that make them as understandable as a clear spoken sentence, while still being guided by visible strategies that show us the signs of conscious craft and complex thinking. They do not pretend that this *is* conversation; even at the peak of rhyme's popularity, people didn't actually *speak* in couplets, and representing words *as if* they were spoken carries a double sense of spontaneity and calculation. Artful heightening can coexist comfortably with an ideal of familiarity and ready accessibility. The tension is even a healthy one: couplet poems are seldom as simple as they may seem; their aim is not transparency but (as in conversation) a surface ease that requires close reading, contemplation, and analytic replaying to come to a full understanding.

The longer answer involves *how* the various artistic strategies work to complicate surface ease. Here for example are the opening two lines of Pope's *The Rape of the Lock* – lines that lay out pretty clearly the issues the poem is going to take up:

> What dire Offence from am'rous Causes springs,
> What mighty Contests rise from trivial Things,
> I sing . . .

Singing is not exactly what Pope does with the issues in the poem; there is music behind the lines, but the better analogue is speaking. This is not one of Pope's most colloquial openings, but it does lay out clearly (the way a conversationalist might) what to expect. And the syntax *is* clear. Here are topic and theme; here is cause, here is effect. But what about the implications?

The most impressive thing about this opening, even more than its neat summary of the plot of this poem and the Homeric *Iliad* whose action it redacts, is the way it sets up our categories. All the elements of opposition and redefinition, naming and sorting, are quickly invoked. Key antithetical terms are asserted at once: "dire Offence"/"am'rous Causes" // "mighty Contests"/"trivial Things." Agency is immediately established in all the varieties of direness and triviality. Important but terrible things happen because they result from human desires and needs; the verbs "springs" and "rise" are powerful in their insistence of causality – as if one thing automatically escalates to another with far greater implications than anyone could predict, and the agents individually do not need to be either important or self-conscious of their might and power to create results well beyond their intention or understanding.

Crucial here is the way the categories of implication and triviality cross and mix; adjectives and nouns dance back and forth in their associations and contaminations. Is Homer about direness and Pope about triviality? How do "am'rous" and "mighty" relate, beyond cause and effect? How does one choose between ancient formulation and modern version, and how do we know which one is mightier, more dire, or more trivial? The oppositions play back and forth across the binary categories. What is set up as initial expectation of categories reverberates and blurs: cause and effect, value and disvalue, old and new move around rather than staying put. The poem becomes an investigation of the process of valuing rather than a standard by which to set a reader's compass, and the very process of complication is engineered by the initial binaries which give the illusion of establishing firm ground. A few lines later the "gentle" and "bold" sexes are similarly polarized, teasingly reversed, then complicated. The "satisfactions" involved in the couplet here are not of neatness and closure but of connection and complication, but the very process of complication is enabled by the simplicities of initial assertion and proposal of categories.[16]

Pope's openings are often quite arresting as well as expressive of the issues he is about to explore, and many of them (like the "Shut, shut the door, good John" opening to *Arbuthnot*) are conversational in the referential sense that someone else seems to be there as interlocutor. *An Essay on Man*, for example, begins with an address to Pope's friend Henry St. John, Viscount Bolingbroke:

> Awake, my St. John! leave all meaner things
> To low ambition, and the pride of Kings.
> Let us (since Life can little more supply
> Than just to look about us and to die)
> Expatiate free o'er all this scene of Man;
> A mighty maze! but not without a plan;
> A Wild, where weeds and flow'rs promiscuous shoot,
> Or Garden, tempting with forbidden fruit.
> Together let us beat this ample field,
> Try what the open, what the covert yield;
> The latent tracts, the giddy heights explore
> Of all who blindly creep, or sightless soar;
> Eye Nature's walks, shoot Folly as it flies,
> And catch the Manners living as they rise;
> Laugh where we must, be candid where we can;
> But vindicate the ways of God to Man.   (I, lines 1–16)

Not only is the friend (who had been a major government official and who, now in involuntary retirement and exile, is an aspiring philosopher and theorist of government) addressed directly here, but he is from the opening word called to attention. Pope's wake-up call, delivered emphatically as common sense – as if Bolingbroke worried too much first about small matters and then too abstract ones – asks his companion to keep his eye on major issues, but to do it carefully, empirically, and by walking bodily through the mazes of this world in a fully grounded way. His theme, he announces quickly, is no less than Milton's in *Paradise Lost* (Milton wanted to "justify the ways of God to man"). But his mode is more down to earth than those who "sightless soar," and his opening sets a tone of openness and alertness to small things and a suggestion that even the hardest issues are approachable through ordinary language and ordinary human observation.

One of Pope's most demanding poems – *An Essay on Criticism*, in which he tries to explain the history of literary criticism, the importance of the classics, the doctrine of mimesis, the reasons why English poetry has developed the way it has, and the relationship between writing and reading – begins in this apparently casual way: "'Tis hard to say, if greater Want of Skill / Appear in *Writing* or in *Judging* ill." Such lines could easily be talked: the opening contraction and colloquial phrasing slide into a complex subject without much fuss. The initial offhandedness and apparent uncertainty – does bad writing or bad reading show more important lacks? – hardly prepares us for the tough-minded (and sometimes difficult) ideas that follow. The whole poem remains in fact similarly accessible even as it explores some very complex issues. Part of the poem's accomplishment is in the very ease and friendliness with which it approaches complexity. In an attempt, for example, to adjudicate between individual tastes and enduring principles of appeal, Pope puts the matter in terms of a deceptively simple analogy that seems to allow for a lot of individual variation: "'Tis with our Judgments as our Watches, none / Go just alike, yet each believes his own" (lines 9–10). Behind the analogy, however (and almost obscured by the easy simplicity and apparently incontrovertible applicability of it), is a powerful metaphor of authority. By what do we set our watches? By the sun's movements, of course; and this is the same sun that orders our whole universe, provides an agreed-on basis for time, gives us the light we live by, and nourishes the whole natural world, including the ripening of the seeds of judgment in our mind. The solar basis of life (as well as of taste) becomes a major theme in the poem – though the imagery of sun, light, and order is never forced upon us and indeed remains submerged through most of the poem – and the authority of standards that cross places, ages, and cultures is thus quietly assumed. The argument here is a deep and difficult one, but its complexities are not teased out in detail; in fact, they do not appear in the poem directly at all but are assumed through the submerged image of solar order.[17] Light in its several senses – as inspiration, learning, discovery, revelation, etc. – is central to the poem, but we may notice only subliminally that its ultimate referent is always an ordering sun that reflects a set divine order and provides sound authority for judgment that remains steady from Greek and Roman times to the eighteenth century, with room only for the few minutes' deviation testified to by variations in individual measuring devices like watches.

Part of the reason that conversation can be a kind of model for poetry is that conversation itself was then regarded as an art, something to be studied, prepared, and practiced.[18] It was not just bursts of unformulated notions, spontaneous outflows of thoughts or feelings, or half-organized attempts to figure out what you were trying to say: the ideal of conversation was to be both clear and elegant – to say something in an organized, persuasive way, to have a point and to speak it eloquently. The conversation of Samuel Johnson, famously recorded by James Boswell, was more than a record of one man's mind, extraordinary though that was; it was an index too of how pointed, serious, and authoritative good talk could be. Poets sometimes make fun of those who fumble such attempts, as Pope does in representing poor inarticulate Sir Plume in *The Rape of the Lock*, when he tries to "argue" for the restoring of the shorn hair:

> (*Sir Plume*, of *Amber Snuff-box* justly vain,
> And the nice Conduct of a *clouded Cane*)
> With earnest Eyes, and round unthinking Face,
> He first the Snuff-box open'd, then the Case,
> And thus broke out – "My Lord, why, what the Devil?
> Z–ds! damn the Lock! 'Fore Gad, you must be civil!
> Plague on't! 'tis past a Jest – nay prithee, Pox!
> Give her the Hair" – he spoke, and rapp'd his Box.
>
> (lines 123–30)

The speaker has the right platform, props, and timing; here he is at a moment of crisis, meaning quite well but having no idea how to cope. He can't speak well because his mind isn't clear; he hasn't "prepared" his conversation. His command is meaningless as well as ineffective, and his mumbling, muttering, stuttering phrasing betrays his addled incoherence and utter physical and social incompetence.

To say that conversation (in both poetry and real life) needs organization and argument to be satisfying and effective is not to say that it is intellectual or even necessarily rational. Argument can often be specious, sometimes consciously so, but the desire to persuade – to take direct aim on the audience and almost to force a reaction or outcome – is very strong in the poetry of the eighteenth century. The careful building up of the case – obvious in longer philosophical, political, or religious poems – is usually there in middle-sized and shorter poems as well, and, if you look carefully at the way the building blocks are laid (usually couplet by couplet) until the edifice stands fully built, you will see a conversation being created, a persuasive argument made, an interaction started between text and reader.

Eighteenth-century poems are often addressed to some specific person, as if that one person were the audience the poet had in mind – and the rest of us were merely reading over his or her shoulder. We have already seen it to be true in two Pope poems (*Arbuthnot* and *An Essay on Man*) in which a friend appears in the very first line to listen, set the tone, and direct traffic; similarly in Pope's epic account of the triumph of literary Dulness in his time, *The Dunciad*, he picks out his friend Jonathan Swift as the ideal reader, dedicates the poem to him, and (in the process) characterizes the dedicatee. Having a specific auditor in mind can help a writer diagnose how to proceed; such a concrete point of reference sets specific expectations of terminology, a presumed level of reading experience and previous knowledge, and grounds for argument. For a reader, the presumed auditor is also a kind of clue to what to expect in terms of subject matter, tone, and intellectual level. A poem addressed to Bolingbroke or Swift is likely to be pretty serious and intellectually demanding, whatever its affability of approach.

Some poems are "addressed" even more directly, as if they were letters to an individual person (again, usually a close friend, but not necessarily so). The commonness of "epistles" among eighteenth-century poems is part of a larger literary and cultural participation in epistolarity and is dependent on the real-life importance of letter-writing at the time.[19] Distances of time and space then could seem very great, and the post (though slow) provided a relatively reliable, private, and intimate means of contact. The care in constructing these private letters – as much care as if they were going to be published[20] – suggests the same kind of dedication to style, organization, and argument that we have seen in conversation and the poetic imitators of conversation. Like talk, letters were at once carefully planned and yet could seem rather informal and even off-hand: personal within a frame of societal expectations. Their style, not surprisingly, could also seem quite conversational since they were quite literally – to use a phrase of Pope's – talking on paper. And perhaps it is also not surprising that a whole subgenre of poems – a very important subset – developed in imitation of letters. They were called verse epistles (many use the term "letter" or "epistle" in their titles),[21] and they have the convenience of seeming a private communication between friends while nevertheless becoming available to readers beyond the addressee, so that readers get the voyeuristic sense of looking over someone else's shoulder and reading his or her private mail.

Some verse epistles are quite personal, although (by definition) they are not really private. Their popularity as a poetic form reflects the broad tendency of the age to give a public edge or direction to even the most private of concerns, and they were useful for the same variety of subjects as poetry in general. They could address ambitious philosophical topics and major events (especially if a poet wanted to offer public advice); the tendency to think in terms of epistolary style is suggested by the fact that Pope's powerful *Essay on Man* was divided into "epistles" rather than "books" or "parts." Pope similarly addressed quite large topics (architecture, gardening, the character of women, the uses of wealth) in his various *Epistles to Several Persons*, although the pretense of writing a letter usually meant that such poems were not overly long (only one exceeds 300 lines). And many epistles are in fact addressed to a particular person on some occasion or other; Pope wrote two poems called "Epistle to Miss Blount," marking important moments in their friendship, and a host of other epistles, many of which were actually sent to the addressee and only published later. Writing "letters" in one's own voice was a common practice among poets (see, for example, Susannah Centlivre's *An Epistle to the King of Sweden* or Helen Maria Williams's *To Dr. Moore, in Answer to a Poetical Epistle*), as was the pretense of writing in the voice of some historical or contemporary figure addressing someone else (as we have seen in Pope's *Eloisa to Abelard*, and which is brilliantly illustrated in Lady Mary Wortley Montagu's *Epistle from Mrs. Yonge to her Husband*).

How close the verse epistle is to an imitation of conversation can sometimes be seen in the way the addressee appears in the poem as a kind of interlocutor, as if the poet imagines the friend saying something in response. Often, of course, the appearance of the addressee to ask a question or make a point (which the poet then has to answer) is just a convenient ploy to change the subject or move the argument along; in Pope's *An Epistle from Mr. Pope, to Dr. Arbuthnot*, for example (which begins as if it is conversation with someone else),[22] Arbuthnot twice appears to interject warnings (at lines 305 and 360), and it is not uncommon for epistles to become, in effect, dialogues – although the best lines almost always go to the poet.

The closeness of the couplet to conversation suggests the crucial quality of voice in the poetry. Different poems project different voices of course, and when we read poems we can (with a little practice) almost begin to "hear" the voices in our heads. It is a good practical habit to try to develop, and reading poems aloud, so that your own voice tries to imitate the voice in the poem, is a good, practical way to hear the syntax and sense of the poem, as well as its voice, tone, and pace. The trick is not to let your voice be too emphatic about the rhyme (or at least not to let it distract you into too rigid divisions between couplets). But hearing yourself (or someone else) read the lines will quickly underscore the point about the couplet's orality and vocal accessibility – and will also allow you to notice how "ordinary" the language of eighteenth-century poetry usually is. There are of course technical terms here and there, but you don't need a learned vocabulary to approach most couplets, which actually tend to use a more limited, common, and accessible vocabulary than most poets in other forms and other ages because the poems talk as if to a familiar friend. Towards the end of the century, a more specifically "poetic" language (specialized, removed, a bit ethereal) developed, and the voice there is sometimes more distant from talk (and the verse often shifts away from couplets). But you will not go wrong by hearing the poetic voice in eighteenth-century couplets directly and simply as if the poet were speaking to you – and then by rereading and analyzing it hard in spite of its easy and accessible qualities that can be mistaken for transparency.

NOTES

1 The relationship between prose and poetry was complicated by the fact that what counted as "literature," or belles lettres, was in flux during the eighteenth century. But it is worth remembering that these terms then were more inclusive than they became later, so that a number of prose "kinds" – e.g. biography, history, philosophical dialogues, sermons, – were regularly considered literary.

2 Print was the usual means to share work in the eighteenth century, but Margaret Ezell reminds us that sharing manuscript work within coteries remained a major practice well into the Restoration; see Margaret Ezell, *Social Authorship and the Advent of Print* (Baltimore: Johns Hopkins University Press, 1999).

3 Quick answers: the author had a servant named John Serle, who answered the door to visitors at Pope's villa in Twickenham, a few miles west of London; the substantial house and grounds (with a cave-like grotto [line 8] where Pope liked to read and write) was accessible by land or via the River Thames by boat ("Chariot" and "Barge," line 10). The intruders are, as the poem makes clear a few lines later, rival poets and hangers-on who want his advice or support with patrons and publishers, and they seem mad with ambition or desperation or poverty or some combination of the three; they are also arrogant and vain.

4 I have summarized in another place what recent scholarship has taught us about literacy then; see *Before Novels* (New York: W. W. Norton, 1990), pp. 61–88.

5 The first coffee house appeared in England (in Oxford) in 1650 and the first in London in 1652; by 1698, there were said to be more than two thousand coffee houses in London alone. See Bryant Lillywhite, *London Coffee Houses* (London: G. Allen and Unwin, 1963), and Paul Kaufman, "Coffee Houses as Reading Centres," in *Libraries and Their Users* (London: The Library Association, 1969), pp. 115–27.

6 On *The Spectator* and its impact see Erin Mackey, *The Commerce of Everyday Life: Selections from The Tatler and The Spectator* (Boston and New York: Bedford/St Martin's, 1998) and Stuart Sherman, *Telling Time: Clocks, Diaries, and English Diurnal Form, 1660–1785* (Chicago: University of Chicago Press, 1996). See also Terry Eagleton, *The Function of Criticism: From The Spectator to Post- Structuralism* (London: Verso, 1984).

7 Coffee houses have traditionally been described as male enclaves (if not male bastions), and they were mostly male-centered. But some women were also a part of the coffee-house culture; see Steve Pincus, "'Coffee Politicians Does Create': Coffee Houses and Restoration Political Culture," *Journal of Modern History* 67: 4 (1995), 807–34.

8 The novel, so called because it was thought to be a new form representing new textual interests in contemporary everyday life, tended to dwell more on the particular, the personal, the individual, and the subjective; in a sense, it claimed these interests from other literary forms, and when (in the Preface to the second edition of *Lyrical Ballads*, 1800) Wordsworth argued that poetry should concentrate more fully on details of ordinary life, he was in part reclaiming for poetry some of the territory the novel had usurped.

9 For Pope's detailed plan, see Miriam Leranbaum, *Alexander Pope's "Opus Magnum," 1729–1744* (Oxford: Clarendon Press, 1977). One way of thinking about eighteenth-century assumptions and methods in comparison to later ones is to compare this poetic project of Pope's with Wordsworth's plan a century later for another epic-length poem: Wordsworth too wanted to be hugely comprehensive and practical, and he also executed only part of his project (*The Prelude* was to be, as its title suggested, only the start of *The Excursion*). Wordsworth's way was to work from personal experience and subjective responses, implying through them more generalized directions and conclusions; Pope, on the other hand, addressed the larger issues directly, and although his method was to proceed empirically by tackling each issue through contemporary examples (note the way the poem opens by insisting on "beating the fields" and otherwise moving through particular observations to more general conclusions), he is anxious not to be merely personal and private, not to call attention specifically to his own reactions and experiences as normative. He would have thought it solipsistic to want to share "the growth of a poet's mind" as a way of explaining the universe.

10 Pope pokes fun at such implications of rhyme (or rather of the naïve belief in them) in *Epistle to Arbuthnot* (lines 25–30), suggesting that a man who has been cuckolded blames Pope because his name rhymes with the word "elope."

11 Isaac Watts, in *The Art of Reading and Writing English* (1721), gives these directions on reading punctuation:

> The *Stops of the Voice* show us where to make a Pause, or rest, and take breath; and are these four . . .
>
> A *Comma* divides betwixt all the lesser Parts of the same Sentence, and directs us to rest while we can tell [i.e., count] two . . .
>
> A *Semicolon* separates betwixt the bigger Parts or Branches of the same Sentence, and directs us to rest while we can tell three . . .
>
> A *Colon* divides between two or more Sentences that belong to the same Sense, and have any proper Connexion with one another; and it requires a Pause a little longer than a *Semicolon* . . .
>
> A *Period*, or full Stop, shows either the Sense, or that particular Sentence to be fully finish'd, and requires us to rest while we can tell five or six, if the Sentence be long; or while we can tell four, if it be short. (pp. 39–41)

12 Older studies such as that of James Sutherland emphasize such qualities as restraint, limitation, and constriction in the poetry (*A Preface to Eighteenth Century Poetry* [Oxford: Clarendon Press, 1948]); newer studies, such as that by Margaret Doody, emphasize freedom, power to choose, celebration (*The Daring Muse* [Cambridge: Cambridge University Press, 1985]). For a recent application of the older position to ideological issues, see Antony Easthope, *Poetry as Discourse* (London and New York: Methuen, 1983).

13 The couplet began to dominate English poetry in the late sixteenth century, and its reign lasted until the beginning of the nineteenth century. During that period of more than two hundred years, the couplet was so dominant that it constituted more of the poetic canon than all other verse forms put together. Deep samplings from the period suggest that something over half, and perhaps as many as two-thirds, of all poetic lines written then were in couplets of some kind, with iambic pentameter couplets outnumbering others by three or four to one.

14 English principle is actually accentual/syllabic (Derek Attridge more precisely calls it syllabic-stress meter), and it is more accurate to count syllables and *then* record the stresses or accents (and then call the couplets decasyllabic rather than pentameter), but the tradition has been to speak in terms of numbers of "feet" or stressed syllables. For a revisionary way of talking about metrics, see Attridge, *Poetic Rhythm: An Introduction* (Cambridge: Cambridge University Press, 1995) or *The Rhythms of English Poetry* (London: Longman, 1982). For a readable (and witty) brief introduction to issues of metrics and rhyme, see John Hollander, *Rhyme's Reason: A Guide to English Verse* (New Haven: Yale University Press, 1981).

15 See John Sitter, *Literary Loneliness in Mid-Eighteenth-Century England* (Ithaca: Cornell University Press, 1982).

16 This paragraph is almost verbatim taken from my essay "Formalism and History: Binarism and the Anglophone Couplet," *Modern Language Quarterly* 61: no 1 (2000), 109–30.

17 See Aubrey Williams, "Submerged Metaphor in Pope," *Essays in Criticism* 9 (1959), 197–201; see also Patricia Meyer Spacks, *An Argument of Images: the Poetry of Alexander Pope* (Cambridge, MA: Harvard University Press, 1971) and David B. Morris, *Alexander Pope: the Genius of Sense* (Cambridge, MA, and London: Harvard University Press, 1984).

18 Conversation manuals, full of practical advice, were very popular; they were published under such titles as *The Art of Pleasing in Conversation* (1691), *The Art of Conversation* (1738), *The Conversation of Gentlemen Considered* (1738), *An Essay on Modern Education, where is contained . . . The Great Advantages of Modern Conversation* (1747), *Models of Conversation for Persons of Polite Education* (1765). Many of them were (or claimed to be) translated from the French or Italian.

19 On the art of actual letters, see Bruce Redford, *The Converse of the Pen: Acts of Intimacy in the Eighteenth-Century Familiar Letter* (Chicago: University of Chicago Press, 1986); on epistolarity issues more generally, see Janet Gurkin Altman, *Epistolarity: Approaches to a Form* (Columbus: Ohio State University Press, 1982). In his detailed study of the verse epistle, which he argues is "the dominant form in eighteenth century poetry" (p. 21), William C. Dowling offers a detailed theoretical rationale for the cultural preoccupation with the poetic epistle (*The Epistolary Moment: the Poetics of the Eighteenth-Century Verse Epistle* [Princeton: Princeton University Press, 1991]).

20 Pope again provides an illustrative case; for an account of his planting of his own letters so that they would be "piratically" printed, see Maynard Mack, *Alexander Pope: a Life* (New York: W. W. Norton, and London: Yale University Press, 1985), pp. 653–58.

21 Examples of titles: Addison, *A Letter from Italy, to . . . Lord Halifax*; Akenside, *An Epistle to Curio*; Leapor, *An Epistle to a Lady*; Finch, "To a Friend, in Praise of the Invention of Writing Letters"; Edward Young, "Letter to Mr Tickell"; Charles Churchill, *An Epistle to William Hogarth*; Fenton, *An Epistle to Mr. Southerne*; Parnell, "To Mr. Pope"; Samuel Rogers, *An Epistle to a Friend*.

22 See pp. 13–14 above.

FURTHER READING

Altman, Janet Gurkin. *Epistolarity: Approaches to a Form*. Columbus: Ohio State University Press, 1982.

Attridge, Derek. *Poetic Rhythm: an Introduction*. Cambridge: Cambridge University Press, 1995.

The Rhythms of English Poetry. London: Longman, 1982.

Doody, Margaret. *The Daring Muse: Augustan Poetry Reconsidered*. Cambridge: Cambridge University Press, 1985.

Dowling, William C. *The Epistolary Moment: the Poetics of the Eighteenth-Century Verse Epistle*. Princeton: Princeton University Press, 1991.

Eagleton, Terry. *The Function of Criticism: From The Spectator to Post-Structuralism*. London: Verso, 1984.

Easthope, Antony. *Poetry as Discourse*. London and New York: Routledge, 1983.

Ezell, Margaret. *Social Authorship and the Advent of Print*. Baltimore: Johns Hopkins University Press, 1999.

Hollander, John. *Rhyme's Reason: a Guide to English Verse*. New Haven: Yale University Press, 1989.

Hunter, J. Paul. "Formalism and History: Binarism and the Anglophone Couplet," *Modern Language Quarterly* 61: 1 (2000), 109–30.

Before Novels. New York: W. W. Norton, 1990.

Kaufman, Paul. *Libraries and Their Users*. London: The Library Assocation, 1969.

Leranbaum, Miriam. *Alexander Pope's "Opus Magnum," 1729–1744*. Oxford: Clarendon Press, 1977.

Mack, Maynard. *Alexander Pope: a Life*. New York: W. W. Norton; London: Yale University Press, 1985.

Mackey, Erin. *The Commerce of Everyday Life: Selections from The Tatler and The Spectator*. Boston and New York: Bedford/ St. Martin's, 1998.

Morris, David B. *Alexander Pope: the Genius of Sense*. Cambridge, MA, and London: Harvard University Press, 1984.

Pincus, Steve. "'Coffee Politicians Does Create': Coffee Houses and Restoration Political Culture," *Journal of Modern History* 67: 4 (1995), 807–34.

Redford, Bruce. *The Converse of the Pen: Acts of Intimacy in the Eighteenth-Century Familiar Letter*. Chicago: University of Chicago Press, 1986.

Sherman, Stuart. *Telling Time: Clocks, Diaries, and English Diurnal Form, 1660–1785*. Chicago: University of Chicago Press, 1996.

Spacks, Patricia Meyer. *An Argument of Images: the Poetry of Alexander Pope*. Cambridge, MA: Harvard University Press, 1971.

Sutherland, James. *A Preface to Eighteenth Century Poetry*. Oxford: Clarendon Press, 1948.

Williams, Aubrey. "Submerged Metaphor in Pope," *Essays in Criticism* 9 (1959), 197–201.

3

CHRISTINE GERRARD

Political passions

Although the eighteenth century is widely regarded as the great age of political verse, that label really applies more strictly to a sixty-year period which cuts across the seventeenth and eighteenth centuries: between the rise of political parties in the 1680s and the fall of Robert Walpole in 1742. During that period the lives and works of most poets were shaped, even defined, by political allegiance. After the mid 1740s poetry was rarely the province of party-politics. With the brief exception of Charles Churchill's pro-Wilkes satires of the early 1760s, few poets tackled political themes with the intensity, even "passion," of the first half of the century. This account must by necessity be weighted heavily toward the earlier period. Yet a political canon centered on the Tory satirists Alexander Pope, Jonathan Swift, and Samuel Johnson fails to convey adequately the complexity of party-political debates played out in the poetry of the period. The Whig party – which dominated eighteenth-century political life and institutions between the powerful cabals of Whig politicians during William III's and Anne's reigns through the twenty-year ministry of Robert Walpole and beyond – attracted and sponsored numerous poets, among them Joseph Addison, Thomas Tickell, Richard Blackmore, and Ambrose Philips. Few of these Whig poets are now read, their names familiar only from Pope's *Dunciad*. Pope and his fellow satirists, best known in their collective identity as the Tory-based Scriblerus Club, were remarkably successful in promoting for posterity the myth that Whig poetry was dull, long-winded, and ignorant. They were fighting a rearguard action against a dominant Whig literary culture and a modern, self-confident British poetry inspired by great contemporary events such as William III's and the Duke of Marlborough's military victories during the Nine Years' War and the War of the Spanish Succession.[1] It is important to reinstate this Whig tradition if only to convey a better sense of the way in which poetic form both mirrored and embodied party-political debate in the early years of the century.

Queen Anne's closing years

Queen Anne's reign was the last in which political loyalty and political debate were polarized along Whig–Tory party lines. Two main issues fueled the "rage of party" – the Tory-led peace negotiations to end Marlborough's wars, culminating in the Treaty of Utrecht (1713), and the crisis over Anne's successor following the death of her only son, the Duke of Gloucester, in 1700. The Whigs threw their support behind the House of Hanover, named in the 1701 Act of Settlement, but many Tories wished to see a Stuart succeed the Stuart Anne. During the last two years of Anne's reign these issues came to dominate, even dictate, literary friendships. When Pope first entered London literary society he prided himself on his non-partisanship, and continued to maintain good relations with both the Whig wits in Addison's circle (writing the prologue for Addison's play *Cato*) as well as with his Scriblerian friends John Gay, Swift, Thomas Parnell, John Arbuthnot, and the Tory minister Robert Harley. But by 1713 this kind of neutrality was impossible to maintain. Addison was no longer on speaking terms with Pope, nor his colleague Richard Steele with Swift, an antagonism between rival literary circles that permeated even ostensibly non-political literary topics such as the appropriate style for pastoral or the popularity of Pope's Homer translations.[2]

War and peace

By 1710 the nation had grown weary of close on two decades of continental war. That year the Whig Marlborough–Godolphin ministry collapsed in the face of a nationwide reaction against its attempt to impeach the High Church Bishop Henry Sacheverell. Swift, who formerly described himself as an "Old Whig" (as a High Church cleric he had no truck with the Whigs' new alliance with religious dissenters), became a leading propagandist for the new Tory ministry headed by the moderate Harley and the High Tory Henry St. John, Viscount Bolingbroke. In *The Examiner* and pamphlets such as *The Conduct of the Allies* Swift argued that the extended Churchill dynasty were bent on raising "the wealth and grandeur of a particular family" through war profiteering.[3] His conspiracy theory centered on the Whig Junto's creation of the Bank of England and the National Debt, measures introduced in William's reign in order to fund the war effort. By Anne's reign they had created "a sort of artificial wealth of funds and stocks in the hands of those who for ten years before had been plundering the publick."[4]

In these prose works Swift laid the foundations for the Tory or Country opposition to the Financial Revolution, the hostility to the new paper-money economy of credit and investment which permeates so many Tory satires of the 1720s and 1730s. But it is arguably in his poems of the same period that his "conspiracy theory" acquires its most powerful mythopoeic form. In *The Examiner* Swift had already taken the risky but necessary step of disgracing the war hero Marlborough by exposing his avarice.[5] In *The Fable of Midas* (1712) Swift develops the analogy between Marlborough and the legendary Phrygian king whose touch turned all to gold. In a musical contest Midas foolishly chose Pan over Apollo: Apollo's punishment – asses' ears – made Midas publicly ridiculous. Swift's poem similarly ridicules Marlborough for siding with Godolphin rather than Harley. But the Midas figure is deeply suggestive. The "magic touch" by which he transforms everything he handles to gold has a satirical application: "Whene'er he chanc'd his Hands to lay, / On Magazines of *Corn* or *Hay*, / *Gold* ready Coin'd appear'd, instead / Of paultry Provender and bread."[6] In December 1711 the commissioners of public accounts had reported to the Commons that between 1702 and 1711 Marlborough had received £62,000 for the contract to supply bread to the army. Yet the satire transcends the merely topical, transforming Whig peculation into some kind of magic which has cheated the people of Britain out of their wealth. So, too, the former Treasurer Sidney Godolphin in *Sid Hamet: or the Magician's Rod* (1710) becomes a wizard or magician, his Chancellor's staff likened to a fantastic, protean conjuring rod, the rod of Hermes, which "o'er a *British* Senate's Lids/ Could *scatter* Opium full as well, / And drive as many *Souls to Hell*."[7] Here Swift borrows what Ronald Paulson defined as the central "fiction of Tory Satire" first created by Dryden in *Absalom and Achitophel* (1681) in which a Whig minister / tempter figure (originally Shaftesbury, first leader of the Whig party) deploys false rhetoric and diabolic or magical powers to dupe an apathetic and gullible people.[8] Such images were given a powerful fillip by the South Sea Bubble in the early 1720s, and reached their apogee in the visual and verbal satire around Robert Walpole.

Whig poets turned such myths back on the Tory ministry itself. In autumn 1711 the Whigs, in alliance with the maverick Tory Nottingham, nearly derailed the peace process by condemning any peace that left Spain and the West Indies in Philip's hands. Harley trumped the Whig majority in the Lords by creating twelve new Tory peers to vote the motion through. Samuel Croxall, a virulent Whig poet, responded with two "Original Cantos of Spencer."[9] In Spenserian stanzas whose archaism veiled political innuendo, Croxall allegorized Britain's martial spirit as Spenser's militant heroine Britomart, bound by a wily magician Archimago (Harley) and guarded by fawning dogs (Tory peers). When the British Bull-dogs (Whig peers) attempt to free her, the wizard simply strikes the ground with his magic stick, conjuring up twelve more loyal cur dogs. Archimago in league with Romania, Sir Burbon (here Catholic France) and Sans Foy, (the Stuart Pretender), contrives to prevent Britomart's marriage to Sir Arthegall (the House of Hanover). Both poems cunningly play on British fears that the Tories were secretly conspiring to bring back the exiled Catholic Stuarts. The Tories devoted an entire issue of *The Examiner* to refuting Croxall's poem by reclaiming Spenser as an "establishment" poet who gave short shrift to anti-government sedition.[10]

The Peace Treaty was finally signed in April 1713 after fifteen months of negotiations. *Windsor-Forest* (February 1713), the most famous poem written in celebration of peace, was initially far less popular than the moderate Whig Tickell's *On the Prospect of Peace* published the preceding autumn. Yet Pope's poem, permeated by a profound sense of historical awareness, is the more memorable. Its debt to Virgil's *Georgics*, a poem with which it is often compared, lies less in the fluidity of its structure (moving between passages of natural description, patriotic emotion, practical rural advice, solitary meditation) than in its sober acknowledgment that the achievements of civilization are founded in past bloodshed. Like Virgil, Pope was writing in the aftermath of a long period of war, and its optimistic vision of a new Pax Britannicum is qualified by a sense of the unending nature of human aggression, which can be redirected, but never eradicated.

Pope also drew heavily on the seventeenth-century royalist topographical poem – Edmund Waller's *On St. James's Park* and especially Sir John Denham's *Cooper's Hill*. Like Denham, Pope describes Britain's past and her national future from the vantage point of the "scenes and prospects around Windsor," a heavily allegorized landscape. Although Pope here, for the first and only time, adopts the voice of the celebratory national poet, his position is in reality strongly partisan.[11] He writes from a Tory, even Jacobite position, suggested initially by the poem's dedication to George Granville, Lord Lansdowne, one of Anne's new Tory peers and a former panegyrist of James II and Mary of Modena, who almost certainly hoped that the Act of Settlement could be set aside. Pope's famous compliment to Anne – "Rich Industry sits smiling on the Plains, / And Peace and Plenty tell, a STUART reigns" (lines 41–42) – links national prosperity firmly to a continuing Stuart dynasty, a tendentious assertion given Anne's poor health and lack of legal Stuart heirs.[12] Pope excised from an earlier manuscript version stronger Jacobite sentiment, but the poem retains a strongly anti-Whig pro-Tory bias. The poem operates through a series of historical analogies linking the barbarous reign of the foreign tyrant William the Conqueror with that of a far more recent "invader," William III. Whereas Whig poetry consistently celebrated William's arrival in 1688 as the start of a new era of British liberty,

Pope by implication depicts It as a return to the dark ages, a period of bloodshed and wasteful war. In his historical survey of the period between the execution of "sacred" Charles I and the accession of Anne, Pope silently assimilates William's reign into "A dreadful Series of Intestine Wars, / Inglorious Triumphs, and dishonest Scars" (lines 325–26). Father Thames's final prophecy of peace indicts Marlborough's victories at Blenheim and at Saragossa in Spain: "No more my Sons shall dye with *British* Blood / Red *Iber*'s Sands, or *Ister*'s foaming Flood" (lines 367–68). *Windsor-Forest* is the irenic Tory response to a decade of extraordinarily bloody Whig poems, such as Addison's *The Campaign*, celebrating Marlborough's victories with "rivers of blood," "floods of gore," and "infants crying in every brake."[13] *Windsor-Forest*'s poignant images of bloodshed and violent death – the pheasant who "Flutters in Blood, and panting beats the Ground," the quails who "fall and leave their little Lives in Air" (lines 114, 134) – function as a mute reproach to the "Battle Hymns of the Junto Whigs."[14]

The succession crisis

The image of Anne as Elizabeth I is central to *Windsor-Forest*: both queens were praised as guardians of British liberty and commerce.[15] At the start of her reign Anne had consciously invited comparisons with Elizabeth by proclaiming that she "knew her heart to be entirely English" and by adopting her motto *semper eadem* ("always the same"). During her last years the irony of the motto was deepened by the ill health of the similarly childless queen. Poets turned to Elizabethan images and poetic forms not merely to celebrate Anne's reign but also to articulate their anxieties over the "mutability" of Britain's future. In 1706 Matthew Prior in his *An Ode Humbly Inscrib'd to the Queen* revived Spenser's Troynovant myth and celebrated Anne as the dynastic heir to the Tudors and Stuarts – a clear rebuff to the "foreign" House of Brunswick.[16] The Whig poet and scholar William Atwood attacked Prior, claiming that his "Dull antiquated Words" not only ridiculed Marlborough (whose victories the poem ostensibly praises) but also slighted the Queen. "To address her *Majesty* in the Stile of Queen *Elizabeth's* Reign may be thought as much a Complement, as a *Jacobite Lady*'s coming to Court on an Inauguration Day, in a *Ruff* and a *Farthingal*."[17] The Jacobite allusion hinted at Whig suspicions of Tory intrigues with the Pretender.

The famous "pastoral war" between the Tory Pope and the Whig Ambrose Philips was as much about the politics of the succession crisis as it was about the appropriate style for pastorals. Both poets had originally had their pastorals published in Tonson's "Miscellanies" (1709). Five *Guardian* essays of April 1713 by the Whig Tickell puffed Philips's rustic Spenserian pastorals to the pointed exclusion of Pope's more polished performances. Pope found revenge in his ironic *Guardian* 40 essay ridiculing Philips's style and praising his own. Philips was Secretary of the Whig Hanover Club, and at least two of his pastorals deal directly with the succession crisis, one lamenting the loss of "Albino" (Anne's last surviving heir, the Duke of Gloucester) and depicting stormy weather ahead.[18] Pope's own pastorals contained encoded Stuart images.[19] John Gay's *The Shepherd's Week* (1713) was written primarily to defend Pope by burlesquing Philips's manner. Yet the comic brio of the eclogues themselves contrasts sharply with the half-playful half-melancholic proem dedicated to Bolingbroke, in which Gay dramatizes himself as a rural swain visiting a court graced by Harley and other Tory peers, fraught with anxiety over the (only just premature) news "that Death / Had snatch'd *Queen* ANNE to *Elzabeth.*"[20]

The Hanoverian accession

Anne's sudden death on 1 August 1714 spelled political death for the Tories, already split by internal division, and triumph for the Whigs, who had thrown their loyalty behind the Hanoverian succession. As Swift lamented, "Too soon that precious Life was ended, / On which alone, our Weal depended."[21] The new Whig ministry impeached a number of leading Tories. Bolingbroke and Ormonde fled to France and the Pretender's service. Harley and Prior ended up in custody. Whig poets celebrated the new regime in panegyric verse, verse given an added force in 1715 by an unsuccessful Jacobite rebellion. But on the whole the early Hanoverians proved more resistant to panegyric than the military hero William III or Queen Anne. They themselves (with the notable exception of Frederick Prince of Wales) had little genuine interest in English literary culture. Robert Walpole, the Whig minister who dominated the English political scene during much of their reigns (roughly 1722–42), was not merely indifferent to poetry, but actively opposed the notion of appointing poets to political sinecures. Thus the extensive network of Whig literary patronage, places, and pensions, which had flourished under William III and continued into Anne's reign, dwindled significantly under the first two Hanoverians. The talented Whig dramatist and poet Nicholas Rowe (poet laureate between 1715 and his death in 1718) was replaced by Lawrence Eusden, a bibulous cleric, and in 1730 by Colley Cibber, a comic actor and stage manager. Colley's mechanical birthday odes (parodied by Swift in his cynical advice to modern poets, *On Poetry, a Rapsody* [1733]), symbolized the nadir of Hanoverian apologetic.

The South Sea Bubble

After 1714 the Whigs steadily consolidated their position by measures such as the Septennial Act of 1716, restricting elections to every seven years. Both the Tories and backbench Country Whigs accused them of corrupt and oligarchic politics, a betrayal of "Old Whig" principles. The event which gave real substance to their accusations was the collapse of the "South Sea Bubble" in 1720.[22] The South Sea crisis marked the culmination of the process begun with the creation of the National Debt under William. In 1711 Harley had proposed that a newly created South Sea Company endowed with a promised monopoly on the profitable slave trade with Spanish America should incorporate the National Debt and pay six percent interest on it to the government's creditors. From the outset its capital was entirely fictitious: the South Sea Company was a financial, not a trading institution. Its directors, including the much vilified John Blunt, issued a series of public subscriptions for stocks which were sold and resold in an upward spiral. They had constructed a financial pump, each spurt of stock being accompanied by an injection of cash to suck it up again, leaving the level higher than before.

The South Sea Company was the most extreme manifestation of the speculating fever which had gripped the nation in the 1710s. Joint stock companies based on all kinds of improbable schemes and projects kept Exchange Alley continually busy in the sale of stocks and shares. By September 1720 South Sea stock prices began to fall, precipitating a run on the banks and London's first ever stock market crash. By December popular fury was directed against parliament and the company directors. In the widespread recrimination that followed, some poets followed *Cato's Letters* (published in the *London Journal*) calling for a return to civic virtue and indicting an entire nation for its contamination by greed and corruption. Hugh Stanhope concluded his lament on the times with an apocalyptic vision of a London in ruin: "Around this spacious City cast your Eyes, / Where Wealth did late, like Thames's River, rise / . . . Gone is our glitt'ring Tide, by which we shin'd, / Left, *Poverty*, and *Dirt*, and Naked Shores behind." Stanhope links the decline of poetry with the seductions of the stock market, "When *Stocks* ran high, and Wit's Productions fell."[23] Poets seeking financial independence were inevitably among those sucked in by the "cheat:" Pope, Swift, and Gay invested in South Sea stock, and all lost money.[24] Yet if their "capital satires" on the bubble were fueled by personal bitterness, the image of the bubble itself provided tremendous poetic capital. Poems such as Swift's "The Bank thrown down," "The Bubble," and Gay's "Panegyrical Epistle to Mr. Thomas Snow" conflate the world of finance and the world of poetic imagination, two kinds of speculative fantasies. "No wonder, if we found some *Poets* there [Exchange Alley], / Who live on Fancy, and can feed on Air." In Gay's poem, the two realms coalesce in the lunatic asylum where a crazed poet and a banker driven mad by his losses do imaginary business together. "Madmen alone their empty Dreams pursue, / And still believe the fleeting Vision true."[25] Swift's *The Bubble* (1720), revised and retitled *The South Sea* (1721), begins by developing his earlier images of Whig "sorcery": "What Magick makes our Money rise . . . / . . . Put in Your Money fairly told; / Presto be gone – Tis here ag'en, / Ladyes, and Gentlemen, behold, / Here's ev'ry Piece as big as ten." Yet the poem moves on through a series of more fluid, morally unsettling "South Sea" metaphors sustained by biblical, classical, and proverbial myths: a Hobbesian ocean dominated by Leviathan-like directors where "Fishes on each other prey," a watery gulf in which subscribers fish for gold and sink without trace, the sea over which Icarus attempts to soar "On *Paper* Wings." [26] The Icarus image combines Faustian aspiration with the paper forms which have replaced real property, an image which anticipates the paper credit that "lends Corruption lighter wings to fly" in Pope's *Epistle to Bathurst*.[27] Swift's deep-seated mistrust of bankers and banking was in 1723–24 famously directed against William Wood, the English ironmonger whom Walpole granted a patent to mint small coins for Irish use. Swift, like other Irishmen, predicted a massive inflation. His *Drapier's Letters* (1724–25), which were remarkably successful in uniting the Irish people to resist the new coinage, earned Swift the sobriquet of Irish Patriot and the lasting hostility of Walpole. The political poems relating to Wood's Halfpence show Swift at his punning best, developing a whole series of mineral analogies between wood, iron, copper, and "brass" – the cheek with which Wood, and by implication Walpole, had attempted to impose an unwanted specie on the Irish people.[28]

The Robinocracy and its opponents

"The Screen of Brass" was, of course, one of the many nicknames given to Robert Walpole, inspired by his broad florid countenance, apparently incapable of a blush, and his ability to "screen" political corruption. In 1720 Walpole managed to deflect criticism for the Bubble away from the royal family as well as restoring government credit. His rapid rise to power came after the sudden deaths of his rivals Sunderland and Stanhope between 1721 and 1722 and his exploitation in 1722 of popular anxiety over a Jacobite plot which led to the impeachment of Pope's friend Francis Atterbury, Bishop of Rochester. Walpole was the most remarkable Whig leader of the century, combining his positions as Leader of the Commons, Chancellor of the

Exchequer, and king's adviser in a prime ministerial role. The "Robinocracy," as Walpole's twenty-year "reign" became dubbed, was a period of unprecedented stability and prosperity for early Hanoverian Britain. This is not how it appeared to some of his contemporaries, who vilified Walpole's corruption, venality, and reluctance to embark on a trade war with Spain as the signs of a nation in rapid moral decline. Among these were virtually all the leading writers of the day: Pope, Swift, Gay, James Thomson, Mark Akenside, Henry Fielding, and the young Samuel Johnson. Walpole's contempt for poets was certainly a contributory factor to their hostility. He reserved funds or sinecures for the journalists hired to defend his policies in the ministerial press. As Swift ironically commented, "A Pamphlet in Sir Bob's Defence / Will never fail to bring in Pence; / Nor be concern'd about the Sale, / He pays his Workmen on the Nail."[29] Even poets such as Pope, who had little need or desire for ministerial patronage, criticized Walpole for his neglect of the arts.[30] Yet it would be too simple to claim that poets attacked Walpole only because he failed to reward them. For Pope and Swift, the Walpole regime marked the culmination of all that they disliked about Hanoverian Whig Britain: the commercialization of the nation, the get-rich-quick ethos, the decline of traditional social bonds. Other poets, such as the Whig James Thomson, who had in 1728 been rewarded with £50 for his praise of Walpole in a elegy to Newton, blasted him the following year in his Britannia for a pusillanimous foreign policy which had damaged Britain's credibility as a trading nation.

Although poets as different as the Tory Pope and the opposition Whig Thomson shared a common concern with civic corruption and cultural decline, there was no organized "literary opposition to Walpole," just as there was no such thing as a monolithic parliamentary opposition to Walpole. Although Walpole faced growing numbers of opponents from the mid-1720s onwards – both backbench Tories and dissident Whigs who left or were dismissed from their government posts – the tensions and conflicts between these different groups prevented a systematic and effective challenge to Walpole's policies. High Church Tories, especially those of latent Jacobite sympathies, often found little grounds for consensus with "turncoat" opposition Whigs. The Craftsman, the leading opposition journal established in 1725 by Bolingbroke and Walpole's former ally William Pulteney, constantly stressed the need for unity. It drew heavily on the civic-humanist tradition of thought which had supplied a platform for country oppositions to the court since the 1670s, and called for the burial of Whig and Tory party labels in the interests of patriotism, an ideal of selfless public activity which found its noblest embodiment in the Roman republican hero Cato. Bolingbroke's Remarks on the History of England and A Dissertation *on Parties*, first serialized in *The Craftsman*, attacked the evils of party and depicted English history as a long struggle between the spirit of liberty and the spirit of faction.[31] In their romanticization of the British past and their call for a return to native virtue, they set the agenda for a body of Patriot opposition poetry far removed from Pope's satires.

The politicization of Pope

By the early 1730s the Scriblerus Club had long since dispersed. Parnell had died in 1722, Gay in 1732. Swift, living in Ireland, contributed little new to the opposition campaign. Pope must, however, remain central to any account of poetry in the Walpole period. His growing alienation from court and ministry inspired an extraordinary body of satirical verse starting with *The Dunciad* of 1728 and ending with the revised *Dunciad in Four Books* in 1743, the year before his death. As the age's greatest living poet, Pope found his writings, conduct, character, and friends constantly held up to political scrutiny. As late as 1730 he was still on fairly good terms with Walpole and the court, despite *The Dunciad*'s implicit critique of the literary culture of Whiggery, a reign of dullness in which "Dunce the second reigns like Dunce the first" (with its sly dig at the succession of George II the previous year).[32] During the early 1730s he embarked on his ambitious *Essay on Man*. This theodicy for the age was dedicated to Bolingbroke: yet his "guide, philosopher and friend" was now playing a leading behind-scenes role in opposition politics.[33]

Such influences are felt in the four *Epistles to Several Persons* of 1731–35, with their uneasy blend of philosophical generalization and sharp social and political commentary. The most pointed of these was the January 1733 *Epistle to Bathurst*, a reprise of Swift and Gay's capital satires of 1720 in its attack on Whig-engineered schemes of finance and ironic allusions to "Much-injur'd Blunt," the disgraced South Sea Company director, John Blunt, who had died the previous year. Pope added new targets in the figures of Walpole's cronies: the crooked financier Peter Walter, Dennis Bond, expelled from the Commons for embezzling Charitable Corporation funds, and Francis Charteris, Walpole's political agent, twice convicted for rape. Pope's resurrection of South Sea Bubble images was highly topical. Between late 1732 and early 1733 the opposition, led in the upper house by Allen, Lord Bathurst, the poem's dedicatee, was pushing for a parliamentary investigation into the use of the forfeited estates of former South Sea Company directors.[34] In the parliamentary sessions of 1733 the issue of South Sea funds was rapidly overtaken by the opposition clamor against Walpole's widely unpopular Excise Bill. A number of Walpole's former supporters, including Pope's friend the Whig peer Richard Temple, Lord Cobham, also opposed the bill. Walpole responded by purging the Lords of the factious Whig peers, among them Cobham, who was also stripped of his regiment. The cashiering of Cobham was widely unpopular. Cobham threw his energies into opposition, using his vast wealth to launch the political careers of his cohort of young nephews. Pope's dedication to Cobham of his 1734 "Of the Characters of Men" was politically pointed, as was his closing paean to Cobham's new-found oppositional patriotism – "'Oh, save my country, Heaven!'"[35]

Between 1733 and 1738 Pope also published his *Imitations of Horace*, a series of loose imitations of the Roman satirist which generate subtle ironies by juxtaposing the manners and mores of Augustan Rome with those of "Augustan" England.[36] The first of these, Satire II.i (February 1733) was unprecedentedly outspoken in its criticism of court and government. Walpole's recent defeat in the excise crisis, the first occasion on which he was forced to withdraw a measure after his Commons majority collapsed in the face of widespread public hostility, emboldened a number of poets, not only Pope, into attack. Paul Whitehead, a lesser satirist, produced in that year *The State Dunces*, dedicated to Pope. Pope's Satire II.i, in which he boldly proclaimed himself "To virtue only and her friends, a friend," also sniped at two of his erstwhile "friends," Lady Mary Wortley Montagu and John, Lord Hervey, both court Whigs. He responded to their subsequent jointly penned riposte, the vicious *Verses Addressed to the Imitator . . . of Horace*, with his *Epistle to Arbuthnot* (1735), his most sustained defence of his "*Person, Morals* and *Family*."[37] Yet the beguilingly personal, confessional tone is belied by the contrivance with which Pope stitches into the poem disparate passages and lines written as much as ten years earlier. The selves Pope dramatizes here are not entirely compatible. The domestic piety of the loyal son who "rock(s) the cradle of reposing Age" (line 409) or the amused tolerance of the Horace figure of the opening lines is at odds with the aggressive glee of the attack on Hervey – "Yet let me flap this bug with gilded wings, / This painted child of dirt, that stinks and stings" (lines 309–10) – as well as with the lofty tones of the satirist who "stoop'd to Truth, and moraliz'd his song," not "for Fame, but Virtue's better end" (lines 341–42). The contrast between Pope's age and Horace's age works to its ironic best in the 1737 *Epistle to Augustus*, a critical survey of English literary history concluding with an ironic mock-panegyric to George Augustus (George II), very unlike Augustus Caesar in both his indifference to verse and a peace purchased at the expense of national pride and national prosperity: "Your country's peace, how oft, how dearly bought!"[38] By 1738, the year in which Pope published the two *Epilogues to the Satires*, he had detached himself from a stance of good-humored Horatian moderation to lash out single-handedly at vice and corruption.

The Patriot opposition

Yet not all opposition poets wrote satire. Some disapproved of its negative tendencies and urged Pope to turn his pen to more positive and inspiring national themes. In 1730 George Lyttelton, Cobham's nephew, wrote an *Epistle to Mr Pope* in which Virgil's ghost tasks the poet to renounce "meaner Satire" and to raise "a lasting Column to thy Country's Praise."[39] Lyttelton, along with his young relatives Richard Grenville, Thomas Pitt, and William Pitt, had all entered parliament by 1735 and gone straight into opposition. Unlike older dissident Whigs they were untainted by former association with Walpole. The "Boy Patriots" or "Cobham's Cubs" are particularly important from a literary perspective.[40] Lyttelton, leader of this group, was a poet and essayist and other members, notably his cousin Gilbert West, were published poets. More importantly, Lyttelton saw himself as a patron of letters, and actively drew into his circle poets such as James Thomson, author of *The Seasons*, his friend David Mallet, and the merchant poet Richard Glover. The Patriots' chief political asset was their intimacy with Frederick, Prince of Wales, disaffected eldest son of George II and Caroline. In 1735 Frederick signaled his growing closeness to this circle and hostility to Walpole by appointing Lyttelton his equerry. Lyttleton played an important intermediary role in drawing poets to the prince's attention. This group of dissident Whig poets and playwrights came closer to recovering the lost ideal of royal patronage lamented by Pope and his friends.

Patriot poetry is very different in form and tone from Tory satire. The Patriots' rejection of satire was part of their larger political-literary agenda which favored the hortatory above the critical, the broad historical sweep over the narrowly topical, and which found expression in such poetic forms as the ode, the ballad, especially the long blank-verse poem. Typical of these were Thomson's five-book *Liberty* (1735–36), which traced the course of Liberty from Greece and Rome down to her "excellent establishment in Great Britain" but which also showed how easily national freedom could be lost and civilization decline. *Liberty* failed to win the same audience as Thomson's earlier *The Seasons*. By the mid 1730s, *The Seasons*, in its revised form, had also begun to mirror Thomson's own political concerns, incorporating paeans to the Patriots Lyttelton and Cobham and a pantheon of "Patriot worthies" – Whig heroes such as Newton, Locke, Hampden, Drake, and Raleigh.[41] Yet *The Seasons* remains rooted in the poet-philosopher's close and loving observation of the natural world – a world apart from

Liberty's lofty abstractions. Thomson saw *Liberty* as his version of an epic poem for the age. Richard Glover, a successful city merchant, followed a previous Whig city-poet turned epicist, Richard Blackmore, in producing his *Leonidas* (1737) an epic on the Spartan's stand at Thermopylae exemplifying love of liberty and patriotic self-abnegation. The poem owed its successful reception to its political timeliness (Prince Frederick was often identified in the role of patriot hero). Yet the Patriot poets, tapping a vein of popular patriotic sentiment, produced some verse closer to the currents of common feeling.

War with Spain

This was especially true of the large body of poems written on the prospect of war with Spain. The years between 1727 and 1739 were marked by steadily mounting pressure on Walpole to declare war over trading rights in the Spanish colonies. In 1727 Spain had originally declared war on Britain for violating the limits of the Asiento clause in the Treaty of Utrecht. In 1729 Walpole, bent on maintaining peace, negotiated the Treaty of Seville. Yet relations with Spain continued to deteriorate in the face of Spanish depredations of English ships. In 1739 parliamentary and extraparliamentary pressure (petitions from merchant communities in Liverpool, London, and Bristol) forced a reluctant Walpole to declare war. Prior to 1728 ministerial poets had written Whiggish paeans to Walpole as defender of trade (notably Young's *Imperium Pelagi*, 1728) but the tide turned with Thomson's *Britannia* (1729) in which the sea-borne goddess indicts ministerial pusillanimity. Poetry played a significant role in fanning war fever. Verses from Mark Akenside's *The Voice of Liberty: a British Philippic*, a rousing Miltonic blank-verse poem, were appended to an inflammatory print of 1738 depicting British soldiers imprisoned by "insulting" Spaniards while Elizabethan naval heroes look down aghast from the skies. Glover's *Admiral Hosier's Ghost* (1740), a rousing ballad recalling the fate of Hosier and his crew, who perished of fever in 1726, disabled by Walpolian scruple from striking down a Spanish gold fleet in the West Indies, proved highly popular, as did Thomson and Arne's "Rule, Britannia," first performed in the *Masque of Alfred* written for Prince Frederick in 1740.

Satire and patriotism

The last four years of Walpole's ministry unleashed political poetry unprecedented in its intensity, vigor, and sheer variety. In 1737 Frederick had gone into open opposition and set up a rival court at Leicester House. Pressure for war seemed to weaken Walpole's position, and in 1738 the Patriot Whigs and Tories led by William Shippen attempted to forge a "broad-bottom" opposition alliance centered on Prince Frederick. It was to this end that Bolingbroke wrote and privately circulated among friends and followers his *Idea of a Patriot King*, a work ingeniously fusing elements of Whig constitutionalism and the Tory romance of kingship in depicting a monarch ruling above party or faction for his people's good. Bolingbroke's treatise, which came close to poetry (*Windsor-Forest* inspired its prophetic conclusion) stirred many poets to produce poems extolling a Patriot king or Patriot prince. Pope, with whom Bolingbroke was then staying, was sufficiently impressed by *The Patriot King* to commission a secret printing: yet Bolingbroke's vein of optimistic messianism rarely entered his own poetry. Never more than lukewarm about Frederick, and skeptical of his potential as national savior, Pope refused to exalt him in verse. Instead he produced two poems distinctive for their combination of patriotic pride and Juvenalian gloom, Dialogues I and II of *The Epilogues to the Satires*, also known by the year of their publication, *One Thousand Seven Hundred and Thirty-Eight*. Dialogue I ends with the magnificently somber cavalcade of the Progress of Vice through the nation: only the poet remains aloof and contemptuous. "Yet may this verse (if such a verse remain) / Show, there was one who held it in disdain" (I, lines 171–2). Dialogue II, outspoken in its support for opposition leaders, contains Pope's most impassioned defence of the satirist's high calling: satire is a "sacred weapon," "To all but heaven-directed hands denied" (II, lines 212, 214). Dialogue II was the last political poem Pope published until *The New Dunciad* of 1742.

He may have been "silenced" by the ministry, whose successful passage of the Stage Licensing Act in 1737 heralded a stricter era of government censorship. In 1739 Paul Whitehead had been arrested and imprisoned for his *Manners*, inspired by the *Epilogue to the Satires*. Another poem of 1738, *London*, an anonymous imitation of Juvenal's third satire (the author was Samuel Johnson) also stirred controversy. During his early years in London Johnson was a violent critic of the ministry, and perhaps of the Hanoverian royal family. Lines in *London* directed at George II have an unmistakable Jacobite thrust in line with the sentiments of two prose satires of the following year, *Marmor Norfolciense* and *A Compleat Vindication of the Licensers of the Stage*.[42] Johnson's indictment of a society in which the outsider is kept out by corrupt patterns of preferment found its counterpart in the poetry directed against Walpole by Johnson's indigent poet friend Richard Savage, a major influence on his politics in this period.[43] *London*'s famous opening lines, in which the disenchanted Thales recalls the lost pride of Elizabethan England ("In pleasing Dreams the blissful Age renew / And call BRITANNIA's

Glories back to view," lines 5–6), combines the heady mood of moral indignation and patriotic nostalgia characteristic of opposition verse in the final years of the Robinocracy.

The fall of Walpole: patriotism betrayed

By January 1742, Walpole faced mounting criticism for his handling of the war. Admiral Vernon's initial victories at Porto Bello had been followed by a series of reversals and losses. Unable to head a working majority, Walpole resigned. He was not replaced, as many hoped, by a Patriot or "broad-bottom" ministry drawn from the best men from both parties, but by a series of less distinguished ministers, such as Wilmington and Pelham, bent on preserving Whig oligarchy. William Pulteney was bought off with a peerage and a seat in the Lords. Poets articulated the widespread mood of cynicism. As early as 1740 Pope had questioned the motives of both court and opposition politicians in the unpublished fragment *One Thousand Seven Hundred and Forty* which opened "O wretched [B]ritain, jealous now of all, /What God, what mortal, shall prevent thy fall?" In 1744 Mark Akenside's bitter *Epistle to Curio* attacked Pulteney for his calculated desertion of Patriot ideals. Pope's *New Dunciad*, effectively a new fourth book to the three-book versions of 1728–29, appeared shortly after Walpole's fall, in March 1742. *The New Dunciad*, the fulfilment of the prophecy of Queen Dulness's universal reign predicted in the original Book III, was far more political in intent and scope than the original version. Pope was looking critically at Hanoverian Britain after twenty years of Walpole's ministry. "Dullness," redefined here more extensively as a moral and spiritual malaise, has, like the triumphal car of Vice in the *Epilogue to the Satires*, spread through the length and breadth of the nation, contaminating her institutions – theaters, schools, universities, the arts and sciences, the church. A pivotal figure is a Walpolian wizard, whose magic cup, a late version of the necromantic potions accorded Whig ministers in Swift's early verse, is also the "*Cup* of *Self-love*, which causes a total oblivion of the obligations of Friendship, or Honour, and of the Service of God or our Country."[44] The next year, Pope revised the entire *Dunciad*, adding to it the fourth book, and – most significantly – replacing the original "hero," Lewis Theobald, with Colley Cibber, the perfect emblem of Walpolian effrontery.

Mid-century directions

The succession of Whig administrations which followed in Walpole's wake failed to throw up any political leader so personally distinctive and charismatic. During the twenty years of the Robinocracy political and visual satire

had gradually built up around Walpole a richly allusive network of historical and tropological correspondences, "the extensive vocabulary of disaffec-
tion minted by the writers of *The Craftsman* and kept bright by continual
rubbing."[45] Walpole's fall, and the "demise" of patriotism as an ideological
force, led many poets not only away from satire but from all politics. With
the fall of Walpole in 1742, and the subsequent deaths of Pope (1744) and
Swift (1745), suggests John Sitter, ended the "Opposition literary contract"
whereby all poets concurred in their opposition to Walpole. Poetry would
no longer be opposed to a particular brand of politics, but to all politics.[46]
Joseph Warton's famous judgment on Pope – "Wit and Satire are transitory
and perishable, but Nature and Passion are eternal" – points to a reordering
of poetic priorities and a redefinition of the poet's role.[47] Poets of the mid
century – Thomas Gray, William Collins, Joseph and Thomas Warton, Mark
Akenside – become more concerned with the power of poetry itself and with
the self-reflexive processes of the poetic imagination. The former Patriot fire-
brand Akenside, for example, turned from strident British Philippics to his
meditative *The Pleasures of Imagination* (1744–54).

Yet poets such as Gray and Collins, who looked to British literary antiquity
rather than to contemporary politics for their inspiration, seemed to be searching for poet-figures with the kind of public and national role which they themselves rejected – or were perhaps denied. As late as 1770, when Gray discussed
poetry with James Beattie, author of the highly popular *The Minstrel* (a sentimental account of the birth of the poet's imagination), he remained convinced that Beattie ought to give his poet-bard Edwin a public and civic role,
that he must perform "some great and singular service to his country . . . (what
service I must leave to your invention) such as no general, no statesman, no
moralist could do without the aid of inspiration and poetry."[48] In formulat-
ing theories about mid-century poetry it is useful to stress continuity as well
as discontinuity. Poets of the Walpole period and figures such as Gray, Collins,
and the Wartons were of overlapping rather than consecutive generations.
Gray's isolated "The Bard," the last of his line, single-handedly defying the
forces of history – "To triumph, and to die, are mine" – bears more than a
passing resemblance to Pope the romantic satirist in *The Epilogue to the
Satires*, single-handedly defying the forces of corruption.[49] One of the final
poems of the Patriots opposition, Gilbert West's *Order of the Garter* (1742),
contains Pindaric odes to a Patriot king sung by choruses of druids and bards
and an antiquarian fantasy of medieval minstrels in "feastful Hall or Bow'r"
– figures that could have walked straight out of an ode by Collins, Gray, or
Joseph Warton.[50] The Patriot emphasis on the earlier stages of the historical
cycle leading to over-civilization and decadence would seem to coalesce with
the mid-century poets' fascination with the primitive and the bardic.

The '45

Mid-eighteenth-century poetry is not entirely apolitical; yet poets addressed topical themes more obliquely and with less sense of certainty than poets of the Walpole period. Collins's "Ode to Liberty," written in the autumn of 1746, shortly after the capture of Genoa and the start of preliminary peace negotiations to end the European War of Austrian Succession, displays an altogether more ambiguous response to war than Thomson's *Liberty*. Collins's Goddess Liberty is finally displaced by the "social" form of the Goddess Concord, perhaps suggesting that Freedom be given a tangible form through peace and reconciliation. The poem opens with a masculine invocation to youths to war – "Who shall awake the Spartan fife" – but ends with a feminized, maternal image of peace, "Before whose breathing bosom's balm, / Rage drops his steel and storms grow calm; / Her let our sires and matrons hoar / Welcome to Britain's ravag'd shore."[51] Britain's shores had recently been "ravaged" by a war closer to home. Collins was writing soon after the Jacobite rising of 1745 had ended in bloody defeat at Culloden. By 1746 Collins cannot confidently proclaim the value of patriotic liberty in a Britain torn by brutal retributions against thousands of her martial youths. The temple of Liberty at the poem's center remains hidden and inaccessible, lost in the realms of myth and time: it only "seems" to rise, no longer a sure source of inspiration.

Collins was not the only poet troubled by the bloodshed. Edward Young, a loyal Hanoverian Whig, raised in his poem to the Duke of Newcastle, "Thoughts, Occasioned by the Present Juncture," the possibility that God was issuing a divine judgment on a corrupt Britain. Young's poem, notably its portrait of Wolsey fallen from power, influenced Johnson's famous *The Vanity of Human Wishes* (1749).[52] Johnson's monumental imitation of Juvenal's Satire x deals with the universal traits of human nature, its restlessness, ambition, desire for power: yet to its author the recent Jacobite rebellion must have seemed a striking and poignant symbol of "the vanity of human wishes." The compassion with which Johnson in this poem treats the fall of princes, notably Swedish Charles XII, a hero in Jacobite eyes, is telling. And the passage between lines 29 and 36, though dealing in generalizations, seems rooted in the recent dynastic conflict:

> Let Hist'ry tell where rival Kings command,
> And dubious Title shakes the madded Land,
> When Statutes glean the Refuse of the Sword,
> How much more safe the Vassal than the Lord,
> Low sculks the Hind beneath the Rage of Pow'r,
> And leaves the bonny *Traytor* in the *Tow'r*,

> Untouch'd his Cottage, and his Slumbers sound,
> Tho' Confiscation's Vulturs clang around.[53]

The italicized word "bonny" (later replaced by the more neutral "wealthy") is distinctively Scottish: the passage clearly alludes to the Scottish lords imprisoned and executed in 1746–47 for their part in the rebellion. The unusually archaic terms "Vassal" and "Hind" also fit in with a Highland context, as does the allusion to the English government's "Confiscation" of land which devastated the Highlands after the '45. Critics have argued fiercely over the extent of Johnson's Jacobitism: this poem shows at least a powerful sense of compassion for the rebels.

The Seven Years' War

Between the '45 and the reign of George III, domestic politics remained relatively tranquil. The clamor for a strong and aggressive policy to defend Britain's American colonies against French power led to the formation of William Pitt's first ministry (1754–61) directing world-wide military operations against the French. The Seven Years' War, especially the successes of 1758–59, which took Canada from France and stripped her of most of her other colonial possessions and which captured Manila and Havana from Spain, fulfilled Britain's long-standing mercantile and imperial aspirations. The Seven Years' War had a profound impact on Britain's conception of herself as a dominant world power, militarily, economically, and intellectually. The poet laureate William Whitehead, Cibber's successor, opened his 1756 "Verses to the People of England" with the hubristic injunction: "BRITONS, rouse to deeds of death! – / Waste no zeal in idle breath!" Yet the poem goes on to stress the essentially humanitarian role of the newly extended British empire in saving the world from French tyranny and Spanish cruelty: "'Let the sordid lust of gain / Be banish'd from the liberal main. / He who strikes the generous blow / Aims it at the public foe."[54] As Kathleen Wilson points out, "Just as both the war and its leaders were celebrated for spreading British freedom and commerce rather than death and destruction over the globe, British imperial ascendancy was glorified as salvation for the world."[55] John Dyer's *The Fleece* (1757), a three-book georgic on Britain's woolen industry, embodies this spirit of benevolent commercial imperialism. Dyer celebrates Britain's commercial energies and depicts her social classes working harmoniously in a shared national purpose. Book III shows Britain as a great historical melting pot, refuge to thousands of Huguenot victims of earlier political oppression. Despite his frequent anti-Gallic declarations, Dyer is rarely merely jingoistic. His patriotism, like that of Pope's *Windsor-Forest*, envisions a world liberated through international trade: "Each clime, each sea, the spacious orb of each, / Shall join their various stores, and amply feed / The mighty brotherhood; while ye proceed, / Active and enterprising."[56]

The early stages of the Seven Years' War had been less promising, marked by Admiral Byng's ignominious loss of the Mediterranean island of Minorca to the French. The debacle provoked an onslaught of popular ballads and satirical prints, as anonymous satirists condemned first the "effeminate" Byng, then Newcastle and Fox, for their corruption and timidity: yet the fact that no major poets addressed the theme suggests the wide gap which now separated the world of politics and the world of "high" culture. It was only in George III's reign that topical politics stirred an intense, if brief, revival of political satire.

Charles Churchill

George III's accession in 1760 was greeted with unprecedented national celebration. The new monarch had imbibed the "Patriot" principles of government above party or faction from his father Frederick, and set about shaking up the Whig oligarchy as well as bringing to a close the glorious but now cripplingly expensive Seven Years' War. In October 1761 Pitt resigned after failing to win Parliamentary support for declaring war on Spain. The resignation was widely blamed on George III's personal adviser and unpopular "favorite," John Stuart, Earl of Bute. Bute took control of the government as first lord of the Treasury on 29 May 1762. The Whig establishment responded by forming the most organized and effective opposition, in both visual and verbal terms, since Walpole's era, in which John Wilkes, the radical MP brought into power on the back of Pitt and the Old Corps Whigs, was the chief player.

Although the campaign against Bute, conducted through a barrage of satirical prints, papers, and poems, bears some resemblance to the campaign against Walpole, both the tone and the target were different. Like Walpole, Bute was accused of being a "royal favorite," of rising from lowly origins, of corrupting the government. Yet Bute, a Stuart accused of encouraging the king's "Jacobite" or absolutist tendencies, was very different from the Whig Walpole. As a Scot, Bute was accused of favoring the Scots and destroying national prestige, and for sexual misconduct with the dowager Princess Augustus. The cartoons and ballads of this period are cruder and less ingenious than those of the Walpole era, mainly focusing on Scottish stereotypes and Bute's sexual organs – "political pornography," as Vincent Carretta calls it.[57] And the satirical poetry generated by the opposition to Bute is again instructively different from the satire directed at Walpole by Pope, Johnson, and Swift. Charles Churchill, its leading proponent, was the most important satirist after Pope. A libertine, hard-drinking rake who pursued his friendship with Wilkes in brothels and the notorious Hellfire Club at Medmenham Abbey, Churchill never attempted, like Pope, to make his personal and domestic morality the ethical basis for his satiric attacks. His early satires, such as *The Rosciad* and *The Ghost*, dealt primarily with literary and theatrical themes, but he and some fellow members of the so-called "Nonsense Club" (George Colman, Bonnell Thornton, Robert Lloyd) joined Wilkes in writing for the anti-Bute paper *The North Briton*.

Between 1763 and 1764 Churchill produced an extraordinary body of satirical verse (twelve published poems in less than a year), including *The Prophecy of Famine*, ironically prophesying a future Scottish invasion of England, the *Epistle to Hogarth, The Candidate, The Duellist* (on the plot to assassinate Wilkes), *Gotham*, and *The Candidate*. The most distasteful of Churchill's satires, the attack on Hogarth, written when the artist was in fact dying, returns satire to the direct and graphic physicality of seventeenth-century lampoons. Yet far more typically his poetry is oblique, rambling, diffuse, even chaotic in form: a sharp contrast to Pope's endless revision and concern for "correctness."[58] Churchill's comically rueful defence of the slipshod productions of his "*slattern* MUSE" – "Rough as they run, the rapid thoughts set down, / Rough as they run, discharge them on the Town" – voices the aesthetic of "spontaneity" cultivated by Nonsense Club members, whose verse is characterized by digressiveness approaching that of *Tristram Shandy*, free associative play, and authorial self-consciousness.[59] This is an odd aesthetic for the political satirist bent on demolishing his adversary. Churchill lacks Pope's tautness and compression, yet his satires are more morally complex than Pope's, substituting a questing ethical relativism for Pope's almost complacent declaration of moral and political certainties. Churchill grew up in the 1740s and shares something of his "adversarius" figures' skepticism about political ideals and political slogans: "When I look backward for some fifty years, / And see Protesting Patriots turn'd to Peers."[60] Whereas opposition poets under Walpole appropriated the slogan of "Independence" – civic virtue premised on the landowning gentry's immunity to parliamentary corruption, or in Pope's case the independence of the poet from political or ministerial patronage – Churchill constantly seeks to question and define its nature and limits.[61] In *The Conference* (November 1763) a threadbare poet and a cynical lord debate the nature of "Virtue," or political integrity. The poet defends his incorruptibility – "Rogues may grow fat, an Honest man dares starve" – but his rhetoric is punctured by the worldly peer who claims that "spite of all You've said, / You'd give Your

Honour for a crust of bread." But after Churchill describes his real-life spell in debtors' prison he throws himself on the mercy of a "gen'rous PUBLIC" which includes the middling classes and even the unruly elements in the populace – a demotic immersion alien to Pope's cultivated circle of aristocrats and authors.[62] Not unlike Samuel Johnson, who rejected Lord Chesterfield's patronage, Churchill asserts an independence founded in the commercial marketplace.

Gotham, the most lengthy and puzzling of Churchill's political satires, is also the most interesting. Gotham was proverbially known as a village notorious for its foolish inhabitants. Churchill's Gotham is an irreverent, carnivalesque, almost utopian fantasy kingdom, a parallel imaginary kingdom to George III's Britain, in which the poet tries out the role of benevolent, paternal monarch, a role that at once parodies and yet seriously parallels the ideal of a Patriot king (a term Churchill continually reiterates) embodied in Bolingbroke's writings and supposedly espoused by George III. Book II's rather more conventional survey of British history (an anti-Bute indictment of Stuart absolutism) gives way to the more personal, lyrical effusions of the "Patriot king" poet. In Book III Churchill's assault on "IGNORANCE" – part of a plea for greater openness in royal and political affairs – leads into a highly personal meditation on the role of "Study" in his life. In depicting himself sitting musing under a "rev'rend oak," "Where with capricious fingers FANCY wove/ Her fairy bow'r," he sounds like any mid-century poet of sensibility.[63] The youthful Churchill wandering "Oe'r hill, o'er dale' reciting his verses to himself while "The clown, his Work suspended, [would] gape and stare, / And seem to think that I convers'd with Air" is second cousin to the "crazed" poet of Gray's *Elegy*.[64]

Churchill's poetry may be hard to characterize, but it would be a mistake to think of it as recondite. His notoriety and irreverence, characteristics of Wilkite popular politics, helped make him the most famous poet of his time: he earned £3,300 in two years before he died (probably from venereal disease) in 1764. Yet its almost romantic subjectivism, even if self-mocking, is very far from the shared ethical language and images which informed the anti-Walpole satires of the 1730s. The times demanded new forms. Behind *The Candidate*'s conventional claim that the age is too corrupt to be reformed by satire lies a tacit recognition that political satire may have had its day. In the 1770s and 1780s social and political protest began to occupy new forms: Churchill's almost Swiftian attack on colonialism and luxury in the opening lines of *Gotham* – the negative consequences of Britain's rapid imperial growth during the Seven Years' War – were to find more elegiac expression in poems such as Goldsmith's *The Deserted Village* (1774) which combines the attack on "luxury" with a more personal, melancholic sense of loss. It was not until the revolutionary fervor of the 1790s that poetry would once again become forged in the crucible of political debate.

NOTES

1 See David Womersley (ed.), *Augustan Critical Writing* (London: Penguin, 1997), pp. xi–xi.
2 George Sherburn, *The Early Career of Alexander Pope* (Oxford: Oxford University Press, 1934), pp. 69–148, contains the fullest account of the literary-political conflicts of the period.
3 *The Prose Works of Jonathan Swift*, ed. Herbert Davis et al. 14 vols. (Oxford: Oxford University Press, 1939–68), VI, 59.
4 Swift, *Prose Works*, VI, 16.
5 See *Examiner*, 23 Nov. 1710 and 8 Feb. 1711.
6 *The Fable of Midas*, lines 15–18, in Swift, *Poetical Works*, ed. Herbert Davis (Oxford: Oxford University Press, 1967), p. 101. The political context is supplied by notes to the poem in Frank Ellis (ed.), *Poems on Affairs of State: Augustan Satirical Verse, 1660–1714* (New Haven: Yale University Press, 1975), pp. 552–8.
7 *Sid Hamet*, lines 40–2, Swift, *Poetical Works*, p. 90.
8 Ronald Paulson, *The Fictions of Satire* (Baltimore: Johns Hopkins Press, 1967), pp. 120–8.
9 Samuel Croxall, under the pseudonym "Nestor Ironside," *An Original Canto of Spencer, Designed as Part of His Fairy Queen, but Never Printed* (1 Dec. 1713) and *Another Original Canto of Spencer* (1714).
10 *Examiner*, 14–16 Dec. 1713.
11 For the most recent political reading, see Howard Erskine-Hill, *The Poetry of Opposition and Revolution: Dryden to Wordsworth* (Oxford: Clarendon Press, 1996), pp. 66–71. See also Earl R. Wasserman, *The Subtler Language: Critical Readings of Neoclassic and Romantic Poems* (Baltimore: Johns Hopkins Press, 1959), pp. 101–68, and Vincent Carretta, *The Snarling Muse: Verbal and Visual Political Satire from Pope to Churchill* (Philadelphia: University of Pennsylvania Press, 1983), pp. 1–19.
12 Pope, *Windsor-Forest*, lines 41–42, in the Twickenham Edition of *The Poems of Alexander Pope*, general ed. John Butt, 11 vols. (London: Methuen and Co.; New Haven: Yale University Press, 1939–69). All quotations from Pope's poetry refer to the TE by line numbers.
13 Joseph Addison, *The Campaign* (London, 1705), in Alexander Chalmers (ed.), *The Works of the English Poets*, 21 vols. (1810), IX, 533–36.
14 Womersley (ed.), *Augustan Critical Writing*, p. xxiii.
15 See Carretta, *The Snarling Muse*, pp. 1–19. For Anne-as-Elizabeth see also Douglas Brooks-Davies, *Pope's Dunciad and the Queen of the Night: a Study in Emotional Jacobitism* (Manchester: Manchester University Press, 1985), pp. 1–11, 33–45, and Toni Bowers, *The Politics of Motherhood* (Cambridge: Cambridge University Press, 1996), pp. 65–71.
16 See Matthew Prior, *Literary Works*, ed. M. B. Wright and M. K. Spears, 2 vols. (Oxford: Clarendon Press, 1959), I, 230–44 and II, 895–98.
17 *A Modern Inscription to the Duke of Marlboroughs Fame. Occasion'd by an*

Antique, In Imitation of Spencer (1706), Preface. For the context, see Prior, *Literary Works*, II, 896, and Ellis (ed.), *Poems on Affairs of State*, pp. 201–7.

18 See Annabel Paterson, *Pastoral and Ideology: Virgil to Valery* (Oxford: Oxford University Press, 1988), p. 212.

19 See John M. Aden, *Pope's Once and Future Kings: Satire and Politics in the Early Career* (Knoxville, TN: University of Tennessee Press, 1978), pp. 62–3.

20 John Gay, *Poetry and Prose*, ed. V. A. Dearing and C. Beckwith, 2 vols. (Oxford: Clarendon Press, 1974), I, 93.

21 *Verses on the Death of Dr Swift*, lines 381–2, Swift, *Poetical Works*, p. 509.

22 The best and most recent study of this subject is Colin Nicholson, *Writing and the Rise of Finance: Capital Satires of the Early Eighteenth Century* (Cambridge: Cambridge University Press, 1994). See also John Carswell, *The South Sea Bubble* (1960, rev. edn. Stroud: Alan Sutton, 1993).

23 Hugh Stanhope, *An Epistle to His Royal Highness the Prince of Wales, occasion'd by the State of the Nation* (London, 1720), pp. 8, 3.

24 See Nicholson, *Writing and the Rise of Finance*, pp. 51–90.

25 "A Panegyrical Epistle to Mr. Thomas Snow," lines 19–20, 34–5, Gay, *Poetry and Prose*, I, 281.

26 *The Bubble*, lines 1–2, 5–8, 69, 45, Swift, *Poetical Works*, pp. 198–204.

27 Pope, *Epistle to Bathurst*, line 70.

28 For poems relating to Wood's Halfpence, see Swift, *Poetical Works*, pp. 198–204.

29 "On Poetry: A Rapsody," lines 187–90, Swift, *Poetical Works*, p. 574.

30 See Bertrand A. Goldgar, *Walpole and the Wits: the Relation of Politics to Literature, 1722–1742* (Lincoln, NE: University of Nebraska Press, 1976).

31 See esp. Quentin Skinner, "The Principles and Practice of Opposition: the Case of Bolingbroke versus Walpole," in Neil McKendrick (ed.), *Historical Perspectives: Studies in English Thought and Society in Honour of J. H. Plumb* (London: Europa, 1974); H. T. Dickinson, *Bolingbroke* (London: Constable, 1970); David Armitage (ed.), *Bolingbroke: Political Writings* (Cambridge: Cambridge University Press, 1997).

32 *The Dunciad* (1728–9), I, 6.

33 *Essay on Man*, IV, 390. For Bolingbroke's influence on Pope, see Brean Hammond, *Pope and Bolingbroke: a Study of Friendship and Influence* (Columbia, MO: University of Missouri Press, 1984).

34 See Earl R. Wasserman, *Pope's "Epistle to Bathurst": a Critical Reading with an Edition of the Manuscript* (Baltimore: Johns Hopkins Press, 1960); Carretta, *The Snarling Muse*, pp. 66–9.

35 Pope, *Epistle to Cobham*, line 265.

36 See Frank Stack, *Pope and Horace: Studies in Imitation* (Cambridge: Cambridge University Press, 1985).

37 Pope, *Epistle to Arbuthnot*, "Advertisement."

38 Pope, *The First Epistle of the Second Book of Horace Imitated: To Augustus*, 397. See Howard Erskine-Hill, *The Augustan Idea in English Literature* (London: Edward Arnold, 1983), pp. 324–34.

39 George Lyttelton, *An Epistle to Mr. Pope, from a Young Gentleman at Rome* (London, 1730), pp. 5–6.

40 For this circle see Christine Gerrard, *The Patriot Opposition to Walpole: Politics, Poetry, and National Myth, 1725–1742* (Oxford: Oxford University Press, 1994).

41 See Thomson, *Spring*, lines 904–62; *Autumn*, lines 1047–80; *Summer*, lines 1479–579, in *Thomson: The Seasons*, ed. James Sambrook (Oxford: Clarendon Press, 1981), pp. 46–47, 188–89, 126–32.

42 See Howard Erskine-Hill, "The Political Character of Samuel Johnson," in Isobel Grundy (ed.), *Samuel Johnson: New Critical Essays* (London: Vision, 1984), pp. 107–36, and his *The Poetry of Opposition*, pp. 119–33.

43 See Richard Savage, "A Poet's Dependance on a Statesman," in *The Poetical Works of Richard Savage*, ed. Clarence Tracy (Cambridge: Cambridge University Press, 1962), and Richard Holmes, *Dr Johnson and Mr Savage* (London: Hodder and Stoughton, 1993).

44 Pope, *The Dunciad* (1743), IV, 515–25, 517n.

45 Maynard Mack, *The Garden and the City: Retirement and Politics in the Later Poetry of Pope, 1731–1743* (Toronto: University of Toronto Press, 1969), p. 128.

46 John Sitter, *Literary Loneliness in Mid-Eighteenth-Century England* (Ithaca, NY: Cornell University Press, 1982), p. 108.

47 Joseph Warton, *An Essay on the Writings and Genius of Pope*, vol. 1 (1756), p. 334.

48 Cited in Irvin Ehrenpreis, *Literary Meaning and Augustan Values* (Charlottesville, VA: University of Virginia Press, 1974), p. 92.

49 Gray, *The Bard*, line 142, in *The Poems of Gray, Collins and Goldsmith*, ed. Roger Lonsdale (London: Longmans, 1969), p. 200.

50 Gilbert West, *The Institution of the Order of the Garter* (London, 1742), p. 53.

51 Collins, *Ode to Liberty*, lines 135–8, *Poems of Gray, Collins and Goldsmith*, p. 454.

52 This argument is drawn from Erskine-Hill, *The Poetry of Opposition*, pp. 146–164, which contains a much fuller account of *The Vanity of Human Wishes*.

53 Johnson, *The Vanity of Human Wishes* (1747), lines 29–36, repr. in *Eighteenth-Century Poetry: an Annotated Anthology*, ed. David Fairer and Christine Gerrard (Oxford: Blackwell, 1999), pp. 263–73.

54 In Chalmers (ed.), *English Poets*, XVII, 230–1.

55 Kathleen Wilson, *The Sense of the People: Politics, Culture and Imperialism in England, 1715–1785* (Cambridge: Cambridge University Press, 1994), p. 194.

56 John Dyer, *The Fleece* (London, 1757), III, 539–42.

57 Carretta, *The Snarling Muse*, p. 232. See pp. 211–47 *passim* on comparisons between anti-Walpole and anti-Bute satire. See also Thomas Lockwood, *Post-Augustan Satire: Charles Churchill and Satirical Poetry 1750–1800* (Seattle: University of Washington Press, 1979).

58 William Whitehead, Churchill's long-standing enemy, addressed some "fragments of verse" to the theme (see Chalmers (ed.), *English Poets*, XVII, 276).

So from his common-place, where Churchill strings,
Into some motley form his *damn*'d good things;
The purple patches everywhere prevail,
But the poor work has neither head nor tail.

59 *Gotham*, I, 177, 173–34, in *Poetical Works of Charles Churchill*, ed. Douglas Grant (Oxford: Clarendon Press, 1956), p. 313. The best account of Churchill in his context is Lance Bertelsen, *The Nonsense Club: Literature and Popular Culture, 1749–1764* (Oxford: Oxford University Press, 1986).

60 *The Conference*, lines 253–4, *Poetical Works*, p. 239.
61 See Brean Hammond and Martin Malone, "Pope and Churchill," in Colin Nicholson (ed.), *Alexander Pope: Essays for the Tercentenary* (Aberdeen: Aberdeen University Press, 1988), pp. 22–38.
62 *The Conference*, lines 80, 91–92, 150, *Poetical Works*, pp. 235, 237.
63 *Gotham*, II, 409, 412–13, *Poetical Works*, p. 342.
64 *Gotham*, III, 401, 403–4, *Poetical Works*, p. 341.

FURTHER READING

Aden, John M. *Pope's Once and Future Kings: Satire and Politics in the Early Career*. Knoxville, TN: University of Tennessee Press, 1978.

Barash, Carol. *English Women's Poetry 1649–1714: Politics, Community, and Linguistic Authority*. Oxford: Clarendon Press, 1996.

Bertelsen, Lance. *The Nonsense Club: Literature and Popular Culture, 1749–1764*. Oxford: Oxford University Press, 1986.

Bowers, Toni. *The Politics of Motherhood: British Writing and Culture, 1680–1780*. Cambridge: Cambridge University Press, 1996.

Brooks-Davies, Douglas. *Pope's "Dunciad" and the Queen of the Night: a Study in Emotional Jacobitism*. Manchester: Manchester University Press, 1985.

Cardwell, John. "Arts and Arms: Political Literature, Military Defeat and the Fall of the Newcastle Ministry 1754–1756." Unpublished D. Phil. thesis, Oxford, 1999.

Carretta, Vincent. *The Snarling Muse: Verbal and Visual Political Satire from Pope to Churchill*. Philadelphia: University of Pennsylvania Press, 1983.

Carswell, John. *The South Sea Bubble*. 1960, rev. edn. Stroud: Alan Sutton, 1993.

Dickinson, H. T. *Bolingbroke*. London: Constable, 1970.

Ehrenpreis, Irvin. *Literary Meaning and Augustan Values*. Charlottesville, VA: University of Virginia Press, 1974.

Erskine-Hill, Howard. *The Augustan Idea in English Literature*. London: Edward Arnold, 1983.

  The Poetry of Opposition and Revolution: Dryden to Wordsworth. Oxford: Clarendon Press, 1996.

  "The Political Character of Samuel Johnson," in Isobel Grundy (ed.), *Samuel Johnson: New Critical Essays*. London: Vision, 1984.

Gerrard, Christine. *The Patriot Opposition to Walpole: Politics, Poetry, and National Myth, 1725–1742*, Oxford. Oxford University Press, 1994.

Goldgar, Bertrand A. *Walpole and the Wits: the Relation of Politics to Literature, 1722–1742*. Lincoln, NE: University of Nebraska Press, 1976.

Hammond, Brean. *Pope and Bolingbroke: a Study of Friendship and Influence*. Columbia, MO: University of Missouri Press, 1984.

Hammond, Brean and Martin Malone. "Pope and Churchill," in Colin Nicholson (ed.), *Alexander Pope: Essays for the Tercentenary*. Aberdeen: Aberdeen University Press, 1988.

Holmes, Richard. *Dr. Johnson and Mr. Savage*. London: Hodder and Stoughton, 1993.

Lockwood, Thomas. *Post-Augustan Satire: Charles Churchill and Satirical Poetry 1750–1800*. Seattle: University of Washington Press, 1979.

Mack, Maynard. *The Garden and the City: Retirement and Politics in the Later Poetry of Pope, 1731–1743*. Toronto: University of Toronto Press, 1969.

Nicholson, Colin. *Writing and the Rise of Finance: Capital Satires of the Early Eighteenth Century*. Cambridge: Cambridge University Press, 1994.

Paterson, Annabel. *Pastoral and Ideology: Virgil to Valery*. Oxford: Oxford University Press, 1988.

Paulson, Ronald. *The Fictions of Satire*. Baltimore: Johns Hopkins University Press, 1967.

Sherburn, George. *The Early Career of Alexander Pope*. Oxford: Oxford University Press, 1934.

Sitter, John. *Literary Loneliness in Mid-Eighteenth-Century England*. Ithaca, NY: Cornell University Press, 1982.

Skinner, Quentin. "The Principles and Practice of Opposition: the Case of Bolingbroke versus Walpole," in Neil McKendrick (ed.), *Historical Perspectives: Studies in English Thought and Society in Honour of J. H. Plumb*. London: Europa, 1974.

Stack, Frank. *Pope and Horace: Studies in Imitation*. Cambridge: Cambridge University Press, 1985.

Urstad, Tone Sundst. *Sir Robert Walpole's Poets: the Uses of Literature and Pro-government Propaganda, 1721–1742*. University of Delaware Press, 1999.

Wasserman, Earl R. *Pope's "Epistle to Bathurst": a Critical Reading with an Edition of the Manuscript*. Baltimore: Johns Hopkins University Press, 1960.

The Subtler Language: Critical Readings of Neoclassic and Romantic Poems. Baltimore: Johns Hopkins University Press, 1959.

Wilson, Kathleen. *The Sense of the People: Politics, Culture and Imperialism in England, 1715–1785*. Cambridge: Cambridge University Press, 1994.

4

BARBARA M. BENEDICT

Publishing and reading poetry

Only a fool, declared Samuel Johnson scrambling to meet his publisher's deadline in the middle of the eighteenth century, would write except for pay. His sentiment expresses a great change in the status of writing and the nature of the activities that surround it: writing, publishing, disseminating literature, and reading. During the eighteenth century, literature was transformed into mass entertainment.

In earlier centuries, virtually only the privileged and highly educated ranks possessed, wrote, or read written texts. This was especially true of poetry partly because its allusions and intricate syntactic techniques traditionally demand from readers a high level of training and close, sustained attention. As long as literacy and leisure remained limited and printing expensive, poetry was largely the province of the elite. If playwrights like Shakespeare wrote drama for a living and poetry in their spare time, by contrast poets enjoyed an idealized image as sophisticated gentlemen who composed in their spare time or so eighteenth-century poets believed. This image is perhaps epitomized by Sir Philip Sidney, the model of the Renaissance nobleman-author: an amateur equally skilled in literature and war, who penned epics between fighting battles and advising princes. Such poets wrote under the patronage of royalty or members of the high nobility. Theirs was a symbiotic relationship: poets need please only their patrons, and their patrons garnered lasting fame from the poetry they encouraged.

In the eighteenth century, this changed. Although writing poetry started to shift into a middle-class profession during the Restoration, when John Dryden and Aphra Behn eked a living from verse, it was in the following century that writing literature transformed into primarily a paid profession in which most literature was produced for immediate publication without the luxury of leisure. New classes of people, particularly those in the middle ranks of society, began to write and publish, and to do so for money. The cultural conception of the writer thus changed from that of a courtly nobleman amusing himself in crafted language, like Charles II's privileged courtier the Earl of Rochester, to that of an ink-stained drone, a lean Grub Street hack as grubby as the street he worked, shivering in his garret as he scribbled sensationalistic pamphlets at the printer's demand. Moreover, the image of literature itself changed since these new writers, aiming to please profit-minded publishers, wrote anything as long as it would sell: scandal, pragmatics, polemic, prose, and also poetry. Rather than meat for contemplative absorption, literature became another fashionable commodity whose main charm was its novelty.

Vital to this transformation of writing was the new mechanism by which books were produced and presented to the public. This mechanism was a revolutionary way of controlling, distributing, and indeed multiplying the production of books: an organized network of artisans and entrepreneurs who, for the first time, created a professional book trade. The business of book production and sale already included different specialists. Before widespread literacy, printers, who were licensed by the government, oversaw in their shops the printing of texts given to them by authors and patrons, and sold these, often to regular clients. Since they were literate, they also often wrote books themselves. Although booksellers who hawked secondhand printed books also existed, they were low-level salesmen rather than producers of culture. As shopkeepers, along with books they sold stationery, medicines, and a range of practical items like boot blacking and pins. For those living in rural areas throughout England, and particularly in the more widely literate Scotland, traveling salesmen or chapmen, like literary vacuum-cleaner hawkers, showed ribbons, penny pamphlets called chapbooks, ballads, and other entertaining items from house to house. Urban printers, however, remained throughout the seventeenth century remarkably independent of the formal mechanisms of patronage; indeed, they were an important avenue for the expression of popular politics and unpopular religion since they could secretly issue, even compose, censored material. Nonetheless, before widespread literacy, most mainly reproduced the texts given to them by authors and patrons.

These established trades, however, were rearranged in the beginning of the eighteenth century through the evolution of a new specialist in the book trade: the publishing bookseller. This new profession was the central innovation that empowered the book trade to monopolize literary production and propelled literature into the center of middle-class consumer culture. These new booksellers were ambiguous professionals: producers of literature yet not themselves authors or printers, booksellers yet highbrow specialists rather than shopkeepers. More than anything else, they were mediators. Reversing the traditional hierarchy of printer and bookseller, they hired printers – and even authors – to produce the works they favored, and sold them to clients themselves. They were devoted to keeping book prices profitably high while selling a lot of books to a lot of people.

Such contradictory goals required flexibility as well as power. Originally, individual booksellers acquired printed books – either from printers or from the frequent auctions of private libraries and of the stock of bankrupt printers – and sold these books from their own shops. Early in the century, however, booksellers in London began to form associations called congers that suppressed competition within the trade. Congers restricted admission to the copyright auctions that were essential for booksellers' survival, and so drove independent booksellers out of business; they also formed alliances so that members of the conger did not bid against each other and drive up the prices. Moreover, they began to acquire copyrights at these auctions, not simply printed copies, a move that allowed them to control the publication of books and began to center book production in their hands. Thus, they engineered a monopolistic hold on both book prices and copyrights. This class of professional bookseller grew into what was known in the nineteenth century as publishers. Under their direction, publishing in the eighteenth century largely evaded governmental censorship, and shifted the cultural center of England away from the court to the entrepreneurial streets of London. Like both authorship and reading literature, publishing became a middle-class activity.

Controlling the production of books ensured fixed prices, but for still greater profits and more security booksellers also required more readers. One technique for building audiences was to improve the distribution of books. Accordingly, congers established trade relations with booksellers all over rural England, as well as the British Isles, Europe, and even North America. This expansion harvested a large, new audience for literature, and incidentally transmitted culture, notably ideas about liberty and government, between nations like France and the North American colonies. This proved immensely profitable. Gradually, an essential part of the bookseller's task became not just finding, but creating new audiences. One important strategy was wide advertisement. Virtually every eighteenth-century book bears at least a single, closely printed sheet at the back announcing other books sold by members of the same conger from multiple (convenient) locations; sometimes, the pages of advertisement outnumber the text, as Pope's footnotes to *The Dunciad* overwhelm his verse. In addition, booksellers began to publish fixed catalogues of books that were always available, and distribute them all over the country. This innovation presented literature as both topical and timeless. It may even have helped to create an audience receptive to the idea of a fixed canon of superior literature that yet coexists with topical verse.

Most significantly, not content merely to disseminate literature, booksellers also intervened in the imaginative creation of literature, for another method of increasing audiences included encouraging the writing of new books and of new kinds of books. Throughout the seventeenth century, the Printing Act had restricted the number and methods of printing books, but when it lapsed in 1695 and was not renewed, the way lay open for a host of hungry businessmen and businesswomen to profit from print by publishing sensitive material. After the Restoration, a new kind of public culture invited writers to try their hands at thinly veiled political commentary. With the new printers, booksellers, and venues for publishing that sprang up all over London came new topics to exploit. Competitively eager to supply a print-hungry public with literary entertainment, booksellers facilitated the development of new genres like the Newgate biographies – prose narratives rushed into print by journalists attending the confessions of criminals from the gallows – which Daniel Defoe imitates in *Moll Flanders*.

Throughout the seventeenth century, illegal publishing persisted. Several printers produced lewd or rebellious works abroad, particularly in Amsterdam, and imported them as foreign books; others printed unauthorized texts secretly under symbolic pseudonyms like John Virtuoso. Although governmental restrictions muffled the printed articulation both of opposition and of prurience, the days of censorship were numbered. Much of the new tolerance resulted from the spread of secular Enlightenment philosophies of the political strength of honesty, man's natural virtue, the moral authority of transparency, and government as a contract with the people. The increasing intermixture of popular and high forms of culture and entertainment, however, also nibbled away at old-fashioned boundaries. In addition, England's own heritage of civil war and the early-eighteenth-century negotiations of political strains between Whig and Tory, and Catholic and dissenter, worked against the strong-armed enforcement of ignorance or moral purity. Despite occasional political spasms, like the Jacobite uprising of 1745, the power and will of the government to control printing steadily weakened throughout the century. The Licensing Act of 1737 repressing plays that opposed the government represents one of the last publicly sanctioned restrictions on publishing until the nineteenth century.

The erosion of governmental restrictions on printing and the rise of publishing as big business thus released previously censored topics for public discussion in print: sex and politics. Booksellers were still subject to prosecution: Edmund Curll, a notorious offender, was convicted of publishing the pornographic *Venus in a Cloister* in 1725–26. Nonetheless, he and others continued to print obscene and politically tendentious works, albeit these were often veiled. Pope's *The Rape of the Lock* (first published in 1712), for example, a tongue-in-cheek poke at the courtship tensions of prominent Catholic families, stands as one of the earliest and most effective exploitations of social scandal and sexual innuendo. Indeed, the metaphorical idiom of poetry enables it particularly to air censored material. Pornography like Hildebrand Jacob's "The Curious Maid" (1720) or Giles Jacob's *Rape of the Smock* (1726) masqueraded transparently as moral fable or satire; poetic rosters naming the liaisons of the famous remained a staple throughout the century. The loss of noble patronage may have enslaved writers under the new yoke of publishers but it also allowed print to become the vehicle of a form of political freedom – or at least, of democratic expression. When writers no longer had to gratify specific patrons but rather faceless readers, they embraced issues of widespread, if not salutary, interest in language the public could understand. Poetry expanded into a genre that encompassed politics, science, and scandal.

At the same time, poetry, rapidly written and produced, was defined as ephemeral: a vehicle of the latest fashion. Booksellers assisted this process by encouraging the retooling of the familiar genres of poetry into forms that would be quick to produce and accessible to a wide readership. They recognized that nothing is so profitable as built-in obsolescence. Traditionally, public poetry at least had been considered the expression of permanent truths, written to last, and books were intended to retain their value in contrast to manuscripts circulated privately, like Rochester's scurrilous verse. Through the course of the century, however, booksellers' practices modified these assumptions. Their rapid publication of rapidly produced works certainly did not vitiate poetry's claim as the expression of a higher truth, but by a material form that presented the topical as the memorable, it did open the door to a new conception of poetry as a blend of high art and popular verse. Under these conditions of production, poetry became as subject to mass-driven fashion as any novelty. As Swift remarks in *Verses on the Death of Dr Swift*, London fashions even in literature change rapidly:

> Some Country Squire to *Lintot* goes,
> Enquires for SWIFT in Verse and Prose:
> Says *Lintot*, "I have heard the Name:
> "He dy'd a year ago." The same . . .
> "To fancy they cou'd live a year!
> "I find you're but a Stranger here . . .
> "His way of Writing now is past;
> 'The Town hath got a better Taste . . .'"
> (lines 253–56, 261–62, 265–66)

Booksellers used other means also to expand the audience for poetry. They recognized that, although long prose narratives attracted readers, poetry traditionally solicited a more exclusive audience. They worked to change that by packaging poetry in ways that would appeal to less confident or leisured audiences. They continued to publish as single works long epics like *Paradise Lost* that, once bought, might take weeks, even months to read – and, worse still, reward a *rereading* that might keep the reader away from bookshops indefinitely. However, they also issued plentiful miscellanies that contained excerpts and patches from longer works, mingled with a variety of short, light, extemporaneous verse. Long scholarly works that won a comparatively small audience, in contrast, were increasingly published by subscription, although well-established publishers did raise their public image by producing high-tone literature. More often, along with collections, booksellers fostered serially-produced newspapers and journals that combined poetry and prose and addressed the current issues on everyone's tongue. These invited a quick read by untrained but curious urban audiences.

Miscellanies or collections of poems themselves helped to change the way poetry was read. Booksellers discovered that the trouble with publishing poems as single items was that the poem had to be good, or at least the poet had to be popular, but then as now good poems and popular poets were in short supply. The plenitude of writers did, however, ensure a large quantity of fairly good poems and moderately popular poets; linked in a miscellany, these works helped to fortify the aesthetic merit of the collection. The whole was more than the sum of the parts. For booksellers, a sheaf of such poems published together as a miscellany proved more profitable than single pieces since they could recycle published works and wring more profit from the copyrights. Readers too seemed to feel they got more for their money. Miscellanies were relatively inexpensive. Although, according to the equivalency tables, *Tom Jones* cost the same as 240 small glasses of gin, miscellanies supplied less dizzying, shorter, and cheaper fare. For authors, however, collections became an important way of establishing a reputation. Collections were signs of a coterie: to be published with Pope made a poet seem comparable with Pope. As public vehicles of poetic unity, miscellanies manifested the connection between writers in print. These compilations of verse thus helped to establish ideological and aesthetic schools of verse. At the same time, they also encouraged readers to compare and rank authors and works. As collections and anthologies reclaimed minor poems from oblivion, they also propelled other poems to stardom. Readers, newly encountering a critically touted poem safely truncated in an anthology, were led to buy fresh editions of the single work or the poet's collected works. Collections paved the way for a canon.

Authors needed to promote themselves in the new, laissez-faire market for literature. These changes in the way books were printed and sold, coupled with demographic and social shifts, speeded up the way books were written.

As London grew to become the hub of a commercial, capitalistic nation, and the practices of enclosure and other legal and social measures drove people from the countryside, many arrived in London to eke out a living writing. Would-be writers, suddenly impoverished wits like Mr. Wilson in Fielding's *Joseph Andrews*, and adventurers who could be writers willingly scribbled off verses for a publisher in a matter of days, and many managed to survive. Writing either for the government's pay or for the pay of a publisher became a quick, if not easy, way to earn a living. For those who wished the public as their patrons, however, competition was fierce. The new kinds of writers, the rush to print, and the resulting volume of printed matter seemed to many to devalue the labor of the writers. Especially to conservative writers, it appeared similarly to devalue the product of literature, forging only waste paper. The Scriblerus Club, particularly Pope and Swift, particularly ridiculed the ponderous, paper-eating labor of unskilled writers in order to clear the way for their style of verse. Moreover, as the increasing professionalization of the book trade made printing fast and cheap, and distribution widespread, quality seemed less profitable than quantity and rapidity. There was simply more of everything – more writers, more readers, more booksellers and printers, and more print.

While pamphlets and newspapers were quite easily attained, however, poetry remained relatively restricted because of the booksellers' stranglehold on copyright. These circumstances provided an irresistible opportunity for piracy: the unauthorized publication of copyrighted material. Particularly in Ireland and Scotland, where different legal provisions paradoxically allowed the production and sale of pirated copies of works in copyright, booksellers regularly produced illegal editions of popular works by fashionable poets. Some were accurate; many were slightly inaccurate, with erroneous words, misplaced stanzas, and misattributed or even deliberately fabricated works, but they steadily sapped the efforts of the London book market to keep poetry a rarified pleasure. They may have disseminated authors' fame, but they did not necessarily fill an author's pockets. Only the piratical booksellers profited for sure.

The power of booksellers over printing, however, was also otherwise challenged. Not only pirates but also entrepreneurs who wanted a piece of the trade challenged congers' hold on the market by printing illegal copies. Key to the power of booksellers over production was copyright. Throughout the eighteenth century, congers battled to preserve, sometimes even to extend, the tenure of copyrights so that they could monopolize the production of books and keep prices high. In 1710, their power exclusively to sell English and foreign language works in England was reconfirmed with the passage of the duplicitously named Act for the Encouragement of Learning. Popularly known as the Copyright Act, this bill masqueraded as a liberal means to open literature by permitting the unrestricted importation of Greek, Roman, and Northern classics, irrespective of extant English editions, and by guaranteeing fair prices for them. That, however, was where the educational encouragement ended. In fact, the committee designed to guarantee the fair prices never bothered to assemble, but the existing restrictions on copyrighting were powerfully reinforced. All copyrights were extended for another twenty-one years, so that those who had the legal power to publish works in high demand like schoolbooks or Dryden's *MacFlecknoe* remained the only publishers licensed to produce them. The Act thus strengthened the congers' monopolies by ensuring that powerful booksellers retained complete control over the printing of new and valuable books.

Throughout the century, this sore issue of copyright reared and was beaten down. Repeatedly, courts reaffirmed that booksellers owned copyrights for indefinite periods – in other words, forever. Needless to say, piracy and more or less blatant infractions multiplied. Most were simply ignored because prosecution was too difficult for booksellers. Authors had little say in the matter. In the scrabble for the right to reprint works, the primary producer, the author, still occupied a lowly place. Formal legislation acknowledging authors' rights did not pass until 1814, and throughout the eighteenth century, authors sold their products outright so that literature became immediately the exclusive property of the copyright holder: Pope sold Lintot the first version of *The Rape of the Lock* for a mere £7; a wiser Young sent Dodsley *Night Thoughts* for £200, but it remained hugely popular throughout the century. Akenside asked Dodsley for £120 for *Pleasures of the Imagination* – which remained popular in the nineteenth century.[1]

Although the main issue remained money, a new set of concerns began to emerge in the rhetoric of the repeated challenges to copyright restrictions. These concerns echo those of contemporary philosophy: the principle of free trade, the public's right to knowledge conveyed in inexpensive and competitive publications, and limping far behind these a hint of the rights of authors over the productions of their intellectual labor. The first two of these issues came to a head in a famous trial in 1774 between Alexander Donaldson, a successful Edinburgh publisher permitted to sell books in Scotland, and Andrew Millar, the London publisher of Fielding and others. In defiance of the law, Donaldson opened a London bookshop and from it sold his own books, notably a copy of James Thomson's *The Seasons*, whose copyright was owned by Millar. When Millar sued, unwisely in a Scottish court, Scottish law lords, arguing that London congers gouged the public and denied them free access to printed literature, promptly overturned the privilege of indefinite copyrighting. More shocking still, when he took the case to the House of Lords they supported the Scottish decision. The *Millar v. Donaldson* case shattered the argument for perpetual copyrights, and opened the floodgates for the competitive reprinting of popular literature. Now that publishers could reissue historical works, literary values again changed. Topicality lost its stranglehold on fashion, and the way was paved for the reverence of the historical canon of English poetry.

Notorious among piratical booksellers in the early years of the century was Edmund Curll. Curll published a mass of topical material, polemical pamphlets and squibs that created controversy as much as they reflected it. Some of these texts he may have written himself, but others he commissioned from his stable of hacks whom he paid per composition. Some publishers supported poets completely. Vicious rumor had it that when he housed his poet William Pattison, Curll starved and worked him to death: certainly he died two months after moving into Curll's house. Curll's favorite target was Pope. Not only did he publish attacks on Pope by intellectual rivals, but he pirated Pope's own poems, publishing cheap versions of famous pieces like *To Miss Blount* and the *Moral Epistles*. In revenge, Pope invited Curll and Lintot out for a frank talk over a tankard in a tavern, and slipped a powerful emetic into Curll's frothing brew. Its physical effects were turned literary, as Curll spilled the story all over the press, characteristically transforming his own humiliation to his profit. Determined to retain control over his own work and to foil Curll, Pope trumped the scurrilous pirate with his own collection. He collaborated with Swift and Lintot to issue an authoritative, three-volume collection of *Miscellanies* (1726–27) of his minor works. Nonetheless, Curll persisted in illegally publishing cut-rate versions of Pope's work, along with duplicitous collections of the works of other copyrighted poets with fallacious titles, incorrect contents, or misattributed poems. These collections, however, mirrored those of more reputable publishers who similarly printed collections of miscellanies to wring more profit out of the same material.

The prevalence of piracy reveals another significant aspect of the production of eighteenth-century poetry. In the first half of the century, a few authors like Pope and Swift were gaining reputations; promoted by friends and enemies alike, they became names to conjure with, and all fashionable readers knew their work. Nonetheless, they remained second cousins to journalists. They were literary workers of an intellectual sort, in an elite social circle, to be sure, but still part of an industry mediated by booksellers. They provided topical entertainment much of whose value depended on quick publication to catch the concern of the day. This status prevented poets from being regarded as creators of timeless art in the way that poets of the Renaissance had been at least in cultural memory, and instead made them subjects of the audience's whim. They were exchangeable, and so was their work. If you couldn't get a satire by Swift on the latest scandal, try for one by Pattison.

Pope's skillful manipulation of his own reputation helped to change this situation. He represented himself as a natural artist subject only to timeless truth:

> Why did I write? What sin to me unknown
> Dipt me in Ink, my parents' or my own?
> As yet a Child, nor yet a Fool to fame,
> I lisp'd in Numbers, for the Numbers came . . .
> Not Fortune's Worshipper, nor Fashion's Fool,
> Nor Lucre's Madman, nor Ambition's Tool,
> Not proud, nor servile, be one Poet's praise
> That, if he pleas'd, he pleas'd by manly ways;
> That Flatt'ry, ev'n to Kings, he held a shame,
> And through a Lye in Verse or Prose the same:
> that not in Fancy's Maze he wander'd long,
> But stoop'd to Truth and moraliz'd his song.
>   (*Epistle to Dr. Arbuthnot*, lines 125–8, 334–41)

Pope's redefinition of the poet as a unique and incorruptible moral monitor of society helped to raise the reputation of poets. So too did his ability to appeal directly to the public, including the new audiences of women and the middle classes, along with the traditional audience for poetry.

The interdependence of publishing and authorship peaks in the mid century in Robert Dodsley's *A Collection of Poems by Several Hands* (1748–58, revised and continued by Pearch in 1775). Dodsley rose from being a liveried footman (a condition he celebrated in his own verse) to one of the most – some claim, *the* most – important publishers in the mid-eighteenth century, printing works by Pope, Swift, Chesterfield, Johnson, both Wartons, Young, Gray, and all the most fashionable poets of the period. Richard Graves in 1756 eulogized "Dodsley's Mint" for stamping verse with the authority that turns it from raw material to sterling.[2] "We have done with patronage," Johnson announced grandly to Boswell in 1773, yet in an earlier letter written on 9 January 1758, he called "Doddy" "my patron".[3] Perhaps because of his background, Dodsley treated his poets with more respect than many previous publishers. For his miscellany, he enlisted their expertise, especially that of George Lyttelton, solicited new works from them, asked their advice, and relied on their evaluations. The project grew from "an inexpensive publishing venture which allowed the bookseller to place a backlog of poetry on the market, to its unprecedented success as the best-selling miscellany of the century, an emblem of polite taste in poetry widely recognized as a signal commercial and literary success".[4] Anchoring new with familiar but popular works like *Grongar Hill*, it became an authoritative collection that set the standard for elite taste in poetry for the literary consumers not only of the time, but for the next hundred years.

Even more significantly, the series redefined publishers as elite mediators – not merely intermediators but people whose contacts with writers, personal preferences, skill, and judgment influenced the production of poetry. Dodsley's collection included Thomas Gray's "Ode on a Distant Prospect of Eton College," "The Progress of Poesy," *Elegy Written in a Country Churchyard* (first published in 1751, and later appearing as the first poem in volume IV in 1755), and "The Bard," all of which became literary staples. In addition, it juxtaposed works by Shenstone and Young that shared Gray's poetic mood. These inclusions could be said to have invented from the collected proto-romantic sensibilities of his authors what critics called the Night or Graveyard School. Dodsley's miscellany also exploited another change in the selling of poetry: the presentation of collections as high art, books designed for gentlemen's libraries rather than quick fixes on the latest topic. Dodsley's second edition is highly ornamented for a mass-market book, full of fine engravings and carefully printed. Other publishers would follow suit.

While Dodsley's series attracted sophisticated readers, it did not especially cater to the growing minority of new readers: middle-class women. That task remained for a publishing duo already experienced in addressing such an audience: the co-authors of *The Connoisseur*, George Colman (the elder) and Bonnell Thornton. Their two-volume *Poems by Eminent Ladies* (1755, reissued in 1773, and reprinted and revised in 1780), ambitiously aimed to define a female canon of eighteenth-century authors equivalent to and consonant with the male poetic tradition. In their preface, the editors announce that their project stands as "proof that great abilities are not confined to the men, and that genius often glows with equal warmth, and perhaps with more delicacy, in the breast of a female."[5] By seeking to "compliment" the "Fair Sex", they also seek female readers, an audience large enough to make their project pay. In its editorial practices, this collection reflects the tastes of this audience and the changes in the way books are produced. Acknowledging that they have selected certain works from each author's opus, the editors explain that,

> as most of their poems were first published by subscription, the bulk, as well as the merit, of the volume was to be considered: on which account several pieces were thrown in merely to fill up so many pages. Besides, most of these Ladies (like many of our greatest male writers) were more indebted to nature for their success, than to education; and it was therefore thought better to omit those pieces, which too plainly betrayed the want of learning.   (p. iv)

By contrasting their selective editing with the indiscriminate publishing of previous miscellanies, Colman and Thornton define their enterprise as a summit of taste. Significantly, they also provide biographical prefaces by Johnson and Cibber, among others. These ways of contextualizing verse reveal that literary collections were transforming from envelopes of ephemeral fashion to anthologies for study.

Poems by Eminent Ladies anticipates later anthologies in other significant ways. Colman and Thornton reprint works already familiar from previous miscellanies, and, like Dodsley, heavily weight authors already familiar to their readers: Aphra Behn appears the most – she is represented by forty-nine selections – whereas many, like the Bluestocking Elizabeth Carter, are allowed only three or four poems. This conservatism did not escape contemporary reviewers. The *Monthly Review* condemns the collection as comprising "very common" texts.[6] Nonetheless, the volumes include eighteen writers: Mary Barber, Behn, Elizabeth Carter, Lady Chudleigh, Mrs. Cockburn, Constantia Grierson, Mary Jones, Anne Killigrew, Mary Leapor, Mrs. Madan (formerly Miss Cowper), Mary Masters, Lady Mary Wortley Montague [sic], the Honourable Mrs. Monk, Duchess of Newcastle, Miss Katherine Philips, Mrs. Laetitia Pilkington, Mrs. Elizabeth Rowe, and Lady Winchelsea. Characteristically, whereas the first volume holds works by only seven poets, the last volume contains many, shorter selections by all the rest. Balancing variety and completeness, this anthology both rivals and complements Dodsley's series.

These anthologies show the beginning of the formation of a canon, a body of works widely accepted as the fundamental standard of literary excellence. The canon as a concept seems largely the invention of critics and booksellers. From the previous century, secondhand booksellers and traders had flourished in London, and they gained more customers throughout the century. The availability of secondhand books may partly have motivated booksellers to contrive their own collections as rivals. But one of the most significant issues was the sheer volume of material to be read. In *The Dunciad*, Pope reviles the swelling flood by moaning, "A Lumberhouse of books in ev'ry head, / For ever reading, never to be read!" Readers needed guides through the clutter, or at least authors and booksellers thought they did. This guidance was provided by authors, critics, and reviewers who offered opinions in print. Powerful as they were, publishing booksellers did not control literature. By the mid century, writers were setting themselves up as monitors of taste. "The Club", a gathering of like-minded artists founded by Samuel Johnson, that met at the Turk's Head in Soho in the winter of 1763–64 and included Oliver Goldsmith, Thomas Percy, Edmund Burke, and James Boswell, formed a coterie influencing literary reputation, but the more formal avenue was periodicals where reviews of current books established a set of standards for the comparative evaluation of poets. By the end of the century, these venues encouraged readers to distinguish – indeed choose – poets by their names and individual styles. Authors in turn, further energized by emerging Romantic ideals of authorship as a sublime task, began to redefine their work as high cultural enterprise, not labor for pay.

From the first decades of the century, authors had fought over how to judge literature. Despite the efforts of the traditionalist Scriblerians like Swift and Pope and the self-styled moderns in the battle of the books – a bitter pamphlet war in the early years of the century over whether classical or modern literature were best – it was not until the middle of the century that a central aesthetic emerged by which all poetry could be judged, and this aesthetic resulted not from the dominance of particular authors, not even Pope's fame, but by means of two, large-scale publishing mechanisms: the anthology and the critical review. Once copyrights had expired, and particularly following *Millar v. Donaldson*, publishers like John Bell could print anthologies of poetry written from the previous hundred years, not only the poetry for which they owned the copyrights. Such anthologies were not entirely new. Early in the century, booksellers had sewn together remaindered poems, slapping a fresh one on the top, and possibly printing a new title page to lure unobservant readers who told books by their covers into buying stale or illegal stock. Now, following Dodsley's authoritative series, booksellers organized dozens of works by date, and issued them in multi-volume series. Joseph Ritson, Thomas Percy, John Bell, John Newbery, and other booksellers published little libraries, sometimes exceeding twenty volumes, each containing a generous collection of a particular genre: English plays, novels, essays, and especially poetry. Rather than the voice of the present, poetry became the testament of England's literate past. The historical anthology was born.

While Dodsley and others commissioned works, the most important patron was the literary consumer, the member of the reading public. Writers in the eighteenth century negotiated a precarious living. The aristocratic systems of patronage that had supported authors as recent as Dryden dried up in the early century, and increasingly even subscription proved untenable in the face of a mobile, restless readership. Subscription, by which an author and bookseller would circulate a proposal describing a new publication to potential buyers and finance the publication with their front money, shrank to become the mechanism for the publication only of works whose audience would assuredly be small. Profit could still be made: Pope published his translation of *The Iliad* by subscription and pocketed over £5,000 by harvesting 575 subscribers at 6 guineas each, and then selling Lintot the rights to additional sales for £200 per volume. In the mid decades Johnson and others engineered subscriptions to support the publications of friends like Richard Savage and Mary Jones. Nonetheless, since profits for both authors and booksellers lay in the wide distribution of texts to an expanding audience, subscription fell into disuse as the century proceeded.

There was, however, the major exception of serial publications. Thanks partly to the establishment of London penny post in 1680, and partly to new printing freedoms, serial publication that relied entirely on subscription flourished throughout the century. Newspapers were immensely popular, if not automatically successful. In the first decade of the eighteenth century, there were already twelve London newspapers, a number which doubled by the mid century; by 1790, there were thirteen morning, one evening, seven tri-weekly, two bi-weekly newspapers.[7] Such a proliferation of print dedicated to reportage and news cleared the way for other serial publications that provided specifically literary entertainment: periodical journals.

Periodicals had a unique function in the eighteenth century as vehicles for both cultural commentary and the expression of popular opinion. From the start of the century, periodicals worked to expand the social conversation beyond politics and reporting to social criticism, cultural affairs, and literature. In the late seventeenth century, the visionary publisher John Dunton had started a periodical called *The Athenian Mercury* whose purpose was entirely to reply to readers' questions. Dunton announced that his club of learned experts could reply to any question, barring obscene or inflammatory political queries, that readers submitted to his bookselling shop. For their ease, he divided knowledge into three categories: spiritual or religious questions, those concerning natural philosophy or science, and those answered by the "Secret Oracle," dedicated to ladies' questions mainly concerning sex. The project was so wildly popular that other writers and publishers imitated the format of inviting readers to respond to their contents throughout the century.

In the eighteenth century, however, readers' contributions to periodicals became increasingly more literary. They shifted away from questions to the submission of essays, fictional vignettes, and poems. Addison and Steele's *Spectator* (1711–12) epitomizes the journal of the early century. Highly topical yet skillfully crafted, it blended news and entertainment, reportage and literature. Among its devices was the invention of literary characters who submitted reports from the countryside. Real readers soon imitated them, submitting essays that were printed in a variety of periodical journals. Stirred by this success, the genre proliferated: by 1745, there were thirty periodical journals, aside from newspapers, and in the next fifteen years forty-five more would appear. Periodicals thus became a new venue for publication by part-time writers, amateur critics, and authors in training. They also became steadily more ideologically specific. As well as supplying printed literary entertainment, they included commentaries on current cultural affairs, and increasingly on books. Book reviews in periodicals could be quite influential, and they gave regular contributors both influence over writers and bargaining power with publishers. As a result, periodicals grew bulkier. Between John Dunton's *Athenian Mercury* in 1691 and Sir Richard Steele's *Tatler* in 1709, the periodical used the format of newspapers: a single, half folio sheet issued two or three times weekly to coincide with the country mails. Only Peter Motteux's *Gentleman's Journal* (1692–94), "forerunner of the magazine," used the longer format which became popular in the mid century of monthly issues of as much as thirty pages.[8] During the course of the century, however, longer periodicals allowed greater space to readers' queries and contributions.

These periodicals drew together, if only imaginatively, an urban population that was growing apart. J. H. Plumb points out that "The size of the audience must not be exaggerated. No more than 3,000 copies of *The Spectator* were ever printed. The *Craftsman* at the height of its popular attacks of Sir Robert Walpole rarely reached 10,000 – the same figure given by Dr. Johnson of the most successful of all eighteenth-century magazines – the *Gentleman's Magazine*."[9] As Johnson's mistaken estimate shows, periodicals seemed ubiquitous because an enormous number of people read the better-known newspapers, periodicals, and magazines by renting them from newspaper clubs, or reading them at coffee houses which regularly subscribed to the most popular serials. The *Gentleman's Magazine*, founded by Edward Cave in 1731 as a periodical news digest, contained reviews, reportage, and commentary. This journal first employed the term "magazine" to describe a periodical. Gradually, it began to specialize in critical essays and to include a greater number of original contributions and records or lists of published materials along with its habitual digests and extracts from contemporary works and parliamentary reports. Debates on cultural and literary issues, like the vexed question of whether Dryden or Pope were the superior poet, found a venue. Edited by the fictional person Sylvanus Urban, it grew to become the centerpiece of London life, printing at its height the correspondence of between six and seven hundred people.[10] This editorial policy propelled poetry into the public sphere as part of fashionable education, and endowed critics with the power to make and break authorial reputations. As England's most popular periodical, the *Gentleman's Magazine* issued 3,500 copies every month. Rival publications also flourished, notably the *Monthly Review* (1749–1845) founded by Ralph Griffiths and its opponent, the Tory *Critical Review* (1756–90) with contributions by Johnson and Goldsmith.

In modern terms, the production of print, books, and serials, remained fairly small: the total production of books in England in the eighteenth century was probably slightly under 110,000, of which the vast majority were printed in London.[11] Still, the perception that urban culture had abruptly turned into a literate culture was not mistaken. Not only were there more books, more people read them. Literacy had leapt forward in the period between the civil war and the mid eighteenth century; David Cressy calculates that whereas 90% of women and 70% of men were unable to sign their names, and thus probably functionally illiterate at the time of the civil war, by the mid century only 60% of women and 40% of men were so disabled.[12] Moreover, these were new readers, including not only the traditional audiences of gentry and elite members of high-ranked professions, but all sorts of professionals, merchants, farmers, tradespeople, skilled artisans, servants, some laborers, and, of course, women of all ranks, but especially the gentry and middle class.

These changes in the way poetry was produced and sold may have influenced the way it was read. Certainly they changed *where* it was read. Poetry was only one of the forms of literature available to readers to peruse for pleasure, and authors of course wrote not only poetry but also journalistic stories, novels, and other prose genres. Reading itself was becoming a leisure activity designed for recreation as much as social advancement or the acquisition of necessary knowledge, and thus more public reading spaces opened up. By 1760, newspapers were distributed all over England. Moreover, coffee houses and taverns kept racks of newspapers, pamphlets, and sometimes ballads for customers to rent or borrow; Plumb estimates that there were 2,000 coffee houses by the reign of Queen Anne.[13] Independent newsrooms also rented customers newspapers to read for a fee. These public venues encouraged the public discussion not only of news, but of literature and literary values.

Poetry also reached audiences through circulating libraries. Increasing in numbers throughout the century, these libraries catered to all kinds of audiences: urban and rural, resident and mobile, female and male. Although they became renowned for supposedly pandering to a taste for cheap sentimental novels that was purportedly female, they also held a great store of poetry and helped to make elite collections like Tonson's "Dryden's Miscellanies" and Dodsley's *Collection* available to readers who could not afford to own them. Unlike coffee houses, these libraries permitted readers to take volumes home. Such practices encouraged a variety of ways of reading: privately, in groups, or aloud. Since these poetic collections and editions of poetry were juxtaposed with prose, even in competition with fashionable novels, readers may also have read them much as they read prose. Such venues may well have influenced the way poets used sound devices like rhyme, alliteration, and assonance, and how they structured their verse.

Unquestionably, however, poets knew they were writing to a new kind of reader. During the eighteenth century, women became a significantly large audience whose particular training, concerns, and venues shaped the way literature was read, as well as written. In the various roles of readers, correspondents, and subjects, women facilitated the construction of a concept of femininity that not only helped to shape the domestic ideal, but also introduced into public print previously private areas of female subjectivity and experience.[14] While the novel explicitly addressed these areas, poetry was also affected. Women readers were also writers whose concerns and questions achieved unprecedented authority by appearing in the printed dialogues published by periodicals like *The Athenian Mercury*; they thus emerged as writing subjects, establishing an identity in print that prompted many to become poets whose anonymity allowed "the public expression of private experience".[15]

These differences in readers and places to read suggest that reading itself may also have changed. Rather than revering poems tested by time, readers were encouraged to consume poems and translations fresh from the press. Moreover, they were encouraged to consume *a lot* of them. Literacy was the mark of fashion; people of widely different incomes and levels of literacy alike wanted the latest pamphlet. As a fashionable pleasure, read for topical interest in public venues, poetry had a social value perhaps even more powerful than that of novels. Wits could quote verse as well as compose extemporaneous verses that often found their ways into published miscellanies; moreover, the knowledge by heart of "beauties," passages of superb artistry, imagery, or sentiment, came as the century wore on to mark the fashionable education and sensitivity of the gently born, particularly marriageable woman. By the end of the century, memorized excerpts from Shakespeare, Pope's *Rape of the Lock*, *The Hermit*, Gray's odes, verse by Parnell and Thomson and others worked to market this well-read woman. More generally, as the sheer volume of publications grew, readers may well have changed the way they read in order to retain their stamp as well-read. Robert DeMaria has suggested that instead of reading a few works intensively, eighteenth-century readers began to skim a great number of works, aiming for wide coverage rather than profound apprehension.[16] Furthermore, the increasing competition between poets and booksellers, as well as the competition for readers in a glutted market, by the late century began to encourage a comparative approach to evaluating literature: since one cannot read everything, readers were told to read only the best. Volumes containing dozens of short poems, magazines and periodicals featuring a medley of different kinds of literary genres, and reviews summarizing the merits of new works all contribute to this new way of reading: for breadth rather than depth.

The shift in poetry's status and subjects to topicality was not dictated by booksellers' practices alone. Rather, a host of economic and social changes prompted a culture of consumption that valued novelty and that extended to literature. The increase in literacy and thus in audiences, cheap printing, the growth of London as the nation's center, and the influx of commodities from the colonies helped to make news central to urban survival. Nonetheless, the new class of publishing booksellers brokered a vital change in literature and culture: the rise of print as the mark of modernity. By facilitating, even initiating, the publication of literature, booksellers became the lynchpin between the two tiers of book-producers, the writers themselves, and the printers who actually produced the material books. At the same time, they mediated readers' desires. This new division of labor proved very successful, at least for booksellers. To the people of the eighteenth century, particularly in the early decades, the world seemed awash in books, yet fresh material always won readers. The topical material in prose and verse that burst from the groaning press changed not only the status, but the nature of poetry. It became a fashionable, topical item produced quickly for consumption by a wide, anonymous audience.

This role itself was to change. In addition to new methods of acquisition, advertisement, production, and distribution, booksellers also packaged poetry in new ways. The professionalization of book production ushered in a new era for the book. No longer the pleasure only of the elite, it transformed into a consumer item, part of a commercialized leisure culture that sold entertainment to a mass audience of newly literate people. As these new audiences, book-trade professionals, and generic forms all matured, however, the topicality that had bolstered poetry as a popular form sprouted a new way of appreciating verse: comparative ranking. This ranking placed both poets and readers in a competition of taste, a competition happily mediated by the new class of publishers issuing anthologies, periodicals, and reviews. Thus, poetry's very popularity in the eighteenth century defined it as a form that blended a chic subject matter appealing to all fashionable readers with, increasingly, a style showing the poet's unique and superior talent that would appeal – so the rhetoric urged – only to the most discriminating of them. Indeed, poetry's very popularity shaped it as the voice of the new, Romantic sensibility in the early decades of the nineteenth century. The eighteenth century's favorite form for a quick read became the next century's revered test of taste.

NOTES

1 Alvin Kernan, *Printing Technology, Letters, and Samuel Johnson* (Princeton, NJ: Princeton University Press, 1987), p. 64.

2 Michael F. Suarez, S.J., "The Formation, Transmission, and Reception of Robert Dodsley's *Collection of Poems by Several Hands*," in Robert Dodsley, *A Collection of Poems by Several Hands*, ed. Michael F. Suarez, S.J. (London: Routledge/Thoemmes Press, 1997), I, 1; Graves's poem appeared in *Aris's Birmingham Gazette*, 20 December 1756, quoted in James Tierney, *The Correspondence of Robert Dodsley, 1733–1764* (Cambridge: Cambridge University Press, 1988), p. 50 (cited in Suarez, p. 103, n. 1).

3 James Boswell, *The Life of Samuel Johnson*, ed. G. B. Hill, rev. L. F. Powell, 6 vols. (Oxford, 1950), I, 326; quoted in Suarez, "The Formation of Dodsley's *Collection*," p. 103, n. 2.

4 Suarez, "The Formation of Dodsley's *Collection*," p. 4.

5 *Poems by Eminent Ladies* (London: R. Baldwin, 1755), I, iii.

6 *Monthly Review* 12 (January–June 1755), p. 512.

7 Jeremy Black, *The English Press in the Eighteenth Century* (Aldershot, Hants.: Gregg Revivals, 1991), p. 14.

8 Kathryn Shevelow, *Women and Print Culture: the Construction of Femininity in the Early Periodical* (London and New York: Routledge, 1989), p. 26.

9 J. H. Plumb, "Commercialization and Leisure," in Neil Mckendrick, John Brewer, and J. H. Plumb, *The Birth of a Consumer Society: the Commercialization of Eighteenth-Century England* (Bloomington: Indiana University Press, 1982), pp. 269–70.

10 Gretchen M. Foster, *Pope Versus Dryden: a Controversy in Letters to "The Gentleman's Magazine"* (Victoria, BC: University of Victoria, 1989), p. 27.

11 Kernan, *Printing Technology*, p. 61, quoted from C. J. Mitchell, "The Spread and Fluctuation of Eighteenth-Century Printing," *Studies on Voltaire and the Eighteenth Century* 230 (1985), 305–21.

12 David Cressy, *Literacy and the Social Order: Reading and Writing in Tudor and Stuart England* (Cambridge: Cambridge University Press, 1980), p. 176.

13 Plumb, "Commercialization and Leisure," p. 270.

14 Shevelow, *Women and Print Culture*, p. 193. Shawn Lisa Maurer, *Proposing Men: Dialectics of Gender and Class in the Eighteenth-Century English Periodical* (Stanford: Stanford University Press, 1998), p. 205.

15 Shevelow, *Women and Print Culture*, p. 78.

16 Robert DeMaria, Jr., "Samuel Johnson and the Reading Revolution," *Eighteenth-Century Life*, n.s. 16:3 (November 1992), 86–102.

FURTHER READING

Benedict, Barbara M. *Making the Modern Reader: Cultural Mediation in Early Modern Literary Anthologies*. Princeton, NJ: Princeton University Press, 1996.

Black, Jeremy. *The English Press in the Eighteenth Century*. Aldershot, Hants. Gregg Revivals, 1991.

Bonnell, Thomas F. "Bookselling and Canon-Making: the Trade Rivalry over the English Poets, 1776–1783," *Studies in Eighteenth-Century Culture* 19 (1989), 53–70.

Chartier, Roger. *The Order of Books: Readers, Authors, and Libraries in Europe between the Fourteenth and Eighteenth Centuries.* Cambridge: Polity Press, 1993.

Darnton, Robert. *The Great Cat Massacre and Other Episodes in French Cultural History.* New York: Vintage Books, 1985. "Readers Respond to Rousseau: the Fabrication of Romantic Sensitivity," 215–56.

DeMaria, Robert, Jr. *Samuel Johnson and the Life of Reading.* Baltimore and London: Johns Hopkins University Press, 1997.

Donoghue, Frank. *The Fame Machine: Book Reviewing and Eighteenth-Century Literary Careers.* Stanford: Stanford University Press, 1996.

Eisenstein, Elizabeth. *The Printing Press as an Agent of Change.* 2 vols. Cambridge: Cambridge University Press, 1979.

Ezell, Margaret. *Writing Women's Literary History.* Baltimore and London: Johns Hopkins University Press, 1993.
  Social Authorship and the Advent of Print. Baltimore and London: Johns Hopkins University Press, 1999.

Feather, John. *A History of British Publishing.* London and New York: Routledge, 1988.

Foxon, David F., and James McLaverty. *Pope and the Early Eighteenth-Century Book Trade.* Oxford: Clarendon Press, 1991.

Johns, Adrian. *The Nature of the Book: Print and Knowledge in the Making.* Chicago and London: University of Chicago Press, 1998.

Kernan, Alvin. *Printing Technology, Letters, and Samuel Johnson.* Princeton, NJ: Princeton University Press, 1987.

Kroll, Richard W. *The Material Word: Literature Culture in the Restoration and Early Eighteenth Century.* Baltimore and London: Johns Hopkins University Press, 1991.

Levine, Joseph M. *The Battle of the Books: History and Literature in the Augustan Age.* Ithaca: Cornell University Press, 1991.

Mayo, Robert D. *The English Novel in the Magazines, 1740–1815.* Evanston, IL: Northwestern University Press, 1962.

Patey, Douglas Lane. "The Eighteenth Century Invents the Canon," *Modern Language Studies* 18:1 (Winter 1988), 17–37.

Raven, James. *Judging New Wealth: Popular Publishing and Responses to Commerce in England, 1750–1800.* Oxford: Oxford University Press, 1992.

Rose, Mark. *Authors and Owners: the Invention of Copyright.* Cambridge, MA: Harvard University Press, 1993.

Shevelow, Kathryn. *Women and Print Culture: the Construction of Femininity in the Early Periodical.* London and New York: Routledge, 1989.

Suarez, Michael F., S.J. "The Formation, Transmission and Reception of Robert Dodsley's *Collection of Poems by Several Hands,*" in Robert Dodsley *A Collection of Poems by Many Hands,* ed. Michael F. Suarez, S.J. London: Routledge/Thoemmes Press, 1997.

5

BREAN HAMMOND

The city in eighteenth-century poetry

How was the city imagined in eighteenth-century poetry? To chart the territory, and measure the distance that the reader traverses in the journey from early to late century, a reader might compare two poems: Jonathan Swift's "A Description of a City Shower," first published in *The Tatler* 238 on 17 October 1710, and William Blake's "London", the eighth poem in the "Experience" section of his *Songs of Innocence and of Experience* (1794). (Texts given at the end of the chapter.)

In Swift's poem, a worsening rain shower becomes a downpour and finally merges with the "flood" of the Fleet River, London's open sewer flowing down from the north towards the Thames. Its serpentine slither collects up the town's effluent disemboguing into the river from Smithfield Market, conveys the rubbish via St. Sepulchre's Church (whose bells would send prisoners under sentence of death on their way to Tyburn to be hanged) and deposits it into the Holborn conduit via Snow Hill stream. At least half-seriously, the topographical organization is also a *moral* organization by the poem's close: the gradually gathering inundation and the term "flood" cannot but suggest the early chapters of Genesis in which Noah's flood is described and, shortly afterwards, the wicked cities are destroyed – London, Swift subliminally suggests, is the new Sodom/Gomorrah. Various *aspects* of city life, realistic observations of the effects of rain on urban dwellers (metonyms) are ratchetted up into metaphors for the *condition* of city life – its squalor, crowdedness, and degradation.

Clearly, however, this is *no more than* half serious. Another form of organization in the poem is a series of classical comparisons that we would term mock-heroic: augury, but here pressed into the service of nothing more important than predicting the weather; rainclouds as a drunkard vomiting, expressed in self-consciously poetic diction:

> Meanwhile the south, rising with dabbled wings,
> A sable cloud athwart the welkin flings;

> That swilled more liquor than it could contain,
> And like a drunkard gives it up again.   (lines 13–16)

and the lengthy mock-Homeric simile that compares a beau in his sedan chair, terrified by the rain, to the apprehensive Greek soldiers concealed in the wooden horse of Troy. Building on a less readily apparent set of allusions to Virgil's *Aeneid* and *Georgics,* Swift's use of the mock-heroic reminds us that his London is, as well as an *actual* city observed with accuracy, a city built out of ancient books. So often, the city in poetry of this period is observed through a template of literary descriptions of ancient cities, perhaps the most obvious case being Samuel Johnson's *London* based on Juvenal's *Satire 3,* about which we will have more to say. For all that Swift's reputation as a writer is based on the quality of savage indignation ("*saeva indignatio*" as inscribed on his gravestone), savagery is entirely lacking in this poem. The poet's voice here is one of easy tolerance. His casual second-person address constructs a reader just as at home in London as he is himself, presumably receptive to the poet's knowingly penny-pinching advice:

> Returning home at night you find the sink
> Strike your offended sense with double stink.
> If you be wise, then go not far to dine,
> You spend in coach-hire more than save in wine.

There is an Olympian detachment behind the comic observation that the rain finds out what really matters to "Triumphant" Tories and "desponding" Whigs – to wit, their wigs, not the significant religious and political divisions of Queen Anne's England. The referral of the beau in his conveyance to that climactic Homeric episode of the wooden horse of Troy suggests a poet entirely at ease with classical and modern culture: so much so that he can risk moustaching the Mona Lisa – letting us see the heroic stratagem that ended the Trojan War in a partially ridiculous light. "A Description of a City Shower" is above all a "polite" poem, as its chosen publication outlet suggests: Steele's *Tatler* was the first salvo in the early-century periodical revolution, preceding *The Spectator* in the campaign to shape new forms of middling- rank perceptiveness and sensibility. Even if the poem's actual locations are the areas of Clerkenwell and Smithfield that, containing the livestock market, Newgate Prison and the Fleet River, could not expect to retain the fashionable citizenry, the insouciant attitudes that shape it seem to belong more to the desirable residential quarters of London that developed in St. James's Square and Bloomsbury late in the seventeenth century. The scene is urban but the voice is urbane. Its good-humored irony is part of the friendly, tolerant conversation promoted by Addison and Steele's periodicals – the cultural arm of a project to prescribe for the whole of middle-class and, if possible, aristocratic society the forms of polite behavior. Swift's evocation of London, despite its focus on the disagreeable, inconvenient aspects of city life and its knowing, comically grumpy tone, is still consistent with his cousin John Dryden's vision articulated in the 1660s in *Annus Mirabilis* of a phoenix rising out of the ashes of the Great Fire, a new Rome that would be a fitting architectural memorial to the restored monarch:

> Methinks already, from this chymic flame,
> I see a city of more precious mould;
> Rich as the town which gave the Indies name,
> With silver paved, and all divine with gold.
>
> Already, labouring with a mighty fate,
> She shakes the rubbish from her mounting brow,
> And seems to have renewed her charter's date,
> Which Heav'n will to the death of time allow.[1]

> (lines 1169–76)

Swift's poem casts a long shadow. At the century's end, it is to Swift's structure that the remarkable Mary "Perdita" Robinson turns (a woman who wrote for bread after having been cruelly abandoned by a husband with whom she endured prison, cast off by two eminent noblemen, and who had given up a career as a prominent actress) when she records her impressions of "London's Summer Morning" (1794?). Robinson sets the sights and sounds typical of the wakening city against a chronological development, and witnesses a dubious transaction as "the old-clothes-man" sells a (possibly purloined) suit. Some lines allude directly to Swift:

> At the private door
> The ruddy housemaid twirls the busy mop,
> Annoying the smart 'prentice, or neat girl,
> Tripping with band-box lightly.[2]

Because it employs blank verse rather than the rhymed couplet, and because it does not deploy mock-heroic at all, by then unfashionable, the poem strikes the reader as more introspective, more pensive than Swift's: and it seems quite fitting when it becomes self-reflexive as a way of closing:

> The porter now
> Bears his huge load along the burning way;
> And the poor poet wakes from busy dreams,
> To paint the summer morning.

In Blake's "London," written at virtually the same time as Robinson's poem, those "busy dreams" have turned to nightmare. No longer the London of the massive church-building program commenced in 1670 and

supervised by Sir Christopher Wren, of the clubs, coffee houses, polite periodicals, pleasure gardens, and places of public display, Blake's city suggests
the effects of industrialization and the drift of people into the cramped con-
centrations of the urban ghetto. Its focus is not merely the discomfort, but
the excruciating misery of being poor in a city the population of which, by
1801, had grown to 900,000. Where Swift's poem, primarily visual, pre-
serves a distance between the observer and the observed, Blake's has the
immediacy of street cries striking the ear with discordant clamor and penetrating the inner recesses of the sensibility. John Gay's treatment of those distinctive sounds made by London's criers and hawkers in his *Trivia: or, the
Art of Walking the Streets of London* (1716) offers a clear comparison. Here,
the cries are a celebration of seasonality, a means of bringing the country into
the city, *rus in urbe*:

> Successive Crys the Seasons Change declare,
> And mark the Monthly Progress of the Year.
> Hark, how the Streets with treble Voices ring,
> To sell the bounteous Product of the Spring!
> Sweet-smelling Flow'rs, and Elder's early Bud,
> With Nettle's tender Shoots, to cleanse the Blood:
> And when *June*'s Thunder cools the sultry Skies,
> Ev'n *Sundays* are prophan'd by Mackrell Cries.
>
> (II, lines 425–32)

Blake's poem, by contrast, might be described as "proto-expressionist": separation of the perceiver from the perceived collapses, and one object bleeds
into another. It is as if the engraver Marcellus Laroon, who depicted the costumes and attitudes of London street criers late in the seventeenth century,
should have his engravings re-inscribed by the expressionist painter Edvard
Munch. E. P. Thompson's brilliant analysis of this poem suggests that there
is here an entirely new way of apprehending urban experience. In contrast
to the way of apprehending the city that comes down to us from classical
antiquity, where the city offers a kind of theater of discrete perceptions and
episodes for the knowing observer – a carnival of follies – this poem offers
the city as a unitary experience.[3] For Thompson, picking up the repetitions
of the words "chartered" and "mark[s]" in stanza 1, Blake's poem speaks
directly to the controversy that arose between Edmund Burke and Thomas
Paine in 1791–92 over the existence of human rights and the nature of the
English constitution. There is a passage in Paine's *Rights of Man* (1791) in
which he repeats several times that charters, far from guaranteeing freedoms
(as they do for London in Dryden's poem quoted above), were originally part
of William the Conqueror's post-conquest bribery system, "to hold the other

parts of [the country] the better subjected to their will."[4] Following this, Paine points to the iniquitous anomalies of political representation (not to be addressed until the 1832 Reform Act), and asks: "Is there any principle in these things? Is there any thing by which you can trace the marks of freedom, or discover those of wisdom?" Blake's London, that is, is most adequately contextualized as a city in near-revolutionary ferment; a city of Jacobins, of Radical Dissent, of apocalyptic sects descended from those flourishing during the English Civil War, of corresponding societies – those radical societies of working men established in London and provincial centers in the 1790s to achieve Parliamentary reform. In contrast to Swift's tongue-in-cheek representation of London as the new Sodom, Blake reads the city through the Book of Revelation and its conjuring with "the mark of the Beast."

Polite London and revolutionary London: two contrasting ideologies between which our discussion will range. "Politeness" in behavior and discourse would, it was hoped, oil the wheels of social intercourse and render different sections of society mutually permeable. Proselytes of the polite such as Addison and Steele did not perceive themselves as promulgating a consciously articulated ideology. Blake, by contrast, was aware that he was taking on the bastions of privilege and power, resisting their capacity to buy and sell human souls as part of the imperatives of capital. Between these extremes of the easy and the angry, of ideology disguised as plain common sense and ideology brandished furiously in the teeth of oppression, there are many intermediate positions – and hence there are many ways of representing the city in eighteenth-century poetry. Let us examine some of them.

Probably the most prominent poem of the early century that featured the city as protagonist was John Gay's *Trivia: or, the Art of Walking the Streets of London* (1716), already briefly mentioned. A "big screen" version of Swift's "Description," in the sense that it presents vastly elaborated material on how to survive the unpleasantness and discomfort of the city as a pedestrian, and in the sense also that it occasionally moralizes that theme, it does not however reach even the apparent and jokey coherence of vision that provides Swift's climax. Gay's friend Dr. Arbuthnot, jesting snidely at the commercial success of *Trivia*, puts his finger (as all good jokers do) on a serious point: "Gay has gott so much money by his art of walking the streets, that he is ready to sett up with equipage."[5] This is an especially good line because the poem sets up a clear, almost Orwellian moral schema – LEGS GOOD, WHEELS BAD – according to which the Walker has not only a health advantage but a clear ethical superiority over those who drive:

> See, yon' bright Chariot on its Braces swing,
> With *Flanders* Mares, and on an arched Spring,
> That Wretch, to gain an Equipage and Place,
> Betray'd his Sister to a lewd Embrace.   (II, lines 573–76).

Arbuthnot counters, however, that Gay's poem (a product of the luxury economy if ever there was one) has actually enabled him to join the ranks of the rich roadhogs that he affects to despise – expressing a paradoxical reading experience to which successive generations of readers also testify. Although it constantly looks as if we will be able to make out of the poem's detail a larger moral or emblematic pattern – for instance a set of instructions on how to live a pure life in the city – such expectations are frustrated. The poem seems to play one poetic mode off against another, implicitly suggesting its own status as a luxury commodity produced only as an entertainment for those who have leisure to read it.[6] Assuredly, short-term investment in incompatible poetic genres is actually a hallmark of a considerable amount of Gay's writing. And Gay, along with Swift and Pope, is the virtual creator of a satiric mode that draws energy from its own targets. True to form in Gay's writing, then, much of *Trivia* offers advice on avoiding the dirt, crime, and immorality of metropolitan life, yet is nevertheless a celebration of the carnivalesque variety that the city offers. But the matter is actually more complex than this: an example. *Trivia* gives us two mock-Ovidian "aetiologies," one of which is an account of how the shoe-blacking service began. The anti-goddess Cloacina (mock-goddess of the sewers) has produced a bastard as the result of a liaison she has had, disguised as a "Cinder-Wench," with a "mortal Scavenger." The child has his sooty parturition "beneath a Bulk" – the folded-down shop-counters that bulk large (pardon the pun) in the myth of eighteenth-century urban poverty after Samuel Johnson tells us that they often furnished sleeping accommodation for his friend Richard Savage. He becomes a shoeblack when the gods take pity on this "Beggar's Brat," answering his prayers by providing him with the instruments of the new trade. The tonal fluctuations of Gay's treatment are quite extraordinary, ranging from cynicism to compassion to a queasy jocularity. Pretending to trace shoe-blacking to its origins enables Gay to play bravura variations on dirt and carbon, to justify arduous occupations such as this one. It is a "beneficial Art" superior to "the canting Art" of beggary, providing an antidote to orphanism. The commodities of a luxury occupation are mystified through the agency of the mock-heroic:

> Each Power contributes to relieve the Poor:
> With the strong Bristles of the mighty Boar
> *Diana* forms his Brush; the God of Day

> A Tripod gives, amid the crouded Way
> To raise the dirty Foot, and ease his Toil;
> Kind *Neptune* fills his Vase with fetid Oil
> Prest from th' enormous Whale;
>
> (II, lines 157–63)

Overall, this attempt to re-fashion Ovidian transformation to meet the demands of urban georgic is doing something almost contradictory. Georgic celebrates the importance of work, particularly agricultural labor, in the building of nations. Gay's passage has an entirely different social agenda, justifying a luxury service by occluding the hardships of the toil and making it the divine answer to a beggar's prayers.

Urban poverty and labor pose further problems for Gay that we might examine in the section "How to know a Whore":

> 'Tis She who nightly strowls with saunt'ring Pace,
> No stubborn Stays her yielding Shape embrace;
> Beneath the Lamp her tawdry Ribbons glare,
> The new-scower'd Manteau, and the slattern Air;
> High-draggled Petticoats her Travels show,
> And hollow Cheeks with artful Blushes glow;
> With flatt'ring Sounds she sooths the cred'lous Ear,
> My noble Captain! Charmer! Love! my Dear!
> In Riding-hood, near Tavern-Doors she plies,
> Or muffled Pinners hide her livid Eyes.
> With empty Bandbox she delights to range,
> And feigns a distant Errand from the *Change*;
> Nay, she will oft' the Quaker's Hood prophane,
> And trudge demure the Rounds of *Drury-Lane*.
> She darts from Sarsnet Ambush wily Leers,
> Twitches thy Sleeve, or with familiar Airs,
> Her Fan will pat thy Cheek; these Snares disdain,
> Nor gaze behind thee, when she turns again.   (III, lines 267–84)

Prostitution is a pervasive feature of eighteenth-century city poetry, increasingly being recognized as the vice that, more than any other, is not merely *a part* of city life but *a symbol* of its condition. Fornication does pretty well on any terrain, but prostitution is less successful in small communities where people's lives are open to constant community surveillance. It thrives on anonymity: a creation of the city's mean streets and huddled housing that provide the ideal conditions for its flourishing, but also a symbol of the human commodification that the city's employment conditions foster. In Gay's poem, however, there is no dawning recognition of this. There is the obvious ambiguity in the caption, "how to know a whore": how to *avoid* one, or how to *procure* one. Beyond that, the prostitute is figured by Gay as an extreme case of the woman who is not "what-you-see-is-what-you-get", to put it in computer-speak. It is a hazard potentially incurred by all those dealing with women who use cosmetics that what you see is not necessarily what you get, and this complaint is therefore a staple of phallocentric satire. Her body unsubjected to the appropriate discipline of "stubborn Stays," she is death-in-life, with her "livid Eyes." Her diabolic power of shape-changing enables her to impersonate even a Quaker, religious "other" to the whore in abstemiousness and anxiety about carnality. Gay's whore is an Eurydice in the urban underworld who will destroy her client if he gives her a second glance. The following passage describes the ruin of a country "Yeoman" at the hands of such a city predator, which attributes all the blame to the soulless "fraudful Nymph" and fails to make any adequate connection between a service and the demand for that service, just as elsewhere in the poem the city's waste and filth are not acknowledged to be related to city activity. Polite literature is here avoiding the enunciation of its own economic premises.

For Gay, we have been saying, the poet's positioning in the cityscape is primarily personal, and the personal is not yet overtly political. One can make a cost/benefit analysis of living in town as against living in the country, as many eighteenth-century poems in the "town mouse and country mouse" mode did. And one can be dimly, contradictorily aware that some of the unpleasantness of city life is not the fault of its immediate agents, but requires a more systematic analysis. Such an apprehension underlies the contradictions of Gay's *Trivia*. But it is not until the melioristic Whig-sponsored politeness program had run for some years that an opposition to it developed. By the 1730s and early 40s, in the poetry of Alexander Pope and the poem *London* that was one of Samuel Johnson's earliest poetic endeavors, London had become a counter in the partisan battle between the Whig establishment and the spectrum of Jacobite Tories, Hanoverian Tories, independents, "Country" supporters, and Whig malcontents who combined to oust Sir Robert Walpole from office. The city's dirt and stink, its roughnecks and its whores, its opportunists and its leaders, are concocted by Johnson and Pope into forms of "corruption" and nemesis that, unchecked, will bring the city to its knees.

Reading *London* (1738) today, one can be a little surprised that contemporaries regarded the poem as a brilliant debut announcing a major new talent when it appears no better than a somewhat mechanical updating of Juvenal's third *Satire*. In Juvenal's poem, the protagonist Umbricius has decided to leave Rome to live in the lonely colony of Cumae, because the capital has become uninhabitable to the ordinary man bent on making a decent living. Crime is rife, the lick-spittle Greeks have insinuated themselves into all influential positions (they become, inevitably, the French in Johnson's version), the city is descending into a chaos of fires, careening traffic, airborne rubbish, and marauding ruffians. Speaking for the poor, freeborn Roman, Umbricius presents him as being tyrannized by plutocrats who make his decent poverty his burden. Johnson adopts much of this social program but it gains impact from being expressed through what, by 1738, had become the unmistakable political code of the so-called "Patriot" opposition to Walpole: opposition to infrequent elections, standing armies, bribery, and manipulation of government employment, all practices that were gathered together under the masthead of "corruption":

> Here let those reign, whom Pensions can incite,
> To vote a Patriot black, a Courtier white;
> Explain their Country's dear-bought Rights away,
> And plead for Pirates in the Face of Day;
> With slavish Tenets taint our poison'd Youth,
> And lend a lye the Confidence of Truth. (lines 51–56)[7]

Passages like this express more than moral disgust at a metropolis that has lost the innocence and tranquillity still to be found in rural life, represented in the poem by the "elegant Retreat" where the refugee from the city can

> prune thy Walks, support thy drooping Flow'rs,
> Direct thy Rivulets, and twine thy Bow'rs . . .

where

> ev'ry Bush with Nature's Music rings,
> There ev'ry Breeze bears Health upon its Wings;
> On all thy Hours Security shall smile,
> And bless thine Evening Walk and Morning Toil. (lines 216–17; 220–23)

Readers would recognize even in something as incidental as the reference to Queen Elizabeth's birth at Greenwich (lines 22ff) a nostalgic glorification of English history that went hand-in-hand with the representation of the present as in the grip of forms of corruption never previously encountered. Walpole's system was stigmatized by his opponents as a highly technical, sinister, and specialized subversion of ancient liberties. The only antidote to it was a return to the courage, wisdom, and strength of the ancient Briton, to the time when:

> A single Jail, in Alfred's golden Reign,
> Could half the Nation's Criminals contain;
> Fair Justice then, without Constraint ador'd

Held high the steady Scale, but sheath'd the sword;
No Spies were paid, no *Special Juries* known,
Blest Age! but ah! how diff'rent from our own!   (lines 248–53)

In Johnson's poem it is not the narrator who is about to depart the city, but his friend Thales setting off for Wales. To some readers, this concealed an allusion to Johnson's hero Richard Savage who was on the point of being sent to Wales by public subscription. Given Savage's Jacobite sympathies as expressed in his early poems, there may be a further spice to Johnson's poem. It may imply an opposition to current political arrangements even more radical than dislike of Walpole – tinged, perhaps, by the poet's difficulty in submitting to the House of Hanover.

In *London*, the sustained condemnation of luxury that is only intermittently and confusedly articulated in Gay's *Trivia* is enunciated clearly and is laid at the door of a corrupt political ascendancy. And Johnson expresses an insight that Pope's *oeuvre*, culminating in *The New Dunciad* of 1742, would develop most systematically: that this nexus of greed, consumption, and suppression of liberty had a propaganda machine in the form of armies of hack writers whose grubby endeavors were retained to legitimize it. When Orgilio's "Palace" goes up in flames, "The Laureat Tribe in servile Verse relate, / How Virtue wars with persecuting Fate; / With well-feign'd Gratitude the pension'd Band / Refund the Plunder of the begger'd Land" (lines 198–201). Before mid century, Pope had developed, and William Hogarth had illustrated, one of the period's most enduring urban myths – the hack scribbling in his garret.

As John Brewer acutely points out in his recent *The Pleasures of the Imagination*, there is a symbiotic relationship between the growth of the cultural marketplace and the prominence of the metropolis as a theme for creative artists. London was "more than a place of streets and houses, rackety districts and aristocratic quarters; it was also a fantastic, imaginary space" which, as it developed, became itself a source of artistic representation as it gained the power to shape the cultural life of the nation as a whole.[8] By the later decades of the seventeenth century, as a result of the emergence of a new middle-class readership with different interests and tastes, leisured women, literate young people, and urban professionals prominent amongst them, an appetite for different kinds of reading materials developed. As part of a much wider process sometimes called "commercial capitalism" that transformed pre-industrial Britain into a mass consumer society in the period between the English Civil War and the mid eighteenth century, there was a demand for leisure-time reading materials. Books were among the possessions that the improving citizens wanted to consume. In symbiosis with the development of a market like this, writers soon emerged in London and the major cities whose level of education was sufficient to enable them to supply it. Newspapers and periodicals, theatergoing, the development of novelistic fiction, growing claims being staked to intellectual property and copyright – these are all indications of the development of a "mass market" for culture. This new readership needed fictional nourishment somewhat different from its aristocratic forebears. The most prestigious kinds of writing – those saturated in the "classics" of Greece and Rome such as epic, high-brow poetry, classical tragedy – were losing their appeal for a reading public who were too impatient or not well enough educated to read classical masterpieces in the original. The new bourgeois commercial sectors, the merchants, successful tradesmen and shopkeepers, manufacturers, financial brokers, and professionals – and their increasingly ornamental wives – were swelling the ranks of the theatergoing and book-buying public. They were achieving enough cultural power to demand that their leisure time be filled by representations of themselves in action. New generations of readers, deriving from different social provenances, wanted to read different stories – stories not concerned with remote, ramrod-stiff heroes but rather, stories colored by humor and concerned with individuals whose destinies might conceivably resemble their own. Works of art therefore begin to reflect, as John Brewer says, "on the circumstances of their creation: the environment they inhabited" (p. 54).

As a young poet moving in Whiggish polite circles, Pope seemed to be entirely at home with these cultural tendencies. His *Windsor-Forest* could culminate in a Drydenesque vision of a newly prosperous London as the center of a commercial empire, dominating the world through trade:

> Behold! Augusta's glittering spires increase,
> And temples rise, the beauteous works of peace.
> I see, I see where two fair cities bend
> Their ample bow, a new Whitehall ascend!
> There mighty nations shall enquire their doom,
> The world's great oracle in times to come;
> There kings shall sue, and suppliant states be seen
> Once more to bend before a BRITISH QUEEN.

(lines 377–84)

Even if he could ironize aspects of the modishness, conspicuous consumption and moral dilution that might result from such a vision in *The Rape of the Lock*, that novelistic poem is still fascinated by beauty and employs the Thames and Hampton Court as dazzling backdrops against which to stage its triumphs and defeats. In maturity, however, Pope developed a much darker vision of the literary marketplace as a barbarian invasion of the precincts of elite culture. In *The Dunciad* of 1728–29, and with greater intensity in the revised and enlarged work of 1742–43, the struggle between the purveyors of low-brow, popular, and irrational culture such as the *Dunciad's* new "hero," Colley Cibber, and those who wish to prevent their infiltration into respectable vicinities, is represented as a struggle over cultural territory. One part of the city of London is set against another, as the "Smithfield muses" migrate westward toward St. James's Palace and Westminster. The opening lines of *The Dunciad*, taken in conjunction with the footnote through which Pope satirizes the scholarly endeavors of journeyman-editors, might illustrate Pope's creation of a geographical myth that locates an army of scribblers, hacks, and dunces in a rectangle of London bounded by Covent Garden and St. Mary le Strand in the west, up to Hockley in the Hole and Bedlam in the north and northeast, and back down to Billingsgate on the eastern Thames:

> The Mighty Mother, and her son who brings
> The Smithfield muses to the ear of kings,
> I sing. (I, lines 1–3)

> [2] *Smithfield* is the place where Batholomew Fair was kept, whose shows, machines, and dramatical entertainments, formerly agreeable only to the taste of the rabble, were, by the hero of this poem and others of equal genius, brought to the theaters of Covent Garden, Lincoln's Inn Fields, and the Haymarket, to be the reigning pleasures of the court and town.

Within a few lines, the source of this cultural pollution is specified to a "cave of poverty and poetry" situated appropriately near Bethlehem Hospital (Bedlam). Pope's fertile imagination licks up felicitous details of London architecture and puts them to work in creating the myth-making of deranged, low-brow artistic production:

> Close to the walls where Folly holds her throne,
> And laughs to think Monroe would take her down,
> Where o'er the gates, by his famed father's hand
> Great Cibber's brazen, brainless brothers stand;
> One cell there is . . . (I, lines 29–33)

> [31] *By his famed father's hand*] Mr. Caius Gabriel Cibber, father of the Poet Laureate. The two statues of the lunatics over the gate of Bedlam Hospital were done by him, and (as the son justly says of them) are no ill monuments of his fame as an artist.

> [33] The cell of poor poetry is here very properly represented as a little *unendowed hall* in the neighborhood of the magnific College of Bedlam; and as the surest seminary to supply those learned walls with professors.

And thus Pope begins to create the prevailing fiction of *The Dunciad* – that London has spawned a publishing industry characterizable as militant, mercenary, and mad, whose collective endeavors will put out the lights of civilization as we know it. Metropolitan topography can be invoked at will as a sympathetic backdrop to the mindless behavior on display, such as in Book II during the heroic games, when various divines, fanatics, and field preachers get involved in an asinine braying contest. Lest the higher seriousness of a passage that has asses responding to nasal preachers be missed, the footnote dignifies it by identifying an allusion to the Virgilian epic:

> There Webster! pealed thy voice, and Whitfield! thine.
> But far o'er all, sonorous Blackmore's strain;
> Walls, steeples, skies, bray back to him again.
> In Tottenham fields, the brethren, with amaze,
> Prick all their ears up, and forget to graze;
> Long Chancery Lane retentive rolls the sound,
> And courts to courts return it round and round;
> Thames wafts it thence to Rufus' roaring hall,
> And Hungerford re-echoes bawl for bawl.   (II, lines 258–66)

> The progress of the sound from place to place, and the scenery here of the bordering regions, Tottenham Fields, Chancery Lane, the Thames, Westminster Hall, and the Hungerford Stairs, are imitated from Virgil, *Aen. vii.* on the sounding the horn of Alecto.

Yet however powerful Pope's indictment of popular culture, however successful his representation of Colley Cibber the playwright, actor, and theatrical impresario as a symbol of marketed, degraded entertainment, *The Dunciad* is finally as much a celebration of metropolitan energy as it is a critique of it. The poem is fed by the swarming, formicating liveliness that it affects to despise. It is a quintessentially urban poem, whose author would have shared the view of London that James Boswell attributed to Johnson:

> Such was his love of London, so high a relish had he of its magnificent extent, and variety of intellectual entertainment, that he languished when absent from it, his mind having become quite luxurious from the long habit of enjoying the metropolis; and, therefore . . . he still found that such conversation as London affords, could be found nowhere else.[9]

Neither Pope nor Johnson was expressing personal or confessional views of the city. Johnson was using the dysfunctional city to articulate an oppositional, anti-government manifesto. Pope's vision of the eclipse of all knowledge in a new age of barbarism shares that manifesto, but transcends it in the creation of a cityscape that mythologizes poor scribblers, those who employ and those who patronize them, as the enemies of civilized culture. Perhaps the first poet who presents a truly personal, confessional account of the alienating effect of the city on an isolated individual is William Cowper. Before turning to his writing, however, let us leave the capital for a while and consider briefly how provincial cities figure in eighteenth-century poetry.

As the previous section has suggested, the synergy between creative writing and the metropolis was not accidental. For a provincial town to develop as a literary and artistic center required a conducive infrastructure in the form of postal systems (hence reasonable transport), good networks of interested and educated people, and a press that opened its columns to writers. In these terms John Brewer explains the rise to prominence in the late century of a writer like Anna Seward, the "Swan of Lichfield." Her interests represent a strong desire to raise the stock of provincial culture and to make regional scenery a proper object of aesthetic attention. To achieve this, she enters into a dialogue with London writers such as Samuel Johnson and with London publications. Thus in the later decades of the eighteenth century, we begin to find poets being associated with the provincial towns and cities in which they lived and in some respects becoming the voices of those communities: Mark Akenside in Newcastle, John Freeth the Birmingham poet, Robert Tannahill the "Paisley Poet," Thomas Chatterton associated with Bristol. But for a city actually to become the substance of poetry, to figure significantly in the content of poems, it needs to strike the imagination distinctively through its architecture and through the forms of social gathering that this architecture enables. Two cities were pre-eminent in their capacity to do this: Bath and Edinburgh.

Literary representations of Bath commence, for the most part, in the later century, which makes Mary Chandler's poem *A Description of Bath. A Poem. Humbly Inscribed to her Royal Highness the Princess Amelia*, first published in 1733, all the more remarkable. Chandler, a milliner living and working in Bath, saw the literary potential of Bath's history, its spa waters and the mores of its visitors before the excavations of the Roman baths commencing in 1755 and the re-planning of the city under the direction of the Woods made it difficult to miss. She draws on a very wide variety of topographical poetic forms ranging from Ausonius and Claudian to Jonson, Denham, and Pope, but these differing traditions are controlled by a structure that takes us on a tour of the main sights. Having imagined the city from the south, she moves in to the center, where Bath Abbey offers her an opportunity to attack priestcraft and Catholicism. We walk with Chandler through the King and Queen's bath, Cross Bath (the marble Cross is another chance to attack popery), West Gate, the main square, Lindsey's gambling rooms, Leake's book shop, Harrison's Banqueting House and finish with a description of Ralph Allen's estate of Prior Park. The poem ends with Chandler wishing she had the gifts of such as Pope with which to praise Allen adequately. Although it has been argued that Chandler defines herself with respect to Pope by means of a non-linear chronological scheme that we might associate with women's writing, it is perhaps more convincing to note Chandler's desire to make her city walk a vehicle for her personal views: on Catholicism, on the House of Nassau that she fervently supports, on temperance . . .[10] We are in the company of a surprisingly opinionated tour guide who takes every opportunity to brandish her information. So that, for example, the prospects afforded by Bath prompt her to invoke Thomas Burnet's eccentric geological theories expressed in his *Sacred Theory of the Earth*, a text that provided Pope and his friends with considerable amusement:

> Thence view the *pendant Rock*'s majestick Shade,
> That speaks the Ruins conqu'ring *Time* has made:
> Whether the *Egg* was by the *Deluge* broke,
> Or Nature since has felt some other Shock;
> Ingenious BURNET, thine's a pleasing Scheme,
> A gay Delusion, if it be a Dream.
> The shatter'd *Rocks,* and *Strata* seem to say,
> Nature is *old,* and tends to her *Decay*[11]

Mary Chandler's Bath is what the reader gets, as the poem becomes a vehicle for her to display knowledge and information very much surplus to requirements in the selling of hats.

Very different from Chandler's poem in which civic pride and personal pride so effectively direct the representation is Christopher Anstey's *The New Bath Guide: or, Memoirs of the B–R–D Family. In a Series of Poetical Epistles*, published in 1766. This is probably the best-known poetic representation of Bath in verse, a work manifestly influential upon Tobias Smollett, whose *The Expedition of Humphry Clinker* (1771) contains the most famous prose vignettes of Bath before Jane Austen. It takes the form of a collection of fifteen verse letters plus epilogues, supposedly written by a "Family during their Residence at BATH." The opening letter from Jenny W–D–R to her friend in the country explains that Lady B–N–R–D (Blunderhead) has proposed a jaunt to Bath so that her son Simkin and her daughter Prue can take the waters, along with Tabby Runt the maid. Cousin Jenny gives a character sketch of Sim that renders him simultaneously foolishly naïve, ignorant of the world's ways, and cleverly satirical and witty. The majority of the letters are written by Simkin in his jog-trotting, six-beat hexameters, but the texture is varied by Cousin Jenny's four-beat octosyllabics and by a single (unwittingly bawdy) letter from sister Prudence describing how she has been converted to Methodism by a vision of Roger, a.k.a. "Nicodemus." Thus the poem can satirize targets such as Methodism associated with urban fashionability while it also celebrates the diversions to be found in Bath:

O the charming Parties made!
Some to walk the South Parade,
Some to Lincomb's shady Groves,
Or to Simpson's proud Alcoves;
Some for Chapel trip away,
Then take Places for the Play.[12]

Cousin Jenny goes on to mention her visits to an artist's studio, to Gill's res-
taurant, and to the toyshop (jewelers). Letter x from Simkin is an amusing
account of the social and societal types to be found in Bath, that he aspires
to join – society women, macaronis (young men whose experience of continental travel had left them with affected taste in dress and manners), men of
taste, critics, dilettantes. Bath in Simkin's eyes is superior to the clodhopping,
trading, and artisanal towns that surround it, towns to which one condes-
cends precisely because they are unlikely to produce poems such as Anstey's
– while at the same time, of course, Anstey's comical poem implies a metropolitan perspective from which Bath itself is something of a joke:

Of all the gay Places the World can afford,
By Gentle and Simple for Pastime ador'd,
Fine Balls, and fine Concerts, fine Buildings, and Springs,
Fine Walks, and fine Views, and a Thousand fine Things,
Not to mention the sweet Situation and Air,
What Place, my dear Mother, with *Bath* can compare?
Let *Bristol* for Commerce and Dirt be renown'd,
At *Sal'sbury* Pen-Knives and Scissars be ground;
The Towns of *Devizes,* of *Bradford,* and *Frome,*
May boast that they better can manage the Loom;
I believe that they may; — but the World to refine,
In Manners, in Dress, and Politeness to shine,
O *Bath!* — let the Art, let the Glory be thine.   (pp.47–48)

This metropolitan perspective is apparent in the incongruous, Breughelian
scenes of the Bath glitterati at play: the portrait, for example of Sir Boreas
Blubber as a dancing hollyhock, fleeting it on his twenty-three-and a half-
stone frame with "Miss CARROT FITZ-OOZER, a Niece of Lord PORUS"
(pp. 83–84).

Such a condescending, infantilizing tone as Anstey frequently adopts is
absent from poems that figure Edinburgh, doubtless because Edinburgh's
citizens were intent upon making it a capital city in the aftermath of an Act
of Union that so many Scots regarded as a political emasculation.
Edinburgh's poets, although they freely, even proudly, admitted to the liber-
tinism and debauchery that their city fostered, could not risk making the city
look ridiculous. Burns's classicizing and personifying apostrophe in his 1786

"Address to Edinburgh" does this unintentionally. It is an anxious example both of an attempt to glorify the city and of an emotionally unconvincing depiction of it as an empty nest for a great royal line. Civic pride at New Town improvements sits uneasily with the nostalgic Jacobitism of the evocation of Holyrood Palace and the ruined Holyrood Abbey founded by David I:

> EDINA! *Scotia*'s darling seat!
> All hail thy palaces and tow'rs,
> Where once beneath a Monarch's feet
> Sat Legislation's sov'reign pow'rs! . . .
>
> Here Wealth still swells the golden tide,
> As busy Trade his labours plies;
> There Architecture's noble pride
> Bids elegance and splendor rise . . .   (lines 1–4, 9–12)

The somewhat mawkish elegiac tone that Burns adopts, incorporating the classical note of alteration or mutability ("alas, how chang'd") and the theme of the downfall of heroes, comes to sound like a confection put together from Oliver Goldsmith's *The Deserted Village* and Thomas Gray's "The Bard." It certainly does not sound like the authentic voice of Scotland:

> With awe-struck thought, and pitying tears,
> I view that noble, stately Dome,
> Where *Scotia*'s kings of other years,
> Fam'd heroes! had their royal home:
> Alas, how chang'd the times to come!
> Their royal Name low in the dust!
> Their hapless Race wild-wand'ring roam!
> Tho' rigid Law cries out, 'twas just!   (lines 41–48)[13]

Far more successful are Burns's predecessor and mentor Robert Fergusson's poetic celebrations of his native city. To do justice to Fergusson's achievement would involve saying a great deal more than is now possible about his combination of Scoto-Latin and Lowland Scots language and culture in the creation of a powerful, original form of Scots urban poetry. For present purposes, we need only refer to his "Auld Reikie" of 1773 (slightly enlarged in 1779), in which he picks up several components of Gay's "pedestrian" poem *Trivia* (see particularly Fergusson's passage on the whore standing "near some lamp-post, wi' dowie face") but expresses them in the fast-moving tetrameter characteristic of Swift. Edinburgh in this poem achieves the status of a metropolis without the aid of the Augustan stilts that Burns continues to need. It is a city of, as David Daiches says, "colour, gaiety and debauchery, dreariness and pretentiousness and weakness, companionship, loneliness and sheer unadulterated humanity."[14] Large enough, like London, to have different areas for different kinds of activity and recreation – so that there is a very strong sense of local geography in the poem–Edinburgh is also a city of clubs and societies such as the Cape, a city of taverns and cozy interiors. Unlike Pope, Fergusson is not superior to the human carnival he portrays. On the contrary, city sights like a cortege can catch the walker unawares and can reach out to grab his vulnerabilities. The coffin reminds him of his own mortality:

> In morning, when ane keeks about,
> Fu' blithe and free frae ail, nae doubt
> He lippens not to be misled
> Amang the regions o' the dead;
> But straight a painted corp he sees,
> Lang streekit 'neath its canopies.
> Soon, soon will this his mirth controul,
> And send d — n to his soul;
> Or whan the dead-deal (awfu' shape!)
> Makes frighted mankind girn and gape,
> Reflection then his reason sours,
> For the neist dead-deal may be ours.

And here is an example also of Fergusson's cultivated combination of broad Scots with classical allusion. Aeneas descending to the underworld is familiarly embraced in the Scottish word "soger" [soldier]:

> When Sybil led the Trojan down
> To haggard Pluto's dreary town,
> Shapes waur nor thae, I freely ween,
> Could never meet the sogers' een.

Much of Fergusson's best poetry is Edinburgh-based, and yet the surrounding countryside has a high profile within it. Edinburgh was, and is, within much closer reach of the country than London, which is perhaps the reason why Edinburgh poetry in the eighteenth century does not counterpose the town and the country so starkly (and routinely) as does English verse of the same period; a contrast which takes us back to the waiting William Cowper.

For it was Cowper who, in his lengthy, digressive and unclassifiable poem *The Task, a Poem, in Six Books* (1785) gave the most striking and forceful expression to the later eighteenth-century orthodoxy that rural living was ethically superior to urban living:

> God made the country, and man made the town.
> What wonder then, that health and virtue, gifts

That can alone make sweet the bitter draught
That life holds out to all, should most abound
And least be threatened in the fields and groves?

(1, lines 749–53)

There is something paradoxical about this individual and idiosyncratic poet
giving us our most memorable, quotable, and universal statement on town
and country in eighteenth-century poetry. Cowper's verse sums up a powerful
strand of eighteenth-century thinking that represents the town as a locus of
luxury and ease certain to destroy the moral fiber of those who inhabit it. The
last line of the passage quoted below is a surprisingly tough-minded, even
harsh formulation for a poet who often strikes readers as mild and introverted:

Possess ye therefore, ye who borne about
In chariots and sedans, know no fatigue
But that of idleness, and taste no scenes
But such as art contrives, possess ye still
Your element; there only, ye can shine,
There only minds like yours can do no harm.

(1, lines 754–59).

Cowper goes on in the passage to compare the creations of "nature" to those
of "art," but reinvigorates that very old literary theme with an oppositional,
them-and-us energy. It culminates in an accusation of cultural effeminacy
leading to an almost Gibbonian apprehension of the decline and fall of great
empires:

Our groves were planted to console at noon
The pensive wand'rer in their shades. At eve
The moon-beam gliding softly in between
The sleeping leaves, is all the light they wish,
Birds warbling all the music. We can spare
The splendor of your lamps, they but eclipse
Our softer satellite. Your songs confound
Our more harmonious notes. The thrush departs
Scared, and th'offended nightingale is mute.
There is a public mischief in your mirth,
It plagues your country. Folly such as your's
Graced with a sword, and worthier of a fan,
Has made, which enemies could ne'er have done,
Our arch of empire, stedfast but for you,
A mutilated structure, soon to fall.   (1, lines 760–74)[15]

Cowper's environmentalist commitment in this passage is an aspect of the
much wider reordering of philosophical and artistic priorities that literary and

cultural historians term "Romanticism." Solitude comes to be valued above society, the country above the city, the private above the public, meditative/conversational poetic forms above declamatory or satirical forms – there is no space, or need, to rehearse all the familiar aspects of Romanticism here. In the later century, London is far less the source and focus of creative energy than it had been previously. Writers such as Charles Churchill (active 1761–65) still depended on it. His poem *The Rosciad*, for example, satirizing all the major figures in London's theatrical world, could not have been written outside a metropolitan milieu, but nevertheless London is not directly its subject. Yet Cowper's formulation is not merely a typical expression of the spirit of the age. Reading it to the end (and certainly, reading it in the overall context of *The Task*) does not sustain the impression that it is a pithy generalization at which we can all nod sagely. Agricultural historians would surely take exception to the apothegm that "God made the country, and man made the town." This is itself as much an urban perception as is its converse. And as it develops, the "green" perspective becomes surprisingly fierce– "There only minds like yours can do no harm" is, as we have noted, a ferocious statement, however quietly uttered. Finally, town luxury (the kind of behavior depicted in *The New Bath Guide*) is not just an affront to the natural music of the birds, causing nightingales and thrushes to abandon their perches. It is a form of effeminacy capable of destroying the empire. Cowper arrives at an apocalyptic vision similar to Pope's in *The Dunciad*, but paradoxically, Cowper holds it much more seriously. Cowper's discovery in nature of a route to salvation was undoubtedly influential on later poets, because his tortured, agoraphobic sensibility was suited to expressing *angst* –loneliness amid the multitude, isolation in a crowd not bound together by traditional ties – that is one of the defining characteristics of modern attitudes to the city. Wordsworth's famous passage on city life in Book VIII of *The Prelude,* where this is expressed more explicitly than anywhere in Cowper, is arguably indebted to him.

The tour that the reader takes through eighteenth-century urban poetry is, then, a dramatic one. In the decades before 1700, especially in the theater, the country is usually represented as a purgatory of exquisite boredom, populated by boorish squires, maiden aunts, and gawkish hoydens. Going to Kent, all of thirty miles from London, is like serving a life sentence. Even where the shortcomings of urban life are acknowledged, as they are in poems like Rochester's *A Ramble in St. James's Park* (c.1680) or Swift's "A Description of a City Shower" or Pope's *Epistle to Miss Blount* (1714), the possibility of actually living elsewhere is never seriously entertained. In more overtly partisan poems such as Johnson's *London* and the later urban poems of Pope, corruption is not perceived as a condition endemic to city living but is an ameliorable situation that a change of government and the revival of the patriotic spirit might address. Yet already in the early eighteenth century, in for example the series of papers Addison wrote for *The Spectator* entitled "Pleasures of the Imagination," there are the beginnings of a new aesthetic valuation of the countryside. Taught to appreciate the beauties of the countryside, middle-class people increasingly visited it, toured it, surveyed it, painted it – finding recreation and solace there. Tobias Smollett's Matthew Bramble expresses the typical sentiments of the propertied country-dweller when he writes to his friend Dr. Lewis:

> What temptation can a man of my turn and temperament have, to live in a place [London] where every corner teems with fresh objects of detestation and disgust? What kind of taste and organs must those people have, who really prefer the adulterate enjoyments of the town to the genuine pleasures of a country retreat?[16]

This suggests how, in the later century, the earlier polarities change and the country is increasingly represented as the only environment that can cherish the human soul and return human being to a sense of its innate worth and purpose. The city is on its way to being a city of dreadful night.

But I will give the last word to a poem, Joanna Baillie's "London" written at the turn of the century (1800?), and undoubtedly influenced by Wordsworth, of which the object is to some extent to deconstruct the city/country binarism. This poem lacks altogether Blake's political radicalism, but in viewing London from Hampstead Heath and in cloudy, rainy conditions, it tries to blur the distinction between the city and the landscape. Clouds, fog and mist transform the London skyline dominated by St. Paul's Cathedral into a sublime mountainscape or seascape:

> With more than natural height, reared in the sky
> 'Tis then St. Paul's arrests the wondering eye;
> The lower parts in swathing mist concealed,
> The higher through some half spent shower revealed,
> So far from earth removed, that well, I trow,
> Did not its form man's artful structure show,
> It might some lofty alpine peak be deemed,
> The eagle's haunt, with cave and crevice seamed.
> Stretched wide on either hand, a rugged screen,
> In lurid dimness, nearer streets are seen
> Like shoreward billows of a troubled main,
> Arrested in their rage.   (lines 19–30)[17]

Such Turneresque transformations at least complicate the relationship between town and country; and as Baillie goes on to say, the "hollow sound" that greets the traveler approaching the city at night, which is "the flood of human life in motion!," can give rise to thoughts "Of restless, reckless man, and years gone by, / And Time fast wending to Eternity." Baillie can hear Wordsworth's "still, sad music of humanity" as audibly in the city as he can above Tintern Abbey.

APPENDIX

Jonathan Swift, "A Description of a City Shower"

Careful observers may foretell the hour
(By sure prognostics) when to dread a shower:
While rain depends, the pensive cat gives o'er
Her frolics, and pursues her tail no more.
Returning home at night, you find the sink
Strike your offended sense with double stink.
If you be wise, then go not far to dine,
You spend in coach-hire more than save in wine.
A coming shower your shooting corns presage,
Old aches throb, your hollow tooth will rage.
Sauntering in coffee-house is Dulman seen;
He damns the climate and complains of spleen.

Meanwhile the south, rising with dabbled wings,
A sable cloud athwart the welkin flings,
That swilled more liquor than it could contain
And like a drunkard gives it up again.
Brisk Susan whips her linen from the rope,
While the first drizzling shower is borne aslope:
Such is that sprinkling which some careless quean
Flirts on you from her mop, but not so clean.
You fly, invoke the gods; then turning, stop
To rail; she singing, still whirls on her mop.
Not yet the dust had shunned th' unequal strife,
But aided by the wind fought still for life,
And wafted with its foe by violent gust,
'Twas doubtful which was rain, and which was dust.
Ah! where must needy poet seek for aid
When dust and rain at once his coat invade;
Sole coat, where dust cemented by the rain
Erects the nap, and leaves a cloudy stain.

Now in contiguous drops the flood comes down,
Threatening with deluge this devoted town.
To shops in crowds the daggled females fly,

Pretend to cheapen goods but nothing buy.
The Templar spruce, while every spout's abroach,
Stays till 'tis fair, yet seems to call a coach.
The tucked-up sempstress walks with hasty strides
While streams run down her oiled umbrella's sides.
Here various kinds by various fortunes led,
Commence acquaintance underneath a shed.
Triumphant Tories, and desponding Whigs
Forget their feuds, and join to save their wigs.
Boxed in a chair the beau impatient sits,
While spouts run clattering o'er the roof by fits;
And ever and anon with frightful din
The leather sounds; he trembles from within.
So when Troy chairmen bore the wooden steed,
Pregnant with Greeks, impatient to be freed,
(Those bully Greeks, who, as the moderns do,
Instead of paying chairmen, run them through),
Laocoon struck the outside with his spear,
And each imprisoned hero quaked for fear,

   Now from all parts the swelling kennels flow,
And bear their trophies with them as they go:
Filth of all hues and odours, seem to tell
What street they sailed from, by their sight and smell.
They, as each torrent drives, with rapid force
From Smithfield or St. Pulchre's shape their course;
And in huge confluent join at Snow Hill ridge,
Fall from the conduit prone to Holborn Bridge.
Sweepings from butchers' stalls, dung, guts, and blood,
Drowned puppies, stinking sprats, all drenched in mud,
Dead cats and turnip-tops come tumbling down the flood.
  Jonathan Swift: the Complete Poems, ed. Pat Rogers (New Haven:
Yale University Press; Harmondsworth: Penguin, 1983), pp. 113–14.

     William Blake, "London"

    I wander thro' each charter'd street,
    Near where the charter'd Thames does flow,
    And mark in every face I meet
    Marks of weakness, marks of woe.

    In every cry of every Man,
    In every Infant's cry of fear,
    In every voice, in every ban,
    The mind-forg'd manacles I hear.

How the Chimney-sweeper's cry
Every black'ning Church appalls;
And the hapless Soldier's sigh
Runs in blood down Palace walls.

But most thro' midnight streets I hear
How the youthful Harlot's curse
Blasts the new born Infant's tear,
And blights with plagues the Marriage hearse.
The Complete Poetry and Prose of William Blake, ed. David V.
Erdman (New York: Doubleday & Co., 1965, 1981)

NOTES

1 John Dryden, *Annus Mirabilis* in *Dryden: a Selection*, ed. John Conaghan (London: Methuen, 1978), p. 78.

2 Quoted from *Romantic Women Poets 1770–1838: an Anthology*, ed Andrew Ashfield (Manchester and New York: Manchester University Press, 1995), p.130.

3 E. P. Thomson, *Witness Against the Beast: William Blake and the Moral Law* (Cambridge: Cambridge University Press, 1993), p.190.

4 Thomas Paine, *Rights of Man: being an Answer to Mr Burke's Attack on the French Revolution* (1791), ed. Mark Philp (Oxford: World's Classics, 1995), p. 125.

5 *The Letters of John Gay,* ed C. F. Burgess (Oxford: Clarendon Press, 1966), p. 27.

6 Stephen Copley and Ian Haywood, "Luxury, Refuse and Poetry: John Gay's *Trivia*," in Peter Lewis and Nigel Wood (eds.), *John Gay and the Scriblerians* (London and New York: Vision Press, 1989), pp. 62–82 (pp. 67, 77).

7 Samuel Johnson, *Complete English Poems,* ed J. D. Fleeman (Harmondsworth: Penguin, 1971), p. 60.

8 John Brewer, *The Pleasures of the Imagination: English Culture in the Eighteenth Century* (London: Harper Collins, 1997), pp. 31, 54–55.

9 James Boswell, *Life of Samuel Johnson*, ed. George Birkbeck Hill and L. F. Powell, 6 vols. (Oxford: Clarendon Press, 1934), IV, 374–75.

10 See Linda Veronika Troost, "Geography and Gender: Mary Chandler and Alexander Pope," in Donald C. Mell (ed.), *Pope, Swift, and Women Writers* (Newark and London: University of Delaware and Associated University Presses, 1996), pp. 67–85.

11 Mary Chandler, *A Description of Bath. A Poem. Humbly inscribed to her Royal Highness the Princess Amelia* (1733; 2nd. edn., London, 1734), p. 8.

12 Christopher Anstey, *The New Bath Guide: or, Memoirs of the B–R–D Family. In a Series of Poetical Epistles* (1766; 3rd edn. London 1766), p. 64.

13 Quoted from *The Poems and Songs of Robert Burns,* ed James Kinsley, 3 vols. (Oxford: Clarendon Press, 1968), I, 308–10.

14 David Daiches, *Robert Fergusson* (Edinburgh: Scottish Academic Press, 1982), p. 114.

15 Quoted from *The Poems of William Cowper,* ed. John D. Baird and Charles

Ryskamp, 3 vols. (Oxford: Clarendon Press, 1995), II, 136.
16 Tobias Smollett, *The Expedition of Humphry Clinker* (1771), ed. Peter Miles (London, Vermont: Dent, 1993), p. 121.
17 Quoted from *Romantic Women Poets 1770–1838: an Anthology*, ed. Andrew Ashfield (Manchester and New York: Manchester University Press, 1995), pp. 100–1.

FURTHER READING

Ashfield, Andrew, ed. *Romantic Women Poets 1770–1838: an Anthology.* Manchester and New York: Manchester University Press, 1995.

Brewer, John. *The Pleasures of the Imagination: English Culture in the Eighteenth Century.* London: Harper Collins, 1997.

Byrd, Max. *London Transformed: Images of the City in the Eighteenth Century.* New Haven: Yale University Press, 1978.

Copley, Stephen, and Ian Haywood. "Luxury, Refuse and Poetry: John Gay's *Trivia*," in Peter Lewis and Nigel Wood (eds.), *John Gay and the Scriblerians.* London and New York: Vision Press, 1989.

Daiches, Donald. *Robert Fergusson.* Edinburgh: Scottish Academic Press, 1982.

Hammond, Brean, *Professional Imaginative Writing in England, 1670–1740: "Hackney for Bread."* Oxford: Clarendon Press, 1997.

Rawson, Claude J. "Nature's Dance of Death, Part I: Urbanity and Strain in Fielding, Swift, and Pope," *Eighteenth-Century Studies* 3 (1970), 307–38.

"The Nightmares of Strephon: Nymphs of the City in the Poems of Swift, Baudelaire, Eliot," in Maximillian E. Novak (ed.), *English Literature in the Age of Disguise.* Berkeley: University of California Press, 1977. 57–99.

Rogers, Pat. *Grub Street: Studies in a Subculture.* London: Methuen, 1972.

Thompson, E. P. *Witness Against the Beast: William Blake and the Moral Law.* Cambridge: Cambridge University Press, 1993.

Troost, Linda Veronika. "Geography and Gender: Mary Chandler and Alexander Pope," in Donald C. Mell (ed.), *Pope, Swift, and Women Writers.* Newark and London: University of Delaware and Associated University Presses, 1996.

Weitzman, Arthur J. "Eighteenth-Century London: Urban Paradise or Fallen City?," *Journal of the History of Ideas* 36 (1975), 469–80.

Williams, Raymond. *The Country and the City.* New York: Oxford University Press, 1973.

6

TIM FULFORD

"Nature" poetry

"English nature," that scenery of rolling hills, oak trees, green pastures, country houses, and churchyards overgrown with moss, is a creation of the eighteenth century. It is a landscape, but it is also a way of feeling – of feeling about native soil, of feeling about the past, of feeling about Englishness itself. Patriotism and nationalism, that is to say, are encoded in a symbolic view of a rural landscape and the way of life that is presumed to have flourished in that landscape. And this view has official sanction: "English Nature" is today the name of the government-sponsored organization responsible for conserving flora and fauna.

The eighteenth century was doubly responsible for the laying down of a landscape of nationalism in English people's consciousness. It was a century of dramatic developments – of the landscaping of estates for the aristocracy who dominated power, of the enclosure of common fields, of agricultural "improvement." But it was also a time in which writing about these developments became a means towards an idealization of social and political order, an idealization with which today's lovers of English nature are frequently complicit. The National Trust, for example, dedicates itself to preserving the houses and parks once owned by great eighteenth-century landowners. It is currently restoring the park at Stowe to the flourishing condition that Alexander Pope celebrated in 1731, when he made it symbolize the moral and aesthetic judgment that, he said, fitted its owner, Lord Cobham, to direct the affairs of state:

> Consult the Genius of the Place in all;
> That tells the Waters or to rise, or fall,
> Or helps th'ambitious Hill the heav'n to scale,
> Or scoops in circling theatres the Vale,
> Calls in the Country, catches opening glades,
> Joins willing woods, and varies shades from shades,
> Now breaks or now directs, th'intending Lines;
> Paints as you plant, and, as you work, designs.
>
> (*Epistle to Burlington*, lines 57–64)[1]

Cobham's judgment was confirmed by nature itself:

> Still follow Sense, of ev'ry Art the Soul,
> Parts answ'ring parts shall slide into a whole,
> Spontaneous beauties all around advance,
> Start ev'n from Difficulty, strike from Chance;
> Nature shall join you, Time shall make it grow
> A work to wonder at – perhaps a STOW.   (lines 65–70)

Working with the "genius" of the place, Cobham ordered nature as he would order the nation: he worked within a recognition of the limits, as well as possibilities, vouchsafed to him by his native land. Pope contrasted his estate, emblem of a consensual body politic, with the landscape of French absolutism. Englishness, that is to say, was defined xenophobically, by opposing its nature to the formal and rigid gardens of its traditional rival:

> Without it, proud Versailles! thy glory falls;
> And Nero's Terraces desert their walls:
> The vast Parterres a thousand hands shall make,
> Lo! COBHAM comes, and floats them with a lake
> (lines 71–74)

A limited constitutional monarchy, in which great landowners governed the people whom they represented as carefully as they managed the land that entitled them to power, was Pope's ideal. He rooted it, for the political education of noble patron and middle-class reader alike, in the soil of the English shires.

Pope had pressing reasons for his political landscaping. At the start of the eighteenth century, the Civil War period of the 1640s was still within living memory. So was the revolution of 1688, when James II had been forced from the throne. Union with Scotland dated only from 1707, and peace remained doubtful while much of the Scottish Highlands supported James's descendants' claim to rule. A rebellion began there in 1715. And when, in 1714, Queen Anne died without surviving issue, it became necessary to import a king from Hanover, who spoke no English. In these uncertain times, peace and prosperity depended on the avoidance of faction, on political cooperation between court and parliament. It was this cooperation that poets urged the landowning classes, who dominated parliament, to deliver. Pope made stability begin at home, on the landowners' estates. John Philips agreed, reminding his readers of the Civil War violence: "Can we forget, how the mad, headstrong Rout / Defy'd their Prince to Arms . . . / . . . And this, once Happy, Land / By home-bred Fury rent, long groan'd beneath / Tyrannic Sway, 'till fair-revolving Years / Our exil'd Kings, and Liberty restor'd."[2]

If political faction was to be replaced with an order laid out in the land itself, then religious controversy was to be superseded by toleration. The Civil War had been a religious one; civil peace demanded the identification of a divine order to which all denominations could subscribe, whatever their doctrinal beliefs. Pope, himself a Catholic, made nature the place where God's order, as well as the landowner's, could be observed: "All are but parts of one stupendous whole, / Whose body, Nature is, and God the soul" (*Essay on Man*, 1, lines 267–68). God was to be inferred from studying nature, and so poets became students of His designing creativity who must, however, accept the limitations mortality placed on their understanding: "In this, or any other sphere, / Secure to be as blest as thou can bear: / Safe in the hand of one disposing Pow'r, / Or in the natal, or the mortal hour. / All Nature is but Art, unknown to thee" (1, lines 285–89).

James Thomson, a Scot who came to London to make his name, was less concerned about human fallibility than Pope. For him, natural order, discovered by empirical observation and the exercise of reason, and reflected in Miltonic blank verse rather than Pope's couplets, disclosed a rational, impersonal, designer God. In *The Seasons* (1726–40), Thomson "observed" the English estates of his politician-patrons, viewing them as places in which God's designing order was reflected in landscape, and in the characters of those shaped by that landscape. Propriety, endurance, and a patriotic concern for the country as a whole (rather than any one faction) were shown to grow naturally from the land. So, at least, it seemed in Hagley Park, seat of Thomson's Whig patron Lord Lyttelton:

> You . . . sit beneath the shade
> Of solemn oaks, that tuft the swelling mounts
> Thrown graceful round by Nature's careless hand,
> And pensive listen to the various voice
> Of rural peace – the herds, the flocks, the birds,
> The hollow-whispering breeze, the plaint of rills,
> That, purling down amid the twisted roots
> Which creep around, their dewy murmurs shake
> On the soothed ear.   (*Spring*, lines 914–22)[3]

Nature prepared Lyttelton to be a statesman:

> From these abstracted oft,
> You wander through the philosophic world;
> Where in bright train continual wonders rise
> Or to the curious or the pious eye.
> And oft, conducted by historic truth,
> You tread the long extent of backward time,
> Planning with warm benevolence of mind
> And honest zeal, unwarped by party-rage,

> Britannia's weal, – how from the venal gulf
> To raise her virtue and her arts revive.　　　　(lines 922–31)

Sheltered by the "solemn Oaks," Lyttelton is nurtured in a natural and political nursery. Nature fosters his paternalistic view: seeing "villages embosom'd soft in Trees" (line 953) from his own hilltop, he will be naturally inclined to protect his land and those who live in it.

It is no accident that Thomson shows Lyttelton's patriotic politics to emerge from his feelings for a view. Throughout *The Seasons*, prospects seen from hilltops show the land laid out before its lord. Thomson gives his patrons commanding views of their estates to emphasize – to them and to his other readers – the extent of their authority and responsibility. These views, however, have a symbolic function too, that of confirming the landowner's right to political power. It was the ability to take a disinterested view that was thought to make landowners fit to govern. Possession of land gave them independent income, ensuring they would not enter politics to feather their own nests. Landowners were supposedly free of self-interest, and so were free to consider the nation's interests with detachment. They were like a man looking at a distant prospect, as Bishop Berkeley put it in 1712: "And if we have a mind to take a fair prospect of the order and general well-being which the inflexible laws of nature and morality derive on the world, we must, if I may say so, go out of it, and imagine ourselves to be distant spectators of all that is transacted and contained in it; otherwise we are to be deceived by the too near view of the little present interests of ourselves."[4] Thomson's prospect-views realize Berkeley's argument on the ground. *The Seasons* turns the viewing of landscape into a confirmation of the landed classes' right to power.

What is omitted from prospect-views is the perspective of those whom the landowners saw from above. Farmers and laborers experienced nature close-at-hand, as a place and a resource in which they lived and worked. Thomson presents them only from afar and *en masse*. Their labor is briefly acknowledged but only insofar as it prepares the land to offer its bounty to men of property. So too in the nature poets whom Thomson influenced. In 1767 Richard Jago published a massive poetic survey of the English Midlands, presented as a series of prospect-views. In *Edge-Hill* the harvest seems to be nature's spontaneous tribute to the Earls of Warwick, who own the land the poet and reader see from above:

> 'Tis well! Here shelter'd from the scorching heat,
> At large we view the subject vale sublime,
> And unimpeded . . .
> 　　　. . . Over all her horn

Fair Plenty pours, and Cultivation spreads
Her height'ning lustre. See, beneath her touch,
The smiling harvests rise, with bending line,
And wavy ridge, along the dappled glebe
Stretching their lengthen'd beds. Her careful hand
Piles up the yellow grain . . .
            . . . The well-rang'd orchard now
She orders, or the shelt'ring clump, or tuft
Of hardy trees, the wintry storms to curb,
Or guard the sweet retreat of village-swain,
With health, and plenty crown'd.   (lines 29–61)[5]

Here the laborer doesn't labor. He is a generalized "happy Swain," a decorative consumer in a scene in which Nature produces without his efforts. Jago's desire to endorse the view of the landowner, and the politics implicit in that view, blinds him to all but the proprietorial perspective of the great and powerful. It is that perspective that he asks readers to share, giving us vicarious access to the commanding and disinterested views that, he argues, make Britain great.

The Englishman's proprietorial love of country had – and has – aggression as part of the scene. Thomson was quite explicit about this. He not only allowed for but gloried in the prospect of Englishness demanding enmity with, and war against, foreign nations. National power, he suggested, depended on the martial success that stemmed naturally from the land. If the oak revealed the English's protective love of their land, it also ensured, literally and symbolically, that they would defeat their trading rivals. Pope, likewise, derived Britain's success as an imperial nation from its native oak, and from what that oak's natural properties said about the national character:

Thy Trees, fair *Windsor*! now shall leave their Woods,
And half thy Forests, rush into my Floods,
Bear *Britain's* Thunder, and her Cross display,
To the bright Regions of the rising Day,
Tempt Icy Seas, where scarce the Waters roll,
Where clearer Flames glow round the frozen Pole;
Or under Southern Skies exalt their Sails,
Led by new Stars, and born by spicy Gales!
            (*Windsor-Forest*, 1713, lines 385–92)

The natural resources of the world, in Pope's vision of empire, are dedicated to the Briton, who will consume them,

For me the Balm shall bleed, and Amber flow,
The Coral redden, and the Ruby glow,
The pearly Shell its lucid Globe infold,

And *Phoebus* warm the ripening Ore to Gold.
The Time shall come, when free as Seas or Wind
Unbounded *Thames* shall flow for all Mankind,
Whole Nations enter with each swelling Tyde,
And Seas but join the Regions they divide;
Earth's distant Ends our Glory shall behold,
And the new World launch forth to seek the Old.

(lines 393–402)

The Briton is happy in the knowledge that his own nature lets him dominate wind, wave, and other nations: "suppliant States" will "be seen / Once more to bend before a *British* QUEEN" (lines 383–84).

Loco-descriptive poems such as *The Seasons* and *Windsor-Forest* derived from the genre of the georgic, based on the Latin poem written by Virgil during his exile from Rome. Thomson and Pope, imitating Virgil, were aiming their poems at a classically educated and, therefore, gentlemanly readership, for whom Virgil's idealization of rural labor was familiar. Among that readership, their nationalistic version of Virgil's nature-description was influential: *The Seasons* was one of the best-selling poems of the century. It spawned a great progeny of poems which also adapted Virgil's rustic ideal to the political circumstances of an increasingly imperial Britain. Virgil had dwelt upon the virtues of rural simplicity. He had made the tending of plants emblematic of a life dedicated to productive order: "Much labour is requir'd in Trees, to tame / Their wild disorder, and in ranks reclaim" (II, lines 85–86).[6] The countryman's attentive care of nature, Virgil concluded, was repaid morally. His was a virtuous, contented life, free from the corruptions of city and court:

Oh happy, if he knew his happy State!
The Swain, who, free from Business and Debate,
Receives his easy Food from Nature's Hand,
And just Returns of cultivated Land!
No Palace, with a lofty Gate, he wants,
T'admit the Tydes of early Visitants . . .
But easie Quiet, a secure Retreat,
A harmless Life that knows not how to cheat,
With homebred Plenty the rich Owner bless,
And rural Pleasures crown his Happiness.   (II, lines 639–58)

Dryden's translation (1697) and Joseph Warton's (1753), made Virgil an example for English poets. Many wrote of agricultural techniques, celebrating traditional and local forms of practical knowledge. In his *Cyder* (1708), Philips applied Virgil's discussion of grafting methods to the apple trees of Herefordshire orchards. John Dyer chose "The care of sheep, the labours of the loom, / And arts of trade" as the subject of *The Fleece* (1757). He described the weaving process in careful detail, risking bathos as a gap opened between his mundane subject matter and his epic diction. But Dyer had reasons for his lofty flights. For him, the processes of rural industry are heroic, because they are the source of national prosperity and imperial power. Rural work establishes a masculine national character that guarantees global success. Other peoples are weak and effeminate in comparison:

> No, ye soft sons of Ganges, and of Ind,
> Ye feebly delicate, life little needs
> Your fem'nine toys, nor asks your nerveless arm
> To cast the strong-slung shuttle, or the spear.
> Can ye defend your country from the storm
> Of strong invasion? . . .
> Can ye lead out, to distant colonies,
> Th'o'erflowings of a people, or your wrong'd
> Brethren, by impious persecution driv'n,
> And arm their breasts with fortitude to try
> New regions; climes, though barren, yet beyond
> The baneful pow'r of tyrants? These are deeds
> To which their hardy labors well prepare
> The sinewy arm of Albion's sons.   (lines 379–96)

The georgic sustains a vision of empire, for a nation competing with France to exploit and colonize India.

Imperial georgic reached its distasteful extreme in James Grainger's *The Sugar Cane* (1764). Here the affection Dyer had lavished on Britain's wealth-generating agriculture is lent to the West Indian colonies. To a modern reader, the celebration of industry and wealth is undermined by the hideous fact that it was slaves who produced the sugar. Grainger, though, is relatively untroubled by this exploitation. His slaves are happy workers, as contented as Virgil's "swains," as long as, like livestock, they are wisely selected and medicined:

> The slaves from Minnali are of stubborn breed:
> But, when the bill, or hammer, they affect;
> They soon perfection reach. But fly, with care,
> The Moco-nation; they themselves destroy.
> Worms lurk in all: yet, pronest they to worms,
> Who from Mundingo sail. When therefore such
> Thou buy'st, for sturdy and laborious they,
> Straight let some learned leach strong medicines give,
> Till food and climate both familiar grow.
> Thus, tho' from rise to set, in Phoebus' eye,

They toil, unceasing; yet, at night, they'll sleep,
Lap'd in Elysium; and, each day, at dawn,
Spring from their couch, as blythsome as the sun.

(IV, lines 99–111)[7]

By the 1780s, the campaign to abolish the slave trade was beginning to stir. To the abolitionists, Grainger's poem demonstrated the evacuation of morality from a genre that had begun as a way of defining the virtuous life. The georgic had become the voice of a complacent mercantile nation which made everything and everyone subservient to prosperity.

Yet it was not gentlemanly georgic, but a more popular genre, that converted the public as a whole to the poets' political myth of national character: it was the song. In 1740 James Thomson's "Rule Britannia" was first performed. It was a rapid success because it made the correspondence between English nature and character so direct:

Still more majestic shalt thou rise,
    More dreadful from each foreign stroke;
As the loud blast that tears the skies
    Serves but to root thy native oak.
        "Rule, Britannia, rule the waves;
        Britons never will be slaves."   (lines 13–18)[8]

Here the symbol of the oak is deployed with new immediacy. Presented starkly, with no surrounding argument, it works directly on the emotions, giving prejudices about British resilience and naval power apparent root in the ruggedness of its native tree. The poem naturalizes patriotism, disguising its arguments as facts about British nature. It became wildly popular: Nelson's sailors sang it before Trafalgar and it was still being taught to schoolboys in the 1930s. Thomson had made from the landscape a nationalist and imperialist ideology with which Britons are still living, even if, with empire lost and loyalties in question, many are now increasingly uneasy with it.

Some were uneasy about it at the time. At the start of the century Ambrose Philips had tried to nationalize the pastoral. With the influential approval of Richard Steele, he brought the idealized shepherds of this classical genre home to England's pastures. His pastorals used local names and a supposedly more realistic setting. To conservatives, Philips had made a mess. He had dumped the knowing artifice of a courtly genre in the mire of real rural work and words. John Gay attacked Philips by taking his avowed faithfulness to contemporary country matters to a parodic extreme: "Thus *Marian* wail'd, her Eye with Tears brimfull, / When Goody *Dobbins* brought her Cow to Bull. / With Apron blue to dry her Tears she sought, / Then saw the

Cow well serv'd, and took a Groat."⁹ Pope joined the fun, undermining
Philips by ironically overpraising him. He set out his own aesthetic in the
Discourse which prefaced his own Pastorals. Classical ideals could not be so
crudely claimed for contemporary Britain: "If we would copy Nature, it may
be useful to take this Idea along with us, that pastoral is an image of what
they call the Golden Age. So that we are not able to describe our shepherds
as shepherds at this day really are, but as they may be conceiv'd then to have
been" (*Pope*, p. 120).

Many poets agreed. Reacting against the easy politicization of nature, they
found a more personal and ambivalent engagement with the rural world.
Not all pastorals were means of glorifying Britain; not all prospect-views
were means of confirming the power of landowners. The young John Dyer,
in *Grongar Hill* (1726), looks down on a scene that tells him of the vanity
of human ambitions. Contemplating a ruined castle, he declares

> Yet Time has seen, that lifts the low,
> And level lays the lofty Brow,
> Has seen this broken Pile compleat,
> Big with the Vanity of State;
> But transient is the Smile of Fate!
> A little Rule, a little Sway,
> A Sun-beam in a Winter's Day
> Is all the Proud and Mighty have,
> Between the Cradle and the Grave.   (lines 84–92)

Picturesque prospects, here, are a source of melancholy moral reflection.
Property and politics become trivial in the wider scheme of things that the
poet sees from his hilltop retreat. Yet if the poet is saddened by his view of
mortality, he has compensations. It is he, after all, who has power. His rural
vantage-point lets him look down on the world of other men. It offers the
satisfaction of gaining exclusive access to truths that are vainly sought in the
city. Retirement offers what business cannot:

> Be full, ye Courts, be great who will;
> Search for Peace with all your skill:
> Open wide the lofty Door,
> Seek her on the marble Floor,
> In vain ye search, she is not there;
> In vain ye search the Domes of Care!
> Grass and Flowers Quiet treads,
> On the Meads, and Mountain-heads.   (lines 146–53)

Nature teaches grave knowledge, but only those who have renounced
worldly ambition learn her quiet truths. Dyer's moral high-ground tells him

this, and he ends the poems sitting comfortably above his fellow men, from a vantage point which later picturesque poets such as James Beattie (in *The Minstrel*, 1771) and Richard Crowe (*Lewesdon Hill*, 1788) were to use for similar ends.

It was left to Thomas Gray to bring Dyer's intimations of mortality home to the poet himself. In his *Elegy Written in a Country Churchyard* (1751), the poet does not sit above, but stands in, the landscape. He has no position of security, and his detachment from the deeds of others does not shield him from his own insights. Nature, he sees, is too indifferent to human concerns to leave the viewer feeling powerful. Although it seems at first to memorialize the dead in its "darkness" and "solemn stillness," nature has, in fact, its own rhythms of renewal, which grimly mock the finality of the grave. The contemplative poet learns of a double loss: death severs human connection and the link that man creates for himself with nature. Morning will break, swallows twitter, woods grow, without the men who invested them with meaning. "Ambition" and the "pomp of power," it follows, can no more imprint their lives on nature than can the "poor." "Annals" and elegies such as this one, which remember the dead, can only be the fragile subjective texts of human memory, unsupported by the world beyond the writer.

The gentleman-poet moralizes about the lives of poor laborers he did not know:

> Far from the madding crowd's ignoble strife,
> Their sober wishes never learn'd to stray;
> Along the cool sequester'd vale of life
> They kept the noiseless tenor of their way.   (lines 73–76)

But the laborers turn the tables on him, viewing him as a man who is as wayward as they, to him, are "sequester'd":

> Hard by yon wood, now smiling as in scorn,
> Mutt'ring his wayward fancies he wou'd rove,
> Now drooping, woeful wan, like one forlorn,
> Or craz'd with care, or cross'd in hopeless love.
>
> (lines 105–8)

Moralizing cuts both ways, it seems, and neither the poet's condescension to the rural poor, nor theirs to him, is necessarily reliable in face of the silence of the grave. In this most profound of poems, eighteenth-century conventions of viewing seem to operate, only to collapse. So do assumptions about the relationship of gentleman to laborer, and of both to nature. By the end, the reader is also left in doubt, left studying an epitaph which the poet imagines being placed over his grave. Texts proliferate, truth and authority flee away; what remains is an impression of the fallibility of all human endeavor in face of a Nature that seems, in its indifference, to have become Death incarnate. After this, the only reliable elegist is one who is himself beyond nature – God:

> No farther seek his merits to disclose,
> Or draw his frailties from their dread abode,
> (There they alike in trembling hope repose)
> The bosom of his Father and his God.   (lines 125–28)

Few poets were as searching as Gray; the *Elegy*, however, is the ultimate concentration of a movement against the blithe self-assurance of poets who identified nature and property. Joseph Warton had set the agenda for this movement, explicitly attacking Cobham's estate at Stowe and Pope's poetic endorsement of it:

> Can gilt alcoves, can marble-mimick gods,
> Parterres embroider'd, obelisks, and urns
> Of high relief; can the long, spreading lake,
> Or vista lessening to the sight; can Stow
> With all her Attick fanes, such raptures raise,
> As the thrush-haunted copse?
>   (*The Enthusiast: or the Lover of Nature*, 1748, lines 1–10)

It was not Warton but William Cowper, however, who most powerfully articulated the gentlemanly reaction against poetry that presented nature as the property of the great. Cowper criticized the rage for landscape gardening and mocked the ambitions of the aristocracy. He also traversed the landscape on foot, exchanging the commanding height of the hilltop for the secure retreats of valleys, copses, and sunken lanes. Like Gray, he made retirement into a moral stance, from which he could both satirize the activity of the city and ponder the ambiguities of his own position – neither a "peasant: nor a squire." Unlike Gray, however, Cowper found in the landscape an emotional home, a place of reassurance capable of holding his depressive and suicidal tendencies at bay.

An Evangelical Christian, Cowper introduced to gentlemanly verse the emotional engagement with a personal God that characterizes the Methodist hymns of Charles Wesley. In Cowper's *Olney Hymns* (1779), co-authored with the ex-slaveship captain John Newton, God is an immediate presence not, as in Thomson and Pope, a remote designer. For Cowper, God works in the lives of men through nature, which displays his love in its beauty and his wrath in its sublimity. Believing himself damned after an earlier suicide attempt, Cowper makes nature a pathetic drama, in which the reprobate yearns for signs of a love that he does not, finally, believe will intervene to save him:

TEMPTATION

The billows swell, the winds are high,
Clouds overcast my wintry sky;
Out of the depths to thee I call,
My fears are great, my strength is small.

O LORD, the pilot's part perform,
And guide and guard me thro' the storm;
Defend me from each threatning ill,
Controll the waves, say, "Peace, be still."

Amidst the roaring of the sea,
My soul still hangs her hope on thee;
Thy constant love, thy faithful care,
Is all that saves me from despair.

Dangers of ev'ry shape and name
Attend the followers of the Lamb,
Who leave the world's deceitful shore,
And leave it to return no more.

Tho' tempest-toss'd and half a wreck,
My Saviour thro' the floods I seek;
Let neither winds nor stormy main
Force back my shatter'd bark again.[10]

At the end of his life Cowper was to imagine himself all at sea again. In "The Castaway" (1799) he pictures his own death. It is a lonely death, in which he finds not a savior across the sea, but the depths of despair. The poet, like the man lost overboard, drowns alone and unredeemed:

No voice divine the storm allay'd,
    No light propitious shone,
When, snatch'd from all effectual aid,
    We perish'd, each, alone;
But I, beneath a rougher sea,
And whelm'd in deeper gulphs than he.   (lines 61–66)

Cowper's cry of anguish is as powerful as any in English poetry. It is all the more so because it remains unspoken, implicit in the imagined events occurring in an unforgiving nature.

New in Cowper's blank verse is a simplicity of diction designed to render observed details as plainly as possible. Diction of this kind illuminates *The Task* (1785), his most influential poem.

The night was winter in his roughest mood,
The morning sharp and clear. But now at noon

> Upon the southern side of the slant hills,
> And where the woods fence off the northern blast,
> The season smiles, resigning all its rage,
> And has the warmth of May. The vault is blue
> Without a cloud, and white without a speck
> The dazzling splendour of the scene below.
> Again the harmony comes o'er the vale,
> And through the trees I view the embattled tower
> Whence all the music. I again perceive
> The soothing influence of the wasted strains,
> And settle in soft musings as I tread
> The walk still verdant under oaks and elms,
> Whose outspread branches overarch the glade.
>
> (VI, lines 57–71)

It is not just Cowper's conversational verse that introduces a new note into eighteenth-century poetry. The closeness of observation, from the shifting viewpoint of a walker, renders nature as a fluid experience, in which time as well as space is organized subjectively, from the consciousness of an individual who finds himself changing as the landscape through which he travels changes. If nature keeps a path for Cowper, it is a path of self-discovery.

> The roof though moveable through all its length
> As the wind sways it, has yet well sufficed,
> And intercepting in their silent fall
> The frequent flakes, has kept a path for me.
> No noise is here, or none that hinders thought.
> The redbreast warbles still, but is content
> With slender notes and more than half suppress'd.
> Pleased with his solitude, and flitting light
> From spray to spray, where'er he rests he shakes
> From many a twig the pendent drops of ice,
> That tinkle in the wither'd leaves below.
> Stillness accompanied with sounds so soft
> Charms more than silence. Meditation here
> May think down hours to moments. Here the heart
> May give an useful lesson to the head,
> And learning wiser grow without his books.   (VI, lines 72–87)

Wordsworth and Coleridge were to tread, quite deliberately, in his footsteps: his pacing out of time and space allowed the Romantic self to be articulated. It remains contemporary.

The need for a rural refuge was not unique to Cowper. In the later eighteenth century poets increasingly yearned for a country idyll to counter the excesses of the city. This yearning was only intensified by changes to the agricultural economy which made that idyll harder than ever to ground in the real world. The drive for prosperity that the georgic poets had celebrated fueled the enclosure and engrossment of common and marginal land. Landowners increased rents to encourage more efficient farming. At the same time, the population increased markedly. Many smallholders and cottagers found themselves deprived of land and reduced to wage laborers for tenant farmers who were striving to pay higher rents. Christopher Anstey protested in these terms: "Proud tenants with rapacious hand / Engross the produce of their land / Usurp the empire of the plains / And lord it over the humbler swains."[11] With the pool of labor thus swollen, wages were depressed. In years when the price of corn was low, or when work was scarce, poverty was widespread. Even in good years, the traditional social structure of the country seemed to have been destroyed, the semi-feudal relationships of squire and tenant to have been supplanted by a cash economy. Such was the argument of Oliver Goldsmith's *The Deserted Village* (1770). Goldsmith portrayed an organic rural community, in harmony with nature, being destroyed by avarice.

> Thus fares the land, by luxury betrayed,
> In nature's simplest charms at first arrayed,
> But verging to decline, its splendours rise,
> Its vistas strike, its palaces surprize;
> While scourged by famine from the smiling land,
> The mournful peasant leads his humble band;
> And while he sinks without one arm to save,
> The country blooms – a garden, and a grave.   (lines 297–304)

He blamed the landowning classes for letting their love of money overcome their traditional duty to those who lived on their estates:

> Where then, ah, where shall poverty reside,
> To scape the pressure of contiguous pride;
> If to some common's fenceless limits strayed,
> He drives his flock to pick the scanty blade,
> Those fenceless fields the sons of wealth divide,
> And even the bare-worn common is denied.   (lines 305–10)

Socially radical in one respect, Goldsmith is nostalgically conservative in another. The community whose destruction he mourns is an idealized idyll, a city-dweller's fantasy, a utopia in which rural innocence equals bucolic ignorance. Thus he pictures the village parson impressing his congregation: "words of learned length, and thundering sounds, / Amazed the gazing rustics ranged around, / And still they gazed, and still the wonder grew, / That one small head could carry all he knew" (lines 215–18).

It was sentimentality of this kind that led George Crabbe to take Goldsmith to task in *The Village* (1783). While Crabbe, like Goldsmith, lamented rural poverty and blamed it on landowners' avarice, he rejected Goldsmith's argument that village life had once been idyllic. In Crabbe's rural world landscape and humankind are both full of strife, waste, and hidden violence. Poverty simply reveals most starkly the facts that Crabbe is determined the rich should acknowledge – that life is full of pain, evil, and disease. The rich, he argues, should stop moaning about their trivial ills; they should cease imagining the country as a vicarious escape from the side-effects of luxury. Villagers are not swains, he insists; they are not innocent shepherds. They are people, good and ill; their distress is real and is exacerbated by landowners' neglect, a neglect that, in practice, goes hand-in-hand with nostalgic yearning for an idyll.

Crabbe confronts his readers, in the name of fact. He strips away pretense and corrects the gentlemanly view of rural life. Yet he still views villagers from above – as a concerned "overseer of the poor" (to borrow Hazlitt's verdict). His is a corrective vision yet still a distant one. He knows as much, asking at the outset "save honest D U C K, what son of verse could share / The poet's rapture and the peasant's care?" (lines 27–28). This alludes to Stephen Duck, the poet who was also an agricultural laborer. Duck's *The Thresher's Labour* (1730) is written from the fields that Thomson, Jago, and others viewed from afar. It speaks confidently, in couplets derived from gentleman-poets (Dryden, Pope, Virgil), of ungentlemanly work. It *seems* to speak for a collective experience, for a whole class of laborers for whom the pleasures of the prospect-view are tied to the demands of work:

> Alas! what pleasing thing,
> Here, to the Mind, can the dull Fancy bring?
> Our Eye beholds no pleasing Object here,
> No chearful Sound diverts our list'ning Ear.
> The Shepherd well may tune his Voice to sing,
> Inspir'd with all the Beauties of the Spring.
> No Fountains murmur here, no Lambkins play,
> No Linnets warble, and no Fields look gay;
> 'Tis all a gloomy, melancholy Scene,
> Fit only to provoke the Muse's Spleen.
> When sooty Pease we thresh, you scarce can know
> Our native Colour, as from Work we go:
> The Sweat, the Dust, and suffocating Smoak,
> Make us so much like Ethiopians look,
> We scare our Wives, when Ev'ning brings us home;
> And frighted Infants think the Bugbear come.   (lines 54–69)

They are also tied to the master for whom they work:

> Week after Week, we this dull Task pursue,
> Unless when winn'wing Days produce a new:
> A new, indeed, but frequently a worse!
> The Threshal yields but to the Master's Curse.
> He counts the Bushels, counts how much a Day;
> Then swears we've idled half our Time away:
> "Why, look ye, Rogues, d'ye think that this will do?
> Your Neighbours thresh as much again as you."
> Now in our Hands we wish our noisy Tools,
> To drown the hated Names of Rogues and Fools.   (lines 70–79)

If Duck restores the facts of labor to the landscape, he also introduces the voice of the laborer. Yet he should not be treated, for this reason, as simply representative of a whole class. Just as he contested the gentlemanly view of the country, so others attacked his. Mary Collier, a washerwoman and gleaner, wrote "The Woman's Labour" to vindicate the work of women – work ignored by gentlemen poets and denigrated by Duck. Collier challenges Duck directly, finding in the process a powerfully detailed counter-argument:

> And you, great DUCK, whose happy Brow
> The Muses seem to fix the Garland now,
> In your late *Poem* boldly did declare
> Alcides' Labours can't with yours compare;
> And of your annual Task have much to say,
> Of Threshing, Reaping, Mowing Corn and Hay;
> Boasting your daily Toil, and nightly Dream,
> But can't conclude your never-dying Theme,
> And let our hapless Sex in Silence lie
> Forgotten, and in dark Oblivion die;
> But on our abject State you throw your Scorn,
> And Women wrong, your Verses to adorn.   (lines 31–42)

Collier effectively reveals the doubly oppressed lot of laboring women, and makes domestic work as worthy of poetic celebration as work in the fields. At the same time, her forceful verse graphically demonstrates what many in the eighteenth century doubted – that women, and laboring women too, could be poets. Other women, including Mary Leapor and Ann Yearsley, were to follow her example.

The order which gentleman poets found, and laborers contested, in the landscape was never easily available to all. The Scottish highlands largely rejected the Hanoverian settlement that England embraced. Wales offered a different landscape and a different language too. In the highlands of the

Celtic cultures, prospect-views did not disclose fertile plains and happy swains, but barren peaks and rebellious clans – at least until 1745, when the Scots supporters of Bonnie Prince Charlie were crushed at Culloden. With the political threat of Jacobitism over, it became possible to admire highland culture without seeming disloyal to Hanoverian rule. Thomson, a lowland Scot writing before 1745, had not enjoyed such security. His work makes Britain and Britishness in the image of England's lowland landscapes, with the exception of a few set-piece descriptions of wilder scenery, like this one seen from the viewpoint of a shepherd lost in a storm:

> . . . cover'd Pits, unfathomably deep,
> A dire Descent ! beyond the power of frost;
> . . . faithless Bogs; of Precipices huge,
> Smooth'd up with Snow; and, what is Land unknown,
> What Water, of the still unfrozen Spring,
> In the loose Marsh or solitary Lake,
> Where the fresh Fountain from the Bottom boils.
> These check his fearful Steps; and down he sinks
> Beneath the Shelter of the shapeless Drift,
> Thinking o'er all the Bitterness of Death
>
> (*Winter*, lines 297–306)

Thomson's exercises in the sublime restage the power of nature so as to leave the reader in terror, admiration, and awe. They have the moral purpose of reminding us of our vulnerability. Yet they remain vignettes, episodes of disorder subsumed within the larger order of the poem as a whole, a poem which finds nature, ultimately, to be providentially ordered to produce peace, plenty, and prosperity. For Thomson, as well as Cowper, "God made the country," and made it to bless man.

Vignettes though they were, Thomson's sublime episodes influenced those no longer prevented by politics from portraying the highlands. After 1745, the supposedly "primitive" Celtic peoples were made heroic. They were made embodiments of the valor that polite Englishmen wished to experience, at least vicariously from the safety of the library. Poets imaginatively repopulated the mountains, replacing the actual clansmen (who were forced from the land after Culloden) with bards and warriors from the past. Set against the sublime backdrop of stormy crags, rushing streams, and barren moors, these figures bespoke the poets' and public's yearning for a controlled dose of wildness which would not overwhelm the broad acres of England and Englishness. Thomas Gray's "The Bard" (1757) was a medieval prophet for his Welsh people. Standing on a "haughty" rock, invoking the "mountains," he mourns the conquest of his culture and its warrior-poets, by the English.

He is wild, like the Welsh landscape by which he is inspired and which sponsors his visionary verse. Yet ultimately the landscape offers him no place to stand, colonized by the English as it now is. At the poem's end the bard commits suicide, casting himself into his sublime landscape: "He spoke, and headlong from the mountain's height / Deep in the roaring tide he plung'd to endless night" (lines 143–44).

Gray's poem is elegiac rather than confrontational. Set firmly in the past, it raises no contemporary banners against English rule. James Macpherson presented a similar version of the Scottish past. Influenced by Gray, he published a series of "translations" from an ancient bard, Ossian, whose Gaelic songs he claimed to have collected. In fact, Macpherson had added to and improved upon the oral poetry he had collected. His *Fingal* (1762) was more a creation of the new vogue for Celtic primitivism than a remnant of the ancient past. A massive success across Europe and America until well into the nineteenth century, it made the Highlands fashionable, as the landscape through which valor, honor, and heroism could still be articulated. Macpherson's Scots warriors are primitive poets: they endow their lives with greatness by comparing themselves with the sublime nature in which they live:

> He fell as the moon in a storm; as the sun from the midst of his course, when clouds rise from the waste of the waves, when the blackness of the storm inwraps the rocks of Ardannider. I, like an ancient oak on Morven, I moulder alone in my place. The blast hath lopped my branches away; and I tremble at the wings of the north. Prince of the warriors, Oscur my son! shall I see thee no more! (*Fragments of Ancient Poetry*, 1760)

New in their primitiveness, Macpherson's ancient poets made rural imagery the sign of authenticity. To sing of nature like a bard was to be truly aboriginal, the desirable opposite to the polite and urban man-of-letters. Macpherson, a university scholar like Gray, was no radical. In bringing his antiquarian research to poetic life, he was not endorsing a revival of clan politics but was searching for an escape from English nature and from the nature of Englishness. So when a vigorous new Scots poet appeared in the present rather than the bardic past, the Ossian enthusiasts welcomed him as a primitive genius, but tried to tame his political radicalism. Robert Burns was patronized as a "native genius," a "Heaven-taught ploughman" warbling "woodnotes wild." He was publicized as a peasant-poet, an untaught son of the soil, a new bard. Such labels ignored the learning and art with which, in fact, he developed both English and Scots models. He imitated Pope and Gray; he revived the ancient tradition of Scottish folksong. In Burns's hands, such songs invested the objects of nature with an individually realized life. In the exquisitely subtle "Now westlin winds," Scots dialect is

the vehicle for a nature so tenderly observed that it quietly empowers the
poet both to oppose the sport of hunting and to woo his beloved.

> Now westlin winds, and slaught'ring guns
>   Bring Autumn's pleasant weather;
> The moorcock springs, on whirring wings,
>   Amang the blooming heather:
> Now waving grain, wide o'er the plain,
>   Delights the weary Farmer;
> The moon shines bright, as I rove at night,
>   To muse upon my Charmer.
>
> The Pairtrick lo'es the fruitfu' fells;
>   The Plover lo'es the mountains;
> The Woodcock haunts the lanely dells;
>   The soaring Hern the fountains:
> Thro' lofty groves, the Cushat roves,
>   The path o' man to shun it,
> The hazel bush o'erhangs the Thrush,
>   The spreading thorn the Linnet.
>
> Thus ev'ry kind their pleasure find,
>   The savage and the tender;
> Some social join, and leagues combine;
>   Some solitary wander:
> Avaunt, away! the cruel sway,
>   Tyrannic man's dominion;
> The Sportsman's joy, the murd'ring cry,
>   The flutt'ring, gory pinion!
>
> But PEGGY dear, the ev'ning's clear,
>   Thick flies the skimming Swallow;
> The sky is blue, the fields in view,
>   All fading-green and yellow:
> Come let us stray our gladsome way,
>   And view the charms o' Nature;
> The rustling corn, the fruited thorn,
>   And ilka happy creature.
>
> We'll gently walk, and sweetly talk,
>   While the silent moon shines clearly;
> I'll clasp thy waist, and fondly prest,
>   Swear how I lo'e thee dearly:
> Not vernal show'rs to budding flow'rs,
>   Not Autumn to the Farmer,
> So dear can be, as thou to me,
>   My fair, my lovely Charmer![12]

Nature accommodates all, the lover of peace as well as of violence, Burns says to "Peggy." But underlying this argument is the association of the lovers with the free, but vulnerable, birds which the farmer hunts. The human lovers' freedom, Burns implies, is closer to nature than the farmer is. It is also more fragile, menaced by man's tyrannic propensity to "dominion." The lovers had better enjoy liberty – and each other's vulnerable bodies – while they can, before the autumn's peace gives way to death.

Burns's poetry is the real thing: the work of a great writer making new an ancient tradition in which he is learned. It is rural; it is Scots. But Burns is no Ossianic primitive bard. Ossian offered a tame ideal in pompous words. Burns offers an achieved art, a lyrical presentation of nature both simple and profound, a version of Scotland which constantly challenges assumptions about land, loyalty, and love. It was a version that, in its more sexually and politically explicit forms, left Ossian's gentlemanly admirers uncomfortable.

Ossian, however, could be discovered further afield. Beyond the landscape park and the tenanted acres, Britons were encountering other kinds of nature, new and old, that were foreign to the Englishness of the epistle and the georgic. It was these encounters, made on the heaths of Huntingdonshire and the fells of Westmoreland, in the snows of the Antarctic and the groves of Tahiti, that poets began to record. Erasmus Darwin, doctor, scientist, and inventor, portrayed the tropical fertility and sexual promiscuity of Polynesia in *The Loves of the Plants* (1789). In this poem the exotic discoveries of explorers met the latest botanical science. Linnaeus had classified plants according to their sexual characteristics. Darwin adapted Linnaeus's system to verse, making free sexual intercourse the creative principle that governed both plant and human behavior.

> A *hundred* virgins join a *hundred* swains,
> And fond Adonis leads the sprightly trains;
> Pair after pair, along his sacred groves
> To Hymen's fane the bright procession moves;
> Each smiling youth a myrtle garland shades,
> And wreaths of roses veil the blushing maids;
> Light Joys on twinkling feet attend the throng,
> Weave the gay dance, or raise the frolic song . . .
> Licentious Hymen joins their mingled hands,
> And loosely twines the meretricious bands. –
> Thus where pleased Venus, in the southern main,
> Sheds all her smiles on Otaheite's plain [Tahiti],
> Wide o'er the isle her silken net she draws,
> And the Loves laugh at all, but Nature's laws.
>
> (IV, lines 287–406)[13]

In Darwin, Pope is transformed. Using Pope's couplets and his mythological machinery, the doctor presented a teeming, licentious nature that exceeded the bounds of propriety and taste. His vision, if not his verse form, was to influence Coleridge and Shelley.

Darwin made sex central to nature in the name of science. Still more threatening to conservative critics, was the work of Sir William Jones, a native of west Wales who found a poetic home in the East Indies. Jurist, administrator, linguist, and poet, Jones, the governor of Bengal on behalf of Britain's East India Company, opened a vast and ancient culture to European eyes. He did so by marrying the styles of Pope and Gray to the mythology of Hinduism. What issued from this union was a neo-classical verse in which nature was metamorphosed by the desire of the gods – as in the account of the holy river in the *Hymn to Ganga* (1785):

> Meanwhile o'er *Potyid's* musky dales,
> Gay *Rangamar*, where sweetest spikenard blooms,
> And *Siret*, fam'd for strong perfumes,
> That, flung from shining tresses, lull the gales,
> Wild *Brahmaputra* winding flows,
> And murmurs hoarse his am'rous woes;
> Then charming GANGA seen, the heav'nly boy
> Rushes with tumultuous joy:
> (Can aught but Love to men or Gods be sweet?)
> When she, the long-lost youth to greet,
> Darts, not as earth-born lovers toy,
> But blending her fierce waves, and teeming verdant isles;
> While buxom *Lacshmi* crowns their bed, and sounding ocean smiles.
>
> (lines 144–56)[14]

If Darwin put sex at the heart of nature and culture, in the name of science, Jones did so in the name of a "heathen" religion. He asked readers to place Hindu scripture on the same elite level as Greek mythology, to grant it heroic status. And in claiming that most European languages derived from an Indian original, he seemed to give Hindu culture priority. To his critics, Jones had "gone native"; to his admirers, including Goethe, Schiller, and Shelley, he had done nothing less than change the status of European history. If European culture derived from Indian, then the lustful gods and teeming jungles of Hindu scripture took precedence over Europe's green and pleasant land.

It is a nice irony that a century which saw gentlemen-poets shaping a national and imperial order from the landscape of England, should have ended with a gentleman-poet, himself a ruler of empire, placing that order in doubt. After Jones, Britannia might still rule the waves, but her people, and the nature they identified themselves with, knew themselves to be part of a Europe that was secondary to the East. In the centuries to come a great many words were to be expended as Britons responded to that knowledge. Not just words, but blood. Many would die to prove what the poets of nature led them to believe, against the voices of the empire:"that there is some corner of a foreign field," as Rupert Brooke would write, "That is forever England."[15]

NOTES

The author wishes to thank John Goodridge and Debbie Lee for their advice on this chapter.

1 *The Poems of Alexander Pope*, ed. John Butt (London: Methuen, 1963), p. 590. Henceforth cited in the text as *Pope*.

2 *Cyder*, II, 498–524 From *The Poems of John Philips*, ed. M. G. Lloyd Thomas (Oxford: Blackwell, 1927).

3 From *Eighteenth-Century Poetry: an Annotated Anthology*, ed. David Fairer and Christine Gerrard (Oxford: Blackwell, 1999). All poems, unless otherwise specified, will be cited from this edition.

4 *Passive Obedience*, in *The Works of George Berkeley, Bishop of Cloyne*, ed. T. E. Jessop, 9 vols. (London, 1948–57), VI, 32–33.

5 In *Poems, Moral and Descriptive* (London, 1784).

6 From *Virgil's Georgics, with the translation by John Dryden* (London, 1949).

7 *The Sugar Cane* (London, 1764).

8 James Thomson, *Poetical Works*, ed. J. Logie Robertson (London, 1908), pp. 422–23.

9 *The Shepherd's Week*, Tuesday, lines 103–6, in *John Gay Poetry and Prose*, ed. Vinton A. Dearing (Oxford: Clarendon Press, 1974), I.

10 *Olney Hymns*, in *The Poems of William Cowper*, ed. John D. Baird and Charles Ryskamp, 3 vols. (Oxford: Oxford University Press, 1980–95), I, 177–78. All Cowper's poems are cited from this edition.

11 *Speculation*, lines 750–53 (1780), in *The Poetical Works of the Late Christopher Anstey* (London, 1808).

12 *Burns' Poems and Songs*, ed. James Kinsley (Oxford: Oxford University Press, 1971), pp. 2–3.

13 *The Loves of the Plants*, 1789 (facsimile reprint Oxford and New York: Woodstock, 1991).

14 *Sir William Jones: Selected Poetical and Prose Works*, ed. Michael J. Franklin (Cardiff: University of Wales Press, 1995), pp. 131–32.

15 During the First World War, Brooke, influenced by Keats, Tennyson, Wordsworth, and thus indirectly by eighteenth-century nature poetry, wrote these words anticipating his own burial in foreign soil. He was indeed to die, as troops from Britain and its colonies invaded Turkey.

FURTHER READING

Barrell, John. *English Literature in History, 1730–1830: An Equal Wide Survey*. London: Macmillan, 1983.

The Dark Side of the Landscape: the Rural Poor in English Painting 1750–1840. Cambridge: Cambridge University Press, 1980.

Chalker, John. The English Georgic: a Study in the Development of a Form. London: Routledge and Kegan Paul, 1969.

Copley, Stephen, and Peter Garside (eds.). The Politics of the Picturesque. Cambridge: Cambridge University Press, 1994.

Crawford, Rachel. "English Georgic and British Nationhood," ELH 65 (1998), 123–58.

Daniels, Stephen. Fields of Vision: Landscape Imagery and National Identity in England and the United States. Cambridge: Polity Press; Princeton, Princeton University Press, 1993.

Erskine-Hill, Howard. Poetry of Opposition and Revolution: Dryden to Wordsworth. Oxford: Clarendon Press, 1996.

Everett, Nigel. The Tory View of Landscape. New Haven and London: Yale University Press, 1994.

Fairer, David. "Thomas Warton, Thomas Gray, and the Recovery of the Past," in W. B. Hutchings and William Ruddick (eds.), Thomas Gray: Contemporary Essays. Liverpool: Liverpool University Press, 1993. 146–70.

Fairer, David, and Christine Gerrard (eds.). Eighteenth-Century Poetry: an Annotated Anthology. Oxford: Blackwell, 1999.

Feingold, Richard. Nature and Society: Later Eighteenth-Century Uses of the Pastoral and Georgic. New Brunswick, NJ: Rutgers University Press, 1978.

Fulford, Tim. Landscape, Liberty and Authority: Poetry, Criticism and Politics from Thomson to Wordsworth. Cambridge: Cambridge University Press, 1996.

Goodridge, John. Rural Life in Eighteenth-Century Poetry. Cambridge: Cambridge University Press, 1995.

Heinzelman, Kurt. "Roman Georgic in the Georgian Age: a Theory of Romantic Genre," Texas Studies in Language and Literature, 33 (1991).

Low, Anthony. The Georgic Revolution. Princeton: Princeton University Press, 1985.

Murphy, Peter T. Poetry as an Occupation and an Art in Britain 1760–1830. Cambridge: Cambridge University Press, 1993.

Watson, J. R. (ed.). Pre-Romanticism in English Poetry of the Eighteenth Century. Basingstoke: Macmillan, 1989.

Williams, Raymond. The Country and the City. London: Chatto & Windus; New York: Oxford University Press, 1973.

Woodman, Thomas (ed.) Early Romantics: Perspectives in British Poetry from Pope to Wordsworth. Basingstoke and New York: Macmillan and St. Martin's Press, 1998.

7

JOHN SITTER

Questions in poetics: why and how poetry matters

Preconceptions

The study of eighteenth-century theories of poetry might be more safely ignored if we knew nothing rather than a little of the subject beforehand. The little learning that may be a dangerous thing, at least for an unbiased reading of the poetry itself, often rests on brief encounters with popular eighteenth-century works, Romantic reactions, and modern generalizations. A few points may loom disproportionately in the memory, for example, from Pope's *An Essay on Criticism*, epigrammatic but easily misconstrued; from Johnson's novel *Rasselas*, in which Imlac recommends "general truths" to poets, over the "streaks of the tulip"; from Wordsworth's retrospective simplification in the Preface to *Lyrical Ballads* of the prior age as artificial, or from later handbook reductions such as "neo classicism," "rules," and "didacticism." Through much of the modern era it has been assumed either that eighteenth-century poetry was inhibited by rigid theoretical principles and succeeded (when it did) by ignoring them. The authors of an influential history of criticism have earnestly insisted that eighteenth-century poetry was largely – and happily – "a hundred years behind the most advanced theory," proceeding more along lines laid down in Renaissance treatises than in newer works such as Edward Bysshe's *Art of Poetry* of 1701. In this light, eighteenth-century criticism "before the rise of romantic theory" produced "only a more or less dismal continuation of the ornamentalist view" of metaphor and poetic language.[1]

Such a view of the period's critical thought is doubly partial, resting on selective reading and unsympathetic interpretation. Eighteenth-century criticism of poetry *is* more firmly tied to the rhetorical tradition than much Romantic writing would be, and Coleridgean "organic form" is *not* central to its vocabulary; criticism of the period tends to find poems more like buildings than plants. But we have good reason to be curious about a body of critical writing that is, like much of our own, unwilling to make transcendental claims for poetry, as Sidney had or Shelley would, a theory of poetry that seeks to defend poetry without mystification. "I can easily admire poetry, and yet without adoring it," wrote Sir William Temple in a genuinely reverential essay of 1690: "I can allow it to arise from the greatest . . . native genius, without exceeding the reach of what is human, or giving it any approaches of divinity."[2] If poetry is unequivocally human and closely allied to rhetoric, it can be taught (within limits) and discussed, not only in relatively uninteresting how-to guides such as Bysshe's, but more importantly as a realm of experience, largely in terms of what would now be considered "reader-response" or affective criticism.

A useful emblem of the pragmatic, rhetorical temper of much of the period's writing about poetry may be found in contrasting late twentieth- and early eighteenth-century treatments of the term "aporia," a word especially prevalent in poststructuralist accounts of indeterminacy. The index entry in the *Princeton Encyclopedia of Poetry and Poetics*, revised in 1993, reads: "APORIA. See DECONSTRUCTION; INFLUENCE." On the other hand, the corresponding entry in Anthony Blackwall's popular *Introduction to the Classics*, 1718, is this: "*Aporia. Vide Doubt.*"[3] The reader who turned to "Doubt" would not find musings on linguistic instability or the anxieties of "undecidability" but an explanation of the rhetorical strategy of pausing in order to appear uncertain of what to say next. Eighteenth-century writers recognized that poetry and oratory were not identical, but they generally declined to oppose them to each other, as would post-Romantic writers such as John Stuart Mill ("eloquence is *heard*; poetry is *over*heard") or William Butler Yeats ("we make out of the quarrel with others, rhetoric, but of the quarrel with ourselves, poetry").[4] Many would see some of the differences as matters of degree, as the mid- seventeenth-century Meric Casaubon had put it winningly in distinguishing rhetorical from poetic decorum: "An Oratour must not alwaies ravish. If he affect it in every part, it is likely he doth it in no part: he is a Fool, or a Child; not an Oratour. But if through exuberance of wit and good language, he happen without affectation, to ravish every where, he is not an Orator, but a Poet."[5]

"Decorum" is one of the words most often invoked, along with "rules" and "neo-classicism" itself, when modern readers cast late-seventeenth- and eighteenth-century critical writing as restrictive. It may be helpful to begin by going past the preconceptions to consider the liberating potential of these terms. "Rules" are descriptive rather than prescriptive for the best eighteenth-century critics, empirical generalizations based on the study of many works of many periods, rather than abstract pronouncements; they were, Pope would say, "*discover'd*, not *devis'd*."[6] And, as suggested already, the idea of "rules" implies that human ends and means are in question and may be debated without immediate appeal to mysteries such as "taste" or "genius," however important those may be. As early as the 1660s Dryden had equated rules with methods: "if nature is to be imitated, there is a rule for imitating nature rightly; otherwise there may be an end, and no means conducing to it."[7] The conviction that poetic means may be better understood through discussion brings criticism – of means and ends – increasingly into the public domain during the century.

While "decorum" could, theoretically, prove a stultifying idea, its more common practical effect was to pluralize poetry in a way that we still have some trouble grasping. Because there is less emphasis, at least in the first half of the century, on Poetry than on *kinds* of poetry, ranging from low to middle to heroic or sublime, a broader range of topics and styles may be allowed than in a putatively more liberal but earnestly monolithic poetic climate. Temple, for example, pragmatically distinguished six recurrent subjects in poetry from the earliest works to his own day: "praise, instruction, story, love, grief, and reproach." It is an inclusive taxonomy, and few authors would have expected the same rules to obtain in the treatment of all of these themes. Most would have thought of decorum as plural and thus less in terms of poetic license than of poetic licenses. Pope's extension of the conventional idea that "Expression is the *Dress* of *Thought*" is often quoted to show the demands of propriety: "For diff'rent *Styles* with diff'rent *Subjects* sort, / As several Garbs with Country, Town, and Court" (*Essay on Criticism*, lines 318, 322–23). But to construe this dictum so narrowly is to forget that a choice of clothing permits one to assume various roles – as Pope's pun on "subjects" suggests – and to choose informality as well as formality.

Some of the period's best-known pronouncements stress, when read carefully and in context, that poetry is an activity, with poet and reader cooperating in cognition and recognition. Pope's couplet on "true wit" is also oft quoted, usually to demonstrate the "ornamentalist view" of poetry that is supposed to have dominated the period: "*True Wit* is *Nature* to *Advantage* drest, / What oft was *Thought*, but ne'er so well *Exprest*." But if the reader merely goes on with Pope to complete the sentence – "*Something*, whose Truth convinc'd at Sight we find, / That gives us back the Image of our Mind" – a deeper meaning begins to emerge, one in which learning is a form of recollection, the remembrance of things we may not have consciously known (lines 297–300). Similarly, when Johnson's Imlac declares that the "business of a poet . . . is to examine, not the individual, but the species; to remark general properties and large appearances" the emphasis is on shared activity, not disembodied abstractions. The poet does not "number the streaks of the tulip" because he does not need to; he draws instead "such prominent and striking features, as *recall the original* to every mind" (*Rasselas*, ch. 10, italics added). For both Pope and Johnson, as for many other writers on the subject, poetry appeals to the whole range of the reader's past experience so artfully that even things beyond it may seem familiar. "Men must be *taught*," said Pope in a statement at once about good coffee-house manners and poetic revelation, "as if you taught them *not*; / And Things *unknown* propos'd as Things *forgot*" (lines 574–75).

Just how poetry goes about teaching "things unknown" – that is, how it has cognitive as well as emotive worth – is the question that underlies most eighteenth-century instances of the "defense of poetry." This chapter will now turn to some of the major arguments made for poetry in the period and some of the problems surrounding their claims; the final section of the chapter will take up a more concrete but far-reaching debate, over the question of "poetic language."

The eighteenth-century defense of poetry

As suggested above, eighteenth-century arguments in defense of poetry tend to be less transcendental than the famous Renaissance statement of Sidney, who declared that poetry created a "golden" world in place of nature's "brazen" one, or the Romantic idealism of Shelley, who pronounced poetry "something divine," and the poet a seer of the "future in the present," a participant "in the eternal," and of course one of the "unacknowledged legislators of mankind."[8] Apart from a few Neoplatonists like the Earl of Shaftesbury, for whom the poet is a "second *maker*, a just Prometheus under Jove,"[9] most of the period's apologists for poetry stay closer to the ground. The phrases from the eighteenth century that seem to anticipate Shelley most closely are ironic in context. When Johnson's Imlac declares that the poet "must write as the interpreter of nature, and legislator of mankind" and must feel himself "superiour to time and place," young Rasselas interrupts this "enthusiastic fit" to remind the sage that by his requirements "no human being can ever be a poet" (chs. 10–11).

Not just the Sidney of *Arcadia* but his scientifically minded contemporary, Francis Bacon, wrote of poetry in terms that might a century later seem somewhat high-flying. Poetry is above reason for Bacon "because it doth raise and erect the mind, by submitting the shows of things to the desires of the mind; whereas reason doth buckle and bow the mind unto the nature of things."[10] Bacon's noble identification of poetry with what Freud might have regarded as the pleasure principle (as opposed to the reality principle obeyed by reason) continues to be invoked from time to time by eighteenth-century critics. But for many intellectuals who had imbibed the skepticism of the

Restoration, the idea of poetry as answerable only to the mind's desires might run uncomfortably close to the sort of imaginative state Swift sardonically termed "happiness" in the section on madness in *A Tale of a Tub*, that is, the "perpetual possession of being well deceived."

The earlier defenses of poetry may have begun to seem outmoded not only because of their philosophical idealism but also because they are in large part apologies for *fiction*. Sidney's insistence that the poet "never lieth" because he "nothing affirms" is part of a necessary argument that the poet's fables are not falsehoods because he tells them "not affirmatively but allegorically." Sidney's is largely a defense of narrative, the highest forms of which happen to be poetic, and he defends narrative poetry negatively and positively: epic and dramatic poems are not lies, and they present models of virtue by portraying heroes and noble actions. But as narrative becomes increasingly associated with the novel in the eighteenth century, poetry can no longer be thought of as primarily narrative in scope; "poetry" is coming less to stand for a set of stories than a way, or set of ways, of using language. Accordingly, vital critical thinking begins to shifts its emphasis away from the truth of poetic fables to the use of poetic figures.

Since the dominant philosopher of the period declared figurative language useless (or worse) in the pursuit of truth, figures needed continual defense. John Locke drew a sharp line in *An Essay concerning Human Understanding* (Book II, ch. 12) between "Judgment" and "Wit," aligning the former with sobriety, good sense, and concern for accuracy, and the latter with figurative language, allusion, "pleasant pictures," pretty "visions in the fancy" – and speciousness. Writers such as Charles Gildon, Joseph Addison, Matthew Prior, and Mark Akenside formulated their defenses of poetry largely in response to Lockean hostility. Looking back from the 1740s, the promising young poet Akenside believed he saw the beginning of a reconciliation of poetry and philosophy, at war for much of the preceding half century. "It is hardly possible to conceive them at a greater distance from each other than at the revolution," he wrote in a note on *The Pleasures of Imagination*, "when Locke stood at the head of one party, and Dryden at the other."[11]

Akenside probably had Locke's *Essay* in view, but one could have turned elsewhere in Locke as well. In *Some Thoughts concerning Education* (1693) Locke criticized the practice of school exercises in writing Latin verse partly because of the impracticality of composing verse in a foreign language but primarily because of the impracticality of composing *in verse*. The practice is unprofitable for two kinds of children: those who have "no *genius* to *poetry*" and those who do. In the latter case, says Locke, "Methinks the parents should labor to have it stifled and suppressed" (p. 132). In *Of the Conduct of the Understanding* (1697; 1706), Locke again warned of the deluding power of similes, through which "fancy passes for knowledge, and what is prettily said is mistaken for solid." Locke says he does not mean to "decry metaphor, or . . . take away that ornament of speech"; it is just that "my business here is not with rhetoricians and orators, but with philosophers and lovers of truth."[12] In a lesser-known work, "Some Thoughts concerning Reading and Study for a Gentleman" (1703), Locke recommends reading in all sorts of subjects – politics, history, chronology, geography, works on the passions – until, nearly last, just before an afterthought on having good dictionaries in one's library, he writes, "There is another sort of reading, which is for diversion, and delight. Such are poetical writings, especially dramatic, if they be free from profaneness, obscenity, and what corrupts good manners."[13] The inclusion seems perfunctory. The one modern author Locke mentions by name is not a poet but Cervantes.

A quarter century after the publication of Locke's *Thoughts concerning Education*, Charles Gildon protests that the low state of modern poetry has led many to "unjustly conclude that the *Art* itself is but a meer Trifle below a serious Thought," and that this view "has drawn Dissuasives from our Study of it, from so great and judicious a Person as Mr. Lock." In his *Complete Art of Poetry* (1718), Gildon contrasts Locke's opinion with that of the Roman author Petronius, "who advises all those who intend to apply their Minds to any thing great, to employ their first Approaches to Letters in the Study of Verse." And he opposes Locke to the emergent counter-tradition of Milton. Had Locke taken as long a view of poetry as Milton did (poetry "handed down to us from *Homer, Virgil, Pindar, Horace, Sophocles, Euripides*, and the like") he would have agreed with *Milton* in recommending the "Poets to the Study of his Pupil, as that admirable Poet does in his Discourse of Education."[14]

Gildon refers to his book generally as a "defence of poetry," and his friendly speakers draw on Sidney, Temple, Addison, and others in countering the charges made against poetry. He invokes Sidney, for example, in clearing the poet from suspicion of lying, for the poet does not contract to say "What is, or is not, but what should, or should not be." He repeats and extends several of Temple's arguments, including the anthropological one; poetry is common, he says, "from China to Peru" (Samuel Johnson would later survey "vanity" over the same span). But the fundamental attack rehearsed by one of Gildon's speakers is on poetry as useless – "All other Arts are of Use in Life; this pretends only to Pleasure" – and his most important defense is of poetry's use, essentially of the use of pleasure. Making an apposite distinction between surviving and thriving, Gildon finds some arts "Necessary to our Ever-Being . . . and others to our Well-Being" (pp. 21, 25, 43, 68). Locke's name disappears from Gildon's work after the Preface, but the new philosopher's low regard for poetry's utility and truth value is the implicit opponent throughout.

Locke's radical distrust of poetic and rhetorical thinking was fully grasped by Prior, judging from his comic "Dialogue between Locke and Montaigne." In this dialogue of the dead (written about 1721 but not published until 1907), Locke is drily professional, dogmatic, self-reflexive to the point of solipsism, a "metaphysician," and humorlessly methodical. The great Renaissance essayist, on the other hand, is deft, earthy, witty, irrepressible: "Method! our life is too short for it," says Montaigne. The dialogue is not about poetry in particular, but it is largely about figurative language. When an exasperated Locke accuses the imaginative Montaigne of offering "Simile upon Simile, no Consequential Proof," Montaigne replies that

> arguing by Simile is not so absurd as some of you dry Reasoners would make People believe. If your Simile be proper and good, it is at once a full proof, and a lively Illustration of your matter, and where it does not hold, the very dispro portion gives you Occasion to reconsider it, and you set it in all its lights, if it be only to find at least how unlike it is. Egad, Simile is the very Algebra of Discourse.[15]

The retort Prior lends to Montaigne is witty but serious: similes and meta- phors have cognitive weight. (Later in the century, George Campbell would note of simile that "all argument is a kind of comparison" and the "distance between argument and illustration" less than "usually imagined."[16]) Putting himself on the side of figurative language, Prior also puts himself on the side of the imagination and the body, on whose senses similes are based. It is odd to think of the contest in these terms, with Locke unmindful of the body, since we often adopt Blake's view of Locke as too limited by the senses. However, it seems clear that for Prior, Locke could just as easily be the Rationalist Descartes – or, to look a few years ahead, one of Swift's Laputan intellectuals who needs a servant to "flap" him to his senses. Less important today than deciding whether the portrayal is fair is understanding that the new philosophy, even Lockean philosophy, could seem abstracted from physical experience and real language use.

The ever diplomatic Addison also found it necessary to subvert Locke's denigration of "wit," although he did so indirectly. In the fifth of the six *Spectator* essays on wit (nos. 58–63), Addison quotes much of Locke's section opposing wit and judgment but suggests that Locke's comparison is merely descriptive rather than evaluative. His larger strategy is to draw his own opposition, between "true" and "false" wit, then relegate most of Locke's criticism to the latter category, and finally constitute "true wit" as a quality that includes rather than opposes "judgment." In not much over

2,500 words, *Spectator* 62 moves from a polite citation of Locke's "admirable reflection" to a ringing declaration (aided by Dominique Bouhours, the "most penetrating" of recent French critics) "that the basis of all wit is truth." The deliberately uncontroversial manner exemplified here has led many to underestimate Addison's critical power. We will return in a moment to his important essays on Milton and the imagination.

The characterization of philosophy as overly abstract, which Prior expresses through his pre-Cartesian Montaigne, is fairly common in the seventeenth and eighteenth centuries. Many of the arguments in defense of poetry imply such a contrast, specifying the function of poetry as its simultaneous appeal to the senses and the intellect. Milton in *Of Education* (the work Gildon appealed to against Locke) had characterized poetry as "less fine and subtle" than logic and philosophical rhetoric but "more simple, sensuous, and passionate." While Milton's general program of education may seem impossibly high-minded to us, he repeatedly recognizes what might now be called the embodied self, whether in recommending exercise and public assemblies "because the spirit of man cannot demean [that is, conduct] itself in this body without some recreating intermission of labor," or in the broader premise that "our understanding cannot in this body found itself but on sensible things." Thus, the "same method is necessarily to be followed in all discreet teaching."[17]

That poetry teaches powerfully because it images sensory things is a claim made again and again through the first half of the eighteenth century. Addison's specification of the Pleasures of Imagination as less "refined" than "those of the understanding" but "not so gross as those of sense" is the starting point for the long essay (in parts) that is essentially his defense of poetry. Through its appeal to the senses, poetry reaches and teaches those unschooled and unskilled in philosophical contemplation, and through its appeal to the passions it moves to action. "Moral writers recommend virtue," said Leonard Welsted, "but poetry adorns it; the moralist gains his reader to approve of it; the poet to be in love with it." Or, as Milton had said in *The Reason of Church-Government*, poetry can make virtue appear with "delight" even to readers of "soft and delicious temper, who will not so much as look on Truth herself unless they see her elegantly dressed."[18]

Milton's emphasis on poetry as suited to our mortal condition – "in this body" – takes a subtle but very interesting historical turn in Gildon, who sees poetry as particularly well suited to the *social* body, that is, to the particular situation of modern society. Even if one grants that poetry is a "meer Diversion," his speaker says, it must also be granted "that it is not possible for Men in the present state of human affairs, to be wholly without Diversion; the Mind must be sometimes relaxed from the Intenseness of

Thought, and the fatiguing Pursuit of Business, or it could never go thro' the Duties incumbent upon it." Poetry is vital precisely because it is among "our Recreations," acting upon us almost unconsciously: "by persuasive Pleasure" it "conveys Virtue to our unguarded Hours" (p. 26). This historical turn is subtle but important; the sense of a uniquely modern condition in which poetry is to play its timely role does not supplant but begins to co-exist with an older idea of its timeless place. The more historically self-conscious argument will grow stronger later in the century, but we can see its seeds in John Dennis's view, as early as 1702, that what Gildon would call the "fatiguing pursuit of business" had grown more invasive in recent decades. Poetry, especially dramatic poetry, is currently in decline, Dennis argues, because the present era is more commercial ("there are ten times more Gentlemen now in business, than in King Charles his reign"), more taxed, more consumed by political "interest." "Now I leave to anyone to judge," Dennis challenges, "whether the imaginative faculty of the Soul, must be more exercised in a Reign of Poetry and of Pleasure, or in a Reign of Politicks and of Business."[19]

Milton had said that the end of education, in which poetry figures so prominently, is to "repair the ruin of our first parents" (*Of Education*, p. 59). Dennis is perhaps even more apocalyptic on poetry's redemptive powers. Whether "the Business of the Tree of Knowledge is literal or allegorical," Dennis writes, it diverted human affections from "God to the Creatures," an act by which the "Harmony of [our] Intellectual and Animal Powers was very miserably broke." But poetry, appealing at once to "the Reason, the Passions, the Senses," can remove "that Discord, and restore the Harmony of the Human Faculties." No other art "provides in such a sovereign Manner as Poetry, for the Satisfaction of the whole Man together." The Edenic possibilities of poetic experience elicit Dennis's loftiest prose:

> Poetry seems to be a noble Attempt of Nature, by which it endeavours to exalt itself to its happy primitive State; and he who is entertained with an acomplish'd Poem, is, for a Time, at least, restored to Paradise. That happy Man converses boldly with Immortal Beings. Transported, he beholds the Gods ascending and descending, and every Passion, in its Turn, is charm'd, while his Reason is supremely satisfied. Perpetual Harmony attends his Ear, his Eye perpetual Pleasure. Ten thousand different Objects he surveys, and the most dreadful please him. Tygers and Lions he beholds, like the first Man, with Joy . . .[20]

That Dennis had so little influence in the eighteenth century cannot be explained simply by the fact that he was satirized by Pope in *An Essay on Criticism* and *The Dunciad*. Douglas Patey has recently noted that by 1710 Dennis had begun to seem "hopelessly old-fashioned" less for his views than because he seemed to embody "captious censoriousness" in an age of emergent "politeness."[21] In any case, his Edenic enthusiasm is not heard again so forcefully in eighteenth- century poetics. Those who share his view of the religious mission of poetry put less faith than he had in the redemptive power of poetry itself; those who might share his faith in poetic power do not share his fundamentally religious framework.

Dennis's analogy of poetry and religion returns a century later in Coleridge's account of poetry as redemptive through psychological integration. Coleridge's terms are secularized but no less utopian, as he characterizes poetry's special power of integrating not only its own several parts but also the reader's several faculties. Where for Dennis poetry provides for the "Satisfaction of the whole Man together," for Coleridge the poet "brings the whole soul of man into activity, with the subordination of its faculties to each other, according to their relative worth and dignity" (*Biographia Literaria*, ch. 14).

It is a short step theoretically from Dennis's satisfaction of the "whole man together" to Coleridge's activation of the "whole soul of man." Or it might have been, had Dennis's position dominated the eighteenth-century debate. But it was Addison's poetic framework, articulated in and disseminated through the widely read *Spectator* that wielded perhaps the greatest critical influence, followed closely by Pope's *Essay on Criticism*. Addison's canonical place as critic as well as stylist became firmly established in the middle and later years of the century. When Akenside sought to close the great "distance" separating philosophy and poetry at the time of the Glorious Revolution, he turned to Addison's great series of essays (*Spectator* 411–21) for the title and much of the subject of his philosophical poem, *The Pleasures of Imagination* (1744). Later in the century, the Scottish rhetorician Hugh Blair would date the beginning of modern "philosophical criticism" of imagination (by now growing more sophisticated in the treatises of Edmund Burke, Alexander Gerard, and Lord Kames) to the work of Addison.[22] Even Johnson, who termed Dryden the "father of English criticism," saw Addison as the originator of much that his own era had come to take for granted. In addition to his famous recommendation of Addison as a prose model (an aspiring English stylist "must give his days and nights to the volumes of Addison"), Johnson cautions against underestimating Addison's intellectual achievement: "It is not uncommon for those who have grown wise by the labour of others, to add a little of their own, and overlook their masters." Johnson's portrait of the critical world before and after Addison pays the author the very high compliment of having been absorbed into the culture and, just as important for our purposes, shows the increasing psychological and historical self-consciousness of later eighteenth-century criticism:

That general knowledge which now circulates in common talk, was in his time rarely to be found. Men not professing learning were not ashamed of ignorance; and, in the female world, any acquaintance with books was distinguished only to be censured. His purpose was to infuse literary curiosity by gentle and unsuspected conveyance into the gay, the idle, and the wealthy; he therefore presented knowledge in the most alluring form . . . His attempt succeeded; inquiry was awakened, and comprehension expanded. An emulation of intellectual elegance was excited, and from this time to our own, life has been gradually exalted, and conversation purified and enlarged.[23]

Although he wrote other criticism, Addison's greatest influence rests on three groups of *Spectator* papers: the six essays on Wit (nos. 58–63) mentioned earlier, some eighteen weekly papers on *Paradise Lost* (beginning with no. 267), and the eleven essays on the "pleasures of the imagination" (nos. 411–21). Milton's literary canonization was already underway when Addison began praising *Paradise Lost,* categorically and then book by book, from January to early May of 1712. But in part because Addison was quietly urbane where Dennis had been stridently enthusiastic, the *Spectator* essays did more to establish Milton as a "polite" author beyond the politics of the previous age.

The *Paradise Lost* essays suggest the general direction criticism of poetry would take as the century progressed. Addison begins firmly in the realm of genre criticism, considering Milton's epic in the light of Aristotle's *Poetics* and the examples of Homer and Virgil; but his essays move steadily toward more affective and expressive concerns, that is, toward the effect of Milton's "sublimity" on the reader and toward an account of the nature of Milton's imagination. We can see Addison's readiness to suspend formalism in exchange for a glimpse of the author in the poem when he refers to *Paradise Lost* as the "greatest production, or at least the noblest work of genius, in our language" (no. 321) There may be a more formally perfect work than Milton's poem but no greater revelation of poetic genius.

Milton also animates Addison's formidable essay on the pleasures of imagination, where he argues that any perceptions or representations which engage our imaginations do so by being "great" (vast, sublime), "beautiful," or "new." Homer, Virgil, and Ovid exemplify these pleasures respectively for Addison, but it is Milton who excels in all three. Milton's magnetic attraction seems to pull the discussion away from the original claim that perceptions (the "primary pleasures" of imagination, largely sight) are superior to representations ("secondary pleasures," imagination in the modern sense), and toward a deeper discussion of the "new creation" (no. 419) that certain kinds of poetry may bring into being. Mimetic "representation" and "description" remain essential, but Addison grows more interested in the imagination's ability to "fancy to itself things more great, strange, or beautiful than the eye ever saw" (no. 418) and to move beyond empirical observation to what Dryden had called the "fairy way of writing." Modern English poets (chiefly Shakespeare and Spenser as well as Milton) have excelled in creating "imaginary persons" and thus demonstrating the power of poetic imagination: "it has not only the whole circle of nature for its province but makes new worlds of its own, shows us persons not to be found in being, and represents even the faculties of the soul with her several virtues and vices in a sensible shape and character" (no. 419).

Two significant implications of Addison's emphasis on imaginative "new worlds" sometimes go unnoticed. The first is the quietly nationalistic modernism that marks an early step in English canonization. Addison, the devout classicist, nonetheless identifies distinctive imaginative freedom with the emergent English trinity, Shakespeare, Spenser, and Milton. The other is its congruence with Addison's thinking about creativity in general. Not only ghosts and personifications show the poet's ability to go beyond the given world of sensation. In the following paper he argues that even in non-fiction writing, "metaphors," "allegories," and "allusions" – all, incidentally, suspicious devices for Locke – bring the ideas of understanding to life in the imagination. Their effective use "sets off all writings in general, but it is the very life and highest perfection of poetry." And in great poetry "It has something in it like creation: it bestows a kind of existence and draws up to the reader's view several objects which are not to be found in being; it makes additions to nature and makes a greater variety to God's works" (no. 420).

Addison's initial junction of both kinds of imaginative pleasure (direct perception and imagining) has the important effect of dignifying each, since the enjoyment of God's artistry is not unlike the enjoyment of human artifacts, and it connects them alike to the reality of the human body. "Delightful scenes, whether in nature, painting, or poetry, have a kindly influence on the body as well as the mind" (no. 411). This practical observation is at least as old as Bacon, as Addison acknowledges; but perhaps its tenuous hold on our consciousness is suggested by the fact that only in the last few years have Western medical studies noticed that patients in hospital rooms with good views recover more quickly. More immediately influential is Addison's description, mentioned above, of the imagination as the accessible middle way between purely abstract thought and physical sensation, conveying pleasures "not so gross" as the latter, "nor so refined" as the former. This formulation is replayed both in what might be considered negative and positive versions in the following decades. In its negative version, poetry is defensible because it speaks to readers for whom philosophy – admittedly finer – would be too abstruse. In its more ambitious version, the defense claims for poetry a power and human scope that philosophy generally lacks.

The distinction between poetry as milder or stronger than philosophy is of course not absolute. One of the growing collection of poetic extracts, Thomas Hayward's *The British Muse*, (1738), announces several goals at once in its sprawling subtitle: "Or, A Collection of Thoughts Moral, Natural, and Sublime, of our English Poets: Who flourish'd in the Sixteenth and Seventeenth Centuries. With several curious Topicks, and beautiful Passages, never before extracted, from Shakespear, Johnson, Beaumont, Fletcher, and above a Hundred more. The Whole digested Alphabetically under their respective Heads, according to the Order of Time in which they wrote; to shew the gradual Improvements of our Poetry and Language." As a collection of *thoughts* on various *topics* (these run from "Abbeys" to "Youth"), Hayward's book aims to function much like collections of aphorisms or many modern dictionaries of quotations. Hayward hopes that he has collected "maxims, sentiments, and reflections best adapted to form the manners, direct the conduct, and enlarge the minds of men." Similarly, Isaac Watts would urge in *The Improvement of the Mind* (1741) that poetry be studied because its memorable passages furnish important ideas "relating to the common prudentials of mankind."[24]

But neither Hayward nor Watts sees poetry as merely moral precepts. "Beautiful" and "sublime" are equally important words for Hayward, and aesthetic concerns join with philological interests and a progressive narrative of literary history. For these writers and many who follow, the idea that poetry "enlarges" the mind is fundamental and flexible. Watts finds in high lyric poetry especially an important cognitive function: its "noble elevations of thought and passion" work to "raise and aggrandize our conceptions" and thus contribute to that "amplitude, or capacity of the mind, which is one of the noblest characters belonging to the understanding." Watts encourages particularly the reading of sublime poems and passages to stretch the mind (examples include God's-eye view passages in *Paradise Lost* and *An Essay on Man*), but he sees that capaciousness comes, so to speak, in many sizes: "even if the subject or matter of the poem does not require such amazing and extensive thoughts, yet tropes and figures, which are some of the main powers and beauties of poesy, do so gloriously exalt the matter, as to give sublime imagination, its proper relish and delight" (pp. 144, 148, 229). Watts's insistence that figures of speech may themselves open the mind more fully is of a piece with Addison's belief that the best figuration "has in it something like creation" for both reader and writer. But Watts's enormously influential work, which went through countless editions up through the middle of the nineteenth century, puts the matter in explicitly educational as well as affective terms. Poetry affords the developing mind a potential for growth not otherwise available.

The critical emphasis moves steadily from "genre" to "genius" as the century progresses. It is not that one concern supplants the other, but that interest in the decorums of kinds yields ground to fascination with imaginative power and creativity considered more generally. Akenside begins *The Pleasures of Imagination* by announcing that he intends to go beyond the now considerable body of poetic criticism prescribing the "laws of each poetic strain" to contemplate the more fundamental – or transcendental – relation of imagination to "all the fair variety of things" (I, lines 31, 78). If Akenside's focus on the mysterious sympathy between the mind and "this goodly frame of nature" suggests Wordsworth's projected celebration of "how exquisitely . . . / The external World is fitted to the Mind" ("Prospectus" to *The Recluse*," lines 66–68), his view of aesthetic pleasure as providential may also foreshadow the assurance of Keats's urn that "truth is beauty, beauty truth":

> Thus was beauty sent from heav'n,
> The lovely ministress of truth and good
> In this dark world: for truth and good are one,
> And beauty dwells in them, and they in her,
> With like participation. (I, lines 372–76)

One can see why Akenside himself was struck by the distance between his assumptions and those of Locke a half century earlier. Instead of being an obstacle to truth, beauty is here its beacon, essential to full cognitive and ethical development. Psychology and morality are not easily distinguished in late-eighteenth-century rhetorical analysis (what we now call psychology was indeed just beginning its disciplinary history as "moral philosophy") when theorists specify poetry's value. Bishop Richard Hurd, certainly a more orthodox Christian than Akenside, shares the general confidence that the energies of poetry speak to an essential human nature:

> For there is something in the mind of man, sublime and elevated, which prompts it to overlook all obvious and familiar appearances, and to feign to itself other and more extraordinary – such as correspond to the extent of its own powers, and fill out all the faculties and capacities of our souls. This restless and aspiring disposition poetry, first and principally, would indulge and flatter, and thence takes its name of *divine*, as if some power above human conspired to lift the mind to these exalted conceptions.

Poetry's fictional and figurative dimensions merge in such formulations. Poems do not need to contain plots and heroes in order to inspire virtue; vivid imagery, description, metaphors, and figures such as personification (the chief way in which the world of poetry is "animated," according to Hugh Blair) all awaken the reader's faculties.[25]

Poetry not only raises the mind but brings it to self-understanding. For Blair, the study of poetry and criticism "open a field of investigation peculiar to themselves." Literary studies "present human nature under a different aspect from that which it assumes to the view of other sciences; they illuminate "various springs of action, which, without their aid, might have passed unobserved; and which, though of a delicate nature, frequently exert a powerful influence on several departments of human life." While careful not to equate aesthetic sensitivity and virtue, Blair closely associates literary appreciation, self-knowledge, and ethical judgment:

> The exercise of taste and sound criticism is, in truth, one of the most improving employments of the understanding. To apply the principles of good sense to composition and discourse; to examine what is beautiful and why it is so; to employ ourselves in distinguishing accurately between the specious and the solid, between affected and natural ornament, must certainly improve us not a little in the most valuable part of all philosophy, the philosophy of human nature. For such disquisitions are very intimately connected with the knowledge of ourselves. They necessarily lead us to reflect on the operations of the imagination, and the movements of the heart; and increase our acquaintance with some of the most refined feelings which belong to our frame. (pp. 13–14 [Introduction])

Vicesimus Knox, whose *Liberal Education* went through some eleven editions between 1781 and 1795, links literary taste and virtue even more firmly: "That delicate faculty which is sensibly delighted with all that is beautiful and sublime, and immediately disgusted with all that is inelegant in composition, must be often affected with similar appearances in the conduct of human life." Knox includes girls and young women in his exhortations, promising that the female reader who studies modern "French and English classics" (such as Milton, Pope, and Boileau) "will have imbibed an elegance which will naturally diffuse itself over her conversation, address, and behaviour" and which will "be favourable to virtue."[26] With small changes in vocabulary, these declarations of the pertinence of literary study to understanding "human nature" and oneself could come from countless present-day educational rationales for the humanities and the study of English.

There is one important difference, however. When we think of literature's psychological and ethical relevance we are likely to give the novel an important, if not dominant, place. The eighteenth-century broadening of the idea of what Knox calls a "classical education" to include *modern*, vernacular "classics" does not, for most contemporaneous critics, include the novel. Hurd regards novels as "abortive poems," products of "sickly imagination." Knox vigorously recommends English *poetry* to the young scholar – in fact he laments the fact that many students enter university without having read Dryden and Pope – but insists that novels compete with rather than complement classical pursuits: "Novels must be prohibited.," he warns darkly. "I have known boys of parts stopped at once in their career of improvement in classical knowledge, by reading novels" (sections xxv, p. 254). If such strictures seem quaint in light of the novel's cultural "rise" during and since the eighteenth century, the desire to distinguish poetry from popular forms reflects more than snobbery. Like Wordsworth's slightly later complaint that great poetry is being "driven into neglect by frantic novels, sickly and stupid German Tragedies, and deluges of idle and extravagant stories in verse," these discriminations indicate that poetry increasingly is being defended not as narrative but nearly in opposition to it.[27]

Most non-narrative poetry is lyric poetry, that is, relatively short poems, usually in the first person, emphasizing the expression of personal emotion over narration or description. As M. H. Abrams long ago observed, the lyric ascends in critical importance, until by the latter part of the eighteenth century it becomes the implicit "poetic norm."[28] Students of Romanticism often see this ascent as unalloyed progress, leading within a few decades to the great lyric achievements of the Romantic poets. But the shift also narrowed the conception of poetry, tending to weaken the ties to rhetoric and mimesis on which much of its defense had rested. When, in his "Essay on the Arts Called Imitative" of 1772, the young and brilliant Sir William Jones flatly rejected the Aristotelian principle that "all poetry consists in imitation," he argued not only that the expression of the passions make up the "finest parts" of poetry, affecting us by "sympathy," but also that only its "inferior parts" are the ones "descriptive of natural objects," since those operate merely by "substitution." While it is surely liberating to recall that poetry is not bound to detailed representation or minute accuracy, the more emphatically such a position is claimed, the more difficult it may be to defend poetry on cognitive grounds. If the poet best "gains his end," in Jones's elegant formulation, "not by imitating the works of nature, but by assuming her power and causing the same effect upon the imagination which her charms produce to the senses," the standard of judgment would seem to be moving inevitably inward and out of the realm of debate.[29] Without imitation as a priority, verisimilitude recedes in importance; so, arguably, does verity.

The proper language of poetry

Jones is significant here because his position, despite his impressive clarity, is not wholly original. Various kinds of lyric poetry were praised highly from the mid-seventeenth century onward, partly under the influence of

Longinus's *On the Sublime* and partly due to growing interest in the poetry of the Bible. What Jones attempts more explicitly than any of his critical predecessors is to establish a clear alternative to Aristotle's *Poetics*, based primarily on drama, and the weighty Aristotelian tradition. His attempt shows the tension perhaps present all along between dutiful allegiances to the *Poetics* and native interest in kinds of poems to which Aristotle (and his commentators, including Horace) gave little attention. From a global perspective, Western criticism is in fact a "minority of one, the odd man out," Earl Miner has recently argued, in being founded on drama rather than lyric.[30] Jones, an early Sanskritist whose essay appeared with his *Poems, Consisting Chiefly of Translations from the Asiatic Languages*, uses the assumption of Dennis and others that poetry must have begun in religious awe to argue anthropologically that poetry praising gods is common to "all nations." Even the admittedly mimetic Greek drama, developed from songs celebrating Bacchus, Jones argues, and thus originates in the need to express a "natural emotion of the mind" rather than to imitate.

The importance of such thinking about lyric poetry is not its emphasis on emotion, with which few earlier critics would have quarreled, but its tendency to minimize imitation or even ignore it altogether. We can see both the continuity and difference between the beginning of the century and the 1770s and 1780s by comparing definitions of poetry given by Jones and Blair with that of Dennis. Jones sees poetry's essence in its emotional genesis: it "was originally no more than a strong and animated expression of the human passions." For Blair, poetry is the "language of passion, or of enlivened imagination, formed, most commonly, into regular numbers" (lecture xxxviii, p. 423). Both of these formulations sound very close to Dennis, who insisted that "Passion is the chief thing in poetry," and that "Poetry is Poetry because it is more Passionate and Sensual than Prose." But when we take Dennis's definition of poetry as a *whole*, we see that the heart of it is what later disappears: "Poetry then is an Imitation of Nature, by a pathetick and numerous Speech" (*Advancement*, ch. 5: Hooker, 1, 215–16). In the later formulations, Dennis's means (passionate speech) becomes both means and end.

We should not imagine that a uniform Aristotelianism existed up to some moment in the century (1745? 1772?) and then dissolved. Earlier critics writing about lyric forms or about poetry as music (versus poetry as painting) tend to stress poetry's affective rather than mimetic benefits, while, on the other hand, many later critics continue to invoke mimesis as fundamental. James Beattie in 1776, for example, is typically "pre-Romantic" in seeking to define "pure poetry" as something quite distinct from rhetoric; but his definition would not have seemed odd to Dennis. What distinguishes such poetry for Beattie is "its aptitude, not to sway the judgment by reasoning, but to please the fancy, and move the passions, *by a lively imitation of nature.*"[31] But if the formula persisted, ideas of imitation and nature had been steadily changing. As the center of gravity moves toward the lyric, so does the sense that "external" nature is less important. The real subject of a lyric poem, Adam Smith was explaining to his rhetoric students in 1763 (and probably for many years earlier), is the "poet's temper of mind" (lecture xxi, p. 127).

Not surprisingly, a greater emphasis on poetry's expressive rather than mimetic dimensions affects assumptions about poetic language. One can see the linguistic implications by recalling that for Dennis in 1704 "Figurative Language" is the "natural Language of the Passions," a belief closely echoed in 1718 by Anthony Blackwall, who grouped figures of speech together as the "Language of the Passions."[32] If in later decades *poetry*, not specifically figuration, is the language of the passions, then a double substitution occurs. The more obvious part is that poetry is associated ever more exclusively with passion (or, as many would say, "sensibility"). The subtler but perhaps deeper meaning is that poetry is coming to be thought of *as figurative language*, that is, not simply as something which may use or license linguistic figuration but as essentially composed of it.

This triangulation of poetry, passion, and figurative language may help us understand why the debate about the proper language of poetry seems to carry so much weight by the time it appears where most modern readers are likely to first encounter it, in Wordsworth's Preface to the *Lyrical Ballads.* For when Wordsworth announces with pride (first in 1800, more fully in 1802) that the *Lyrical Ballads* contains "little of what is usually called poetic diction," indeed that he has "taken as much pains to avoid it as others ordinarily take to produce it," more seems to be at stake than word choice.[33] The issue seems to have become a moral one, with the use of "real language" being somehow crucial to the integrity and fate of poetry. How did the argument reach this point and what does Wordsworth have in mind? We have partly answered the first question already. Two developments converged to give the issue of diction such weight: poetry was increasingly equated with its language (that is, its passionate and therefore figurative language), and poetry had become a more singular concept by the late decades of the century (that is, an idea with resonance beyond the many kinds of poetry). This point bears on the question of what Wordsworth had in mind, because he surely knew that the sort of "arbitrary" and "artificial" elegancies that he avoided, in favor of language more "necessary" and "natural," were common only in certain *kinds* of eighteenth-century poetry. Writers of most satires, epistolary poems, and songs – sub-genres comprising much of the period's poetry – freely use informal and "low" language.

Where elevated and often fixed phrases are common in eighteenth-century poetry is in the epic (including, for comic effect, mock-epic), pastoral and descriptive poetry, and the ode. Typical examples – and by Wordsworth's day, tired ones – are periphrastic phrases such as "finny tribe" (for fish), "feathered kind" (birds), or "fleecy care" (sheep). As Geoffrey Tillotson and others have demonstrated, even the more easily caricatured formulae were often used to combine allusiveness and novelty or particularity and generality. "Feathered kind," meaning creatures with wings, is not just a euphemism for birds but a way of looking at them as a link in the Great Chain of Being. "Fleecy care" may, depending on the pastoral context in which it appears, call attention to sheep as *the* care of otherwise carefree shepherds or, as in Pope's early lines, to the sheep's collectively bright appearance against a green field at just the moment when

> Two swains, whom Love kept wakeful, and the Muse,
> Pour'd o'er the whitening vale their fleecy care.[34]

Poetic precision and tact of this sort are presumably what Johnson means – rather than the "distorted language" and "adulterated phraseology" Wordsworth hears (Preface, Appendix) – when he celebrates Dryden for establishing English poetic diction. The terms in which Johnson praises Dryden for having "refined the language" of English poetry are significant: "There was . . . before the time of Dryden no poetical diction, no system of words at once refined from the grossness of domestic use, and free from the harshness of terms appropriated to particular arts. Words too familiar, or too remote, defeat the purpose of a poet. . . Those happy combination of words which distinguish poetry from prose had been rarely attempted".[35]

The issue of whether language itself is what should distinguish poetry from prose is complex and to some degree perennial. Distinctive diction is clearly not sufficient, but is it necessary? Coleridge would soon differ publicly from Wordsworth (*Biographia Literaria*, chs. 14, 17–20) about "real" language, and Hopkins would argue, in an undergraduate essay written in the middle of the nineteenth century, a position close to that espoused in the middle of the eighteenth by Thomas Gray, who remarked that the "language of the age is never the language of poetry." Gray's position not only irritated Wordsworth but is likely to irritate contemporary readers committed to the principle that nothing should be off-limits to the artist, including all of the "language of the age."[36] In fact, most periods appear in retrospect to have had a noticeably restricted poetic idiom. Whatever writers of various eras may have declared, their quests to avoid the hazards of cliché and jargon that Johnson identified (words "too familiar" or "too remote") have often taken them to the rather narrow range of choices discerned later as period styles.[37]

What we tend now to overlook is the play and flexibility of eighteenth-century poetic language. The heroic couplet employed in so much of the period's poetry could, of course, be a medium for heroic poetry, especially in translation. But couplets, both pentameter and tetrameter, could also allow for great freedom in less lofty modes. The couplet's master, Pope, was committed to rhyme partly for this reason, not on putatively neo-classical or doctrinal grounds. Late in life, he remarked disarmingly to Joseph Spence that his preference for rhyme has been wholly pragmatic:

> I have nothing to say for rhyme, but that I doubt whether a poem can support itself without it in our language, unless it be stiffened with such strange words as are like to destroy our language itself.
>
> The high style that is affected so much in blank verse would not have been borne even in Milton, had not his subject turned so much on strange out-of-the-world things as it does.[38]

In other words, rhyme itself can provide music and stylization enough to obviate forced elevation. What Milton had called the "bondage" of rhyme (Preface to *Paradise Lost*), Pope sees as potential freedom from unnatural diction. Much of the poetry of Pope's day and after confirms his insight: post-Miltonic, this-worldly poets generally adhere more closely to common language when freed not from but *by* rhyme.

The debate over the proper language of poetry was not resolved in the eighteenth century, of course, or in the nineteenth or twentieth. Wordsworth's characterization of most of the eighteenth century's poetry as "unnatural" and his own as "natural" tells us more about his aspirations than his predecessors' achievements. Vitally important as manifesto, Wordsworth's Preface as literary history is inaccurate and somewhat naive. From the Renaissance onward, most generations have seen themselves as less conventional than the last. It is worth recalling that Johnson grows impatient with the Metaphysical poets not because they were too daring (the impression often given in literary surveys and handbooks) but too coldly academic. "Seldom natural" in their thoughts, "always analytic" in their descriptions, they wrote "rather as beholders than partakers of human nature."[39] The point is not whether Johnson's experience matches ours – likely to be based, incidentally, on a more select body of Metaphysical poetry than Johnson had in mind – but to understand the complexity and variability of appeals to "nature" and common usage.

It is hardly the case that eighteenth-century poetic theory on the whole was overly "ornamentalist." We might even say that it sometimes grew, as many other eras' poetics have grown, too essentialist, tending to equate poetry with one of its important features, such as "passion" or figurative language.

In any event, anthropological evidence as well as literary history suggests that artistic practice is in fact ornamentalist. To recognize as much is not to diminish great poetry but to broaden our idea of what counts as aesthetic. Ellen Dissanayake's recent cross-cultural study of artistic behavior, *Homo Aestheticus: Where Art Comes from and Why*, mounts an impressive argument for the category of "making special" as a universal in cultural life: a kind of behavior that might be thought of as non-utilitarian but necessary. Her catalogue of such activities may put some of the debates we have been examining in a larger perspective. The behaviors she describes ethnologically as those that human beings use to separate some activities from simple self-preservation are these: "engaging in song, dance, poetic language, drama with costumes and masks, music, self-adornment, and embellishing personal and public artifacts."[40] Many eighteenth-century critics would have understood the logic of including poetic language with other modes of stylization and adornment. As Joshua Reynolds put it, poetry uses a language "in the highest degree artificial" as a way of "deviating from actual nature, in order to gratify natural propensities."[41] In other words, poetry speaks to a natural need for artifice.

NOTES

1 William K. Wimsatt, Jr., and Cleanth Brooks, *Literary Criticism: a Short History* (New York: Alfred A. Knopf, 1957), pp. 233, 245–46.

2 "Of Poetry," in J. E. Spingarn (ed.), *Critical Essays of the Seventeenth Century* (Oxford: Clarendon Press, 1909), III, 75.

3 A. Anthony Blackwall, *Introduction to the Classics*, 5th edn. (1737), index and p. 191.

4 Mill, "What Is Poetry?" (1833), rpt. in Daniel G. Hoffman and Samuel Hynes (eds.), *English Literary Criticism: Romantic and Victorian* (New York: Meredith Publishers, 1963), p. 197. For Yeats's distinction see the "Anima Hominis" chapter of *Per Amica Silentia Lunae*, rpt. in *Mythologies* (New York: Collier Books, 1969).

5 *A Treatise Concerning Enthusiasme* (1656), ed. Paul Korshin (Gainesville, FL: Scholars' Facsimiles & Reprints, 1970), p. 271.

6 *An Essay on Criticism*, line 88 All quotations from Pope are from the one-volume Twickenham Edition, ed. John Butt (New Haven: Yale University Press, 1963, rev. 1973).

7 Dryden, "Defence of An Essay of Dramatic Poesie," *Of Dramatic Poesy and Other Critical Essays*, ed. George Watson, 2 vols. (London: Dent, 1962), I, 122.

8 Sir Philip Sidney's work was written in the 1580s and published twice in 1595 as *An Apology for Poetry* and the *Defense of Poesie*; Shelley's *A Defence of Poetry* was written in 1821 and published in 1840.

9 Anthony Ashley Cooper, Earl of Shaftesbury, "Soliloquy: Or Advice to an Author" (1710) in John M. Robertson (ed.), *Characteristics* (Indianapolis: Bobbs-Merrill, 1964), I, 136.

10 *Advancement of Learning*, Book II, quoted from the Oxford Authors *Francis Bacon*, ed. Brian Vickers (Oxford and New York: Oxford University Press, 1996), p. 187.

11 Akenside's note to *The Pleasures of Imagination*, II, 30; see *The Poetical Works of Mark Akenside*, ed. Robin Dix (Cranbury, NJ, and London: Associated University Presses, 1996), p. 162.

12 *Of the Conduct of the Understanding*, ed. Francis W Garforth (New York: Teachers College Press [Columbia University], 1966), pp. 100–1.

13 "Some Thoughts Concerning Reading and Study for a Gentleman," in *Locke: Political Essays*, ed. Mark Goldie (Cambridge: Cambridge University Press), p. 355.

14 *The Complete Art of Poetry In Six Parts* (1718), Preface (unpaginated).

15 *The Literary Works of Matthew Prior*, ed. H. Bunker Wright and Monroe K. Spears, 2nd edn. 2 vols. (Oxford: Clarendon Press, 1971), I, 625. I have slightly regularized Prior's manuscript spelling and punctuation.

16 George Campbell, *The Philosophy of Rhetoric* (1776) (Philadelphia, 1818), p 88.

17 The first two quotations in this paragraph are from *Of Education*, the third from *The Reason of Church-Government*, in *Aereopagitica and Of Education*, ed. George H. Sabine (Arlington Heights, Illinois: AHM Publishing, 1951), pp. 59, 68, 80.

18 Gildon, *The Complete Art of Poetry*, p. 30; Welsted, "Dissertation concerning the Perfection of the English Language" (the preface to his *Epistles, Odes, &c, Written on Several Subjects*, 1724) in Scott Elledge (ed.), *Eighteenth-Century Critical Essays* (Ithaca: Cornell University Press, 1961), p. 339; Milton, *Reason of Church-Government*, p. 79.

19 Dennis, "A Large Account of the Taste in Poetry," in Willard Higley Durham (ed.), *Critical Essays of the Eighteenth Century, 1700–1725* (New Haven: Yale University Press, 1915), p. 136.

20 *The Advancement and Reformation of Modern Poetry* (1701), in *The Critical Works of John Dennis*, ed. E. N. Hooker (Baltimore: Johns Hopkins University Press, 1939–43), I, 257, 264.

21 Douglas Patey, "The Institution of Criticism in the Eighteenth Century," in H. B. Nisbet and Claude Rawson (eds.), *The Cambridge History of Literary Criticism*, vol. IV (Cambridge: Cambridge University Press, 1997), p. 18.

22 Blair, *Lectures on Rhetoric and Belles Lettres* (New York, 1814), p. 31 (lecture iii).

23 Johnson, "Life of Addison," in *Lives of the English Poets* (London: J. M. Dent, 1925), I, 365–6.

24 Thomas Hayward, *The British Muse* (1738), p. xv; Watts, *The Improvement of the Mind* (Boston, 1833), p. 229 (ch. 20, section xxxvi).

25 Richard Hurd, *A Dissertation on the Idea of Universal Poetry* (1766), in Elledge (ed.), *Eighteenth-Century Critical Essays*, II, 862–63; Blair, lecture xvi, pp. 172–75

26 Vicesimus Knox, *Liberal Education: or, a Practical Treatise on the Methods of Acquiring Useful and Polite Learning*, 1781; quotations are from the seventh edition (1785), pp. 207, 277–78 (sections xxi and xxv).

27 Adam Smith deems poetry superior to "novels" because it does not appeal to the reader's mere "curiosity" or appetite for "newness" of incident; see his *Lectures on Rhetoric and Belles Lettres*, ed. J. C. Bryce (Oxford: Oxford University Press, 1983), p. 97 (lecture xvii). Similar distinctions have continued from the eighteenth century to now. Mill sees narrative interest as derived "from incident" and

poetic interest "from the representation of feeling" ("What Is Poetry?" p. 194). More recently, Alice Fulton writes – in *Feeling as a Foreign Language* (St. Paul, MN: Graywolf Press, 1999) – that "Narrative is about what happens next. Poetry is about what happens now" (p. 7).

28 See M. H. Abrams, *The Mirror and the Lamp: Romantic Theory and the Critical Tradition* (New York: Oxford, 1953), esp. pp. 84–88.

29 Jones's brief, provocative essay is available in Elledge (ed.), *Eighteenth-Century Critical Essays*, II, 872–81.

30 Miner, *Comparative Poetics: an Intercultural Essay on Theories of Literature* (Princeton: Princeton University Press,1990), p. 8.

31 James Beattie, *Essays* (Edinburgh, 1776), p. 288, italics added. Very helpful on the question of imitation is P. W. K. Stone, *The Art of Poetry: Theories of Poetic Composition and Style in the Late Neo-Classic and Early Romantic Periods* (London: Routledge & Kegan Paul, 1967), especially pp. 65–83.

32 Dennis, *Grounds of Criticism in Poetry*, ch. 4, in Hooker (ed.), vol. I, 359; Blackwall, *Introduction to the Classics*, p. 182.

33 The various editions of the Preface and its Appendix are available in R. L. Brett and A. R. Jones (eds.), *Lyrical Ballads* (London: Methuen, 1963, rev. 1965). The quotation is on p. 251.

34 Pope, *Spring*, lines 18–19 This example and many others are discussed most perceptively in Geoffrey Tillotson, *Augustan Poetic Diction* (London: Athlone Press, 1964).

35 Appendix to Preface, *Lyrical Ballads*, p 315; Johnson, "Life of Dryden," in *Lives of the English Poets*, I, 231.

36 Gray, *Correspondence*, ed. Paget Toynbee and Leonard Whibley (Oxford: Clarendon Press, 1935), I, 98. Hopkins essentially agreed; see his remarkable undergraduate essay on "Poetic Diction" in *The Note-Books and Papers of Gerard Manley Hopkins*, ed. Humphrey House (London: Oxford University Press, 1937), pp. 92–94.

37 An unusually broad historical perspective informs Charles Kingsley's mid-nineteenth-century recognition of "this new poetic diction into which we have now fallen, after all our abuse of the far more manly and sincere 'poetic diction' of the eighteenth century"; quoted in Geoffrey Tillotson, *Augustan Poetic Diction*, p. 49.

38 Joseph Spence, *Observations, Anecdotes, and Characters of Books and Men*, ed. James M. Osborn (Oxford: Clarendon Press, 1966), I, 173 (June 1739, number 365).

39 "Life of Cowley," *Lives*, I, 11–12

40 *Homo Aestheticus* (New York: Free Press, 1992), p. 32; see also Dissanayake's ch. 3, "The Core of Art: Making Special," pp. 39–63.

41 Reynolds, Discourse XIII, in *Discourses* (Harmondsworth: Penguin), p. 288.

FURTHER READING

Bate, W. Jackson. *The Burden of the Past and the English Poet*. Cambridge, MA: Harvard University Press, 1970.

Durham, Willard Higley (ed.). *Critical Essays of the Eighteenth Century, 1700–1725*. New Haven: Yale University Press, 1915.

Elledge, Scott (ed.). *Eighteenth-Century Critical Essays*. Ithaca: Cornell University Press, 1961.

Engell, James. *Framing the Critical Mind: Dryden to Coleridge*. Cambridge, MA and London: Harvard University Press, 1989.

Mahoney, John L. *The Whole Internal Universe: Imitation and the New Defense of Poetry in British Criticism, 1660–1830*. New York: Fordham University Press, 1985.

Marks, Emerson R. *The Poetics of Reason: English Neoclassical Criticism*. New York: Random House, 1968.

   Taming the Chaos: English Poetic Diction Theory since the Renaissance. Detroit: Wayne State University Press, 1998.

Marsh, Robert. *Four Dialectical Theories of Poetry: an Aspect of Neoclassical Criticism*. Chicago and London: University of Chicago Press, 1965.

Monk, Samuel H. *The Sublime: a Study of Critical Theories in XVIII-Century England*. 1935. Ann Arbor: University of Michigan Press, 1960.

Nisbet, H. B. and Claude Rawson (eds.). *The Cambridge History of Literary Criticism*. vol. IV, Cambridge University Press, 1997.

Parker, Blanford. *The Triumph of Augustan Poetics: English Literary Culture from Butler to Johnson*. Cambridge University Press, 1998.

Sherbo, Arthur. *English Poetic Diction from Chaucer to Wordsworth*. East Lansing: Michigan State University Press, 1975.

Spingarn, J. E. (ed.). *Critical Essays of the Seventeenth Century*, vol III: *1685–1700*. Oxford: Clarendon Press, 1909.

Stone, P. W. K. *The Art of Poetry, 1750–1820: Theories of Poetic Composition and Style in the Late Neo-Classic and Early Romantic Periods*. London: Routledge & Kegan Paul, 1967.

Sutherland, James. *A Preface to Eighteenth Century Poetry*. Oxford University Press, 1948.

Tillotson, Geoffrey. *Augustan Poetic Diction*. London: Athlone Press, 1964.

8

CLAUDIA THOMAS KAIROFF

Eighteenth-century women poets
and readers

During the eighteenth century, British women poets built upon and varied the repertory of styles and topics bequeathed them by their foremothers. They also entered the literary marketplace in ever-greater numbers. The rising number of women poets may seem to have been predictable, given the increased access to print by writers of both sexes after the seventeenth-century lapse of laws circumscribing the press. Professional male writers were soon so numerous that the hack, that ubiquitous feature of late-seventeenth- and eighteenth-century satire, was an established cultural icon. In fact, however, numerous factors challenged aspiring women poets. Chief, perhaps, was the conservative ideology governing notions of femininity, a trend that became ever more restrictive throughout the century. Women of middling and upper status were encouraged to define themselves as mothers and household managers rather than as active contributors to their family economies. These roles sanctioned women's pursuit of domestic activities such as childhood education but inhibited their participation in such public business as politics and scholarship. The marketing of one's literary productions was another process that involved some transactions within the public domain. If all women writers had heeded the advice that conduct books so assiduously inculcated throughout the century, few would have ventured beyond the occasional birthday tribute enclosed in a letter, or the funeral elegy confided to a journal.

Instead, increased leisure, access to books and hence to male and female models, and availability of publishers combined to lure women writers of every social status toward the literary marketplace. Conscious of the expectations governing feminine behavior, women nevertheless participated in all the major literary trends of the century, from the politically charged writings characteristic at its outset, through a growing preference for verse influenced by classical and Christian precedents, and on to the later tastes for gothic and romantic lyricism. In doing so, they revealed themselves as assiduous readers of English writers, past and present, as well as of the French writers

most privileged English women were trained to read. Their literary productions reveal them to have been studying the writings of predecessors for instruction, competing with each other and with their predecessors. For eighteenth-century women, reading and writing were complementary activities. Their writings reveal their reading, and their reading inspired their writing. Frequently separated from spouses, children, and friends while residing in the country or on lengthy visits, women maintained relationships through correspondence that simulated the pleasure of reading together through exchanges of critical opinion. As the century progressed, periodicals allowed women to share their verses with other readers. While different social and literary trends influenced women as they did men, reading loomed large in the training of women writers because independent, even furtive, reading often substituted for the formal education accorded their privileged brothers.

As the eighteenth century opened, many poets were still active who had commenced their careers in the seventeenth. All women poets inherited the literary topics and styles characteristic of the Williamite era, a period of considerable political turmoil following the Glorious Revolution. For a brief period, women benefited from the legal consequences of the Revolution, as laws were reinterpreted in the context of King James's "divorce" from his people. Married women more freely sued for separate maintenance rather than endure abusive marriages, for example, claiming the precedent of England's separation from James. While this trend persisted, men and women argued publicly on behalf of women's education and legal rights; Mary Astell, for example, published her proposal for a female seminary in 1697–97. Among women poets, Lady Mary Chudleigh (1656–1710) corresponded with Astell and joined her in advocating female education in "The Ladies Defense" (1701). In her *Poems on Several Occasions* (1703),[1] she counseled women to avoid marriage, because "Wife and servant are the same" (line 1). Sarah Fyge Egerton (1670–1723) – who had published *The Female Advocate* as a teenager in 1686 – was noteworthy for poems such as "The Emulation," included in her *Collection of Poems on Several Occasions* (1703),[2] that exclaims, "From the first dawn of life unto the grave, / Poor womankind's in every state a slave" (lines 3–4). Concluding that men tyrannize women for "fear we should excel their sluggish parts" (line 19), Egerton advises women to turn the tables on them: ". . . we'll be wits, and then men must be fools" (line 39).

Poets such as Chudleigh and Egerton might claim, in addition to the glimpse of potential changes inspired by William and Mary's ascension, the inspiration of two female monarchs. Although Mary had died in 1694, Anne Stuart succeeded her brother-in-law William in 1702 and reigned, the last of

the Stuart monarchs, until 1714. Astell, Chudleigh, and Egerton all dedicated writings to Anne, claiming her authority for their own public expressions. Chudleigh's and Egerton's poems culminated the tradition of coterie writings centered on the Stuart court, extolling and defending its monarchs.[3] Women's poems had pledged loyalty to Charles II during his exile, and now praised Anne in her domestic role of mourning mother as well as in her public persona of warrior-queen. Pro-Stuart sympathy had sustained a community of women who read each other's writings, understood the ideological and stylistic requirements for membership, and participated as unofficial laureates when occasions required. With Anne's death ceased a long-standing rationale for women's public expression of political opinions. Not only did women lose the monarch as precedent for their public speech, but they lost an entire canon of politically charged writings that would have provided a context for ongoing participation in civic debates. As a result and in a changing social climate, women wrote fewer explicitly political poems in the course of the century. For many, the vocabulary of political engagement became a foreign tongue as such writings by women fell into obscurity.

Not every woman poet, however, had looked to William and Mary and then to Anne for inspiration. Anne Kingsmill (1661–1720) served as a Maid of Honor to Mary of Modena, second wife of James II, and married Col. Heneage Finch, a Gentleman of the Bedchamber. The couple's lives were forever altered by the court's flight; they retired soon afterward to Eastwell Park in Kent and spent most of their remaining years in seclusion. Finch eventually became a Lady of the Bedchamber to Queen Anne, but when her husband became Earl of Winchilsea in 1712, he never served in the House of Lords. He preferred to remain a non-juror, refusing to swear allegiance to William and Mary and loyal to the ideals of the previous monarch. Anne Finch's poetry reflects her melancholy due to the Revolution, and her efforts to construe what was for a time, in effect, internal exile as a Horatian retreat from the corruption that ensued after James's departure. Like women poets of the previous century, she appropriated the language of poems in which men celebrated their deliberate retreat from the city to eulogize the typical feminine life of rural seclusion. Her poems about the idyllic grounds of Eastwell are some of the loveliest of the century.[4] Among these, "A Nocturnal Reverie" is her best known, a celebration of the landscape "when darkened groves their softest shadows wear, / And falling waters we distinctly hear" (lines 23–24). During these precious hours, "Their short-lived jubilee the creatures keep, / Which but endures whilst tyrant man does sleep" (lines 37–38). Some readers have discerned in these lines, describing the transient sights, sounds, and smells encountered by a solitary walker, hints of the restiveness experienced by a woman equally fettered by the customs of "tyrant man."

Finch, however, enjoyed a happy and supportive marriage; her husband not only encouraged and transcribed her writings but sponsored the publication of her *Poems on Several Occasions* in 1713. She enjoyed the friendships of Nicholas Rowe and Jonathan Swift and a mentor-like relationship with Alexander Pope. Yet Finch was well aware of the conventions discouraging women's literary performances; she chastised Pope for his suggestion, in *The Rape of the Lock*, that women's "Hysteric or Poetic Fit[s]" are equally caused by spleen (IV, line 59).[5] A veteran sufferer from spleen – most likely depression – herself, she resented Pope's assertion that women's creativity was rooted in illness. An early manuscript poem, "The Introduction," remains among the century's strongest expressions of women's plight:

> Alas! a woman that attempts the pen,
> Such an intruder on the rights of men,
> Such a presumptuous Creature, is esteem'd,
> The fault, can by no vertue be redeem'd . . .
> To write, or read, or think, or to enquire
> Wou'd cloud our beauty, and exhaust our time . . .
> Whilst the dull mannage, of a servile house
> Is held by some, our utmost art, and use.
>
> (lines 9–12, 16–17, 19–20)

Although Finch resolves in "The Introduction" to avoid criticism by embracing retirement (line 59), she evidently became comfortable enough to circulate her poems among friends, permit some to appear in miscellanies, and finally, perhaps sustained by her new aristocratic title, to publish a collection under her name. "The Introduction," nevertheless, reiterates women's resentment of boundaries that continued to discourage their publications for decades. Women's writing, reading, and thinking were sometimes deplored even by female acquaintances who preferred to maintain the traditional identification of literature and scholarship as masculine.

Finch wrote in a great variety of genres, from ambitious Pindaric odes ("The Spleen," "Upon the Hurricane") to pastoral lyrics, to fables. These bespeak as great a variety of reading, from translated classics and the Bible to male and female contemporaries. The esteem in which contemporaries held her verse may owe much to the subtlety with which she veiled all political allusions, a practice typical of John Dryden, Aphra Behn, and other supporters of James II after his abdication. By the 1720s, few women were publishing politically charged verse; an ideal of femininity withdrawn from public concerns had gained wide acceptance. Because many prominent women writers of the past half-century (Behn, Centlivre, Manley to name three) had avidly supported political parties in an era when professional

Pope's availability as a model coincided with other influences to encourage a growing number of women poets in the second quarter of the century. Some ladies apparently felt compelled to salute the reigning bard in their own volumes. Mary Masters, for example, addressed her patron, the Earl of Burlington, in the first poem of her *Poems on Several Occasions* (1733),[10] but she digressed to praise her fellow Burlington protégé: "O happy *Pope*, blest with auspicious Fate!" Although a staunch feminist in many of her letters and poems, Masters deferred in this instance to her male rival for Burlington's approval. But Masters's appearance in print represents another phenomenon favorable to middling- and lower-status as well as genteel women writers of the period: publication by subscription. Formerly a publication method chosen by, for example, scholars and their booksellers, subscriptions guaranteed a market for esoteric works; sustained writers throughout lengthy projects; and reduced writers' dependence on single patrons. The same factors encouraged women writers, whose volumes often appeared risky ventures due to their relative obscurity and lack of educational credentials. Because their lives were chiefly absorbed in domestic pursuits, moreover, mid-century women writers had fewer opportunities to ingratiate themselves with patrons through such traditional means as political journalism. Subscriptions not only assured booksellers some return on women's publications; they also circumscribed an initial readership and thus appeared more appropriate to many women than the appearance of their volumes in the open market. Throughout the century, women could and did seek patrons by publishing elegies and panegyrics on eminent figures, and published their works commercially as in the successful case of Charlotte Smith. But by somewhat preserving their privacy while permitting them to profit from their labors, subscriptions beckoned many women into print who might have otherwise confined their efforts to the pages of common place books.

The second quarter-century, then, witnessed a number of volumes by women of middling and lower social status. Mary Barber (ca.1690–1757), wife of a Dublin merchant, published successfully her *Poems on Several Occasions* (1734)[11] after amassing a lengthy subscription-list through the aid of Swift and his influential friends. She corresponded with her printer, Samuel Richardson, regarding his novels, and her poems reveal her to have been an avid reader of authors from Plato to her fellow members of Swift's circle. Barber is remembered, however, for poems such as one ostensibly spoken by her son on his transition to adult male attire: "What is it our mammas bewitches, / To plague us little boys with breeches?" (lines 1–2). Such verse, with its attentive yet unsentimental observation of childhood, exercises an appeal beyond Barber's didactic intention. Two years later marked the third edition, augmented with miscellaneous poems, of Mary Chandler's *The Description of Bath. A Poem* (1736).[12] Chandler (1687–1745) kept a milliner's shop in Bath, where her title poem – a topographical celebration of the city's attractions – proved so popular with tourists as to attract a compliment by Alexander Pope and to achieve eight editions by 1767. Like Barber's, Chandler's poems reveal her keen reading and study of contemporaries, particularly of Pope, for whom she evidently felt an affinity due to their mutual deformity and rather anomalous social standing. Jane Brereton (1685–1740), a lady of straitened means following separation from her abusive and spendthrift husband, published steadily throughout the period, but her assembled *Poems* (1744) did not appear until four years after her death. Her verses allude to Ovid and Horace, if only to observe that both wrote best in a prosperity unknown to herself. In a poem first published in The *Gentleman's Magazine* in response "To the Gentleman who offer'd Fifty Pounds to any Person who should write the best Poem by May next on five Subjects, viz. Life, Death, Judgment, Heaven, and Hell," she lamented that even her contemporaries "old Swift, Dan Pope, and Young, / Those leaders of the rhiming Throng, Are better paid for Meditations / On the most trifling Occasions" (lines 9–12).[13]

Mary Jones (?-1778), dependent sister of a clergyman in Oxford, represents both the lingering obstacles and the rewards before women poets. The Reverend Oliver Jones disapproved of women's writing and discouraged his sister's efforts, perhaps fearing a consequent loss of status. Jones apparently desisted from sharing her work with Oxford acquaintances. She nevertheless circulated her poems in letters and manuscripts among a network of aristocratic friends, including Martha Lovelace, a Maid of Honor to Queen Caroline. Jones's letters and poems record her efforts to maintain pride and independence among a circle of much wealthier acquaintances. When, in 1750, her admirers sponsored a volume of her *Miscellanies in Verse and Prose* – with well over a thousand subscribers, including Princess Amelia – Jones endeavored to maintain her stance as an amateur, scribbling only for private amusement.[14] In an epistle "Of Desire," she claimed that her sole wish was "to live unknown, / In some serene retreat, my time my own, / To all obliging, yet a slave to none" (lines 171–73). By modeling her persona on Pope's, who made a similar claim in his *Epistle to Dr. Arbuthnot*, Jones established her dignity in relation to distinguished friends, much as Pope had claimed his status as a leisured gentleman, entitled to the friendship rather than the patronage of aristocrats. Throughout her volumes, she alludes to Pope's poetry, creating a vigorous and authoritative voice. Unfortunately, after the success of her volume, Jones refrained from further composition, exercising the preference for leisured retirement she claimed in "On Desire."

The poems bespeak Jones's ambition, particularly in their echoes of Pope's self-confidence as cultural arbiter, but she evidently felt that a lady's independence, unlike a man's, required withdrawal from, rather than participation in, the marketplace.

Another self-taught poet of genuine promise whose career was cut short, this time through early death, was Mary Leapor of Brackley (1722–46). Leapor's recognition as a poet was even more unlikely than Jones's. A nurseryman's daughter, Leapor worked as a maid in two households until her dismissal from Edgecote House (allegedly because she neglected her duties as cook-maid while reading) the year before her death. Encouraged by Bridget Freemantle, a local clergyman's daughter, Leapor devoted herself to poetry during her last year, maturing phenomenally as a writer while Freemantle campaigned for subscriptions on her behalf.[15] Freemantle later described her protégée as having loved reading from childhood, but possessing fewer than twenty books, including some Pope, Dryden's fables, and several plays. Her scant personal holdings confirm the assiduity with which Leapor must have perused her employers' libraries when permitted to do so. Leapor, like Jones, was considerably indebted to Pope for her style and opinions, but her range was wider and her ambition more intrinsic. Capable of emulating Pope's epigrammatic style ("A friend too soft will hardly prove sincere; / The wit's inconstant, and the learn'd severe"; "Essay on Friendship," lines 31–32), Leapor also wrote nostalgically about Edgecote House as the comic but doomed "Crumble-Hall," and passionately about Pope in "On the Death of a justly-admir'd Author." "Dorinda at her Glass" modulates from zestful satire at the expense of aging ladies ("Her careless locks upon her shoulders lay / Uncurl'd, alas! Because they half were gray," lines 25–26) to an earnest plea that such women might recognize their foolishness and embrace virtue. Leapor's references to Freemantle's subscription efforts are self-deprecating (her muse refuses to assist her effort to appear in print, and instead offers "a Maid of less Degree / . . . Whose Voice, tho' hoarse, is loud and strong"; "The Proposal," lines 30, 33). The amount of work she left at her death, leading to a second volume (1751) after the first appeared posthumously in 1748, attests to her ambition as a maturing artist before her death from measles.

Leapor was fortunate in the patronage of "Artemisia" Freemantle. Like those of male poets of the century, her prospects were considerably enhanced by the assistance of a sympathetic, resourceful, well-connected mentor who encouraged her reading as well as writing. Mary Collier (ca. 1690–1762), another laboring-class poet, was not so lucky. Collier published her rebuttal of Stephen Duck's "The Thresher's Labour" (1730) at her own expense in 1739.[16] Unlike Duck, who aggrandized both rural laborers and their masters through Homeric metaphors, Collier found little to redeem the grueling efforts of female day-laborers such as herself. "The Woman's Labour" bitterly laments the rigors of cleaning and laundering for the local gentry before returning home to care for children and uncooperative husband. "While you to *Sysiphus* yourselves compare, / With *Danaus' Daughters* we may claim a share" (lines 239–40). While Duck forestalled apprehensions of rebellion by suggesting the relative passivity of his threshers, as well as their inevitable role as part of a natural cycle, Collier adopted a resentful tone. She excoriated her mistress for accumulating needless luxuries at the expense of those burdened with their care, and for begrudging her assistants their meals and pay. It is little wonder that unlike Duck, rewarded by the Queen herself, Collier was ignored by her intended audience. Collier and Leapor, nevertheless, represent the limited but palpable opportunities available even to women laborers during a century when a flourishing print culture demanded materials for consumption, and when even a manifestly overworked laborer had enough access to books to enrich her own poem with allusions to Greek myth.

After the death of Alexander Pope, female as well as male poets experienced both the exhilaration of release from his ubiquitous influence and the challenge of establishing new modes of poetry. While living, Pope had seemed to some women a potential mentor and to others an adversary. When Anne Ingram, Lady Irwin (ca. 1696–1764), read Pope's newly published *Epistle to a Lady, on the Characters of Women* (1735), she quickly responded with an "Epistle to Mr. Pope. Occasioned by his Characters of Women," printed in the *Gentleman's Magazine* of December 1736.[17] Lady Irwin's poem appropriates Pope's style in order to argue against his narrow view of women's psychology as well as his failure to suggest any strategy for ameliorating their whimsical personalities. Echoing Pope's well-known examples, Lady Irwin observes that women are not essentially different from men; both thrive when educated and when engaged in meaningful activities. She concludes by asking Pope to propose the antidote to the situation his satire described: "Wou'd you . . . / Bestow some moments of your darling ease, / To rescue woman from this *Gothic* state . . .?" (lines 111–17). Her poem resembles those of a number of contemporaries who apparently felt that Pope was amenable to their suggestions or, at least, likely to read their productions much as they read and were influenced by his. Pope's death in 1744 thus struck some women poets as a personal loss, inspiring tributes such as Mary Leapor's plaintive elegy: "Ev'n we condemn'd at distance to admire / Bewail the Hopes that with our Guide expire" ("On the Death of a justly-admir'd Author," lines 35–36).

Women gradually overcame their dependence on Pope as chief model, a trend inaugurated by the appearance of Elizabeth Carter's admired *Poems on Several Occasions* (1762).[18] This volume included revised versions of poems Carter (1717–1806) had earlier published when a frequent contributor to the *Gentleman's Magazine*, the journal that had promoted her reputation as a woman of letters. One poem in particular, "On the Death of Mrs. Rowe," praised the deceased poet as an apt model for contemporary women writers, as distinguished from Pope's dangerous influence. "On the Death of Mrs. Rowe" alludes to Pope's verses mainly to establish their opposition to a more pious, edifying female tradition. Her conclusion, for example, echoes Pope's address to the rakish, skeptical Lord Bolingbroke as his "guide, philosopher, and friend" in the *Essay on Man* (IV, line 390). Carter, however, adopts Rowe's spirit as "my genius and my guide below" (line 42), vowing to "regulate" her own verse by comparison with the "spotless" performances of her predecessor (line 44). Accordingly, Carter's poems celebrated the joys of platonic friendship in lines encouraging the piety of her addressees. While Pope's fallen heroine, Eloisa, lasciviously mourned the "lov'd Idea" of her lost Abelard (*Eloisa to Abelard*, line 12), Carter invoked the "lov'd Idea" of an absent friend in "To —," asking heaven to ensure that "Thro' flow'ry Paths securely may she tread, / By Fortune follow'd, and by Virtue led" (lines 51–52). Occasional poems such as "On a Watch" directed *memento mori* reflections to specifically female readers: "Destructive Years no Graces leave behind, / But those, which Virtue fixes in the Mind" (lines 27–28). In "Ode to Melancholy," first published in 1739, Carter develops a popular theme later elaborated by Edward Young in his *Night Thoughts*: a walk amidst the "midnight horrors" (line 19) of a graveyard leads to reflections on "the last morn's fair op'ning ray" heralding "the bright eternal day" (lines 77–78).

Through such orthodox verse, Elizabeth Carter augmented her already formidable reputation as a linguist, becoming a nationally recognized model for aspiring young women. Her rise to prominence was accomplished in large part by her regular contributions to Edward Cave's popular *Gentleman's Magazine*. Established in 1731, "The Mag" rapidly became a venue for publication of verse by amateur as well as professional writers, and by provincial as well as London-based men and women. Cave encouraged literary submissions by his readers, many of which were published under pseudonyms that allowed ladies and gentlemen to maintain anonymity while reaching a large audience. Some of these contributors, such as Carter – who published as "Eliza" – secured a large following, engaging in correspondences under their pseudonyms and later publishing their collections. Cave mentored those contributors he thought promising, writing letters of advice and introducing them to each other, establishing networks of mutual support and friendship.

Besides Mary Barber, Lady Irwin, and Elizabeth Carter, Jane Brereton and her daughter Charlotte (born ca.1720), Elizabeth Teft (fl.1741–44), Mary Whateley Darwall (1738–1825), Anna Seward (1742–1809), Mary Scott (ca. 1752–93), and Catherine Jemmat (fl. 1750–66) and many more female poets published in the *Gentleman's Magazine*. All were indebted to the encouragement and sponsorship of Edward Cave, who thus played a critical role in assisting women's emergence in the literary marketplace.

Samuel Johnson, too, followed Cave's example and encouraged women to publish. Although some critics have suggested that Johnson inhibited women from testing the open marketplace by urging them to publish by subscription, his advice was given to contemporaries who often shrank from the exposure of their names and even texts on bookstalls. Johnson reminded female acquaintances of their right to profit from their writings, assurance welcome to some who needed to earn their livings and were hampered by the lack of employment options appropriate for ladies. Johnson's efforts were furthered by his female acquaintances, whose growing literary reputations enabled them to campaign effectively on behalf of their less-well-known protégées. Johnson and Carter cooperated, for example, in procuring subscribers to Anna Williams's (1706–83) *Miscellanies in Prose and Verse* (1766),[19] and Carter subscribed to the volumes of Sarah Dixon (fl.1716–45), Jane Brereton, Mary Jones, Mary Masters, and Mary Whateley Darwall, among others. Indeed, Carter had an "extreme partiality for writers of her own sex"[20]:

> Though she detested the principles displayed in Mrs. Woolstonecraft's [sic] wild theory concerning the "Rights of Women," . . . yet she thought that men exercised too arbitrary a power over [women], and considered them as too inferior to themselves. Hence she had a decided bias in favour of female writers, and always read their works with a mind prepared to be pleased . . .
> (1, 448)

Well-connected and aristocratic women had previously taken part in the subscription campaigns of Dryden, Pope, and a host of poets, but increasingly, women writers engaged in patronage of their fellow women through this method, which enabled those of moderate means to experience the pleasure as well as responsibility of fostering literary productions.

A group of women who exercised considerable influence upon female literary productions belonged to the Bluestocking Circle of Elizabeth Montagu (1720–1800). Montagu, known not for poetry but for her prose defense of Shakespeare against the strictures of Voltaire, sponsored periodic gatherings at her home at which such acquaintances as Johnson and Edmund Burke, Carter and Hester Mulso Chapone (1727–1801) engaged in conversation.

As "Queen of the Blues," Montagu exercised considerable influence, not simply over her friends' tastes, but also over their objects of patronage. This situation could provide mutually satisfactory support, as with Anna Williams, or Montagu's encouragement of her sister, the novelist Sarah Scott. On the other hand, when Hannah More (1745–1833) later emulated Montagu and marshaled a subscription on behalf of the poet Ann Yearsley (1752–1806),[21] disaster befell when More attempted to control the profits she had worked to amass. But the Bluestocking Circle provided a nexus of support to many women writers for whom Montagu, Carter, Chapone, More, and their friends undertook subscription efforts. The letters of all demonstrate that these women not only enjoyed reading their contemporaries; they enjoyed participating in the life of letters through self-expression and patronage.

By the opening of the third quarter of the century, enough women had achieved distinction as poets that George Colman and Bonnell Thornton published a two-volume anthology entitled *Poems by Eminent Ladies* (1755).[22] Although Katherine Philips, the Duchess of Newcastle, Anne Killigrew, and Aphra Behn were represented in their collection, the remaining fourteen writers had been productive during the first half of the eighteenth century. In their preface, the editors observe that "There is indeed no good reason to be assigned why the poetical attempts of females should not be well received, unless it can be demonstrated that fancy and judgment are wholly confined to one half of our species; a notion, to which the readers of these volumes will not readily assent" (p. iii). Although they acknowledge that "like many of our greatest male writers," their authors were usually "more indebted to nature for their success, than to education" (p. iv), Colman and Thornton intended their volumes for a wide readership, indicated by their modernization of the earliest texts and the simplified typography throughout. The headnotes for most authors are borrowed from recent sources such as George Ballard's *Memoirs of Several Ladies of Great Britain who have been Celebrated for their Writings* (1752)[23] and Robert Shiells's *The Lives of the Poets* (1753).[24] *Poems by Eminent Ladies* is often called the first canon of women writers in English; as such, it is notably inclusive. Not only are aristocrats such as Lady Mary Wortley Montagu and Lady Winchilsea represented, as well as middling-rank writers such as Constantia Grierson (a Dublin printer's wife, ca. 1705–32), Mary Barber, Mary Jones, and Elizabeth Rowe. Mary Leapor is admitted into the canon, as well as Aphra Behn and Laetitia Pilkington, both of questionable reputation. Mary, Lady Chudleigh, Alicia Cockburn (wife of an Edinburgh advocate; ca. 1712–94), Judith Madan, Mary Masters, and Mary Monck (daughter of

Viscount Molesworth, ca. 1678–1715) complete the anthology. As the anthology went through successive editions, its selections were pruned as literary taste became more sentimental and decorous, and different genres emerged. Nevertheless, Colman and Thornton's initial gesture provided a benchmark against which proceeding generations of women poets could measure their progress in the realm of literary reputation.

By the close of the third quarter of the century, women had apparently gained enough ground as writers that Mary Scott (ca. 1752–93) wrote a supplement to *The Feminiad*, a tribute to accomplished women that John Duncomb had published in 1754.[25] In *The Female Advocate* (1774), Scott laments that "Lordly Man" still wishes "Alone to bow at wisdom's sacred shrine" (lines 21–22). Nevertheless, she argues, more women than have been previously recognized have attained excellence in the arts and learning. She intends her poem to complete and extend Duncomb's attempt so that women's abilities will be fully appreciated and their future efforts encouraged. Scott softened her addresses to "Lordly Man" with notes explaining she advocated an adequate education for all women but encouraged only gifted women to pursue literature. Nevertheless, the few passages in *The Female Advocate* resembling the complaints of such predecessors as Lady Mary Chudleigh were enough to ensure Scott a critical drubbing. The conservative ideology governing femininity was already established, making statements such as Scott's seem not merely dated but dangerous. While women continued to pour into the literary marketplace as the century drew to a close, they rarely chose to express themselves in a tone as adamant as Scott's. Instead, female wit was extolled more decorously, as in the youthful Hannah More's *A Search after Happiness*.[26] Published the year before *The Female Advocate*, More's pastoral drama closes with a celebration of the Bluestocking ladies' achievements. Nevertheless, she adds, ". . .though Learning's cause I plead, / One virtuous sentiment, one generous deed, / Affords more genuine transport in the heart / Than genius, wit, or science can impart" (lines 37–40). More's prominent disclaimer would increasingly provide a model for women who wrote for publication.

As the century drew to a close, numbers of women published volumes of poetry. Although the novel, with its greater financial rewards and lesser status, had gained ascendancy as the genre of choice for women writers, more women than ever emerged as poets. In fact, many women writers practiced both genres; the heroines of Ann Radcliffe (1764–1823), for example, compose extemporaneous sonnets as they gaze upon sublime landscapes or muse upon their fates. Charlotte Lennox (ca. 1729–1804), Charlotte Smith (1749–1806), and Hannah More all composed verse and prose. Women incorporated into both genres the current taste for the sublime, the sentimental, the rural, and

the gothic, as compared with the affinity of previous generations for the satirical, the urban, and the classical. Joanna Baillie's (1762–1851) *Poems* (1790)[27]
are typical in featuring both "The Storm-Beat Maid. Somewhat after the style
of our old English ballads" (lines 97–107) and "A Story of Other Times.
Somewhat in imitation of the poems of Ossian" (lines 143–69). Nowhere are
these influences more clearly observed than in the popular *Elegaic Sonnets* of
Charlotte Smith, first published in 1784.[28] Although Smith alludes to Pope in
the first sonnet of the sequence, paraphrasing an enigmatic statement in *Eloisa
to Abelard* to the effect that "those paint sorrow best – who feel it most!"
(line 14), the following sonnets indicate the predominant reading of her generation. Rousseau and Goethe merit allusions, while Thomson, Young, and
Thomas Gray are important influences. Milton and Thomas Otway are fore-
most among Smith's chosen forebears, while Pope's prophetically gothic
Eloisa to Abelard sustains his importance for Smith, as for so many contemporaries. Addressing the Arun river in Sussex, she extolled its best-known
local writer as well as two recent, critically acclaimed poets:

> Banks! Which inspired thy Otway's plaintive strain!
>   Wilds! – whose lorn echoes learn'd the deeper tone
> Of Collins' powerful shell! Yet once again
>   Another poet – Hayley is thine own!
> Thy classic stream anew shall hear a lay,
> Bright as its waves, and various as its way!
>   ("To the River Arun," lines 9–14)

Smith's sonnets succeeded because, like those of many great practitioners,
they created for contemporaries the impression of genuine passion despite
adhering to the rigid fourteen-line form. Crucial to their impact are Smith's
frequent allusions to texts that epitomized, for herself and her community of
readers, grief and yearning, as well as a sensitive response to the landscape,
to humanity, and to experience. Smith in fact endured years of grief while
supporting ten children and a feckless husband, but her sonnets' evocative
power owes as much to cannily chosen allusions as to the genuine tribulations at which they hint.

One of Smith's chief critics and rivals, Anna Seward, was not merely an
avid but a voracious reader. Nothing if not opinionated, Seward engaged in
a lengthy *Gentleman's Magazine* debate (1789–91) over the relative merits
of Dryden and Pope.[29] In the wake of Joseph Warton's *Essay on the Genius
and Writings of Pope* (1756) which proclaimed him a second-rate poet,
Seward argued vigorously on his behalf against the argument that the more
rugged verse of Dryden was superior to the refined, hence less sublime,
poems of his successor:

> If from Pope's Homer lines can be produced mean and wretched as those which Dryden has, in his Aeneid, put into the mouth of the Empress of Heaven, and if it cannot be proved that such vulgar language occurs on almost every page in Dryden, I will give up the point in contest; which, on my part, goes no farther than to assert, that the poetic writers of *this* day have done honour to their art, by avoiding the botching vulgarities of Dryden's style, and emulating the polished graces of his successor.   (p. 64)

Passages such as this capture something of Seward's self-confidence as a critic, and her poetic output was equally fearless. Seward wrote Horatian epistles and essays in the manner of Pope, but she as often challenged her precursor as emulated him.[30] Her "Epistle to Cornelia" rebukes his version of female psychology in *Epistle to a Lady*, observing the inaccuracy of the society portraits Pope describes as metaphors for women's minds. Instead, Seward compares women to the good-hearted Sarah Young of Hogarth's *The Rake's Progress*, thus suggesting that women are generally flawed but loyal and charitable. As prolific a poet as she was a prose-writer, Seward experimented with most extant genres, from sonnets that rival Smith's in their evocation of melancholy ("Misfortune's victim hails, with many a sigh, / Thee, scarlet Poppy of the pathless field") to the fragment of an epic based on Fenélon's *Telemachus*. Dispatching verse and critical proclamations to London from her Lichfield stronghold, she achieved fame throughout Britain while confirming that women in the provinces were fully capable of critical reading and writing.

Seward also stated, at the century's close, an opinion that few women would have dared venture at its beginning: that the learned languages were no longer crucial components of genteel education. "The writers of Great Britain equal, in every style of composition, the proudest literary boasts of Greece and Rome, or those of any living language. I cannot suppose that the being able to read thoughts and sentiments, either of verse or prose, in foreign tongues, which in equal force and beauty may be found in our own, any great advantage to the understanding or imagination."[31] Seward's declaration occurred in a letter to Walter Scott estimating David Garrick's education, and no doubt reflects her resentment of Johnson's condescension toward his former pupil. Hers is also the attitude toward "unlettered genius" espoused by many male and female patrons, particularly if they lacked a classical education themselves. But with characteristic bravado Seward declared a liberating principle that earlier writers – for example, the youthful Lady Mary Wortley Montagu, furtively teaching herself Latin and Greek – could never have formulated, much less uttered.

Seward, a clergyman's daughter, preferred her social eminence in Lichfield to the lesser status and literary competition she would have endured in

London. At the century's close, other, less privileged women also achieved reputations while remaining at a distance from the capitol. Ann Yearsley survived her altercation with Hannah More, publishing two further volumes of poems as well as other writings. More had originally claimed that Yearsley's only reading consisted of some Shakespeare, Milton, Pope, and Young, but the milk-vendor's verse develops the emphasis on sensibility and the sublime that most readers of her generation found irresistible. While Yearsley began her career as a representative "untutored" poet, several other women emerged in another variant of the same trend. *The Poetical Works of Janet Little, the Scotch Milkmaid* (1792)[32] capitalized on the popularity of Robert Burns, and of poems in archaic and rustic dialect. But although publicized as a rural muse, Little had read such recent, major publications as Samuel Johnson's *The Lives of the Poets*, to which she referred in some autobiographical lines "Given to a Lady who asked me to write a Poem":

> Swift, Thomson, Addison, an' Young
> Made Pindus echo to their tongue,
> In hopes to please a learned age;
> But Dr. Johnson, in a rage,
> Unto posterity did shew
> Their blunders great, their beauties few.
> But now he's dead, we weel may keen;
> For ilka dunce maun hae a pen,
> To write in hamely, uncouth rhymes;
> An' yet forsooth they please the times.   (lines 11–20)

In fact, Little praised Burns for his achievement ("Even folks, who're of the highest station / Ca' him the Glory of our nation," lines 25–26), and emulated his style. Her poems often comment on other texts, as in "On Reading Lady Mary Montague and Mrs. Rowe's Letters," in which the moon of Rowe's pious creativity eclipses the Venus of Montagu's brilliant prose. Such verse demonstrates the extent to which reading was available even to laborers in their leisure hours. It also suggests that many women of all classes acknowledged the tradition of pious female writers descended from Katherine Philips to Elizabeth Rowe and hailed by Elizabeth Carter.

By the close of the century, Hannah More had inherited that tradition and its authority. While radicals such as William Blake invoked apocalyptic imagery to sanction the revolutionary movement in France, More preached acceptance of Providence to the British laborers who read the poems in her *Cheap Repository Tracts*. While poet-novelist Helen Maria Williams (ca. 1761–1827) hailed the destruction of the Bastille in a series of *Letters from France*,[33] More bade her readers to await their heavenly rewards or risk eternal punishment. While many modern critics find More's verse hopelessly retrograde, there is little dispute that she found in print a powerful tool with which to maintain social order through evangelism. Her writings complete another trajectory initiated in the previous century. Early-seventeenth-century women often confided their spiritual autobiographies to private journals, using biblical readings as patterns for their private revelations. More invited thousands to construct private spiritual journeys patterned on her readings of scripture. The long, slow development of a private, domestic exercise into a public medium characterized female writing throughout the century. Women did not, however, progress from being "passive" readers to "active" writers; rather, reading and writing were inextricably intertwined activities as women scrutinized, studied, and responded to, as well as promoted, challenged, and contributed to, the poetry of the eighteenth century.

NOTES

1 Lady Mary Chudleigh, *The Poems and Prose of Mary Lady Chudleigh*, ed. Margaret Ezell (New York: Oxford University Press, 1993).
2 Sarah Fyge Egerton, *Poems on Several Occasions, Together with a Pastoral* (London: J. Nutt, 1703).
3 See Carol Barash, *English Women's Poetry, 1649–1714: Politics, Community, and Linguistic Authority* (Oxford: Clarendon Press, 1996), for a full discussion of this topic.
4 Anne Finch, Countess of Winchilsea, *Selected Poems of Anne Finch, Countess of Winchilsea*, ed. Katharine M. Rogers (New York: F. Unger, 1979).
5 Alexander Pope, *The Rape of the Lock*, in *The Poems of Alexander Pope*, ed. John Butt et al., 10 vols. (London: Methuen, 1967), II, 185–86.
6 Elizabeth Singer Rowe, *The Miscellaneous Works in Prose and Verse of Mrs. Elizabeth Rowe*, 2 vols. (London: R. Hett and R. Dodsley, 1739).
7 Isobel Grundy, "Books and the Woman: an Eighteenth-Century Owner and Her Libraries," *English Studies in Canada* 20:1 (March 1994), 1–22.
8 See Lady Mary Wortley Montagu, *Essays and Poems and Simplicity, a Comedy*, ed. Robert Halsband and Isobel Grundy (Oxford: Oxford University Press, 1977).
9 Judith Cowper Madan, "To Mr Pope," in Alexander Pope, *Miscellany Poems*, 2 vols., 5th edn. (London: B. Lintot, 1726) I, 26–29.
10 Mary Masters, *Poems on Several Occasions* (London: T. Browne, 1733), pp. 5–7.
11 Mary Barber, *Poems on Several Occasions* (London: C. Rivington, 1734).
12 Mary Chandler, *The Description of Bath . . . With Several Other Poems*, 3rd edn. (London: H. Leake, 1736).
13 Jane Brereton, *Poems on Several Occasions: By Mrs. Jane Brereton. With Letters to her Friends, and an Account Of Her Life* (London: Edward Cave, 1744), pp. 215–16.
14 Mary Jones, *Miscellanies in Prose and Verse* (Oxford: Dodsley et al., 1750).
15 Mary Leapor, *Poems Upon Several Occasions* (London: J. Roberts, 1748).
16 Mary Collier, "The Woman's Labour," ed. Moira Ferguson (1739; rpt. Los Angeles: Augustan Reprint Society, 1985).

17 Anne Ingram, Lady Irwin, "An Epistle to Mr. Pope, Occasioned by his Characters of Women," *Gentleman's Magazine* 6 (1736), 745.

18 Elizabeth Carter, *Poems on Several Occasions*, 2nd edn. (London: J. Rivington, 1762).

19 Anna Williams, *Miscellanies in Prose and Verse* (London: T. Davies, 1766).

20 Montagu Pennington, *Memoirs of the Life of Mrs Elizabeth Carter*, 2 vols., 2nd edn. (London: F. C. and J. Rivington, 1808).

21 Ann Yearsley, *Poems, on Several Occasions, by Ann Yearsley, a milkwoman of Bristol* (London: T. Cadell, 1785).

22 George Colman and Bonnell Thornton (eds.), *Poems by Eminent Ladies*, 2 vols. (London: R. Baldwin, 1755).

23 George Ballard, *Memoirs of Several Ladies of Great Britain who have been Celebrated for their Writings*, ed. Ruth Perry (1752; rpt. Detroit: Wayne State University Press, 1985).

24 Robert Shiels, *The Lives of the Poets of Great Britain and Ireland*, 5 vols. (1753; rpt. Hildesheim: Verlagbuchhandlung, 1968).

25 Mary Scott, "The Female Advocate" (1774; rpt Los Angeles, Augustan Reprint Society, 1984).

26 Hannah More, *A Search after Happiness: a Pastoral in Three Dialogues* (Bristol: S. Farley, 1773).

27 Joanna Baillie, *Poems; wherein it is attempted to describe certain views of nature and of rustic manners* (1790; rpt. Oxford: Woodstock Books, 1994).

28 Charlotte Smith, *The Poems of Charlotte Smith*, ed. Stuart Curran (Oxford: Oxford University Press, 1993).

29 Gretchen M. Foster, *Pope Versus Dryden: a Controversy in Letters to The Gentleman's Magazine, 1789–1791* (Victoria, BC: University of Victoria Press, 1989).

30 Anna Seward, *The Poetical Works of Anna Seward, with extracts from her literary correspondence*, ed. Sir Walter Scott, 3 vols. (Edinburgh: Ballantyne, 1810).

31 Seward to Walter Scott, 24 August 1807. In Hesketh Pearson (ed.), *The Swan of Lichfield, being a Selection from the Correspondence of Anna Seward* (London: Hamish Hamilton, 1936), p. 299.

32 Janet Little, *The Poetical Works of Janet Little, the Scotch Milkmaid* (Ayr: John and Peter Wilson, 1792).

33 Helen Maria Williams, *Letters from France*, 2 vols. (London: G. G. and J. Robinson, 1790).

FURTHER READING

Armstrong, Isobel, and Virginia Blain (eds.). *Women's Poetry in the Enlightenment: the Making of a Canon, 1730–1820*. Basingstoke: Macmillan; New York: St. Martin's Press, 1999.

Barash, Carol. *English Women's Poetry, 1649–1714: Politics, Community, and Linguistic Authority*. Oxford: Clarendon Press, 1996.

Demers, Patricia. *The World of Hannah More*. Lexington, KY: The University Press of Kentucky, 1996.

Ferguson, Moira. *Eighteenth-Century Women Poets: Nation, Class, and Gender*. Albany: State University of New York Press, 1995.

Greene, Richard. *Mary Leapor: a Study in Eighteenth-Century Women's Poetry.* Oxford: Clarendon Press, 1993.

Griffin, Dustin. *Literary Patronage in England, 1650–1800.* Cambridge: Cambridge University Press, 1996.

Grundy, Isobel. *Lady Mary Wortley Montagu: Comet of the Enlightenment.* Oxford: Oxford University Press, 1999.

Hinnant, Charles H. *The Poetry of Anne Finch: an Essay in Interpretation.* Newark, DE: University of Delaware Press, 1994.

Landry, Donna. *The Muses of Resistance: Laboring-Class Women's Poetry in Britain, 1739–1796.* Cambridge: Cambridge University Press, 1990.

Lonsdale, Roger (ed.). *Eighteenth-Century Women Poets: an Oxford Anthology.* Oxford: Oxford University Press, 1989.

Myers, Sylvia Harcstark. *The Bluestocking Circle: Women, Friendship, and the Life of the Mind in Eighteenth-Century England.* Oxford: Clarendon Press, 1990.

Thomas, Claudia. *Alexander Pope and His Eighteenth-Century Women Readers.* Carbondale: Southern Illinois University Press, 1994.

Waldron, Mary. *Lactilla, Milkwoman of Clifton: the Life and Writings of Ann Yearsley, 1753–1806.* Athens: University of Georgia Press, 1996.

9

DAVID FAIRER

Creating a national poetry: the tradition of Spenser and Milton

During the middle years of the eighteenth century there was a fruitful intimacy between English poetry and what we now think of as "literary history." Earlier poets had been conscious of their illustrious predecessors among whom they hoped to find a place, and in that sense the idea of a poetic canon is a very old one.[1] Chaucer's position as the "Father" of English poetry had long been a commonplace, and by 1700 Spenser and Milton were seen as completing a classic pantheon of great writers, with Dryden clearly in contention. Pope's remark to Joseph Spence in 1736 was offered as a truism: "'Tis easy to mark out the general course of our poetry. Chaucer, Spenser, Milton, and Dryden are the great landmarks for it."[2] But of those "landmarks" Chaucer was virtually unread in the original, and Spenser very little. Their status as canonical English classics was based on reputation rather than reading;[3] their language was generally regarded as outdated and even barbarous, and when being subjected to parody, imitation, or modernization, it was their distance from the present that was being exploited.

By the 1760s, however, a rather different concept had developed whose implications are still with us: a national literary history. This was a more capacious and historicized notion than the old fixed canon of great writers, and it encouraged a living sense of continuity. Spenser and Milton came to be seen as offering much more than fine thoughts and images wrapped up in an outdated language. As poets began to explore their work, use some of their vocabulary, and experiment with the Spenserian stanza and Miltonic blank verse, the old poets seemed to open up a richer poetic language and more varied possibilities in subject-matter. Chaucer, Spenser, Milton, and increasingly Shakespeare, came to be viewed not just as individual "greats" but part of a continuing tradition of poetry with which modern poets wanted to be associated. These native classics were being edited and annotated with this in mind, and readers began to encounter other less familiar names and recognize allusions and influences. A figure like Milton, admired as a sublime genius, could also be valued as a transmitter of the earlier tradition and not just as a unique phenomenon. Rather than setting up predecessors who might overawe an aspiring writer, this more complex sense of "literary history" offered something closer to a varied family tree in which a young poet might experiment with different voices and enter into conversation with the authentic British past:

> The *British* muse in *Chaucer* first began . . .
> The Tree he planted took a gen'rous Root,
> Shot into Boughs, and bent with golden Fruit;
> Under whose fair auspicious Shade were seen
> *An Eden lost and won*, a *Fairy Queen*[4]

These lines by Richard Daniel from 1706 are an early example of how a benign interconnectedness could be seen in the native poetic tradition. This British tree had remained a vital organism and produced "Off-spring of a Manly Grace; / Whose vast Athletick Limbs, and wondrous Fire, / Still own'd the brawny Vigour of the Sire"; but in recent times, says the poet, the potency has ebbed away, and "The puling Brat scarce lifts its foolish Eyes." In contrast, six years earlier another writer had used an inversion of the child-man image to celebrate modernity and assert his own distance from the past: "We can only say, that [Chaucer] liv'd in the Infancy of our Poetry, and that nothing is brought to Perfection at the first. We must be Children before we grow Men."[5] This is Dryden in 1700 (the year of his death) voicing what had by then become the dominant theory of literary development: one of progressive refinement. According to this, English poetry had emerged from an earlier barbarity into modern correctness and elegance. It followed that to look back into its history was something quaintly antiquarian or merely futile.

The two images offered by Daniel and Dryden seem incompatible, but what we nowadays understand as literary history would come from an engagement between them. The rather complacent modernist narrative had to be superseded in favor of a more open and complex reading of older literature that would do justice to the past. Through a combination of scholarly knowledge and historicized "sympathy," the nation's poetic ancestry could be understood more on its own terms. But any history is as much about the present as the past, and my title, "Creating a national poetry," is intended to highlight not just the development of a richer understanding of the nation's historic achievement in poetry, but also an ambition in the poets of the eighteenth century to contribute to it – to understand themselves historically.

It used to be thought that many mid-century poets fell under the "spell" of Spenser and Milton, with all that implies of surrendering to another's power. Concepts such as "the burden of the past" or "the anxiety of influence"[6] tended to represent the phenomenon as sapping the strength of eighteenth-century verse and turning what had been sharp, confident, and clear into something gloomy, indolent, and self-indulgent. Where Homer, Virgil, Horace, or Juvenal bred healthy imitators, it is implied, Spenser and Milton's children were helpless and gullible, unable to find their own voice or direction.[7] This model will no longer do. Once we widen the issue and speak of a national tradition of English poetry ("English" in linguistic terms only, as it tended to be British in outlook) we can see the poets' engagement with it as a token of their curiosity and confidence rather than their weakness.

From the 1740s ambitious and experimental poets (sometimes very young) were becoming conscious of the rich body of English poetry that predated the Restoration of 1660, when a French neo-classicism had become preeminent. After eight decades of elegance, classical imitation, smooth-running heroic couplets, and verbal wit, they felt they wanted to widen poetry's scope and recapture the more daring imagery of the past; they wanted especially to be able to "hear" poetry again – to be surprised by its rhythms and harmonies. In discovering their native tradition, poets like Collins, Akenside, and the Wartons felt they were simultaneously recovering a more pristine classicism which had become overlaid by the prescriptions of the "petits maîtres" of French criticism. Just as a romance/Gothic line of inheritance was waiting to be recovered, so the primal Doric of the Parthenon was somewhere to be found under the grandiloquent façade of Versailles. This concern with getting back to original sources also involved forging links between the national poetry and the language of the Bible.[8] In rediscovering a continuity with their medieval and Elizabethan inheritance, eighteenth century poets were putting themselves in touch with an English classical line that was sympathetic to ancient Greek and Old Testament traditions, and they valued the connections between them. The present essay is able to convey only part of this complex wider picture: it will focus on the particular influence of Spenser and Milton, and attempt to show how their example worked to develop and enrich English poetry, and how their admirers helped establish a native literary history. The concept of a national poetry that was being built up during these decades was neither insular nor merely nostalgic: its emphasis was on the recovery of the past, rather than its loss. The movement towards reestablishing continuity with the literature of former ages was a broad one, with political and social as well as aesthetic implications; criticism and scholarship would also play their part, and some of the most significant poets were literary historians themselves.

Dryden venerated Chaucer and understood the family resemblance in the

Chaucer–Spenser–Milton line, but he valued his own independence from it. He noted: "*Milton* was the Poetical Son of *Spencer* [sic] . . . *Spencer* more than once insinuates, that the Soul of *Chaucer* was transfus'd into his Body; and that he was begotten by him Two hundred years after his Decease. *Milton* has acknowledg'd to me, that *Spencer* was his Original." But Dryden does not present himself as the current embodiment of this poetic transmigration. He pushes all three of them back into the past by regretting their obsolescent language. Milton, who had been "digging from the Mines of *Chaucer*, and *Spencer*" had brought this on himself: "His Antiquated words were [Milton's] Choice, not his Necessity; for therein he imitated *Spencer*, as *Spencer* did *Chaucer*." Dryden offers himself as a contrast to Milton in having chosen the verbal currency of the present.[9] If there is to be continuity, it will come from Dryden assisting Chaucer to speak in the new polished tongue, as he does in his elegant modernizations of *The Wife of Bath's Tale*, *The Knight's Tale*, and *The Nun's Priest's Tale*. It was in these versions that most eighteenth-century readers encountered Chaucer, and Dryden was widely praised for having brought the old poet back to life: "And *Chaucer* shall again with Joy be Read, / Whose Language with its Master lay for Dead."[10] If nothing could be done to resuscitate the language of the old poet, then at least his "sense" could be rescued and preserved before it entirely disappeared.

In a similar way, by 1700 the language and intricate stanza form of Spenser's *Faerie Queene* were viewed as disabling difficulties which only the poet's genius had overcome – they were certainly not to be imitated. In 1687 an anonymous "Person of Quality" published *Spenser Redivivus*, a rewriting of Book One in heroic couplets. The preface commented that Spenser's "obsolete Language and manner of Verse" had been removed, so that he could join the modern polite world on the arm of his translator "in more fashionable *English*." Such modernizings of the English classics were symptomatic of a widespread embarrassment at the barbarity of the native literary past. As Joseph Addison elegantly wrote in his "Account of the Greatest English Poets" (1694):

> Old *Spenser* next, warm'd with poetick rage,
> In ancient tales amus'd a barb'rous age . . .
> But now the mystick tale, that pleas'd of yore,
> Can charm an understanding age no more[11]

Typically, Spenser is being simultaneously canonized and discarded.

If the language or mode of the "olde" poets was revived at all, then it tended to be for comic or satiric purposes to make coded comments on contemporary events, like Matthew Prior's Chaucerian imitation, "Earle

Robert's Mice" (1712) seeking a sinecure from Prime Minister Harley, or *Brown Bread and Honour, a Tale. Moderniz'd from an Ancient Manuscript of Chaucer* (1716),[12] which indignantly lamented the new Hanoverian corruptions. The collection, *Chaucer's Whims: Being some Select Fables and Tales in Verse, Very Applicable to the Present Times* (1701),[13] offered a series of moralized beast fables on dangerous subjects like "The *Succession*," "The *Non juring Clergyman*," and "The *Impeachment*," but made no attempt to imitate Chaucer's style. In the early years of the century, Spenser was particularly exploited as a voice from the past which could be redirected for prophetic or admonitory purposes. For the Tory Prior, in *An Ode, Humbly Inscrib'd to the Queen* (1706), he was used to glorify the Stuart dynasty, while the Whig Samuel Croxall in 1713–14 produced two newly discovered "Original Cantos" of *The Faerie Queene* in which the Spenserian allegory seemed to accuse the Tory Prime Minister of treason. Without precisely documented historical contexts, and carrying a dim aura of strangeness, old texts with a vague canonical authority could enter public debate as prophetic voices from Gothic antiquity and contribute to the quarrels of the present.[14] To be of use, the poetry either had to be refurbished for the polite market, or have its quaint antiquity exploited for others' ends. There was no attempt to engage with Spenser's poetic character.

Towards the middle of the eighteenth century, however, a different attitude is noticeable, particularly in Spenserian imitations. The art of imitation seems to become something closer to absorption as poets discover new possibilities of subject, vocabulary, and rhythm. William Thompson's *Hymn to May* (1746–47), for example, weaves through more than five hundred lines a rich descriptive tapestry with images of returning life and love. The *Faerie Queene* stanza (eight iambic pentameters followed by a final alexandrine, rhyming ababbcbcc), or variations on it, begins to develop a life of its own beyond the parodic. One of the most popular imitations of the century, William Shenstone's *The School-Mistress* (1737) is a case in point. At this date the poem offered just twelve Spenserian stanzas celebrating a village teacher, and much of the amusement came from applying the quaint old language to an everyday subject:

> In evrich Mart that stands on *British* Ground,
> In evrich Village less y-known to Fame,
> Dwells there, in Cot uncouth a far renown'd,
> A Matron old, whom we *School-Mistress* name . . .[15]

This opening sounds patronizing and self-conscious (an Oxford student putting on a funny voice), but something begins to happen as Shenstone revisits his childhood in the leisurely pace of the Spenserian stanza. The nine lines give him room to ponder and notice things – as if he has been freed from the tighter responsibilities of the heroic couplet where each thought tends to be shaped into a point. The Elizabethan burnish in the language has the effect of suggesting both the encrustations of memory, and the magic of a child's perspective – here after a boy has been beaten:

> The other Tribe aghast, with sore dismay
> Attend, and conn their Tasks with mickle Care:
> By turns astony'd evrich Twigg survey,
> And from their Fellows furrow'd Bum beware;
> Knowing, I wist, how each the same may share.

The word "sore" is uncomfortably apt, and the children are torn between concentrating on the lesson and glancing fearfully at the caning twigs.

Over the years Shenstone enlarged the poem to twenty-eight stanzas in 1742, and finally to thirty-five in 1748. He removed some of the mock-antiquity (such as *evrich* and *y-known*) and exploited further the descriptive qualities for which Spenser was particularly admired.[16] He went on to lavish three stanzas of suggestive detail on the herbs found in the schoolmistress's garden, in the process transforming her cottage into a place of wonder: "Lavender, whose spikes of azure bloom / Shall be, ere-while, in arid bundles bound; / To lurk amidst the labours of her loom, / And crown her kerchiefs clean, with mickle rare perfume."[17]

The seductive fullness poets seem to have found in Spenser was exploited most memorably in James Thomson's *The Castle of Indolence* (1748), which began as a few stanzas "in the way of raillery" on himself and his friends, but grew into a two-canto exploration of poetry's delights and responsibilities. In the first canto all the richness of Spenserian description is lavished on the castle and its pampered guests. Thomson leaves direct imitation behind and begins to absorb the allegorical world of enchantment to create a spell of his own:

> Aereal Music in the warbling Wind,
> At Distance rising oft, by small Degrees,
> Nearer and nearer came, till o'er the Trees
> It hung, and breath'd such Soul-dissolving Airs,
> As did, alas! with soft Perdition please:
> Entangled deep in its enchanting Snares,
> The listening Heart forgot all Duties and all Cares.

(1, lines 345–51)

(This is Spenser as filtered through the dangerous poetry of Milton's *Masque*.) If the first canto recognizes how Spenser's imagination can create a world of alluring artifice, then the second canto challenges that world by turning towards Spenser the moralist (the "sage and serious" poet whom Milton admired[18]). With a sudden change of mood, Thomson introduces the "Knight of Arts and Industry," a venerable figure who combines in himself "all the Powers of Head and Heart" (II, line 77). The knight is determined to destroy the castle with its "soul-enfeebling" corruptions and is helped by a Bard who sings a rousing song on the importance of public virtue and "Godlike Reason," accompanied by his *British* Harp." The Bard declares that a literary tradition can play a part in building a civilized society. Both need energy and ambition, otherwise

> The Wits of modern Time had told their Beads,
> And monkish Legends been their only Strains;
> Our MILTON's *Eden* had lain wrapt in Weeds,
> Our SHAKESPEAR stroll'd and laugh'd with *Warwick* Swains,
> Ne had my Master SPENSER charm'd his *Mulla*'s Plains.
>
> (II, lines 464 68)

Thomson's message is that a thriving and morally healthy country needs a national poetry and must cultivate the conditions for its encouragement. But Spenser's position is more ambiguous than the above roll call suggests. In his two-part poem Thomson draws out of *The Faerie Queene* both its pleasurable magic and its spiritual and moral dimension – its poison and its power to heal. *The Castle of Indolence* combines the world of Spenser's Bower of Bliss with that of its destroyer, Sir Guyon (Temperance). Thomson understands the complexity of his source and employs Spenser the moralist to challenge Spenser the enchanter.

The awareness that Spenser's poetic character included both romantic imagination and native vigor made him ideal as an instrument of education. He could capture the young with his romantic Fairy-land, but also lead them out of it to public responsibility and social morality.[19] This is the dynamic theme of James Beattie's *The Minstrel* (published in two books, 1771 and 1774). In a dual structure indebted to Thomson's *Castle of Indolence*, the poem follows the education of young Edwin the harpist, a child of nature who delighted in "Whate'er of lore tradition could supply / From Gothic tale, or song, or fable old," and scanned every aspect of the natural world "with curious and romantic eye" (I, lines 517–19). In the second book Edwin meets a philosophical hermit who leads him from the innocent delights of youth towards a sterner and more rigorous poetry. Beattie recognizes the implications for his own language, and adjusts his instrument accordingly:

> So I, obsequious to Truth's dread command,
> Shall here without reluctance change my lay,
> And smite the Gothic lyre with harsher hand;

> Now when I leave that flowery path for aye
> Of childhood . . .   (II, lines 19–23)

For his imitators in the eighteenth century Spenser offered more than just a faery world of imaginative delight: a Spenserian style, as we have seen, would often include severer tones and a national dimension. Gilbert West used his Spenserian imitation, *Education* (1751), to call for educational reform and the renewal of the nation's self-confidence; and in Robert Bedingfield's *The Education of Achilles* (1747) the future Greek hero absorbs his lessons from various allegorical figures such as Modesty, Exercise, and Temperance, who (in a duality characteristic of Spenserian writing) "temper stern behests with pleasaunce gay." Bedingfield's description of the grotto where the boy is schooled ("A lowly habitation, well I ween, / Yet sacred made by men of mickle fame, / Who there in precepts wise had lesson'd been")[20] could almost be a description of what the Spenserian stanza had become by the 1770s.

More than any other, it was the heroic figure of Milton which helped to define and strengthen the concept of a national poetry in the mid eighteenth century. His influence was so various and pervasive, and has been so well charted by literary scholars, that only a brief outline can be attempted here.[21] By the 1770s Milton had become, along with Shakespeare, a universal favorite with all classes of reader; *Paradise Lost* was "read with Pleasure and Admiration, by Persons of every Degree and Condition," and Dr Johnson had to concede grudgingly that Milton was an author "with whom readers of every class think it necessary to be pleased."[22] *Paradise Lost* was published over a hundred times between 1705 and 1800, and as well as scholarly editions and popular reprints there were grammatically simplified versions, prose versions, and some editions especially for children, many of whom read the poem at school. The War in Heaven in Book VI was evidently popular for younger readers.[23]

To his admirers at the beginning of the century Milton was the one English poet fit to stand in the company of Homer and Virgil as having created an epic poem that was both national and universal. As if to make this very point, Joseph Trapp, Oxford's Professor of Poetry, translated *The Aeneid* into Miltonic blank verse, and then Milton's epic into Virgilian hexameters.[24] In *Paradise Lost* Britain offered the world the most universal poem of all. In his epic, Milton explored not only the widest possible reach of history and geography, but also the basic human experiences and emotions in their primal form: the first nature and growth, the first sinning and dying, the first questioning and arguing, the first marriage, the first pride, ambition, sexual desire, betrayal, guilt, forgiveness, the first heroism, and the first pathos; the universal sweep of his poem seemed to establish a totality containing all the world's material, divine and human. The Miltonic model was not limiting: for most poets it opened up new fields of exploration and represented range, variety, power, and daring. Thomas Marriott concluded: "Who reads lost Paradise all Knowledge gains, / That Book of *Milton* ev'ry Thing contains."[25] To engage with cosmic struggle or domestic dispute meant somehow engaging with Milton, and for a poet like Pope the eternal issues of Miltonic epic lay as much behind the choices that faced Belinda in *The Rape of the Lock* (1714) as behind his image of the apocalyptic "universal darkness" at the climax of *The Dunciad* (1743). As with Spenser, but more profoundly, the poet was widely imitated and then increasingly absorbed until he became part of the nation's literary bloodstream, so that his individual influence took its place within the embrace of a national literary history.

During the early years of the century two critical developments occurred simultaneously: Milton's reputation soared, and the reading public came to be fascinated by "the Sublime." This was no coincidence, as the poet and the theory seemed made for each other. In a ground-breaking critical discussion, Joseph Addison devoted a series of eighteen *Spectator* papers between January and May 1712 to an appreciation of *Paradise Lost*, and it was as a work of "Sublime Genius" (no. 303) that he particularly praised it. Addison demonstrated Milton's ability to "raise and terrifie the Reader's Imagination" and create astonishment with his bold thoughts and descriptions. In the opening decades of the century it was this Milton who was especially influential – not just in the Sublime, but also in its inversion, the mock-sublime or "heroicomical" mode. The same year, 1723, saw the publication of Thomas Newcomb's vast blank-verse epic, *The Last Judgment of Men and Angels. A Poem, in Twelve Books: After the Manner of Milton* (whose 12,383 lines outran its model) but also *The Bog-House, a Poem in Imitation of Milton*:

> Of Man's Important Bus'ness, and his Work
> Of Nature, late and early, ev'ry Day,
> Sing, my *Pierian* Muse, in Numbers sweet
> As is my Subject, voiding all thy Wit
> Uncostive, flowing forth in happiest Strains . . .[26]

It is useful to remember that Milton did not offer merely a heroic style to be parodied, but himself provided a model for how a formal poetic language could stretch itself from delight or terror to comedy and burlesque, and how those modes might be mixed. Episodes in *Paradise Lost* which show the perverting of heroic energies, such as the mining of Hell, the war in Heaven, or the building of Hell's bridge to Earth, exploit elements of grim burlesque.

Unlike Homer and Virgil, Milton develops a mock-epic of Lucifer and his followers at the heart of his true Christian epic, with one travestying the other: Satanic pride sinks to pettiness, an angel turns into a toad, a heroic speech becomes a humiliating hiss. Milton's divine Father is an ironist who watches Satan boast, rage, and busy himself in vain, much as Pope surveys the activities of his tribe of dunces. The Augustan satirists from Dryden onwards learned much from Milton about how to locate layers of pride and self-deception within a heroic language.

They did not, however, copy Milton's verse form. During the decades after Milton's death in 1674 the rhymed heroic couplet was supreme, and it was through Milton's early admirers that blank verse began to find a niche for itself in non-dramatic poetry. At this time, blank verse and "Miltonic verse" were practically synonymous.[27] The poet who did most to establish it as a popular poetic medium was John Philips, and it is significant that he inaugurated his career as Milton's poetical son through parody. In *The Splendid Shilling* (1701), one of the century's favorite comic poems,[28] a down-at-heel poet recounts his delights and disasters. Using the language of Britain's native epic he transforms his daily routine into a heroic struggle with the forces of nature: his well-worn breeches

> An horrid Chasm disclose, with Orifice
> Wide, Discontinuous; at which the Winds
> *Eurus* and *Auster*, and the dreadful Force
> Of *Boreas*, that congeals the *Cronian* Waves,
> Tumultuous enter　　　　　　　　　　　(lines 124–28)

As the stirring Miltonic paragraphs unfold, the garret-dweller finds a voice of increasing confidence and mastery which struggles free of rueful self-irony; swept up in his poetic aspirations he risks a final epic simile with its vivid picture of a shipwreck, but whereas the vessel "sinks found'ring in the vast Abyss" (line 143) the poem ends buoyantly, having generated its own linguistic confidence. There is no return to the garret. Philips's friend Edmund Smith remarked on how Milton's example had encouraged the poet's youthful boldness (setting him in opposition to some of the coffee-house wits), and how this was part of Philips's sense of his native literary inheritance:

> Rail on ye Triflers, who to *Will's* repair
> For new Lampoons, fresh Cant, or modish Air;
> Rail on at *Milton's* Son, who wisely bold
> Rejects new Phrases, and resumes the old:
> Thus *Chaucer* lives in younger *Spencer's* Strains[29]

The word "resumes," with its suggestion of returning, after an interruption, to the native tradition, is particularly telling. For the young Philips, says his earliest biographer George Sewell, Milton was the gateway to "the Force and Elegancy of his Mother-Tongue . . . by the Example of his Darling *Milton*, [he] searched backwards into the Works of our Old *English* Poets, to furnish himself with proper, sounding, and significant Expressions, and prove the due Extent, and Compass of the *Language*. For this purpose he carefully read over *Chaucer* and *Spenser*," and in his next poem, *Blenheim* (1705), written to celebrate Marlborough's victory, Philips showed that "he could use the same sublime and nervous Style as properly on a serious and heroick Subject."[30] The term "nervous" (what we would now call *sinewy*, a combination of strength and flexibility) was used to celebrate the controlled energy of Miltonic blank verse, and it was easy to see the patriotic implications of this native style: Edmund Smith paid the poet of *Blenheim* the ultimate compliment of surpassing Nicolas Boileau-Despreaux, the leading French poet of the day: "His nervous Verse great *Boileau*'s Strength transcends, / And *France* to *Philips*, as to *Churchill*, bends."[31]

At a time when English poetry seemed to have settled for competing with the French on their own neoclassical terms, Milton offered poets a confident voice and an unfettered style that could colonize new subjects. To the early Miltonists, rhyme was fussy, jingling, and restrictive,[32] whereas blank verse was able to project and explore, and build more ambitious structures. Isaac Watts spoke of Milton as "The noble Hater of degenerate Rhyme" who "Shook off the Chains, and built his Verse sublime, / A monument too high for coupled Sounds to climb."[33] With its suitability for accumulating material and growing substantial paragraphs of description or thought, the Miltonic voice seemed to catch the mood of national expansiveness. It was the natural choice for the seventeen-year-old Mark Akenside when he published his rousing call for a war with Spain, *The Voice of Liberty; or, a British Philippic. A Poem, in Miltonic Verse. Occasion'd by the Insults of the Spaniards* (1738):

> Yet, *Britons*, are ye cold?
> Yet deaf to Glory, Virtue, and the Call
> Of your dear, wrong'd, insulted Country? – No,
> I see ye are not; ev'ry Bosom glows
> With native Greatness, and in all its State
> The *British* Spirit rises. Glorious Change![34]

Satanic vaunting could be redeemed by youthful patriotism. In the pro-Wilkes *Liberty. A Poem. In Imitation of Milton* (1763) the anonymous author ends by invoking Miltonic epic, looking forward to the day when Britons will reclaim their freedoms and "Dear LIBERTY at last, by us REGAIN'D, / With its Attendants, Virtue, Plenty, Peace, / Fully atones for

Paradise once Lost." Blank verse could appropriately be associated with British liberty and with the nation's recovery of a more pristine classicism untainted by the French. One poet praised Milton's followers as those "Bold British Bards, who re-assume / The free-born Rights of Greece and Rome; / While slavish France in jingling Strain / Drags on, yet hugs the servile Chain."[35] Milton himself had given warrant for this by declaring in a prefatory note that his epic was "an example set, the first in *English*, of ancient liberty recoverd to Heroic Poem from the troublesom and modern bondage of Rimeing." One critic, Daniel Webb, describes his sense of rhyme's restrictiveness in contrast to the liberating possibilities that blank verse offered:

> The perpetual returns of similar impressions lie like weights upon our spirits, and oppress the imagination. Strong passions, the warm effusions of the soul, were never destined to creep through monotonous parallels; they call for a more liberal rhythmus; for movements, not balanced by rule, but measured by sentiment, and flowing in ever new yet musical proportions.[36]

This passage combines two principles crucial to the eighteenth-century Miltonic tradition: the dynamic and the organic. Miltonic writing is particularly interested in movement and growth, and in conveying a sense of continuity. Webb suggests that blank verse is an appropriate medium for the "more liberal rhythmus" of Sensibility; but such possibilities are also useful for a philosophical poem like Mark Akenside's *The Pleasures of Imagination* (1744), which explores "what high, capacious pow'rs / Lie folded up in man" (1, lines 222–23) and how the Platonic divine mind lovingly extends itself into an organic creation. It is ironic that some of the best examples of eighteenth-century Miltonism are deeply inimical to Milton's own political and religious convictions – while some of the worst are wholly in tune with them.

In no area are the principles of movement and growth more notable than in the genre of blank-verse georgic. John Philips was once again the innovator here, and his Miltonic *Cyder* (1708) set a fashion for poems (based on the *Georgics* of Virgil) describing the cultivation of nature's raw materials and the processes used to transform them. The English georgic poem showed how a less heroic and more varied strain could be drawn from *Paradise Lost*, particularly from those books describing life in the garden. Through this genre, patriotic fervor worked a richer and quieter seam during the century. Britain's natural resources were celebrated alongside the human energies that harnessed them. In its early years the georgic poem represented the world of labor into which Adam and Eve had walked at the close of Milton's epic. But it offered a landscape that looked towards redemption. Philips's favorite cider-apple is the Red Streak, whose "pulpous Fruit" is "Tempting, not fatal" (1, line 515), and whose inspiration even compensates for its ancestor's role in the Fall: "I perceive / Her sacred Virtue. See! the Numbers flow / Easie, whilst, chear'd with her nectareous Juice, / Hers, and my Country's Praises I exalt" (1, lines 520–23). The direct echo of Eve's fatal address to her tree suggests the redemptive possibilities linking nature and Miltonic verse in eighteenth-century Britain.[37] But the most extreme statement of the spiritual potential of blank verse came from Milton's admirer, Edward Young, when he declared it to be "verse unfallen, uncurst; verse reclaim'd, reinthron'd in the true *language of the Gods*."[38]

James Thomson was the poet who best exploited the capacity of Miltonic verse to range from the soaring and sonorous to the detailed and observant. In *The Seasons* (1730) he employs less a "middle" style than one which uses to the full the range of resources that the eighteenth century recognized in their national poem – the freedom it offered to explore the world before them. In this Thomson happily associated himself with Milton and his heir, "PHILLIPS, *Pomona*'s Bard, the second thou / Who nobly durst, in Rhyme-unfetter'd Verse, / With BRITISH Freedom sing the BRITISH song" (*Autumn*, lines 645–47). Placing his poem in the line of succession, Thomson celebrates that "active" and "various Spirit" of the apple which, inherited from Milton, had been Philips's "*Native* theme, and boon Inspirer" (644). The same organic principle informs Thomson's verse. His nature is simultaneously an expansive force and a more hidden power working within:

> By Nature's swift and secret-working Hand,
> The Garden glows, and fills the liberal Air
> With lavish Fragrance; while the promis'd Fruit
> Lies yet a little Embryo, unperceiv'd,
> Within its crimson Folds.   (*Spring*, lines 97–100)

Thomson's verse exemplifies Daniel Webb's "movements . . . measured by sentiment," an organic concept of poetic form in which thought and feeling find their shape across the lines and speech rhythms play against the pentameter pulse – as at the moment of Adam and Eve's parting in *Paradise Lost*: "Thus saying, from her Husbands hand her hand / Soft she withdrew" (IX, lines 385–86). Thomson learned from Milton how words or phrasal units can be reordered and juxtaposed so as to elicit their full significance, and an adjective made palpable as a noun:

> Th'uncurling Floods, diffus'd
> In glassy Breadth, seem thro' delusive Lapse
> Forgetful of their Course. 'Tis Silence all,
> And pleasing Expectation.   (*Spring*, lines 159–62)

Even at a moment of extreme calm, Thomson is aware of the latent energies stored within language.

Later writers of blank-verse georgics such as William Somerville in *The Chace* (1735), John Armstrong in *The Art of Preserving Health* (1744), and Christopher Smart in *The Hop-Garden* (1752), deliberately stretched their poems to include digressive, even exotic, elements, or took up technical subjects which demanded an ingeniously wrought vocabulary; the results may sometimes be awkward, but the linguistic daring is undoubted. John Dyer's *The Fleece* (1757) celebrates "ev'ry airy woof, / Cheyney, and bayse, and serge, and alepine, / Tammy, and crape" (III, lines 480–2) as if they are a roll-call of angels. In poems like these, Milton's example suggests that no subject is out of poetry's reach, and a work need not be an epic in order to accommodate the widest range of tones and topics. One of the greatest poems in the Miltonic tradition, Cowper's *The Task* (1785), sets itself the challenge of finding a way from the mock-heroic sofa of its beginning out into the wider fields of politics and philosophy, and Cowper (who had studied *Paradise Lost* in depth) develops from the Miltonic tradition a blank verse that is immensely supple and resourceful. But it is his late fragment, *Yardley Oak* (1792), which best illustrates how much this tradition had by the century's end become part of a poet's sense of his nation's history:

> While thus through all the stages thou hast push'd
> Of tree-ship, first a seedling hid in grass,
> Then twig, then saplin, and as century rolled
> Slow after century, a giant bulk
> Of girth enormous with moss-cushion'd root
> Upheav'd above the soil, and sides imboss'd
> With prominent wens globose, till at the last
> The rottenness which Time is charged to inflict
> On other Mighty Ones found also Thee–   (lines 60–68)

At the heart of this unfolding passage, time itself moves with a Miltonic tread ("as century rolled / Slow after century"); the venerable oak with its "wens globose" and "excoriate forks deform" demands a vocabulary with ancient roots, just as the root-system of the tree, however corrupt its superstructure, remains sound ("The Spring / Thee finds not less alive to her sweet force," lines 132–33). By the 1790s, the recovered voices of Spenser and Milton had helped create a living root-system for English poetry, and Keats and Wordsworth would draw sustenance from it, both directly and through the eighteenth-century tradition.

During the second half of the century the achievement of Alexander Pope complicated this picture of a single continuous line of poetic development.

A delighted reader of Chaucer and Spenser from his early teens, Pope learned his craft by reworking them as well as Homer and Virgil. That said, the years immediately following Pope's death in 1744 saw a generation of young poets enter the scene who shared a curiosity about their English literary past and an interest in recovering its language, but for whom Pope was an uneasy and ambivalent presence.[39] One text in particular reveals how difficult it seemed to place Pope's recent achievement within the native tradition.

In a belated tribute the young Cambridge poet, William Mason (1724–97), published his pastoral elegy *Musæus: a Monody to the Memory of Mr Pope* in 1747. In imitation of the procession of mourners in Milton's *Lycidas* (1637), the dying Pope is visited in his grotto by Chaucer, Spenser, and Milton. Each speaks to Musaeus (Pope) in turn, and in his own distinctive style. Chaucer laments that his language has suffered decay over the centuries: "Old Time, which alle things don maliciously, / Gnawen with rusty tooth continually, / Gnattrid my lines, that they all cancrid ben" (p. 9), and he praises Pope's youthful versions of *The Merchant's Tale* and *The Wife of Bath's Prologue* for making his verses flow smoothly again. Next Spenser, in the stanza of *The Faerie Queene*, praises *The Rape of the Lock* as an allegorical fable surpassing his own: Pope's heroine outshines his Una and Florimel ("Belinda far surpast my beauties sheen, / Belinda, subject meet for such soft lay I ween," p. 11). A different note is then struck by Milton ("a bard of more exalted tread") who congratulates Pope on having won him back to rhyme:

> I such bonds
> Aim'd to destroy, mistaking . . .
> Thou cam'st, and at thy magic touch the chains
> Off dropt, and (passing strange!) soft-wreathed bands
> Of flow'rs their place supply'd: which well the Muse
> Might wear for choice, not force; obstruction none,
> But lov'liest ornament.   (p. 15)

Then, as if turning aside from his great epic, Milton looks around admiringly at Pope's grotto and begins to speak in the language of his own early *Masque* ("all these slowly-dripping rills, / That tinkling stray amid the cooly cave"). Both poets are reminded of the freshness of their youthful verses, and are put in touch with their more fanciful earlier selves. But at this intriguing moment Pope jolts into life and interrupts Milton disapprovingly in rather preachy couplets:

> Ah! why recall the toys of thoughtless youth?
> When flow'ry fiction held the place of truth;
> When fancy rul'd; when trill'd each trivial strain,
> But idly sweet, and elegantly vain.   (p. 17)

Jarring against the lyric note that has just been sounded, this language emphasizes poetry's responsibility to uphold morality and "sway the judgment." Pope presents himself as the didactic poet of *An Essay on Man* who celebrated Virtue and the "moral plan." None of his three visitors is heard from again. The response comes from a fourth arrival, the female figure of "Virtue," who suddenly swoops down to declare Pope her champion, and the poet dies in her arms. After this intervention and the intrusive didactic note of Pope's couplets, which have disrupted his own elegy much as St. Peter's speech interrupted *Lycidas*, the poem reverts for its final lines to pastoral elegy and the imagery of Spenser and the early Milton:

> Then wept the Nymphs; witness, ye waving shades!
> Witness, ye winding streams! the Nymphs did weep . . .
> And now down-dropt the larks, and ceas'd their strain:
> They ceas'd, and with them ceas'd the shepherd swain.
>
> (pp. 20–22)

Mason's *Musæus* is an oddly contradictory poem. It praises Pope but ends by distancing him from his predecessors. The generous concessions all three visitors make (Chaucer on Pope's elegant modernizations, Spenser on his sophisticated Belinda, and Milton on his rhyming couplets) tend to stress the eighteenth-century poet's difference from them. Most startlingly, Pope disowns his pre-1717 poetry (which included *The Rape of the Lock* and *Eloisa to Abelard*) written when he was most under their influence. If Mason wanted to make the encounter an uneasy one, then he succeeded. His Pope is content to embrace Virtue rather than his fellow-poets. Ostensibly a warm tribute to a dead genius, Mason's poem is also a young man's bid for poetic fame. Chaucer, Spenser, and Milton speak through him, and he is able to show off his mastery of their individual rhythms, vocabulary, phrasing, and imagery. By the end of the poem it seems as if this young poet is more the true heir of the immortals than Pope himself.

Mason gives us the older poets in their own language, and this is significant. Rather than merely apply an antique cast to their words he takes artistic care in capturing the original inflections of each voice, while remarkably managing to show a familial resemblance between them. Chaucer's beautiful image of how Pope smoothed out his "rough song" to make it flow ("this lite rivere / Stealen forth by, making plesaunt murmere") shows what Spenser would take from the fourteenth-century poet, and Mason's other recreated passages reveal similar continuities between Spenser and Milton: Mason understands how *Lycidas* and the *Masque* echo Spenserian pastoral and romance. His reworkings push beyond parody and antiquarianism: in a creative way they combine imaginative sympathy with a sense of literary history.

Mason was just one of several young men in the 1740s who stepped forward to claim the discarded mantle of the old poets. In the same month as *Musæus*, and via the same publisher, the nineteen-year-old Thomas Warton published a poem suffused with the imagery of Spenser and Milton, *The Pleasures of Melancholy* (1747), in which the speaker turns away from civilized society and finds imaginative excitement in searching out traces of the "Antick" and "Barb'rous" at a series of abandoned places. As if reaching back beyond a century of sociable civility to the uncouth poetic language of the past, Warton's melancholy man looks for inspiration in caves, ruins, and charnel-houses, places that seem to speak only of loss and decay, but which can reanimate the poet. For him they represent excited discovery and imaginative arousal. This is what the recovered old poetry came to mean for many young writers of mid century. It was the opposite of mere decoration ("Trickt in Antique Ruff and Bonnet," as Dr. Johnson sneeringly remarked[40]), but represented an imaginative stimulus that challenged the tastes of the former generation, Addison's so-called "understanding age."

The Pleasures of Melancholy repeats Mason's comparison between Pope's Belinda and Spenser's Una, but decides the outcome differently:

> Thro' POPE's soft song tho' all the Graces breath,
> And happiest art adorn his Attic page;
> Yet does my mind with sweeter transport glow,
> As at the foot of some hoar oak reclin'd,
> In magic SPENSER's wildly-warbled song
> I see deserted Una wander wide
> Thro' wasteful solitudes, and lurid heaths,
> Weary, forlorn, than when the fated Fair,
> Upon the bosom bright of silver Thames,
> Launches in all the lustre of Brocade . . .   (lines 153–62)

The passage ends with a satiric swirl: Belinda's restless glitter belongs to art, not nature. For Warton in his guise as the melancholy visionary it is Spenser who opens the magic casement of the poet's imagination into a world of romance. His response to Spenser is not passive, but argumentative and experimental: there is something daring in the way Warton seizes on the most unanimating ideas – the aimless, wasteful and weary – to show that poetry need not be full of busy present things, but can stretch the imagination to a world more distant. His return from this wilderness to Belinda's sudden glory takes the extra risk of setting sprightly Popean wit alongside his own languid sublime. While playing this aesthetic game, however, the poet grounds himself at the foot of an ancient oak tree – an image of strength and continuity with its historic roots in the native soil.

It was partly through the work of the Warton brothers that a concept of literary history began to have an impact on poetry during the 1740s and 50s. Their historical scholarship and literary criticism helped redirect poetic taste towards the romance tradition. It could even be said that they had a joint project to turn the tide against politeness and wit. Thomas Warton's *Observations on the Faerie Queene* (1754) represents the earliest full-scale example of English historical literary criticism, discussing Spenser's poem sympathetically within its period context of Elizabethan courtly entertainments and romance narratives. Rather than judge Spenser by classical rules, Warton recontextualizes him as a "Romantic Poet" who draws on myth and legend, medieval metrical romances, Ariosto, and the Arthurian story of Malory's *Morte Darthur*. In a thirteen-page digression he offers a brief narrative of literary history, placing *The Faerie Queene* as the culmination of a visionary allegorical tradition that stretches from Chaucer through Shakespeare and the early Milton to the Restoration of 1660, at which point, he says, "imagination gave way to correctness; sublimity of description to delicacy of sentiment, and striking imagery to conceit and epigram."[41]

Where his brother advanced the cause of Spenser, Joseph Warton set out to demote Pope. In his *Essay on the Writings and Genius of Pope* (1756) he argues that by pursuing the didactic and moral vein Pope had cut himself off from the "first class" of English poets, "our only three sublime and pathetic poets; Spenser, Shakespeare, Milton." It was they who represented what Warton liked to call "pure poetry,"[42] and his inclusion of Shakespeare reflects the extent to which the great dramatist was being assimilated into the native poetic tradition at this period (he was not one of Pope's "landmarks" in 1736). In making this judgment Warton was developing views he had expressed in the "Advertisement" to his *Odes on Various Subjects* (1746): "as he looks upon Invention and Imagination to be the chief faculties of a Poet, so he will be happy if the following Odes may be look'd upon as an attempt to bring back Poetry into its right channel." In describing his poems as "fanciful and descriptive" Warton hardly needed to mention Spenser and the early Milton in order to define what the "right channel" was, and to suggest that the nation's poetry had lost its way over the previous hundred years. If critics at the beginning of the century had rejected the language of Spenser and Milton as being no longer "current," Warton intends to show that it is they who have cut themselves off from the current of true poetry. His dynamic image presents the task as rechannelling poetry in order to connect it with its true sources.[43]

Joseph Warton's opening "Ode to Fancy" ("Fancy" and "Imagination" were interchangeable at this period) celebrates the volume's presiding spirit. His immediate model is Milton's diptych of *L'Allegro* and *Il Penseroso*, and in reworking these youthful poems, which are a tissue of allusions to earlier poets including Chaucer, Spenser, Shakespeare, Jonson, and Drayton, Warton is also tapping into the native poetic tradition. Imagination is the connecting link:

> Then lay me by the haunted stream
> Wrapt in some wild, poetic dream,
> In converse while methinks I rove
> With SPENSER thro' a fairy grove   (p. 7)

In imitating Milton the poet feels he is conversing with Spenser and being introduced to the spirit of romance, to "Such sights as youthfull Poets dream / On summer eeves by haunted stream" (*L'Allegro*, lines 129–30). As Warton's imagination guides him through various scenes and emotions he beckons Fancy away from Shakespeare's tomb ("On which thou lov'st to sit at eve, / Musing o'er your darling's grave") towards the present age so that she can inspire some eighteenth-century poet, who "May boldly smite the sounding lyre, / Who with some new, unequall'd song, / May rise above the rhyming throng." The poem ends with Warton's vision of a revived national poetry:

> Teach him to scorn with frigid art
> Feebly to touch th'unraptur'd heart . . .
> With native beauties win applause,
> Beyond cold critic's studied laws:
> O let each Muse's fame encrease,
> O bid BRITANNIA rival GREECE!   (p. 11)

The Wartonian agenda for a national poetry on the ancient Greek model can only be achieved by reviving the "native beauties" of the Chaucer–Spenser–Shakespeare–Milton tradition. The Wartons' poetry of echoes plays repeatedly across this stave, as if to define a lost music which they want people to hear again.

The odes of Thomas Gray and William Collins explore the difficulty and excitement of catching these notes from the literary past. Collins's "Ode on the Poetical Character" (1747) is a rueful recognition that Milton may be the last poet to speak with godlike power, but it is also a young poet's dedication of himself to Fancy ("to me Divinest Name") in whose gift that power is. In Gray's ode, "The Progress of Poesy" (1757), the speaker hesitantly takes up the "Lyre divine" and wakes it to music; but "The Bard" (1757) ends with the old poet hearing the sounds of Spenser, Shakespeare, and Milton in the distance as he plunges to his death: what are Gray's voices of the past are for him the voices of the future. The old magic songs may continue beyond his hearing.[44]

In the introduction to his edition of Milton's early poems (1785), Thomas Warton looked back at the developments in the national poetry over the previous forty years:

> A visible revolution succeeded in the general cast and character of the national composition. Our versification contracted a new colouring, a new structure and phraseology; and the school of Milton rose in emulation of the school of Pope.[45]

Leaving unfinished his mighty *History of English Poetry* (3 vols., 1774–81), Warton had turned to edit Milton partly in reaction to Samuel Johnson's *Lives of the Poets* (1779–81), in which the critic set out to devalue, and even dismantle, the eighteenth-century tradition springing from Spenser and Milton. In *Rambler* 121 Johnson had attacked imitators of Spenser: "they seem to conclude, that when they have disfigured their lines with a few obsolete syllables, they have accomplished their design." The *Lives*, however, caused particular offence to Milton's admirers with their harsh treatment of the poet's character and the tart comments on popular works such as *Lycidas*, the *Masque,* and *Paradise Lost* ("The want of human interest is always felt. *Paradise Lost* is one of the books which the reader admires and lays down, and forgets to take up again . . . Its perusal is a duty rather than a pleasure").[46] Striking at Milton's role as the great national poet, Johnson criticized his "foreign idiom,"[47] and throughout the *Lives* showed his strong distaste for the poets of Warton's "school of Milton," the "brethren of the blank song."[48] For Johnson, blank verse was by nature undisciplined, with a tendency to become "crippled prose";[49] it was unsuited to common subjects, betrayed thought into self-indulgence, and was usually "in description exuberant, in argument loquacious, and in narration tiresome."[50] Imitating Milton encouraged two things Johnson hated: the distortion of a natural word-order and the importation of obsolete words. His comments on John Philips's *Blenheim* are representative:

> Deformity is easily copied; and whatever there is in Milton which the reader wishes away, all that is obsolete, peculiar, or licentious is accumulated with great care by Philips. Milton's verse was harmonious, in proportion to the general state of our metre in Milton's age, and, if he had written after the improvements made by Dryden, it is reasonable to believe that he would have admitted a more pleasing modulation of numbers into his work.[51]

Johnson brings us back to Dryden's response to Milton's outdated language. In the *Lives* he advances his conviction that the work of Waller, Dryden, and Pope in refining poetry during the century before 1744 had been the true national achievement, and the Spenser–Milton tradition a regrettable falling away. On the matter of versification, Pope's heroic couplets were supreme:

"New sentiments and new images others may produce, but to attempt any further improvement of versification will be dangerous."[52] To an acute observer of the literary scene in 1782, it was clear from Johnson's *Lives* and the responses to them that two schools of poetic taste were in opposition:

> I think it is not difficult to perceive, that the admirers of English poetry are divided into two parties. The objects of their love are, perhaps, of equal beauty, though they greatly differ in their air, their dress, the turn of their features, and their complexion. On one side, are the lovers and imitators of Spenser and Milton; and on the other, those of Dryden, Boileau, and Pope.[53]

Vicesimus Knox devotes the rest of his essay to bringing the two sides together and seeing excellences in both. But he feels that Johnson has missed a golden opportunity to present "the Body of English Poetry" by leaving out Spenser and Shakespeare, and his contemporaries Goldsmith, Beattie, Mason, and the Wartons. For Knox, as he draws the two schools into a single embrace, the national poetry is a rich and varied historical legacy that continues to flourish, and the disputes over the canon are in fact a sign of its greatness: "the active and polished genius of this nation seems capable of surmounting all obstacles in letters, as its manly spirit has ultimately borne all before it in the unhappy contests of war."[54]

NOTES

1 See Trevor Ross, "The Emergence of Literature: Making and Reading the English Canon in the Eighteenth Century," *ELH* 63 (1996), 397–422; and Richard Terry, "Literature, Aesthetics, and Canonicity in the Eighteenth Century," *Eighteenth-Century Life* 21 (Feb 1997), 80–101; see also pp. 102–7 and the resulting "Forum on Canon Formation, Part II," 21 (Nov. 1997), 79–99.

2 Joseph Spence, *Observations*, ed. James M. Osborn (Oxford: Clarendon Press, 1966), I, 178.

3 Trevor Ross, in *The Making of the English Literary Canon* (Montreal and Kingston: McGill–Queen's University Press, 1998), charts the shift from a "rhetorical" to an "objectivist" canon for consumers.

4 Richard Daniel, *The British Warriour, a Poem* (1706), p. 3 (Foxon D27). John Hughes remarked: "we have two Antient *English* Poets, *Chaucer* and *Spenser*, who . . . seem to have taken deep Root, like old *British* Oaks, and to flourish in defiance of all the Injuries of Time and Weather" (*Works of Edmund Spenser* [1715], I, xxvi).

5 John Dryden, Preface to *Fables Ancient and Modern* (1700), sig B2v.

6 See W Jackson Bate, *The Burden of the Past and the English Poet* (London: Chatto & Windus, 1971); Harold Bloom, *The Anxiety of Influence: a Theory of Poetry* (New York: Oxford University Press, 1973).

7 For Paul Sherwin, for example, "There is no purer instance of the adolescent experience in English literature than Collins's poetic life (and death) cycle" (*Precious Bane: Collins and the Miltonic Legacy* [Austin: University of Texas Press, 1977], p. 4).

8 See Howard D. Weinbrot, *Britannia's Issue: the Rise of British Literature from Dryden to Ossian* (Cambridge: Cambridge University Press, 1993), pp. 405–74.

9 *The Satires of Decimus Junius Juvenalis Translated into English Verse* (1693), pp. l, viii. Cf. Francis Atterbury's description of Spenser's vocabulary as "like old Coyns, one must go to the Antiquary to understand their true meaning and value" (*Edmund Spenser: the Critical Heritage*, ed. R. M. Cummings [London: Routledge, 1971], pp. 302–3).

10 "To Dr Samuel Garth" (anon.), in *Luctus Britannici: or the Tears of the British Muses; for the Death of John Dryden, Esq.* (1700), p. 55.

11 *The Miscellaneous Works of Joseph Addison*, ed. A.C. Guthkelch (London, 1914), I, 31–2.

12 London: John Morphew, 1716 (Foxon B501).

13 Probably by William Pittis (Foxon P431).

14 For an account of how Spenser was exploited for political purposes between 1706 and 1742, see Christine Gerrard, *The Patriot Opposition to Walpole* (Oxford: Clarendon Press, 1994), pp. 174–84.

15 William Shenstone, *Poems upon Various Occasions* (Oxford, 1737), p. 17.

16 "Spenser is the most descriptive and rural of all our English writers" (William Thompson, *A Description of May* [1746–47], preface).

17 [Dodsley] *Collection of Poems* (2nd. edn., 1748), I, 252.

18 *Areopagitica* (1644), *Complete Prose Works of John Milton*, ed. Don M. Wolfe et al., 8 vols. (New Haven: Yale University Press, 1953–82), II, 516.

19 *The Faerie Queene* tended to be enjoyed by the young: Cowley, Dryden, Pope, Thomson, Thomas Warton, and Chatterton all read it as children. See Richard C. Frushell, "Spenser and the Eighteenth-Century Schools," *Spenser Studies* 7 (1986), 175–98.

20 [Dodsley] *Collection of Poems* (2nd. edn., 1748), II, 120.

21 Still valuable is R. D. Havens, *The Influence of Milton on English Poetry* (Cambridge, MA: Harvard University Press, 1922); an argument for Milton's creative influence is Dustin Griffin, *Regaining Paradise: Milton and the Eighteenth Century* (Cambridge: Cambridge University Press, 1986).

22 William Massey, *Remarks upon Paradise Lost* (1761), p. iii, quoted by Havens, *The Influence of Milton*, p. 25; *Lives of the English Poets*, ed. George Birkbeck Hill (Oxford University Press, 1905), II, 147 (Addison).

23 See Havens, *The Influence of Milton*, pp 3–43.

24 *The Æneis of Virgil*, 2 vols. (1718–20); *Johannis Miltoni Paradisus amissus*, 2 vols. (1741–44).

25 Thomas Marriott, *Female Conduct: Being an Essay on the Art of Pleasing* (1759), p. 99.

26 *Serious and Cleanly Meditations upon a House of Office . . To which is added, The Bog-House, a Poem in Imitation of Milton* (1723), p. 11. Not listed by Good or Havens.

27 See Havens, *The Influence of Milton*, p. 78.

28 In *Tatler* 249 (11 Nov 1710) Addison praised *The Splendid Shilling* as "the finest Burlesque Poem in the *British* Language." In 1719 Francis Peck remarked on "the Novelty of Blank Verse, with the Beauties of which the generality of Readers (before *Milton* and *Philips* appeared) were so little acquainted, that they hardly

knew what it was" (*Sighs Upon the never enough Lamented Death of Queen Anne. In Imitation of Milton*, p. xi).

29 Edmund Smith, "A Poem to the Memory of Mr John Philips," in *The Works of Mr. Edmund Smith* (1714), p. 81.

30 *Poems Attempted in the Style of Milton. By Mr. John Philips. With his Life by Dr. [George] Sewell*, 10th. edn. (London: E. Curll, 1744), pp. vii, xv.

31 *Works of Edmund Smith*, p. 78.

32 See the material gathered by Havens, *The Influence of Milton*, pp 44–53, and by John Walter Good, *Studies in the Milton Tradition* (Urbana: University of Illinois Press, 1915), pp. 203–8 (Illinois Studies in Language and Literature, vol. I, nos. 3–4). In the preface to his *Sighs* (1719) Francis Peck commented that Dryden "doated upon Rhime, and was charmed with the Tinkling of his Chains" (p. xvi).

33 Isaac Watts, "The Adventurous Muse," lines 48–50, in *Horae Lyricae* (2nd. edn., 1709), pp. 210–13.

34 In a later *British Philippic* (1756), Joseph Reed also used Milton as a stick to beat his contemporaries: "Th'immortal Bard . . In vain would strike his Epic Lyre, to raise / Th'inactive Spirit of this drousy Isle / To that unconquerable Height, to which / Our venerable Ancestry aspir'd" (pp. 7–8).

35 [Anon], "To the Hon. Lieut. Gen'l Cholmondeley," quoted by Good, *Studies in the Milton Tradition*, pp. 66–67.

36 Daniel Webb, *Observations on the Correspondence between Poetry and Music* (1769), p. 113.

37 See Griffin, *Regaining Paradise*, pp. 101–33.

38 Edward Young, *Conjectures on Original Composition* (1759), p. 60.

39 The implications of this are explored by Robert J. Griffin, *Wordsworth's Pope: a Study in Literary Historiography* (Cambridge: Cambridge University Press, 1995).

40 Recorded by Mrs. Piozzi. See *Samuel Johnson: the Complete English Poems*, ed. J. D. Fleeman (New Haven: Yale University Press, 1971), pp. 132, 223.

41 Thomas Warton, *Observations on the Faerie Queene* (1754), p. 237.

42 *Essay*, pp. xi, iv. Joseph Warton admired Pope's great example of the "sublime and pathetic," *Eloisa to Abelard*. This Ovidian epistle steeped in the visionary melancholy of Milton's *Il Penseroso* tended to become a favorite with those who found most of Pope uncongenial.

43 In his preface to *Winter* (1726) James Thomson urged: "let POETRY, once more, be restored to her antient Truth, and Purity."

44 "The Progress of Poesy" (originally entitled "Ode in the Greek Manner") and "The Bard" were influenced by Gray's researches for a history of English poetry abandoned in 1762.

45 Milton, *Poems upon Several Occasions*, ed. Thomas Warton (1785), pp. x–xi.

46 *Lives*, I, 183 (Milton) "His treatment of Milton is unmercifull to the last Degree," Cowper–Unwin, 31 Oct. 1779 (*The Letters and Prose Writings of William Cowper*, ed. James King and Charles Ryskamp [Oxford: Clarendon Press, 1979], I, 307).

47 *Lives*, I, 190 (Milton).

48 *Lives*, III, 418 (Akenside).

49 *Lives*, II, 320 (Somerville).

50 *Lives*, III, 418 (Akenside). Johnson, however, admired *The Seasons*, arguing that Thomson's blank verse was not Miltonic: "His numbers, his pauses, his diction, are of his own growth, without transcription, without imitation" (*Lives*, III, 298).

51 *Lives*, I, 318 (John Philips).

52 *Lives*, III, 251 Probably also in response to Johnson's *Lives*, Joseph Warton completed and published the second volume of his *Essay on Pope* (1782). See James Allison, "Joseph Warton's Reply to Dr Johnson's *Lives*," *Journal of English and Germanic Philology* 51 (1952), 186–91.

53 Vicesimus Knox, *Essays Moral and Literary* (1782), II, 186 (no. CXXIX, "On the Prevailing Taste in Poetry"). The dispute over the status of Pope would continue into the next century with the controversy between Lord Byron and the Wartons' protégé, William Lisle Bowles. See James Chandler, "The Pope Controversy: Romantic Poetics and the English Canon," *Critical Inquiry* 10 (March 1984), 481–509.

54 *Essays*, II, 188.

FURTHER READING

Bate, W. Jackson. *The Burden of the Past and the English Poet*. London: Chatto & Windus, 1971.

Bloom, Harold. *The Anxiety of Influence: a Theory of Poetry*. New York: Oxford University Press, 1973.

Chalker, John. *The English Georgic: a Study in the Development of a Form*. London: Routledge & Kegan Paul, 1969.

Dowling, William C. "Ideology and the Flight from History in Eighteenth-Century Poetry," in Leo Damrosch (ed.), *The Profession of Eighteenth-Century Literature: Reflections on an Institution*. Madison: University of Wisconsin Press, 1992. 135–53.

Frushell, Richard C. "Spenser and the Eighteenth-Century Schools," *Spenser Studies* 7 (1986), 175–98.

   "Imitations and Adaptations, 1660–1800," *The Spenser Encyclopedia*, gen. ed. A. C. Hamilton. Toronto and Buffalo: University of Toronto Press, 1990. 396–403.

Good, John Walter. *Studies in the Milton Tradition*. Illinois Studies in Language and Literature, vol. 1. nos. 3–4. Urbana: University of Illinois Press, 1915.

Griffin, Dustin. *Regaining Paradise: Milton and the Eighteenth Century*. Cambridge: Cambridge University Press, 1986.

Griffin, Robert J. *Wordsworth's Pope: a Study in Literary Historiography*. Cambridge: Cambridge University Press, 1995.

Guillory, John. *Poetic Authority: Spenser, Milton, and Literary History*. New York: Columbia University Press, 1983.

Havens, R. D., *The Influence of Milton on English Poetry*. Cambridge, MA: Harvard University Press, 1922.

Johnston, Arthur. *Enchanted Ground: the Study of Medieval Romance in the Eighteenth Century*. University of London: Athlone Press, 1964.

   "Poetry and Criticism after 1740," *History of Literature in the English Language*, vol. 4: *Dryden to Johnson*, ed. Roger Lonsdale. London: Barrie & Jenkins, 1971. 357–98.

Kramnick, Jonathan Brody. *Making the English Canon: Print-Capitalism and the Cultural Past, 1700–1770*. Cambridge: Cambridge University Press, 1998.

Kucich, Greg. *Keats, Shelley, and Romantic Spenserianism*. University Park: Pennsylvania State University Press, 1991.

Levine, Joseph M. "Eighteenth-Century Historicism and the First Gothic Revival," *Humanism and History*. Ithaca: Cornell University Press, 1987. 190–213.

Moore, Leslie E. *Beautiful Sublime: the Making of* Paradise Lost, *1701–1734*. Stanford: Stanford University Press, 1990.

Patey, Douglas Lane. "The Eighteenth Century Invents the Canon," *Modern Language Studies* 18 (1988), 17–37.

Ross, Trevor. *The Making of the English Literary Canon*. Montreal and Kingston: McGill–Queen's University Press, 1998.

Sitter, John. *Literary Loneliness in Mid-Eighteenth-Century England*. Ithaca and London: Cornell University Press, 1982.

Uphaus, Robert W. "Vicesimus Knox and the Canon of Eighteenth-Century Literature," *The Age of Johnson* 4 (1991), 345–61.

Wasserman, Earl R. *Elizabethan Poetry in the Eighteenth Century*. Illinois Studies in Language and Literature, vol. 32: nos. 2–3. Urbana: University of Illinois, 1947.

Weinbrot, Howard D. *Britannia's Issue: the Rise of British Literature from Dryden to Ossian*. Cambridge: Cambridge University Press, 1993.

10

RALPH COHEN

The return to the ode

But if I may be allowed to speak my mind modestly, and without injury to his [Cowley's] sacred ashes, somewhat of the purity of English, somewhat of more equal thoughts, somewhat of sweetness in the numbers, in one word, somewhat of a finer turn and more lyrical verse, is yet wanting.

John Dryden, "Preface to *Sylvæ*"

In December 1746, Joseph Warton published *Odes on Various Subjects*, and later in the same month his friend William Collins published *Odes on Several Descriptive and Allegoric Subjects*. Joseph Warton, in his "Advertisement" introducing his odes, urged readers to look upon these poems "as an attempt to bring back Poetry into its right channel." These odes were examples of "invention" and "imagination"; and they were his effort to restore British poetry to its classical heritage. The "Advertisement" read as follows:

> The Public has been so much accustom'd of late to didactic Poetry alone, and Essays on moral Subjects, that any work where the imagination is much indulged, will perhaps not be relished or regarded. The author therefore of these pieces is in some pain least certain austere critics should think them too fanciful and descriptive. But as he is convinced that the fashion of moralizing in verse has been carried too far, and as he looks upon Invention and Imagination to be the chief faculties of a Poet, so he will be happy if the following Odes may be look'd upon as an attempt to bring back Poetry into its right channel.[1]

That Joseph Warton and William Collins chose the "ode" in which "to bring back Poetry into its right channel" was a considerable challenge. Although Dryden and Pope had written formal odes to music and Cowley had written irregular Pindaric odes, the ode as a form was little used by the Augustans. Mark Akenside in his *Odes on Several Subjects* published in 1745 remarked in his "Advertisement": "From what the ancients have left of this kind, perhaps the Ode may be allow'd the most amiable species of poetry; but certainly, there is none which in modern languages has been generally attempted with so little success."[2] The question for Akenside, Warton, and Collins was why attempt the ode that had proven so unsuccessful for modern poets yet so successful for the ancients. Akenside's answer was given in his ode "On Lyric Poetry," "lyric" referring to classical poetry accompanied by the lyre. After mentioning classical ode writers such as Anacreon, Alcaeus, Sappho, and Pindar, Akenside concluded his poem with an assertion of his poetic self, a self whose "prophetic mind" was beyond the poet's capacity to control:

> But when from envy and from death to claim
> A hero bleeding for his native land;
> When to throw incense on the vestal flame
> Of liberty my genius gives command,
>   Nor Theban voice nor Lesbian lyre
>   From thee, o Muse, do i require;
>   While my presaging mind,
>   Conscious of powers she never knew,
> Astonish'd grasps at things beyond her view,
> Nor by another's fate submits to be confin'd.   (lines 111–20)[3]

The failure of others did not prevent him from undertaking the writing of odes because such writing stemmed from powers beyond those of his muse. Whatever the claim for the return to the ode, Akenside did not feel confined by the failure of others. Paul Whitely quotes the passage and writes that the poet "needs no 'Theban voice' to sing the praise of liberty." But this statement does not take account of the fact that the poet does not need the help of the muse because his ode at such times grasps at things beyond the muse's view. Yet Whiteley does have a sense "of Akenside being more concerned to create a poetic refuge, to withdraw from the real world into the world of Greek lyric."[4] It is not only the world of the Greek lyric into which Akenside and ode writers withdraw. It is a world of the origin of poetry, of the universality of poetic language and feeling.

What led Warton and Collins and Gray to turn to the ode? How did they and eighteenth-century critics define odes? What new possibilities did the poets find in the ode that made them engage in its practice? What was the situation in the 1740s that initiated this poetry and set it in contention with sung poetry such as the ballad, hymns, psalms, catches, and songs? The ode that Warton, Collins, and Gray practiced was derived from a classical tradition and from the Hebrew scriptures, but ballads and street songs were derived from the lives and work of often unlearned poets who preferred or were relegated to anonymity. The turn to the sublime ode was undertaken by learned university poets, and their version of the ode differed in aims and procedure from the "lesser" kinds of ode that characterized popular poetry, such as poems of natural description, of love, and of hymns, psalms, and elegies. This chapter explains the "turn" to the ode by indicating first the separation of these two poetic practices and then the consequences that followed from their interaction. What follows, therefore, is a study of the generic identity of the ode and its relation to and contention with other genres.

The first ode in Joseph Warton's *Odes* is entitled "To Fancy" and although he invokes the conventional muse of poetry, he wishes her to inspire him to unconventional poetry. He urges her to empower "some chosen swain" to write "some new, unequall'd song." He writes:

> O queen of numbers, once again
> Animate some chosen swain,
> Who filled with unexhausted fire,
> May boldly smite the sounding lyre,
> Who with some new, unequall'd song,
> May rise above the rhyming throng.   (lines 129–34)

His reference to the "chosen swain" was "once again" to create a new song. His aim for the ode was to invent some new impassioned view of nature and the human situation. Warton's odes have as their subjects liberty, health, superstition, evening, spring, and nightingales; his aim, however, was to remove these from the everyday life of which they were a part and to create imagined worlds in which they functioned, a world of active personification of inanimate nature and abstract ideas.

The variety of Warton's odes suggests that this particular kind of poetry could treat subjects found in other poetic kinds such as eclogues, elegies, georgic, and satiric poetry. But the new ode was to treat its subjects with "invention" and "imagination." In so far as landscape poetry, for example, had been descriptive and empirical or poetry about health had been preceptive, the ode sought to treat these as allegorical, as situations that were states of mind or passions of the soul inherent in the religious originary powers of poetic language. This interpretation of the imagination turned the ode from ordinary to extraordinary subjects. It distinguished what came to be called the "sublime" ode from the "lesser" ode, but even the lesser odes were structured to suggest the universal power of nature, the rotation of the day and the seasons.

William Collins's "descriptive" and "allegoric" odes were experiments in creating a kind of poetry that moved from natural description – too often rooted in the clichés derived from classical poetry – to a poetry that dealt with changes in nature and human passions. In his "Ode to Evening" he took a subject often handled by his predecessors in descriptive poems about night or landscape and converted it to a poem about the contesting forces within nature, the enduring stability of evening during the ever changing cycle of the seasons. Converting evening into a muse, "chaste Eve," Collins made his ode into a poem about the soothing power of poetry. In wind or rain, in the cycle of the seasons, the poet celebrated the gentle influence of evening in its gradual transformation to night. This aspect of "chaste Eve" endures even through the violence of winter that

> rudely rends thy robes;
> So long, sure-found beneath the sylvan shed,
> Shall Fancy, Friendship, Science, rose-lipped Health,
> Thy gentlest influence own,
> And hymn thy favourite name!   (lines 48–52)[5]

In spite of the irregularity of the metrical pattern and the unusual absence of rhyme, the ode provides a soothing comfort for the reader. Despite its description of seasonal change, winter's conflict with "chaste Eve" nevertheless invokes a gentleness that only an imaginary world can produce.

The ode as a poetic kind was marked by radical shifts of person, of subjects, of passions. In one respect it arose as an answer to satirical poetry and its moralizing conclusions. In another the turn to the ode was to produce a poetry that while dealing with the association of ideas and feelings nevertheless possessed a unity. The ode included innumerable connections among incidents and subjects. The ode writers included in their odes references and quotations from and allusions to the poetry of earlier writers. This was not a new procedure. Dryden had noted the practice of Ben Jonson in including quotations from the ancients in his works, and Pope and Thomson continued the procedure. But the ode writers used it to demonstrate their learning and to establish a fictive British poetic tradition and progress.

It is, however, important to distinguish the kinds of intertextuality poets establish in the ode. It is one thing for Collins to introduce in an ode stanzaic patterns from Pindaric odes, another to share with Joseph Warton images of evening in their odes to evening. One points to fragments of the sublime ode, the other to shared views of diurnal and cyclical time. The procedure of intertextuality in these poems, in so far as quoting from contemporaries is concerned, establishes a community of reference, a community that shares aims, educational backgrounds, and literary knowledge.

Collins's "Ode on the Poetical Character" begins with a reference to Spenser and his "school":

> As once, if not with light regard
> I read aright that gifted bard,

> (Him whose school above the rest
> His loveliest Elfin Queen has blessed) . . .　　　　(lines 1–4)

In his "An Ode on the Popular Superstitions of the Highlands of Scotland, Considered as the Subject of Poetry" he writes of the need to preserve the poetic legends of the highlands:

> Proceed, in forceful sound and colours bold
> The native legends of thy land rehearse;
> To such adapt thy lyre and suit thy powerful verse
> 　　　　　　　　　　　(lines 185–87)

The odes of the 1740s are often poems about poetry and the poet. In his "Ode on the Poetical Character" Collins connects the creation of poetry with God's creation of the world (lines 23–40). "Fancy" or "imagination" creates a poetry that derives from the very sources of language and religious devotion. The significance of this claim was to restore the ode as the highest and most original poetic kind. And this claim was buttressed in 1753 by Bishop Robert Lowth's Latin *Lectures on the Sacred Poetry of the Hebrews* (translated into English in 1787). There Lowth declared "the origin of the ode may be traced into that of poetry itself, and appears to be coeval with the commencement of religion, or more properly to the creation of man."[6]

Although the new ode writers connected their poems with the origins of poetry, they took as their sources Greek and Latin models. Gray's "The Progress of Poesy" and "The Bard" are Pindaric odes and "The Progress" begins with the Greeks, not the Hebrews. Nevertheless, the structure of hymns and psalms shared many features with ancient Greek lyrics. Indeed Bishop Lowth argued that the Hebrew term "Shir" and the Greek term "Ode" were synonymous: "both these words have exactly the same power and signification" (II, 186).

The relation between "ode" and "lyric" has puzzled critics in our time,[7] but it was not without contradictions for eighteenth-century writers. Early in the century, Joseph Trapp in his Latin *Lectures on Poetry* delivered at Oxford in 1712 and 1713 (the lectures were translated into English in 1742, the decade initiating the ode revival) noted that the ode was "the most ancient Kind of Poem"[8] Examples of the ode were hymns and psalms, sung with or without musical instruments. This kind of poem "was the boldest of all other Kinds, full of Rapture, and elevated from common Language the most that is possible. . . .." These poems were constructed with digressions and excursions, with abrupt beginnings and endings "and are carried thro' a Variety of Matter with a sort of divine Pathos, above Rules and Laws, and without the common Forms of Grammar" (p. 204).

Horace's odes, which were the models for Trapp of "lyric" poetry, were of varied kinds. Trapp wrote, "Upon the whole, then, we see that the Ode may be either Sublime, or of the lower Strain; jocose or serious; mournful or exulting, even satirical sometimes, epigrammatical never. It may consist of Wit, but not of that Turn which is the peculiar character of Epigram" (p. 214). When Trapp came to his own time, he had little respect for the "Songs and Catches" that were set to music.

As mentioned before, in noting that the ode "may be either Sublime, or of the lower Strain," Trapp granted that the latter could be "jocose" or "serious." The kind of poem it was, therefore, could be a parody or a landscape poem. The ode could be "mournful"; it could, therefore, be an elegy. It could be "exulting" or a poem in admiration of a hero or a victory. The point is that Trapp conceived of the lower strain of the ode as including many mixed forms that were identified as independent "kinds" rather than as species of the ode, though they were both.

The Greek ode writers who served as guides for the 1740s ode writers were identified by Akenside and the other poets as Anacreon, Alcaeus, Sappho, and Pindar and the Latin model was Horace. These and especially Horace included in their odes poems that could or did belong to independent kinds. David West, for example, points out that some of Horace's odes are, in our sense, dramatic monologues (Book I, 5, 9, and 27), that his odes include love poems and drinking poems as well as sacred poems, and that within his odes there are allusions to and quotations from other kinds.[9] The ode itself was "greater" or "lesser" and within each of these kinds were particular species. Odes could be composed of numerous particular species; ode, therefore, whether "sublime" or "lesser" was a collective designation, a genus which contained numerous species. These species underwent changes over time, changes that included subjects, language, characters, and even aims. The return to the sublime musical ode and to lesser odes on health, birds, travel, and similar subjects signaled changes in the poetry of the 1740s and 1750s. The nationalistic and aesthetic changes that occurred at this time were not only an avoidance by the ode of Popean moralizing poetry; they were also indicative of national, religious, and social changes that were taking place in society as a whole. These changes were confronted in such works as David Hume's *A Treatise of Human Nature* (1739–40) and the various theories of associationism. One extensive example of the latter was David Hartley's *Observations on Man* (1749). I can only point out here that the problems of interpreting generic changes and reversals – from genus to species and the reverse – formed the concern of Hume in his study of the passions in Book II of the *Treatise* and the rewriting of it in his essay "Of the Passions" in *Four Dissertations* (1757). In the latter volume in the essay, "Of Tragedy" he also applied his theory of passions in everyday life as they were transformed to aesthetic passions in tragedy. Generic interactions in poetry no less than in human behavior stimulated philosophical, aesthetic inquiries at mid century. The interrelation of genres within the ode and the contention between odes and other literary genres led to a return to the ode at mid century. But by the end of the century, these practices subverted the versions of the ode they had initiated.

Chambers in his *Cyclopaedia* (5th. edn. 1743)[10] pointed out that "Among the antients [sic] *ode* signified no more than a *song*, with us they are different things. The antient *odes* were generally in honor of the gods . . .," although he acknowledged that there were odes on other subjects by Anacreon, Sappho, and other classical poets. Chambers, like Trapp, used the term "ode" as a collective noun that included poems of different kinds and different subjects. A similar situation applied to lyric. According to Chambers, the term "lyric" applied "to the antient odes and stanza's [sic]; which answer to our *arias* and *songs* and may be played on instruments." Originally "lyric" was synonymous with the sublime ode: "This species of poetry was originally employed in celebrating praises of Gods and heroes; though it was afterwards introduced into feasts and public diversions . . . it appears from scripture to have been in use above a thousand years before that poet [Anacreon]." The use of the term "lyric" was synonymous with "ode" in referring to classical poetry, and the distinguishing character of the "ode" as the "lyric" was identified by Chambers as "sweetness."

Chambers's view that "sweetness" or a soothing effect was the distinguishing characteristic of the ode was in contradiction to the rapture and diversity that Trapp attributed to the varied kinds. The attempt to fix a single distinguishing character to the ode in all its variations was not shared by other eighteenth-century definitions. Johnson's *Dictionary* (1755) was traditional in dividing the ode into two kinds, the sublime ode and the lesser ode, and only the latter was marked by "sweetness" and ease.[11] Bishop Lowth divided the ode into three kinds: the sublime, the lesser, and a mixture of the two. Robert Potter divided the ode into four kinds later in the century.[12]

To understand why the ode writers of the 1740s turn to this genre despite so debatable a critical history, we need to note that their definitions all agree that odes are songs or have the possibility of being sung with or without instruments. The poets stress the aural as well as the oral character of language. They experiment with metrical variations that often remove their poetry from the repetition of the heroic couplet. They also insist on the classical sources of the ode, thus providing a historical basis for their turn. Consequently, much of their poetry is about poetry.

Originally the ode was not a poem about the poet's feeling but about the public expression of admiration for Gods and heroes and the community. In demonstrating the poet's heroic role, Gray's bard in "The Bard, a Pindaric Ode" prophesies his own fate and that of the tyrannical King Edward:

> ". . . I see
> The different dooms our fates assign.
> Be thine despair and sceptered care;
> To triumph, and to die, are mine."
>
> He spoke, and headlong from the mountains' height
> Deep in the roaring tide he plunged to endless night.
>
> (lines 139–44)[13]

The poet is a significant figure in Warton's odes and the poet's voice in the ode of Akenside arises unusually from his autobiographical, his private "genius." The poet is given power and authority in Collins's odes on poetry. But Collins's references to the poet were neither personal nor autobiographical. Neither Gray's bard nor Warton's "chosen Swain" belonged to the world of patrons and publishers in which the author lived. The poets were part of the imagined world created by the ode writers; it was a world beyond the ordinary. When they made reference to ordinary events like the presence of a country churchyard or a description of evening, they created visions of their social desires or fantasies of remembered experience. In creating such visions they did not always call their poems odes; the *Elegy Written in a Country Churchyard* was in an earlier state – the Eton manuscript – called "Stanza's [sic] Wrote in a Country Churchyard." The final poem, though called an "Elegy," creates a world that characterized the construction of sublime odes. In its beginning it makes reference to the characteristic description of evening and in its conclusion it introduces the imagined figure of the autobiographical poet.

The *Elegy* begins at the time when day turns into night – a time selected by both Warton and Collins to soothe the poet and the reader – and thus describes changes in nature and in the rural work tasks. The sight of the churchyard cemetery leads to the poet's imaginary vision of the lives no longer lived. The poet knows none of the buried dead and makes no reference to the particularities of their activities, only to the merit of their sustained inconsequence. The poem is not about the lives lived or unlived, but about the need or desire for memorialization.

> On some fond breast the parting soul relies,
> Some pious drops the closing eye requires;
> Ev'n from the tomb the voice of nature cries.
> Ev'n in our ashes live their wonted fires.   (lines 89–92)

Gray is not concerned with the way in which members of the hamlet actually lived, suffered, or succeeded, but with the way the poet imagines them.

The poem envisions the imagined world as uncontroversial, as different from the actual world. But the dying need memorials in order to become part of a future imagination. They leave tokens for others to imagine what their world was. The poem is about the poet who not only memorializes the unhonored dead, but who in his own death urges the reader not to inquire about his life. Rather, the reader should ponder the peace of the future world; the hope of the dead poet is to lie in "the bosom of his Father and his God."

Long before Gray published his version of the lives of rural working people, there had been popular poems that dealt in various kinds of actual situations, many of which were lesser odes in the Horatian sense. Street poems like the ballads and catches were songs that dealt often with narratives that described actual and historical incidents. But it was not until 1711 that the ballads were treated as legitimate literary forms. Joseph Addison in *The Spectator* (nos. 70 and 74) analyzed the ballad of Chevy Chase as a Virgilian epic and approved of the ballad, "Two Children in the Wood," that, despite "a despicable Simplicity in the Verse," was "able to move the mind of the most polite Reader with inward Meltings of Humanity and Confession" (no. 85). Ballads, he argued, can deal with sentiments and passions that appeal to people of all classes, not excluding polite responders. And as songs they can be considered among the lesser odes. The progress of the ballad from street performance to the stage in *The Beggar's Opera* to the printed page occurs in the first half of the eighteenth century. But the ballad was not a genre practiced by the ode writers, whose special language of the ode was not suited to the common, sometimes vulgar, language of the ballads.

The psalms and hymns, unlike the ballad, were ancient forms, part of the Hebrew scriptures. They formed part of Christian services and in translation were examples of lesser odes. The psalms of David, for example, were translated in 1719 by the dissenting minister Isaac Watts, who sought to provide a version for his followers; his volume was entitled *Psalms of David Imitated in the Language of the New Testament and Apply'd to the Christian State and Worship*. These poems and the religious songs published by the Wesleys formed part of the turn to a poetry of impassioned feeling. But neither the moralistic, satiric writers like Pope and Swift nor the ode writers like Warton and Collins composed many hymns or psalms.

As learned poets, Gray and Warton, Collins and Akenside continued the tradition which stated that the language of the ode was necessarily different from ordinary language. Since the greater ode was sometimes called the sublime ode, it is obvious that the language of sublimity was not the language of quotidian behavior and expression. Gray's famous letter of 8 April 1742, supported this view and extended it to the "language of poetry."

As to matters of stile, I have this to say. The language of the age is never the language of poetry, except among the French, whose verse, where the thought or image does not support it, differs in nothing from prose. Our poetry, on the contrary, has a language peculiar to itself; to which almost every one, that has written, has added something by enriching it with foreign idioms and derivatives: Nay sometimes words of their own composition and invention.[14]

Whether Gray would apply this dictum to ballads or to the poetry of unlearned writers such as Stephen Duck or Mary Collier is certainly questionable. These poets using as poetic subjects incidents and situations from their own lives expressed their feelings in a language drawn from everyday experiences. These experiences were also to be found in the novels' prose mixtures that dealt with the life histories of criminals, servants, and other members of the lower classes. By 1740 it was obvious that the publication of novels was encroaching upon, even reducing, the publication of poetry.

It was in 1740 that a novel was published that demonstrated a very special subordination of poetry to prose. It also illustrated the intimate relation between the poet and the poet's personal situation in a prose text. It illustrated the function of poetry as self-expression as well as entertainment. It treated poetry as public expression and as private expression that becomes public. It demonstrated that even when one deals with a religious ode one can convert it into a language that mixes the received language with ordinary prose. The novel that manifested these claims was *Pamela* (1740). It is the story of a servant girl who not only writes prose epistles to her parents about the sexual pursuit by Mr. B, but composes poetry at significant moments in her life. Her poetry is written in the language of her prose discourses, her epistles, and journal entries. Her poetry arises from the situations in which she finds herself. The acts of imagination that permit the ode writer to avoid the situations of everyday life lead Pamela to dwell upon them. They provide her with occasions for expressing intense feeling, especially as they reflect changes in her situation.

Pamela's poems are songs and the first one she composes is a farewell ballad to her friends, the household help, when she believes she is leaving them to return to her parents' home. It is entitled "Verses on my Going Away" and it begins as follows:

I.

My Fellow servants dear, attend
   To these few Lines, which I have penn'd:
I'm sure they're from your honest friend,
   And Wisher-well, Poor *Pamela*.

I from a state of low degree
Was plac'd in this good Family.
Too high a Fate for humble me,
The helpless, hopeless *Pamela*.[15]

This initial effort hardly merits the designation "poetry," but it occurs early in the novel. It draws attention to Pamela's childishness and artistic simplicity. It is an effort at a formal farewell written in quatrains, with the first three lines of each stanza rhyming and followed by a fourth that is a refrain. It moves from personal sincerity to self-abasement to self-congratulation. The poem is addressed to her fellow servants and its naïveté of vocabulary and sentiments is appropriate to her audience. In contrast, the ode writers addressed their poems to a learned audience. Gray's two Pindaric odes needed notes to be understood and Collins's "Ode on the Poetical Character" and his other odes, including the "Ode to Simplicity," deliberately contain references that require classical and literary knowledge.

The ballad structure of Pamela's poem not only reveals her childishness and simplicity, it also shows her naïveté in admiring the situation in which she find herself.

For oh! We *pity* should the great,
Instead of *envying* their estate;
Temptations always on 'em wait,
Exempt from which are such as we.   (I, 118)

If we compare these lines with the later sophisticated sentiments in Gray's *Elegy* we can note the sympathy, not the envy, of the serving girl for the "great," her personal resistance to temptation and the learned poet's abstract construction of rural workers who remained content with their situation:

Far from the madding crowd's ignoble strife
Their sober wishes never learned to stray;
Along the cool sequestered vale of life
They kept the noiseless tenor of their way.   (lines 73–76)

Still there is an irony in Pamela's recital that is absent from Gray's lines. For as she sees herself exempt from temptation she is nevertheless not exempt from abduction and terrorizing by the great Mr. B.

In 1740, in *Pamela*, the mixture served to demonstrate the creativity of the serving girl. Pamela can express herself in prose and poetry. Her turn to poetry exhibits a public sensibility in which she converts received attitudes and language into personal statements. In this respect, her turn to personal feeling does for her class what the ode writers do when they return poetry to originary claims about poetry and the poet – except that they are addressing an audience from a different class.

It is not surprising that the ode writers should disdain some of the lesser odes like the ballad and public songs and catches since these lack the credentials of a classical tradition. They are also the expressions by members of a lower class. A similar conflict existed at mid century with regard to hymn writing and singing – though that conflict began earlier. Richard Arnold quotes from tracts, pamphlets and articles against Methodism and specifically about Methodists' hymn-singing.[16] The hymn, as Robert Lowth pointed out, was traditionally identified as an ode and the conflict was between the received Anglican hymns and the new Methodist contributions. The latter were more personalized and human, and they were sung outside as well as inside the church. Unlike the learned ode writers, the hymn writers addressed an audience in a language not unlike Pamela's. Their change of the religious ode offered a change in language and feeling that was antithetical to the aesthetic directions that were taken by the university ode writers, even though in the example of Christopher Smart, a composer of lesser odes could also compose sublime ones.

Pamela's version of Psalm 137 is an example of the change that was taking place in religious odes. Pamela's rewriting of the psalm removes it from its historical reference and makes it, as she says, "somewhat nearer to my case." Her case was the result of her abduction and confinement in Mr. B's distant manor under the guardianship of Mrs. Jewkes. Her revision of the psalm is cited twice, once when she composes it and a second time when Mr. B, having decided to marry Pamela, arranges a recital for his guests of her revision. He and Mr. Wilson engage in responsive reading, in which Mr. Williams reads the standard version of Psalm 137 and Mr. B reads Pamela's revision. The last two stanzas of the received psalm read as follows:

IX

Ev'n so shalt thou, O *Babylon*!
  At length to Dust be brought.
And happy shall that Man be call'd
  That our Revenge hath wrought.

X

Yea, blessed shall that Man be call'd
  That takes thy little ones
And dashes them in Pieces small
  Against the very Stones.

Pamela's version reads:

IX

Ev'n so shalt thou, o wicked one! [Mrs. Jewkes]
   At length to Shame be brought,
And happy shall all those be call'd
   That my Deliv'rance wrought.

X

Yes, blessed shall the Man be call'd
   That shames thee of thy Evil,
And saves me from thy vile Attempts,
   And, thee, too from the D—l.   (II, 110)

The psalm of bitterness and revenge is converted into a personal song of bitterness and forgiveness. Pamela's revision substitutes "shame" for destruction, "to dust be brought." It substitutes for an appeal to God's anger, an appeal to God through one's personal mercy. In this respect a turn to the personal involves an optimistic hope that mercy will lead to reformation.

Pamela's personal version conforms to the practice of revising the text of the psalms. Christopher Smart's publication in 1765 of *A Translation of the Psalms of David* contains a version of Psalm 137, the last stanza of which reads as follows:

But he is greatest and the best,
Who spares his enemies profest,
And Christian mildness owns;
Who gives his captives back their lives,
Their helpless infants, weeping wives,
And for his sins atones.[17]

Christopher Smart rewrites rather than revises Psalm 137 and he exhibits a skill and understanding superior to Pamela's poetic range. His *A Song to David* (1763) demonstrated what the sublime ode of adulation could achieve as it exemplified the combinatory qualities of a religious hero.

One further example in Richardson's novel needs to be mentioned. When Mr. B wishes to express his love for Pamela, he writes a love poem and sings it to her. It is a "sweet" song, a lesser ode. Although love poems were not frequently written in the first half of the eighteenth century, some of these "sweet" forms like the ballad and songs were written. The ballad, as I have indicated, came to be a sophisticated form.

But one lesser ode, the sonnet, was not written. In Johnson's *Dictionary* this poem was defined as "a short poem consisting of fourteen lines of which the rhymes are adjusted to a particular rule." The definition added, "It is not very suitable to the English language, and has not been used by any man of eminence since Milton." A study of the avoidance of the sonnet and its resumption in 1748 is especially pertinent to an analysis of the turn to the ode because it is in the sonnet form that a direct attack was launched against Warton's aims regarding poetic language and imagination. The attack occurred in Charlotte Smith's sonnet entitled "To Fancy," the same title that Warton gave to his poem in *Odes on Various Subjects*. Smith's poem was published in an enlarged edition of her *Elegiac Sonnets* and it contained the following lines:

> Thro' thy false medium then, no longer view'd,
>   May fancied pain and fancied pleasure fly,
>   And I, as from me all thy dreams depart,
> Be to my wayward destiny subdued . . .   (lines 9–12)[18]

Smith rejected Warton's view of the imagination and his view of the language of poetry as averse to ordinary language. The poet was not a heroic bard nor were the passions of poetry other than those felt by the poet. Smith turned to the sonnet because it was a deliberate rejection of the classical models that ode writers followed. Smith's use of the sonnet based on autobiographical experiences was a continuation of the practices of poets who did not insist on odes as necessarily using a language different from ordinary prose. She demonstrated this in her novels *Emmeline*, *The Old Manor House*, and *Celestina* in which sonnets were included in the prose text. Not only in the novels of Charlotte Smith but in those of Ann Radcliffe and other practitioners of the novel did poetry play a subordinate but distinctive part.

Stuart Curran believes that the rebirth of the sonnet "coincides with the rise of a definable woman's literary movement".[19] Certainly Smith's sonnets were followed by those of Anna Seward, Mary Robinson, and others. Paula R. Feldman and Daniel Robinson modify this claim by writing that "These women poets were largely responsible for the sonnet revival of the 1780s and 1790s and established a tradition that important women sonnet writers would follow well into the nineteenth century".[20] It is well to remember, however, that Charlotte Smith in her 1784 preface refers to William Hayley as an exceptional sonnet writer and that although William Lisle Bowles modeled some of his sonnets after Smith, Wordsworth's attack on Gray's poetic diction in his sonnet independently arrived at a position not dissimilar from Smith's attitude to Joseph Warton.

The ode writers had avoided writing the lesser ode, the sonnet. There are only two instances of their sonnet practice: in 1739 William Collins's poem entitled "Sonnet" was published in the *Gentleman's Magazine* 8, and

Thomas Gray actually composed a sonnet. Collins's poem consisted of two quatrains about love. To him, "sonnet" merely meant a short song (Johnson's second definition); it also meant the same to Pamela, who concluded her Verses – "and so my sonnet ends."

Thomas Gray's sonnet on the death of his friend Richard West (written in 1742) is formally correct, but he refused to publish it; it remained for William Mason to publish it posthumously in 1775. Whatever Gray's reasons for withholding the sonnet, his act coincided with the received views that the sonnet was not part of the progress of poetry transmitted to Britain. The poem was, moreover, about the emotion that Gray probably felt; as such, it was in contradiction to his poetry of the imagination that avoided these particular actualities of experience.

Gray's refusal to publish his sonnet may have been his belief that it was a "bad" poem, but if this was his judgment it was buttressed by at least a half century of disregard, even avoidance, of this genre. The reasons for this neglect are historically significant in understanding the shaping of an English poetic tradition. Sonnets had been composed by Shakespeare, Spenser, Sidney, and Milton, but the sonnet was not a classical form. Neither was it an indigenous form since it was invented by Italian poets and reused by English Renaissance poets. In their usage they introduced a less complicated rhyme scheme though they continued to use the sonnet as predominately a love poem with a rule-governed structure. It was, in its brevity, inhospitable to the freedom and variety of incidents in a changing political society. The reason Johnson gave for its unsuitability to the English language was noted earlier by Akenside and repeated by Warton with regard to the ode. Warton wrote in his *Essay on the Genius and Writing of Pope*: "The moderns have, perhaps, practised no species of poetry with so little success, and with such indisputable inferiority to the ancients, as the Ode, which seems owing to the harshness and untuneableness of modern languages, abounding in monosyllables, and crowded with consonants. This particularly is the case with English . . . ."[21]

But Warton and his colleagues had experimented with odes despite the so-called harshness and unmusicality of the language. The major writers of the Renaissance and Milton had successfully written sonnets and, paradoxically, the willingness of the university ode writers to experiment with song in the ode led writers to experiment with the sonnet. The resumption of sonnet writing began in 1748 when Thomas Edwards published thirteen sonnets in the second edition of Robert Dodsley's *A Collection of Poems by Several Hands*.[22] His sonnets were in effect odes, lesser odes of praise and admiration of friends and eminent individuals. The revival of sonnet writing thus began with poems to or about individuals; consequently it fits into a

tradition of odes of praise or dispraise. Additional support for the membership of the sonnet in an English tradition occurred with Thomas Percy's
Reliques of Ancient English Poetry (1765) that included popular ballads and
even incomplete poems in tracing the refinement of English poetry from
medieval times. The sonnet could legitimately be treated as poetry contributing to the progress of refinement. The revising and rewriting of received
hymns and psalms supported the composition of short forms dealing with
personal experience. And in 1782, when Robert Dodsley's *Collection* was
printed for the last time, the ready availability of odes by the ode writers
ceased.

Only two years later, 1784, Charlotte Smith published her *Elegiac Sonnets
and other Essays*. In this early effort she felt the need to defend her use of
the sonnet.

> The little Poems which are here called Sonnets have, I believe, no very first
> claim to that title: but they consist of fourteen lines, and appear to me no
> improper vehicle for a single sentiment. I am told, and I read it as opinion of
> very good judges that the legitimate Sonnet is ill calculated for our language.
> The specimens Mr. Hayley has given, though they form a strong exception,
> prove no more than that the difficulties of the attempt vanish before uncom-
> mon powers.
>
> Some very melancholy moments have been beguiled by expressing in verse
> the sensations those moments brought.[23]

The defense appeared almost as an apology. Her sonnets were a specified
number of lines in a language that she claimed only skilled poets could make
musical and moving. The subjects of her sonnets were personal moments,
and the poems aimed at the communication of her melancholy feelings. The
personal nature of her poems and their favorable reception encouraged her
to continue to write them.

Smith's return to the sonnet may be seen as analogous to the turn to the
ode by the ode writers. Although she deliberately opposed Warton's view of
the imagination and substituted and argued for her personal experience as
the source of her language and feelings, not some invention of fancied pain
and pleasure, her sonnets continued some of the practices of the ode writers.
Adela Pinch points out that Smith's sonnets are "echo chambers, in which
reverberate direct quotation, ideas and tropes from English poetry." This
procedure signals the allegiance of her sonnets to a poetry that is formally
made out of other poems.[24] In this she continued the practice of the ode
writers. She provided in her poems the learning that Pamela lacked. But
Smith insisted on the single sentiment of the sonnet; her construction of these
poems was aimed at avoiding the complicated and often complex changes

within the odes. She sought to avoid their shifts in sentiment, their depiction of imagined other worlds. Many of her sonnets addressed particular variants of melancholy. It is as though her sonnets represent a fracturing of the great ode, selecting one experience or sentiment or passion to constitute a poem in itself.

Smith was not alone in turning away from the imagined worlds of the ode writers. George Crabbe attacked the imagined rural worlds of earlier poets.[25] Christopher Smart in his rewriting the psalms of David, in his songs, especially *A Song to David* and *Jubilate Agno*, embedded personal feeling with public religious professions. The process that had been implicit in the turn of the ode writers – the recognition that a form like the ode could also be an elegy, that eclogue could also be a song, that the ode could also be a description or allegory – became explicit in titles like "Elegiac Sonnets" and "Lyrical Ballads." Subject and structure were intertwined rather than distinguished as individual features.

If one compares Collins's "Ode Occasioned by the Death of Mr. Thomson" (1748) with Wordsworth's early poem "Remembrance of Collins Composed upon the Thames near Richmond," written in 1789 and published in 1798, a shift becomes apparent from pastoral imagery to actual observation, from learned to ordinary language, from mythic imagination to private prayer. Collins's poem is a typical example of the ode writing of the 1740s. It is a poem in which the poet is treated as a poet-prophet, a Druid; in the first line the Druid is unidentified – "In yonder grave a Druid lies." In the last line the poet has become a national hero pointed to in future times by the musing Briton: "In yonder grave your Druid lies!"

The poem creates an imagined pastoral world in which the poet's grave becomes a place of mythical mourning for maids and youth, a place in which the moving sounds of Thomson's poetry continue to reverberate. The ode is written in a literary language many terms of which make reference to vocabularies of other poems – "airy harp," "sedge-crowned Sisters," "lorn stream" – as well as to Thomson's own poetry. The poem contains personifications of nature, of pity, of ease and health, of remembrance.

> Remembrance oft shall haunt the shore
> When Thames in summer wreaths is dressed,
> And oft suspend the dashing oar
> To bid her gentle spirit rest!   (lines 13–16)

There are changes of address – to the dead poet, to the Thames – and a change of voice from the poet to the future Briton, as the latter addresses the "vales and wild woods." It is indicative of the "turn" of Collins's poem that even though written about his friend Thomson, it honors him by placing him in an imagined world very different from the often specific nature that Thomson described in *The Seasons*.

Wordsworth's "Remembrance of Collins" is an ode praising a poet who had died thirty years earlier, in 1759. In it he indicates his tribute to and his revision of Collins's practices. His ode, though it is not entitled an "ode," is an example of the inward turn he gives to some of Collins's imagery. His reference to Collins's quatrain beginning "Remembrance oft shall haunt the shore" suggests that continuity is present but that it is reimagined.[26]

Wordsworth admires the address to the Thames, but his example involves rejection of the inflated image of the river – "Vain thought." Such inflation is vain both because the river cannot function to make all minds operate with the depth of the river and because it is vain of a poet to think so. Wordsworth limits the multiplicity of personifications. He recognizes the importance of Collins's elegiac tribute but he avoids the pastoral tradition. He also finds Collins's pity a limited conception of mourning. He avoids in the language of the ode any attempt at a "literary" language. The sentence he quotes from Collins – "And oft suspend the dashing oar" – he converts to a reference to Collins, "For him suspend the dashing oar." Collins uses this moment to bid Thomson's spirit rest. Wordsworth uses it as a prayer. The last two lines of his poem function as the concluding couplet in a sonnet, an epilogue to the poem and a reference to Collins's description of darkness, a darkness that veils the view – "Dun night has veiled the solemn view!" (line 34). – Wordsworth's poem concludes: "–The evening darkness gathers round/ By virtue's holiest Powers attended" (lines 23–24). Wordsworth's emendation, if his religious moralism can be so called, is that darkness does not veil the view but illuminates it. In "Remembrance" he depicts with respect Collins's practices, but he clearly separates his own poetic aims from them.

This chapter has traced the (re)turn to the ode in the 1740s, illustrating the significance of this poetic kind in redirecting British poetry. I have tried to explain generic changes by examining the practices of the poets themselves. They identified the genres they used with social, religious, and aesthetic aims. The ode writers began by rejecting what they considered an overabundance of the moralizing poetry of Pope and his followers, and they sought to reestablish the primacy of a classical genre. They were intimidated by what the Greek and Latin writers had accomplished in the ode, and they therefore developed it as a learned form dependent upon a specialized language with references to prior odes and related poetry. Their contribution was the creation of imagined worlds, experiments with meter and rhyme, the insistence on the musical or song character of the ode, and the impassioned praise of poets and their view of poetry. They contributed these emphases in opposition to the novel and in disregard of the lesser kinds of ode and popular song.

At the same time there existed a popular poetry that consisted of lesser odes of ballads, songs, hymns, and psalms. This poetry was also involved in a turn, in the expression of the personal feelings of the poet within conventional kinds. Not only were forms like the psalms and hymns and ballads undergoing change, but the sonnet was recuperated after being rejected for half a century. These poems often set themselves against the odes of the university poets, against their concept of imagination and against their specialized language.

This opposition and contention among the genres gradually altered their interrelations. The special language of the ode became mixed with the ordinary language of prose. The imagination that in the great ode revealed a universal, originary world became in the lesser ode associated with the private world of the poet. The poet, prophet, bard of the great ode, the heroic figure, was joined by a speaker in the lesser odes often troubled, awed, or overwhelmed by thoughts and dreams of the surrounding life. The lesser odes such as the ballad and the sonnet came into frequent use and served to erode the mixtures that separated the two species of ode. And the very term "lyric" that originally in classical use referred to the musical accompaniment of the ode became the name for all poetry that expressed the personal, passionate feeling of the poet no longer created by the sounds of music. The ode at the end of the century thus became one kind of lyric although in the 1740s its lyricism had been only one aspect of the ode.

NOTES

1 Joseph Warton, *Odes on Various Subjects* (1746), ed. Joan Pittock (Delmar, NY: Scholars' Facsimiles and Reprints, 1977), p. 3.
2 The complete "Advertisement" read as follows:
   From what the ancients have left of this kind, perhaps the Ode may be allow'd the most amicable species of poetry; but certainly there is none which in modern languages has been generally attempted with so little success. For the perfection of lyric poetry depends, beyond that of any other, on the beauty of words and the gracefulness of numbers; in both which respects the ancients had infinite advantages above us.
   Mark Akenside, *The Poetical Works*, ed. Robin Dix (Rutherford, NJ: Fairleigh Dickinson University Press; London: Associated University Presses, 1996), p. 475. The "beauty of the words" was a reference to the relation of words to the music which accompanied them and so, too, was the "gracefulness of numbers."
3 *The Poetical Works*, p. 289.
4 "Gray, Akenside and the Ode," in W. B. Hutchins and W. Ruddick (eds.), *Thomas Gray Contemporary Essays* (Liverpool: Liverpool University Press, 1993), p. 185.
5 Roger Lonsdale (ed.), *The Poems of Thomas Gray, William Collins and Oliver Goldsmith* (Oxford: Oxford University Press, 1969); all poems by Collins are cited from this edition.

6 Robert Lowth, *Lectures on the Sonnet Poetry of the Hebrews*, tr. G. Gregory, 2 vols. (London, 1787), II, 192. John Ogilvie, in "An Essay on the Lyric Poetry of the Ancients" in *Poems on Several Subjects*, agreed with Lowth and Trapp on the ancient origin of lyric poetry: probably "the first rude draughts of Poetry were extemporary effusions either descriptive of the scenes of pastoral life, or extolling the attributes of the Supreme Being . . . To paint those objects which produce pleasure was the business of the pastoral, and to display those which cause admiration was the task assigned to the Lyrick Poet" (IX). See also Richard Shepherd, *Odes Descriptive and Allegorical* (1761). He writes of his odes:

> of the descriptive and allegorical Ode the Writings of the Ancients offered no Examples . . . This species of Writing is in almost every Circumstance different from the *Pindarick* Ode, which has its Foundation in Fact and Reality, that Fact worked up and heightened by a studied Pomp and Grandeur of Expression; it not only admits of, but requires bold Digressions, abrupt and hasty Transitions; while the other is built intirely upon Fancy, and Ease and Simplicity of Diction are its peculiar characteristics.

Shepherd apparently did not understand the distinction between the greater and the lesser ode. Quoted in Howard Weinbrot, *Britannia's Issue: the Rise of British Literature from Dryden to Ossian* (Cambridge: Cambridge University Press, 1995), p. 374.

7 Mark Jeffreys's assumption that "only in the nineteenth and twentieth centuries was it [the lyric] mythologized as the purest and oldest of the poetic genres and thus transformed into a nostalgic ideological marker" needs correction in the light of eighteenth-century criticism of the ode. "Ideologies of Lyric: a Problem of Genre in Contemporary Anglophone Poetics," *PMLA* 110:2 (March 1995), 157. More satisfactory discussions of mid-century poetry can be found in John Sitter, *Literary Loneliness in Mid-Eighteenth-Century England* (Ithaca and London: Cornell University Press, 1982), and Douglas Lane Patey, "'Aesthetics' and the Rise of the Lyric in the Eighteenth Century," *Studies in English Literature* 33: 3 (Summer 1993), 587–608. It is ironic that the volume entitled *Lyric Poetry*, ed. Chaviva Hosek and Patricia Parker (Ithaca: Cornell University Press, 1985), does not contain a single essay on the English ode or lyric in the eighteenth century.

8 Joseph Trapp, *Lectures on Poetry* (1742) (Hildesheim: Georg Olms, 1969), p. 203.

9 David West (ed.), *Horace Odes*, 2 vols. (Oxford: Clarendon Press, 1995–98).

10 Chambers's entries for "ode," "lyric," and "song" indicate that a change has taken place historically in the characteristics attributed to the ode; especially to the difference between the sublime ode and the lesser ode. He does not, however, deal in detail with what these historical changes were.

11 In Johnson's *Dictionary*, the definition of the "ode" was: "a poem written to be set to musick; a lyrick poem. The ode is either of the greater or the less kind. The less is characterised by sweetness and ease; the greater by sublimity, rapture and the quickness of transition."

12 Norman MacLean discusses in detail the views of the ode as these undergo change in his article "From Action to Image: Theories of the Lyric in the Eighteenth Century," in R. S. Crane (ed.), *Critics and Criticism* (Chicago: University of Chicago Press, 1952). See also Robert Potter, *An Inquiry into Some*

Passages of Dr Johnson's Lives of the Poets: Particularly His Observations on Lyric Poetry and the Odes of Gray (London, 1785).

13 From Lonsdale (ed.), *The Poems of Thomas Gray, William Collins and Oliver Goldsmith*; all poems by Gray are cited from this edition.

14 My quotation is taken from Richard Terry's article, "Gray and Poetic Diction," in Hutchings and Ruddick (eds.), *Thomas Gray Contemporary Essays*, p. 79.

15 *Pamela*, 4 vols. (Oxford: Blackwell, 1929), I, 116. Hereafter references given in the text.

16 Richard Arnold, *The English Hymn: Studies in a Genre* (New York: Peter Lang, 1995), p. 66.

17 *The Poetical Works of Christopher Smart*, vol. III. *A Translation of the Psalms of David*, ed. Marcus Walsh (Oxford: Oxford University Press, 1987).

18 *The Poems of Charlotte Smith*, ed. Stuart Curran (New York and Oxford: Oxford University Press, 1993), p. 44.

19 Stuart Curran *Poetic Form and British Romanticism* (New York and Oxford: Oxford University Press, 1986), p. 30.

20 Paula R. Feldman and Daniel Robinson (eds.), *A Century of Sonnets* (Oxford: Oxford University Press, 1999), p. 10.

21 Joseph Warton, *An Essay on the Genius and Writings of Pope* (London, 1806), 5th. edn., I, 62–63.

22 Thomas Edwards, "Sonnets," Robert Dodsley's *A Collection of Poems by Several Hands*, 1748 edition; for a modern edition see *A Collection of Poems by Several Hands [compiled by] Robert Dodsley; with a new Introduction, Notes, and Indices by Michael F. Suarez*, 6 vols. (London: Routledge/Thoemmes Press, 1997).

23 Curran (ed.), *Poems*, p. 3.

24 Adela Pinch, *Strange Fits of Passion: Epistemologies of Emotion, Hume to Austen* (Stanford: Stanford University Press, 1996), pp. 60, 61.

25 George Crabbe, *The Village* (London, 1783).

26 *The Poetical Works of William Wordsworth*, ed. E. de Selincourt, vol. 1 (Oxford: Clarendon Press, 1940).

FURTHER READING

Arnold, Richard. *The English Hymn: Studies in a Genre*. New York: Peter Lang, 1995.

Davie, Donald. *Augustan Lyric*. London: Heinemann Educational, 1974.

Feldman, Paula R. and Daniel Robinson (eds.). *A Century of Sonnets*. Oxford: Oxford University Press, 1999.

Jeffreys, Mark. "Ideologies of Lyric: a Problem of Genre in Contemporary Anglophone Poetics," *PMLA* 110:2 (March 1995), 196–205.

Lonsdale, Roger (ed.). *The New Oxford Book of Eighteenth Century Verse*. Oxford: Oxford University Press, 1984.

  The Poems of Thomas Gray, William Collins and Oliver Goldsmith. Oxford: Oxford University Press, 1969.

MacLean, Norman. "From Action to Image: Theories of the Lyric in the Eighteenth Century," in R. S. Crane (ed.), *Critics and Criticism*. Chicago: University of Chicago Press, 1952. 408–60.

Ogilvie, John. "An Essay on the Lyric Poetry of the Ancients," *Poems on Several Subjects*, London, 1762, reprinted by Augustan Reprint Society. Ed. Wallace Jackson, William. A. Clark Memorial Library, 1970.

Pinch, Adela. *Strange Fits of Passion: Epistemologies of Emotion, Hume to Austen.* Stanford: Stanford University Press, 1996.

Sitter, John. *Literary Loneliness in Mid-Eighteenth Century England.* Ithaca and London: Cornell University Press, 1982.

Smith, Adam. *Lectures on Rhetoric and Belles Lettres*, ed. John M. Lothian. Edinburgh: Thomas Nelson and Sons, 1963.

Suarez, Michael F. (ed.). *A Collection of Poems by Several Hands [compiled by] Robert Dodsley; with a new Introduction, Notes, and Indices by Michael F. Suarez*, 6 vols. London: Routledge/Thoemmes Press, 1997.

Terry, Richard, "Gray and Poetic Diction," in W. B. Hutchings and William Ruddick (eds.) *Thomas Gray Contemporary Essays.* Liverpool: Liverpool University Press, 1993.

Weinbrot, Howard. *Britannia's Issue: the Rise of British Literature from Dryden to Ossian.* Cambridge: Cambridge University Press, 1995. 350–401.

Whiteley, Paul. "Gray, Akenside and the Ode," in W. B. Hutchings and William Ruddick (eds.), *Thomas Gray Contemporary Essays.* Liverpool: Liverpool University Press, 1993.

DAVID B. MORRIS

A poetry of absence

A poetics of absence appropriate to the eighteenth century would take as its distinctive image not the void or abyss – where the rich material world encounters its opposite state of nothingness – but the ruin. Ruins are the trace of something that has vanished. As eighteenth-century poets employ the image, a ruin is less the sign of a distinct past, like the famous monument commemorating the London fire, than an evocation of something lost beyond recovery while nonetheless still persisting in fragments, remnants, and flashes of recollection. The ruin gives absence, so to speak, a material dwelling: a rock-solid site that, paradoxically, embodies a sense that the world is also porous, uncertain, and insubstantial. Its power in eighteenth-century poetry derives from this implicit doubleness combining solidity with evanescence, like Rome as Piranesi depicted it in his *Vedute di Roma* (begun in the late 1740s), with shrubs sprouting from tumbledown classical arches, fallen statues beside overgrown temples, wooden shacks propped against the cenotaphs. John Dyer created his own version of this imagery in *The Ruins of Rome* (1740):

> the solemn scene
> Elates the soul, while now the rising sun
> Flames on the ruins in the purer air
> Tow'ring aloft, upon the glitt'ring plain,
> Like broken rocks, a vast circumference;
> Rent palaces, crush'd columns, rifled moles,
> Fanes roll'd on fanes, and tombs on buried tombs.[1]

An encounter with such embodiments of absence – traces of something lost or vanished beyond recovery – evokes the mingled surprise, melancholy, awe, sadness, and occasional elation that the poetry of the period finds implicit in the experience of loss. Although ruins and their allied insignia grew so popular that architects rearranged the landscape to feature crumbling walls and blasted oaks, such follies show how deeply the era of

Enlightenment progress and of Palladian grandeur also needed to encounter images that bear a reminder of something lost, missing, lacking, immaterial, or absent. These traces create a persistent subtext in the poetic treatment of dreams, death, and desire.

Although desire has recently come to occupy a central place in discussions of the novel, its place in eighteenth-century poetry is relatively unexplored terrain, with the exception of a few Ovidian arias such as Pope's *Eloisa to Abelard* (1717). The fate of verse with less classically sanctioned erotic pedigrees is suggested in Johnson's response to Pope's "Elegy to the Memory of an Unfortunate Lady" (1717): poetry, he wrote, has seldom been worse employed than in dignifying "the amorous fury of a raving girl."[2] Whereas eighteenth-century novelists openly explore the permutations of individual desire, poets seem to focus elsewhere, on gardens, morals, satire, treatises, or states of being such as solitude or happiness. This truism has three main defects in addition to being only half true. It prevents us from asking what poets understood by desire; it prevents us from recognizing the wide spectrum of desire that they explored; and, most seriously, it prevents us from seeing how desire gives a distinctive character to the absences at the heart of eighteenth-century verse.

Absence is a precondition of desire. Desire, in effect, feeds on absence. This formula might sound suspiciously like postmodern razzle-dazzle, but if so Johnson in his *Dictionary* (1755) illustrates his one-word definition of desire ("wish") with a very postmodern quotation from Locke's *Essay concerning Human Understanding* (1690). Desire, writes Locke, is the "uneasiness a Man finds in himself upon the absence of any thing, whose present enjoyment carries the *Idea* of Delight with it."[3] Here at the fountainhead of so much eighteenth-century thought is a statement that explicitly identifies desire with lack or absence. Further, the operation of desire demands not just that something is missing. We must be aware of its absence; what is absent must be associated with pleasure or delight; and our awareness of its absence creates uneasiness. Poetic versions of this process abound. An uneasiness accompanying the absences intrinsic to desire, for example, is what drives the modest psychodrama unfolding within much minor Horatian verse – as in John Pomfret's "The Choice" (1700) – which employs strategies of containment designed to secure a happiness whose chief enemy is desire. Such poems instruct the reader that contentment flows from desiring little or, even better, from renouncing desire. Yet, this minimalist solution to the uneasiness of desire cannot resolve a paradox fundamental to eighteenth-century verse. Poetry in its more ambitious moments is always entangled with desire, including the poet's desire to give pleasure and to secure fame. Poems

expressing, exploring, or evoking desire cannot remain long or wholly free
from the anxieties it generates, which leave their traces in even the most successful acts of containing desire and dispelling absence. The ubiquitous eighteenth-century occasional poem on some profoundly inconsequential topic
– a bird cage or a lady's fan – seems in retrospect to derive its satisfactions
from an engagement with the present moment so absorbing in its absolute,
unamplified materiality that absence and desire cannot possibly creep in.
"Of all the discoveries of the Augustans," writes scholar Blanford Parker,
"the idea of the *literal* is the most important."[4]

The spectrum of desire explored by eighteenth-century poets includes a
sharply diminished band for love. The new dynamic of middle-class courtship makes Marvell's courtier and Donne's lover look like waxwork
antiques. Even the Restoration rake quickly fades. The diminished fate of
erotic verse is confirmed in Pope's rough satire dealing with sex and adul-
tery, "Sober Advice From Horace" (1734), where in preference to unsatis-
fied longing the speaker recommends a "tight, neat Girl" who will "serve the
Turn" (line 151). The ensuing lines praise Pope's aristocratic friend Bathurst
for his choice of any "willing Nymph" so long as she is "Extremely clean,
and tolerably fair" (lines 161–62). Bathurst's choice signals a near erasure of
desire: it is as if, at dinner, he simply attends to the satisfaction of an appetite. At an opposite extreme, appetite almost disappears in the commodified
world of Pope's *Rape of the Lock* (1714), where pocket watches and silk
brocade replace Belinda as the real object of desire. (The coquette, in a more
sober reading, becomes the symbol or centerpiece of a society where commerce has united commodities and desire in a perfect closed circle.) Family
patterns were also changing, especially with the advent of the "companionate" marriage, in which a marital bond of affection replaces or softens earlier
property-centered marriages.[5] Unfortunately, the companionate marriage
leaves poetic traces mainly in satires and epistles where women record their
disappointments. Female desire inspires cries for social opportunity as often
as for love, and women poets increasingly depict marriage through images
of legalized slavery, as the traditional amorous battle of the sexes yields to
more grinding metaphors of tyranny and oppression. The coldness of a
neglectful marriage eventually takes its toll in the pained tones of *Address to
her Husband* (1730?), by Mehetabel Wright, the talented sister of Methodist
founders John and Charles Wesley, wed to a London tradesman who spends
his nights in the tavern:

> O thou, whom sacred rites designed
> My guide, and husband ever kind,
> My sovereign master, best of friends,
> On whom my earthly bliss depends;

If e'er thou didst in Hetty see
Aught fair, or good, or dear to thee,
If gentle speech can ever move
The cold remains of former love,
Turn thee at last – my bosom ease,
Or tell me *why* I cease to please.[6]

It is a heart-breaking poem – alternately tender, pleading, furious, self-condemning – its hobbled octosyllabic couplets employing the same verse form that Marvell employed with fluid grace in "To His Coy Mistress" (1681). Few poems suggest more clearly why the troubled emotions, changing social roles, and discordant expectations of eighteenth-century courtship did not generate a love poetry that resembles or rivals earlier modes.

Desire might be said to shift its focus in eighteenth-century verse from love to nature. There is nothing in the country-house poems of the seventeenth century or in earlier loco-descriptive poems – such as Sir John Denham's famous "Cooper's Hill" (1655) – that predict the epic sweep of James Thomson's *The Seasons* (1730–46). As his Miltonic style implies, Thomson seeks to transform the middle-style loco-descriptive poem into a new kind of heroic magnum opus. His vision of nature demands no less:

Nature! great parent! whose directing hand
Rolls round the seasons of the changeful year,
How mighty, how majestic are thy works!
With what a pleasing dread they swell the soul!
That sees, astonished! and astonished sings!

(*Winter* [1726], lines 106–10)[7]

The language of this passage echoes contemporary discussions of "the sublime," a critical-poetic standard that soars in prestige during the early eighteenth century. The well-known critics John Dennis and Joseph Addison soon elevated *Paradise Lost* to preeminence as the modern masterpiece of the sublime. Thus readers understood the serious act of emulation at stake when *The Seasons* in 1730 first appeared in its full (although not yet final) four-book form, rewarding subscribers with a lavish, illustrated quarto edition that embodies its claims to Miltonic stature. Nature, Thomson implies, holds the same innate grandeur as the mysteries of Christian revelation held for Milton, including similar potential for the restoration of poetry from its fallen state. The desire for a new poetry of nature feeds upon the lack Thomson perceives in contemporary writing. "Let poetry," he urges in his Preface to *Winter* (1726), "once more be restored to her ancient truth and purity; let her be inspired from heaven, and in return her incense ascend thither; let her exchange her low, venal, trifling subjects for such as are fair, useful, and magnificent; and let her execute these so as at once to please, instruct, surprise, and astonish; and then of necessity the most inveterate ignorance and prejudice shall be struck dumb, and poets yet become the delight and wonder of mankind."[8] This Miltonic vision of poetry as centered on inspiration and sublimity is exactly what seems absent in the Age of Pope.

The eighteenth-century revolution in attitudes toward nature implies vast changes not only in poetry but also in the history of desire. Two absences are crucial to notice in this redirection of desire toward nature. First, an increasing number of readers now lived in cities, where nature is conspicuously absent or violently subordinated to human needs. (It was an eighteenth-century poet, William Cowper, who penned the famous line "God made the country, and man made the town.") The new longing for nature is a desire for something in visible retreat. Second, the pressing swarm of new writers all focusing on daily social life – epitomized in the Grub Street subculture – left an almost palpable vacancy where contemporaries saw the absence of great poetry like Milton's. Pope, after an early flirtation with epic, settled into ethical writing and social satire that involved regular skirmishing with his enemies: his early ambitions for a national epic on the founding of Britain were not so much unrealized as abandoned. The generation of writers who grew up during Pope's ascendancy felt strongly that something was amiss. Poet and critic Joseph Warton – born when Pope was in his early thirties – in his own early thirties dedicated the first volume (1756) of his *Essay on the Genius and Writings of Pope* to fellow mid-century proponent of poetic change, Edward Young, to whom he addressed the following provocative volley: "The sublime and the pathetic are the two chief nerves of all genuine poesy. What is there transcendently sublime or pathetic in Pope?"[9]

The desire for a poetry transcendently sublime and pathetic led Warton, like Thomson, to nature. What we need to recover in Warton's poem *The Enthusiast; or the Lover of Nature* (1744–48) is the sense in which the term "lover" is no metaphor. The poet's desire has found a new object. Nature now openly occupies the place once held in earlier literature by women:

> All-beauteous Nature! by thy boundless charms
> Oppressed, O where shall I begin thy praise,
> Where turn th' ecstatic eye, how ease my breast
> That pants with wild astonishment and love!

Nature, further, has taken over the female role of muse and is represented as infusing the poet with imaginative power. Warton depicts this imaginative power, personified as Fancy, nursing the infant Shakespeare in a hidden cave beside the winding, willowed banks of the Avon. This access to the nourishing and untrammeled power of nature is what seems to Warton missing in

Pope and his contemporaries. Pope described how in his early years he followed the advice of his mentor to become England's first "correct" poet. The "enthusiast" sees the poetic challenge differently: "What are the lays of artful Addison, / Coldly correct, to Shakespeare's warblings wild?" Even the rejection of rhyme reflects a desire for new forms of poetic expression recovering the imaginative power that Warton links in Shakespeare with whatever is sinuous, passionate, untamed, and, in a word, natural. What we might not expect to find in this turn to a poetry of natural description is how far it reaches. In his "Ode to Fancy" (1746), Warton urges the absent creative power of fancy – "O warm, enthusiastic maid" – to "hither come" in a union of poetry and nature that holds benefits for the nation as well as for the poet: "O let each Muse's fame increase, / O bid Britannia rival Greece!" The desire for personal fame is thus linked explicitly with wider desires for national grandeur. Within ten years of Warton's "Ode to Fancy" Britain's overseas empire expanded to its all-time limit. Thomson, in a fantasia of desire that rivals Warton's, created no doubt the most notorious poem that links nature with claims of national grandeur: "Rule, Britannia" (1740). Even the wild and violent sea – nature as raw power – here obligingly accepts the role of imperial subject.

Nature in the eighteenth century holds an inseparable connection with religion and with religious feeling, so that the desire for nature is often inseparable from a desire for God. Thomson depicted nature even in its most violent moods as the handiwork of God. (As he writes in *Spring*: "though concealed, to every purer eye / The informing Author in his works appears" [lines 859–60].) The only passages in Pope's *Essay on Man* (1733–34) that Warton deemed sublime are descriptions of God's presence in nature. In criticism and poetry, the sublime was early associated with God's power expressed in nature, and the one universally recognized illustration of sublimity in the eighteenth century is the *fiat lux* from Genesis: "God said, Let there be light, and there was light." From the instantaneous flood of light at the Creation to the awesome force of whirlwinds and volcanoes, nature cannot be understood in the eighteenth century except as the handiwork of God. Newton insisted on this point no less than the Deists. Desire in the eighteenth century even when occupied in counting the streaks of a tulip simultaneously engaged readers and writers in varieties of experience that can only be called religious.

Historians sometimes depict religion in the eighteenth century as marked by an arid turn toward rationalism, but this claim cannot stand up. The century's most popular form of literature was the sermon. If some sermons strike us as dryly argumentative, the arguments once glowed with intensity and answered to a desire that left readers uneasy without good arguments.

Moreover, argument was not the sole staple of sermon literature and religious discourse. Anglicanism faced its most serious challenge not from outside
but from internal division. The division concerned, among other rancorous
matters, the value of feeling and the validity of personal devotion.
Methodism began as a movement within the Anglican Church, and the
threat it posed to traditional Anglican practices – especially through its emotional appeal to women, craftsmen, apprentices, and the lower classes in
general – finally led to the expulsion of its leaders. Uneasiness takes few more
urgent forms than an ardor driving clergy and parishioners outside the
church that has assured their salvation. In the middle and late eighteenth
century, the perceived absence of God in an individual life proves a powerful source of desire.

John and Charles Wesley, leaders of the breakaway Methodist movement,
are not generally considered poets, perhaps for the same reason that hymns
are not considered poems. This prejudice impoverishes our understanding of
eighteenth-century poetry and religion.[10] The Wesleys – along with other distinguished religious writers of the period – breathe new life into the hymn as
an expression of spiritual desire. John Wesley's plainly titled "Hymn"
(1738), for example, begins with an explicit account of uneasiness – inward
pain whose source lies in an absence so vast that its dimensions are unfath-
omable:

> Thou hidden love of God, whose height,
>   Whose depth unfathomed no man knows,
> I see from far thy beauteous light,
>   Inly I sigh for thy repose;
> My heart is pained, nor can it be
> At rest, till it finds rest in thee.

Religious experience in the Methodist hymn often focuses on the absence of
repose, on the sinner's sense of loss, on a restless unfulfilled desire for God.
The restlessness of religious loss and separation turns into terror in "The
Castaway," written in 1799 by the Evangelical poet William Cowper, who
describes his own spiritual desolation through the struggle of a "wretch"
washed overboard and lost at sea. Desire finds many voices in eighteenth-
century religious poems, from Christopher Smart's extraordinary impulse to
praise God through a meticulous and somewhat eccentric inventory of divine
works and creatures in A Song to David (1763) to the less successful emulation of Miltonic sublimity in endless blank-verse biblical epics and odes.
Many eighteenth-century poets were clergymen, and many clergymen wrote
verse, including Isaac Watts, Jonathan Swift, Thomas Parnell, Joseph
Warton, Edward Young, and Robert Blair, to name just a few. Poems on

explicitly religious subjects – from Pope's "Messiah" (1717) to Cowper's "Walking with God" (1779) – constitute one of the more powerful forms that desire takes in eighteenth-century verse.

Death has long maintained an open or underground commerce with desire. These complex interconnections extend, as Jonathan Dollimore has shown, from the ancient world, where intense desire is represented as unbinding or wrecking the self, through the ecstatic union of love and death in British and German Romantic writers.[11] Death is also deeply paradoxical as both the most frightening of presences (when we encounter the dead) yet something we can never know in ourselves and thus always elusively absent and enigmatic. Strangely, Dollimore's learned historical study of connections among death, desire, and loss in effect skips over the eighteenth century. Our challenge is to recognize in what ways eighteenth-century culture helped decisively to reconfigure the experience of death. This reconfiguration, in which poetry played an indispensable role, gives a distinctive cast to the literature of the age well before Keats in his "Ode on Melancholy" recounts his midnight whispering to death, in the manner of a lover, as he called it "sweet names."

The eighteenth century inherited and greatly expanded a philosophical–religious reflection on death expressed in the famous writings known as *ars moriendi*. Death from this perspective was not just something that happened – an abrupt, outrageous intrusion into the ordinary flow of life – but a premeditated action. The act of dying of course did not normally take place sequestered in hospitals, which in the eighteenth century were mostly charitable institutions for the poor. Instead, the deathbed held a semi-public status. Death was, ideally, a performance, an event, subject to the same artful preparations as any serious action performed on the stage, and like any stage performance it also held the power to move and to edify its audience. Addison in his last days, for example, summoned his profligate son-in-law to witness the peace and consolation of a Christian death. Death was the revelation of a truth. It exposed a solid core beneath the social masks and continuous changes of human character, as Pope argued in *To Cobham* (1733). It did away with evasion. Thus Boswell paid a visit to the dying David Hume curious to know whether the great thinker would act out the final scene in ways that contradicted his skeptical philosophy. In law, deathbed confessions held the status of fact. A variety of eighteenth-century poems confirm and extend this view of death as the summarizing truth of a life.

The elegy and epitaph have nearly passed from notice in contemporary criticism, except for a few remarkable works, like Auden's famous monody on the death of Yeats. We still read poems at funerals – a sign of the marginal but still elevated status assigned to poets – although death is no longer an occasion for writing poetry. The eighteenth century, by contrast, looked upon death as demanding a poetic voice to remember and to commemorate the dead. This serious acceptance of a memorial function for poetry in part reflects a sense – equally distinctive in the period – that the destructive forces of mutability and loss now take the shape of a consuming blankness that threatens to swallow up everything in oblivion. Dryden's *MacFlecknoe* (1682) and Pope's *Dunciad* (1743) both explore a satiric mythos in which degraded poets help push civilized life backward toward an unremembered chaos. The revitalized poetry sought by Dryden and Pope takes as a major goal the primal act of fending off oblivion. For eighteenth-century poets, the poetic, commemorative voice demanded by the forgetfulness of death not only gives increasing prominence to the elegy and epitaph but also infuses these traditional funerary genres with something like new language. If death is the summarizing truth of a life, the truth must emerge in a stark and simple style that proclaims its absolute distance from the mere flattery and lies of fiction.

The change in style marking the English epitaph and elegy indicates a revolution in thought. For example, the baroque christianized mythology and intricate pastoral machinery of Milton's *Lycidas* (1637) gives way to the restrained diction and sparing but resonant classical allusions underpinning Dryden's "To the Memory of Mr. Oldham" (1684). The restraint and refusals typical of Dryden's elegy create a template for the similarly straightforward epitaphs and elegies by Pope and Johnson. Johnson's "On the Death of Dr. Robert Levet" (1783) dispenses with allusion altogether in order to create a plain, direct memorial appropriate for an unassuming man who spent his long life quietly tending the poor. The elegy in its style is a direct rebuke to the poetic tributes Johnson describes as "lettered arrogance." Of course, any genre built for seriousness is also, in the eighteenth century, open to parody or mock-heroic play, as in Gray's ornate "Ode on the Death of a Favorite Cat, Drowned in a Tub of Gold Fishes" (1748) or Goldsmith's prankish "Elegy on the Death of a Mad Dog" (1766). The bogus or overflowery verse staged to commemorate the death of animals points obliquely to the changed attitude toward human death. The truths spoken in the name of death have now proved either too plain or too stark and serious for traditional poetic ornament.

The truths spoken in the name of death reach beyond an accurate depiction of the individuals who have died. The voices of women writing on the regular deaths of children and newborns express at times a general weariness, as in Hetty Wright's "To an Infant Expiring the Second Day of Birth" (1733), where in her "anguish" she pleads to join her dying child. John Gay's brief auto-obituary, "My Own Epitaph" (1720), gives to such weariness a wry, witty, mordant edge: "Life is a jest, and all things show it; / I thought so once, but now I know it."

Here too, in contrast to the uncertainties and mere probabilities of life, Gay represents death as providing access to truth, although it is a dark truth that exposes a radical emptiness where we are accustomed to plenitude. Perhaps Gay's witty couplet implies that the proper response to life's emptiness is wit, not solemnity. It is death, however, that now gives wit an added edge. Indeed, death in eighteenth-century verse has a way of challenging and altering ordinary perception. In *Eloisa to Abelard*, Eloisa's long vacillation between duty and desire – between God and Abelard – reaches a decisive turning point only when she suddenly imagines her own death. The vision of death now changes everything: "O death all-eloquent! you only prove / What dust we doat on, when 'tis man we love" (lines 335–36). Johnson's first definition of the verb "dote" is "To have the intellect impaired by age or passion; to be delirious." Death alone, Eloisa tells us, holds the power to correct our vision and to expose the most potent human desire as a mere fixation on dust. The supreme eloquence of death lies in reducing every other claim to silence. Death in this understanding is far more than the terminus to an individual life. It is a force that, directly or indirectly, infiltrates the vision and alters the whole tenor of eighteenth-century life and writing.

The particular ambience that death casts over eighteenth-century life is nowhere more visible than in the literature of melancholy. It is a writing with precedents in the brooding darkness, flapping rooks, and spiky towers of Milton's *Il Penseroso* (1645) and its various early eighteenth-century derivatives, such as Pope's "Elegy to the Memory of an Unfortunate Lady" and Thomas Parnell's "Night-Piece on Death" (1721). Something happens around mid century, however, that concentrates this scattered imagery of pensiveness into a new death-centered literature for which the prevailing mood is melancholy. Thomas Warton's *The Pleasures of Melancholy* (1747) offers a reliable introduction to this new literature with its solitary speaker, lit only by the dim glare from a candle, walking at midnight through the burial vaults of a "ruined" abbey:

> while airy voices talk
> Along the glimm'ring walls; or ghostly shape,
> At distance seen, invites with beck'ning hand
> My lonesome steps . . .

The dead here – if only through their presence to the imagination – intrude among the living in ways that ultimately redirect eighteenth-century writers.

Death, for example, could be considered a major character in the gothic novel, and it is certainly central to the literature of melancholy, where it dominates such popular poems as Edward Young's *The Complaint, or Night Thoughts on Life, Death and Immortality* (1742–45) and Robert Blair's *The Grave* (1743). We cannot fully grasp the significance of melancholy in eighteenth-century verse, however, without looking briefly at the almost simultaneous transformations of death.

The distinguished historian Philippe Ariès provides both a vocabulary and a context for thinking about eighteenth-century changes through his distinction between "tame" and "savage" death.[12] He explains much of the social and theological life of the Middle Ages as devoted to removing death from a savage state in which humankind is prey to the unmediated ferocity of the natural world. Burial customs such as covering the face of the corpse, along with numerous Christian rites and consolations, helped move death toward a state in which its previous ferocity is somewhat controlled and tamed. Death, so domesticated, attained a familiarity that distanced its fearsomeness. It was not unusual, Ariès reports, for people to predict correctly the day of their death. Death would now in effect come when called. We can interpret the eighteenth-century epitaph as in part an extension of this medieval program to tame and domesticate death, much like the eighteenth-century reinvention of the cemetery, which replaced urban medieval graveyards with picturesque countrified landscapes. Thomas Gray's *Elegy Written in a Country Churchyard* (1751) is a monument in this ongoing transformation of death. The opening "ivy-mantled tow'r" and "moping owl" (lines 9–10) create gentle ties with the literature of melancholy – his imagined epitaph says of the speaker that "*Melancholy marked him for her own*" (line 120) – and the poem in its quiet portraits of rural life succeeds in drawing the forgotten dead back into the community of the living.

The eighteenth-century transformation of death, however, pointed also in another direction where melancholy revealed its darkest links with terror. Ariès explains how the savage death staged a comeback as Enlightenment science, in a near confirmation of Swift's laconic vision of watching a woman flayed, relentlessly stripped the body of its familiar domestic coverings. New terrors suddenly emerge to trouble the popular imagination, such as burial alive. Indeed, the death that Gray so carefully domesticates in a peaceful country setting of lowing cattle now affirms a ferocious new connection with cities and machines, which the English observe horrified as the Enlightenment in France spirals uncontrolled into the efficiency, chaos, and bloodshed of the guillotine. Premonitions of this urban and scientific reemergence of savage death doubtless help reinforce the gentle melancholy that in effect reaffirms the familiar values to which Gray gives voice. When Johnson wrote (twenty

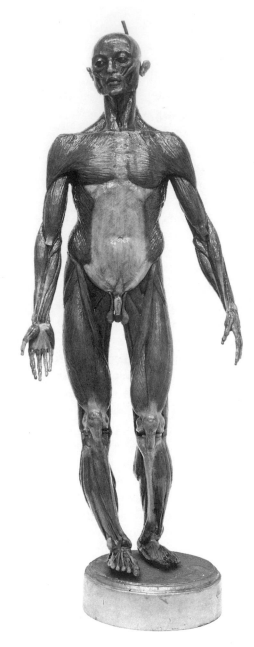

Figure 1. Anatomical figure in wax showing superficial muscles, anterior view

years after its appearance) that Gray's elegy abounds "with sentiments to which every bosom returns an echo," he referred in part to the widespread sentimental transformation of death which the poem did much to secure.[13]

The savage death that infiltrates later eighteenth-century thought does not have a major place in poetry, where its presence would risk overwhelming any structure that poets could create to contain it. We find it breaking through, however, at moments, in glimpses, uneasily countered by reassurances finally less than absolute or convincing. Its most common appearance comes in changed representations of the rural poor, who increasingly do not resemble fellow citizens in Gray's community of "rude forefathers" but outcasts, misfits, and refugees from economic turmoil. We find glimpses of such lone and broken rural figures in *The Deserted Village* (1770) by Oliver Goldsmith and in *The Village* (1783) by George Crabbe. Less well known is the protagonist in Robert Southey's "The Widow" (1799), wandering at night, destitute and weary, over the cold, shelterless downs:

> "Once I had friends, – but they have all forsook me!
> Once I had parents, – they are now in heaven!
> I had a home once – I had once a husband –
> Pity me, strangers!"   (lines 13–16)

The rattling chariot and horseman that pass by cannot hear her cries through the loud wind. She lies down in the snow, where a traveller finds her the next morning, dead. "God had released her," Southey writes in his final line, but neither the pious last line nor the controlled sapphic stanzas can erase a sense that the poor inhabit a world that looks increasingly savage. Arguably, one purpose of Southey's poem – a strategy basic to sentimental writing – is to evoke and to exercise compassion in the reader, thereby widening the moral community to enfold impoverished outcasts. The image of an old rural pauper found frozen to death in a country ruled by industrial values might also bring to mind the demystified, unsentimental, cold rage of William Blake's "The Human Abstract" (1794): "Pity would be no more, / If we did not make somebody poor."

Dreams have received considerable attention in the work of Romantic writers, but we know very little about their appearance in the poetry of the eighteenth century.[14] As a biological state, dreaming is of course set apart from normal, waking consciousness, so for writers in every period it easily absorbs values associated with a departure from everyday reality. On the other hand, religion and philosophy have often criticized everyday reality as an insubstantial or fraudulent substitute for an absent higher state, recognizable especially in dreams and visions. One dream, then, transports us to a region of truth, while another traps us in illusion and falsehood. One dream offers an alternative to the emptiness of life, while another fritters life away in barren images and wishful thinking. This basic doubleness finds expression in the Homeric myth that posits two gates – ivory and horn – through which dreams enter the world: dreams that pass through the ivory gate are false and deceiving, whereas dreams passing through the gate of horn are prophetic and true. All very simple – except that dreams also interrupt the binary thinking that divides the world into opposing compartments labeled false and true. Eighteenth-century poets are drawn to dreaming in ways that greatly complicate any simple dichotomy between delusion and truth.

Eighteenth-century analysts emphasize both the psychological faculties responsible for dreams as well as a surprising link between waking and dreaming states. "Dreams are certainly the Result of our waking Thoughts," *The Spectator* (no. 586) affirmed in 1714, "and our daily Hopes and Fears are what give the Mind such nimble Relishes of Pleasure, and such severe Touches of Pain, in its midnight Rambles."[15] Pope articulates the common belief (supported by twentieth-century research) that the dream assembles images present to the mind during consciousness, and he emphasizes the equally common belief that what produces dreams is the mental faculty called fancy or imagination. Imagination in the eighteenth century normally refers to the mind's power to make or receive pictorial images. As mainly pictorial compositions, dreams not only communicate with unusual speed and vividness but also maintain a strong link with the emotions. "[T]he Passions affect the Mind with greater Strength when we are a-sleep," wrote Addison in an essay on dreaming, "than when we are awake. Joy and Sorrow give us more vigorous Sensations of Pain or Pleasure at this time, than at any other" (*Spectator*, no. 487). Dreams, however, are more than an arresting compound of vivid and emotionally powerful images encountered in sleep. They take their defining character from the absence of another mental faculty: reason.

Dreams as the sign of reason absent, suspended, overturned, or disordered make a regular appearance in eighteenth-century satire, where they are frequently elided with madness. Madness in this context is both a clinical and a moral category. Its public exemplars are the two stone statues of Raving and of Melancholy Madness positioned above the gates of Bethlehem Royal Hospital ("Bedlam") that preside over the opening of Pope's *Dunciad*. In *The Dunciad* madness is represented less as a personal malady than a social force threatening to consolidate its powers and to overwhelm the polite world in a spectacle of mass irrationality. Bethlehem Royal Hospital was designed not for cure but for confinement, and London spectators paid a small fee to observe the mad confined in Bedlam, much as they paid to see the lions kept at the Tower. Pope's many satiric references to madness develop the picture of a world (and certainly a poet) threatened by swarming irrationality, as in the opening lines of his *An Epistle from Mr. Pope to Dr. Arbuthnot* (1735):

> Shut, shut the door, good *John*! fatigu'd I said,
> Tye up the knocker, say I'm sick, I'm dead,
> The Dog-star rages! nay 'tis past a doubt,
> All *Bedlam*, or *Parnassus*, is let out:
> Fire in each eye, and Papers in each hand,
> They rave, recite, and madden round the land.[16]

The connection between Parnassus and Bedlam is more than a convenient way for Pope to denigrate his poetic enemies. Poets and madmen both face dangers implicit in an active imagination.

It was a poet, Imlac, to whom Johnson assigned the famous speech in *Rasselas* (1759) warning against the "dangerous prevalence" of imagination. Prevalency – which Johnson defines as "superiority; influence; predominance" – holds dangers because the imagination gives us real pleasure, and pleasure helps confirm its dominance. "Then," continues Imlac, "fictions begin to operate as realities, false opinions fasten upon the mind, and life passes in dreams of rapture or of anguish."[17] Dreamers lost in rapture or in anguish become another distinguishing mark of eighteenth-century satire. Book III of *The Dunciad* opens with the hero, Cibber, resting his head on the lap of Dulness and slipping off to sleep:

> Then raptures high the seat of Sense o'erflow,
> Which only heads refin'd from Reason know.
> Hence, from the straw where Bedlam's Prophet nods,
> He hears loud Oracles, and talks with Gods:
> Hence the Fool's Paradise, the Statesman's Scheme,
> The air-built Castle, and the golden Dream,
> The Maid's romantic wish, the Chemist's flame,
> And Poet's vision of eternal Fame.   (lines 5–12)

The absurdist visions that Cibber, delighted, beholds in his ensuing dream – conveyed "on Fancy's easy wing" (III, line 13) – represent Pope's judgment on the moral, political, and literary follies of his day. What unites many of these follies with the deluded alchemist, scheming statesman, bedlamite prophet, and poet dreaming of eternal fame is the way in which individuals and groups give themselves over to a near total absorption in the rapturous and unchecked inner world of images.

The attractions of the dream world pose a special risk for poets because poetry demands a commerce with fancy. As Hobbes wrote in 1650,

"Judgment begets the strength and structure, and Fancy begets the orna-
ments of a Poem."[18] This mechanistic division of labor at least set in place
the crucial terms and values so basic to early eighteenth-century poetic
theory. Often employing a silent or explicit analogy between poetry and
painting, critics commonly describe judgment as providing the design or
outline, while fancy adds the color. Fancy in this context appears as a
dreamlike, insubstantial, secondary power occupied mainly with decoration, dress, and style. Its acknowledged facility in linking disparate images
could seem to resemble delirium or fever. Here is how Isaac Watts described
his mental state in "The Hurry of the Spirits, in a Fever and Nervous
Disorders" (1734):

> If I but close my eyes, strange images
> In thousand forms and thousand colours rise,
> Stars, rainbows, moons, green dragons, bears, and ghosts,
> An endless medley. . . .   (lines 21–24)

Dreams in this context become a synonym for delusion and error: "Nor is it
Homer Nods," writes Pope in *An Essay on Criticism* (1711), contesting a
critical commonplace about Homeric faults, "but *We* that *Dream*" (line
180). Poets early in the century recognize that poems cannot dispense with
the dreamlike coloring and variety that fancy provides, but they emphasize
the active, indispensable guidance of a wide-awake judgment.

Two complications skew this fairly straightforward picture of dreams.
First, eighteenth-century critics increasingly acknowledge that the greatest
poetry is simply uncontainable within the Hobbesian matrix of fancy and
judgment. They write increasingly of genius, rapture, fire, and sublimity. The
concept that Pope employs in praising Homer is invention: a copiousness of
mind that approaches what we mean by creativity. "It is to the strength of
this amazing invention," Pope writes in 1715, "we are to attribute that
unequaled fire and rapture which is so forcible in Homer that no man of a
true poetical spirit is master of himself while he reads him."[19] Ten years later,
Pope singles out originality as Shakespeare's defining trait. "If ever any
author deserved the name of an original," he writes in highest praise, "it was
Shakespeare. Homer himself drew not his art so immediately from the foun-
tains of nature . . ."[20] Writers in the generation after Pope enrich the discussion of originality and of invention, linking both concepts with a vastly
revised understanding of fancy. No longer is fancy a permanent junior
partner in the Hobbesian firm of Strength, Structure, & Ornament. The creative power newly attributed to fancy finds expression not only in the so-
called "greater" genres such as tragedy and epic but also throughout the
lesser range of lyric verse down to the smallest fragment of the sublime. This

new understanding of fancy is also highly visible in the changed status now attributed to dreams and dreaming.

Edward Young – author of the alternately argumentative and ecstatic popular poem *Night Thoughts* – offers a clear instance of the changes at mid century. In his *Conjectures on Original Composition* (1759), he writes passages of praise that Pope might well have included in footnotes to *The Dunciad*. "In the Fairyland of Fancy," he writes in supporting originality over imitation, "Genius may wander wild; there it has a creative power, and may reign arbitrarily over its own empire of Chimeras." Not only the matter of poetry but also the experience of the reader is reshaped through the writer's creative power. "[O]n the strong wing of his Imagination," Young writes of the original author, "we are snatched from *Britain* to *Italy*, from Climate to Climate, from Pleasure to Pleasure; we have no Home, no Thought, of our own; till the Magician drops his Pen: And then falling down into ourselves, we awake to flat Realities, lamenting the change, like the Beggar who dreamt himself a Prince."[21] Reading, like writing, is now akin to an immersion in dream. Dreams, moreover, have lost their negative aura of delusion and assume a positive kinship with vision and prophecy. William Collins begins his "Ode on the Poetical Character" (1746) with a Spenserian tale about a "magic girdle" worn only by the fairest. The gift of poetry, he concludes, is also sparingly bestowed:

> Young Fancy thus, to me divinest name,
>> To whom, prepared and bathed in heav'n,
>> The cest of amplest pow'r is giv'n,
>> To few the godlike gift assigns,
>> To gird their blest prophetic loins,
> And gaze her visions wild, and feel unmixed her flame!

> (lines 17–22)

The poetical character, for Collins, is endowed with a godlike, heavenly gift and power bestowed by fancy upon prophetic, visionary souls. The visions of poetry need not be in fact divinely inspired or religious in content. What matters is that mid-century poets increasingly see their role as an excursion into dreamlike realms – even a dreamlike past such as James Macpherson recreated in the bardic Ossian prose poems – that Pope for the most part consigned to dunces.

This fancy-centered, mid-eighteenth-century "poetry of vision" – while often including passages of natural description – differs from earlier landscape verse because it typically employs an almost cinematic dissolve in which the speaker's immediate surroundings become the trigger for an excursion into dream, memory, or imagination. Thomas Gray's "Ode on a

Distant Prospect of Eton College" (1747) offers a particularly effective version of this technique for bringing absence into the present. Gray's title invokes the genre of eighteenth-century "prospect" poems, which normally offer a visual and spatial inventory of the landscape, enriched perhaps by relating the history of local sites. In this case, the immediate surroundings of Gray's speaker include the "distant spires" of Eton College, and this spatial vision provides the trigger for an imaginative journey through a temporal prospect even more remote. The poem, in fact, dwells not upon Eton College and its picturesque landscape but upon an unseen, inescapable, grim future awaiting the young students:

> Lo, in the vale of years beneath
> A grisly troop are seen,
> The painful family of Death,
> More hideous than their Queen . . .   (lines 81–84)

The verb "seen" is important. William Blake's illustration to this passage, while the work of an exceptional visionary artist, offers a helpful indication of the rich pictorial resources that eighteenth-century poets and critics recognized as implicit in the literary technique of personification. Personification transforms something absent and abstract (the idea of death or old age) into a concrete pictorial image carrying an emotional charge and often performing an action, albeit minimalist and highly ritualized. Although it invokes a literary heritage reaching back to Chaucer's *Hous of Fame* (c. 1379), the dream-vision in eighteenth-century poems is often a vehicle to initiate the fanciful, visual encounter with absent personified beings.

The second major complication that disrupts any simple formula linking dreams with falsehood and delusion is a growing interest in the operations of the mind. The first works that resemble modern psychology appear during the eighteenth century, and the new interest in mental phenomena affects the discussion and status of dreams, which have a place in the work of John Locke, David Hartley, George Berkeley, and Dugald Stuart. Popular works such as Andrew Baxter's *Enquiry into the Nature of the Human Soul* (1733) and John Bond's *Essay on the Incubus* (1753) show how dreams come to hold a fascination not as simply the derelict obverse of reason but as forms of mental life with their own validity and logic. Pope's friend Jonathan Richardson, for example, between 1726 and 1728 wrote a quartet of remarkable poems entitled together "On My Late Dear Wife." One poem is followed with the annotation "*Really dreamed, July 14–15, 1726*"; another is annotated "*Dreamed, Sept. 10–11.*" These dream-encounters with his dead wife give the grieving Richardson a joy represented in the poems as undamaged by his knowledge that her image is unreal:

Figure 2. William Blake, illustration for Thomas Gray's "Ode on a Distant Prospect of Eton College"

Slumb'ring disturbed, appeared the well-known face,
Lovely, engaging, as she ever was;
I kissed and caught the phantom in my arms,
I knew it such, but such a shade hath charms!   (ii, 1–4)

This complex experience conveys a feeling quite different than the spectacle of Pope's dunce booksellers giddily clutching after the phantom of a plump poet. Richardson's poems, clearly written for his own purposes and not published until fifty years later, reflect the growing power that dreams possess to claim attention not as delusion but as authentic fragments of human mental and emotional life.

The changing interest in dreams may be measured by the difference between Addison's ten successive *Spectator* papers known as The Pleasures of the Imagination (1712) and their later poetic counterpart, Mark Akenside's *The Pleasures of Imagination* (1744–71). Addison has nothing to say about dreams – mentioning them once as an instance of Lockean wit – whereas Akenside describes the creative process in a language deeply indebted to dreams, with their familiar combination of night, garish images, and unregulated profusion. Here, for example, is Akenside's description of the poet at work surveying his inner memory-bank of images:

> Anon ten thousand shapes,
> Like spectres trooping to the wizard's call,
> Fleet swift before him. From the womb of earth,
> From ocean's bed they come: th' eternal heav'ns
> Disclose their splendours, and the dark abyss
> Pours out her births unknown. With fixed gaze
> He marks the rising phantoms.   (i, 48–54)

Akenside's poet compares, blends, divides, and varies the images – uncertain of his aim – until at last, as judgment fixes upon a general plan, "Lucid order dawns" (i, 61). The arrival of this metaphoric dawn, concluding the dream-like or reverie stage of poetic composition, might remind us that gothic novelists and visionary painters would soon attribute a truth-telling, revelatory power to night and its disorderly dreams. Henry Fuseli in his painting "The Nightmare" (1781) – a copy of which Freud kept on display – depicts night and its dreams as exposing sexual desires or fantasies that elude the decorous world of daylight order. Dreaming here represents not so much the opposite of reason – the folly or madness that ensues when reason lets go – as the revelation of a hidden truth that reason would seek to deny and suppress. Fuseli's exposure of suppressions and denials is not so distant, after all, from the phantasmagoric and feverish underworld in Pope's *Rape of the Lock* – a truth-telling variant on distortions native to the beau monde –

Figure 3. Henry Fuseli, *The Nightmare*

where "pow'rful Fancy works, / And Maids turn'd Bottels, call aloud for Corks" (IV, 53–54).

The complex trajectory that dreams assume in eighteenth-century verse points toward significant developments in the work of later poets, such as Coleridge's "The Pains of Sleep" (written 1803), Byron's "Darkness" (written 1816), or Crabbe's "The World of Dreams" (written c. 1817). Like death and desire, dreams find new uses and expressions among Romantic writers, but not entirely new. Pope in *An Epistle to Mr. Jervas* (1716) had depicted his friendship with the portrait painter Charles Jervas as a union of two spirits both moved with a vision of British poetry and painting restored through the reassertion of a classical ideal. Although Greece rather than Italy becomes the preferred Romantic origin, Pope's lines to Jervas depict a rich combination of dream, death, and desire all brought into contact through the resonant image of the eternal city, once the summit of arms and arts, reduced in the eighteenth century to a site of prodigious remnants and debris:

> What flatt'ring scenes our wand'ring fancy wrought,
> *Rome*'s pompous glories rising to our thought!
> Together o'er the *Alps* methinks we fly,
> Fir'd with ideas of fair *Italy*.
> With thee, on *Raphael*'s Monument I mourn,
> Or wait inspiring dreams at *Maro*'s Urn:
> With thee repose, where *Tully* once was laid,
> Or seek some ruin's formidable shade;
> While fancy brings the vanish'd piles to view,
> And builds imaginary *Rome* a-new.   (lines 23–32)

Here the young Pope, who never in his life left England, imagines himself at Virgil's grave seeking inspiration through dreams or reposing in the shade of a ruin while fancy creates an image of classical Rome in all its greatness. Desire seems ready to propel the poet beyond human limits, fired by a vision of the power of art, only to end (in the final couplet) with an elegiac recognition of the absolute, inescapable fact of absence: "Alas! how little from the grave we claim?/ Thou but preserv'st a Face and I a Name." Fragments, remnants, traces: a poetics of absence is what creates some of the more compelling moments in eighteenth-century British verse.

NOTES

1 John Dyer, *The Ruins of Rome* (1740), in *Poems by John Dyer* (London, 1761), p. 20. See Laurence Goldstein, *Ruins and Empire: the Evolution of a Theme in Augustan and Romantic Literature* (Pittsburgh: University of Pittsburgh Press, 1977).

2 Samuel Johnson, *Lives of the English Poets* (1779–81), ed. George Birkbeck Hill, 3 vols. (Oxford: Clarendon Press, 1905), III, 101.

3 John Locke, *An Essay concerning Human Understanding* (1690), ed. Peter H. Nidditch (Oxford: Clarendon Press, 1975), p. 230 (II.xx.6).

4 Blanford Parker, *The Triumph of Augustan Poetics: English Literary Culture from Butler to Johnson* (Cambridge: Cambridge University Press, 1998), p. 20.

5 Lawrence Stone, *The Family, Sex and Marriage in England, 1500–1800* (London: Weidenfeld and Nicolson, 1977).

6 In *Eighteenth-Century Women Poets*, ed. Roger Lonsdale (Oxford: Oxford University Press, 1989), p. 112.

7 In *The New Oxford Book of Eighteenth-Century Verse*, ed. Roger Lonsdale (Oxford: Oxford University Press, 1984). All poems, unless otherwise specified, are cited from this edition.

8 James Thomson, Preface to *Winter* (1726), in *Eighteenth-Century Critical Essays*, ed. Scott Elledge, 2 vols. (Ithaca, NY: Cornell University Press, 1961), I, 407.

9 Joseph Warton, "To the Reverend Dr Young, Rector of Welwyn, in Hertfordshire" (1756), *An Essay on the Genius and Writings of Pope*, in *Eighteenth-Century Critical Essays*, ed. Elledge, II, 719.

10 See Donald Davie, *The Eighteenth-Century Hymn in England* (Cambridge: Cambridge University Press, 1993).

11 Jonathan Dollimore, *Death, Desire and Loss in Western Culture* (New York: Routledge, 1998).

12 Philippe Ariès, *The Hour of Our Death* (1977), trans. Helen Weaver (New York: Knopf, 1981), pp. 602–14.

13 Johnson, *Lives of the English Poets*, ed. Hill, III, 441.

14 See Jennifer Ford, *Coleridge on Dreaming: Romanticism, Dreams and the Medical Imagination* (Cambridge: Cambridge University Press, 1998).

15 *The Spectator*, ed. Donald F. Bond, 5 vols. (Oxford: Clarendon Press, 1965).

16 *The Poems of Alexander Pope*, ed. John Butt (New Haven: Yale University Press, 1963), pp. 597–98; all citations are from this edition.

17 Samuel Johnson, *The History of Rasselas, Prince of Abissinia* (1759), ed. Geoffrey Tillotson and Brian Jenkins (London: Oxford University Press, 1971), p. 115 (ch. 44).

18 Thomas Hobbes, "The Answer of Mr Hobbes to Sr Will. D'Avenant's *Preface before Gondibert*" (1650), in *Critical Essays of the Seventeenth Century*, ed. J. E. Spingarn, 3 vols. (1908–1909; rpt. Bloomington: Indiana University Press, 1957), II, 59.

19 Alexander Pope, Preface to the Translation of the *Iliad* (1715), in *Eighteenth-Century Critical Essays*, ed. Elledge, I, 258.

20 Alexander Pope, "The Preface of the Editor" to *The Works of Shakespeare* (1725), in *Eighteenth-Century Critical Essays*, ed. Elledge, I, 279.

21 Edward Young, *Conjectures on Original Composition* (London, 1759), pp. 37, 13.

FURTHER READING

Butler, Marilyn. *Romantics, Rebels and Reactionaries: English Literature and its Background 1760–1830*. New York: Oxford University Press, 1981.

Castle, Terry. *The Female Thermometer: Eighteenth-Century Culture and the Invention of the Uncanny*. New York: Oxford University Press, 1995.

Carson, Anne. *Eros the Bittersweet*. Princeton: Princeton University Press, 1986.

Davie, Donald. *The Eighteenth-Century Hymn in England*. Cambridge: Cambridge University Press, 1993.

Doody, Margaret Anne. *The Daring Muse: Augustan Poetry Reconsidered*. New York: Cambridge University Press, 1985.

Etlin, Richard A. *The Architecture of Death: the Transformation of the Cemetery in Eighteenth-Century Paris*. Cambridge, MA: MIT Press, 1984.

Goldstein, Laurence. *Ruins and Empire: the Evolution of a Theme in Augustan and Romantic Literature*. Pittsburgh: University of Pittsburgh Press, 1977.

Hobson, J. Allan. *The Dreaming Brain*. New York: Basic Books, 1988.

Irlan, Shaun. *Elations: the Poetics of Enthusiasm in Eighteenth-Century Britain.* Stanford: Stanford University Press, 1999.

Knapp, Steven. *Personification and the Sublime: Milton to Coleridge.* Cambridge, MA: Harvard University Press, 1985.

McGann, Jerome. *The Poetics of Sensibility: a Revolution in Literary Style.* New York: Oxford University Press, 1996.

Morris, David B. *Alexander Pope: the Genius of Sense.* Cambridge, MA: Harvard University Press, 1984.

Mullen, John. *Sentiment and Sociability: the Language of Feeling in the Eighteenth Century.* Oxford: Clarendon Press, 1988.

Stewart, Susan. *On Longing: Narratives of the Miniature, the Gigantic, the Souvenir, the Collection.* Durham, NC: Duke University Press, 1993.

Sitter, John. *Literary Loneliness in Mid-Eighteenth-Century England.* Ithaca: Cornell University Press, 1982.

Todd, Janet. *Sensibility: an Introduction.* London: Methuen, 1986.

Weiskel, Thomas. *The Romantic Sublime: Studies in the Structure and Psychology of Transcendence.* Baltimore: Johns Hopkins University Press, 1976.

PATRICIA MEYER SPACKS

The poetry of sensibility

To designate a body of literature "the poetry of sensibility" aligns it not only with a kind of feeling but with a cultural movement. An intricate culture of sensibility flourished in late eighteenth-century Britain. It affected the behavior of men and women, the conception and development of social reform, and the nature of prose and poetry. It expressed a set of assumptions and values that operated in philosophy as well as fiction and influenced even politics. It had profound consequences long after it had largely disappeared as a social movement.

Sensibility, the *Oxford English Dictionary* tells us, is "emotional consciousness; glad or sorrowful, grateful or resentful recognition of a person's conduct, or of a fact or a condition of things." Again, it is defined as "Quickness and acuteness of apprehension or feeling; the quality of being easily and strongly affected by emotional influences." And yet again: "Capacity for refined emotion; delicate sensitiveness of taste; also, readiness to feel compassion for suffering, and to be moved by the pathetic in literature or art." Sensibility always involves emotion, and it always entails willingness and ability to respond to others. From a twentieth-century point of view, its responses may seem excessive. Marianne Dashwood, in *Sense and Sensibility*, rhapsodizing over dead leaves, offers a comic version of its possible extremity. But Marianne requires chastening. Her sensible sister makes fun of her extravagances, and her creator arranges the plot to reeducate her. Her predecessors in fine feeling, in contrast, won admiration from many of their contemporaries.

The culture of sensibility depended on subtle discriminations. Not every kind of feeling, or feeling expressed in every way, testified to the fine responsiveness that guaranteed rare emotional capacity. Stereotypically, men and women of sensibility reacted compassionately to the sufferings of others – including animals. They wept readily. They blushed and fainted, registering in their bodies the delicacy of their feelings. They behaved in these ways on the pages of novels, but contemporaneous essays and sermons suggest that the ethic of fine feeling flourished also in actual experience, particularly among young women powerfully influenced by their reading of fiction.

If the cultivation of feeling for its own sake lends itself readily to mockery (and mockery of it thrived right along with all the tears and blushes), as a literary and as a social fact it also reveals important currents in the community. Humanitarian issues became vivid in the second half of the eighteenth century. The injustices of slavery, the brutalities of the penal system, and the suffering of the poor all attracted increasing attention. The new consciousness coexisted with an increasingly emphatic individualism. Intensifying awareness of the value of particular persons made it harder to dismiss such broad human categories as the poor or the imprisoned, which obviously contained suffering individuals. Social conscience thus deepened along with self-consciousness. And the sensibility that burgeoned in literary works as well as, arguably, in human hearts involved social as well as personal feeling.

This fact is crucial in understanding sensibility as social and as literary event and in differentiating its poetry from other kinds of verse controlled by emotion. The poetry of sensibility belongs peculiarly to the late eighteenth century. Although scholars of Romanticism sometimes claim as their own the practitioners of sensibility, these poets reveal preoccupations quite different from those of their nineteenth-century successors. Northrop Frye long ago claimed sensibility as a defining aspect of the second half of the eighteenth century.[1] His important essay emphasized the fluidity and the stress on process associated with sensibility, and argued for the concept's formal implications. But sensibility determines content as well as form. The content of its poetry consistently emphasized the social, even when a poem appeared to be the complaint of a single suffering individual. More consistently than the Romantic poetry that followed it, the poetry of sensibility flourishes on the symbiosis and the tension of the social and the personal. Poets like Thomas Gray and William Cowper constructed personae who wrestled with the nature of interpersonal obligation. Charlotte Smith used social upheavals as correlatives for their personal counterparts and proclaimed her escape from individual suffering through communal concern. Explicit poetic statements about sensibility emphasized its inherent connection with "sympathy," that quality drawing human beings together. Yet this poetry's emotional repertoire turns out to include a range of angry and aggressive feelings.

The asserted connection between sensibility and sympathy largely accounts for the moral weight often assigned, in the eighteenth century, to a quality that from our chronological vantage point may look like mere self-indulgence and self-display in its ostentatious performances of grief or longing. The development of individualism inevitably generated concomitant anxiety lest self- preoccupied individuals neglect their social obligations.

The ideal of sympathy, however, posited a kind of feeling that would necessarily extend outward, from self to family to society at large. Theorists like Adam Smith (*Theory of Moral Sentiments*, 1759) elaborately delineated the workings of the human capacity for perceiving resemblance between self and other, thus for feeling the suffering of others by analogy with what the experience would mean for the self. Such feeling provided a foundation for compassion and for benevolence. And a theory of felt connection among human beings helped to resolve the potential conflict between self-love and outward-reaching love. When Pope, as early as 1733, in the *Essay on Man* sketched a social universe where self-love and social might coincide, he outlined a kind of reconciliation upon which many writers after him would depend – or toward which they might aspire.

The importance of sensibility as an issue for poets of the later eighteenth century registers in the considerable number of poems written explicitly about the subject. Best-known among these is Hannah More's lengthy *Sensibility: a Poetical Epistle*, published in 1782, which both praises sensibility for its moral effects ("Unprompted moral! sudden sense of right! / Perception exquisite! fair virtue's seed!" [lines 238–39]) and warns against "counterfeits" of the quality (line 266). More's poem, indeed, comprises a compendium of important attitudes toward and assumptions about sensibility, and it exemplifies aspects of the quality in its own poetic practice.

More associates sensibility specifically with imagination, and thus with poetry.

> Yet what is wit, and what the Poet's art?
> Can genius shield the vulnerable heart?
> Ah no! Where bright imagination reigns,
> The fine wrought spirit feels acuter pains.   (lines 65–68)[2]

She also identifies it, importantly, with energy, a quality assigned high value during this period. According to her argument (which appears also in other poems on the subject), possessors of sensibility feel great pain, but since their most intense pain comes from the sorrows of others, suffering itself includes a kind of pleasure, the moral and aesthetic gratification implicit in the action of sympathy. Moreover, the capacity to feel powerful pain implies corresponding capability for pleasure.

> Wou'd you renounce such energies as these
> For vulgar pleasures or for selfish ease?
> Wou'd you, to 'scape the pain, the joy forego,
> And miss the transport to avoid the woe?   (lines 181–84)

Although she praises sensibility elaborately and at length, More also expresses anxiety lest it drive away such "sterner virtues" as "Fair Truth, firm Faith, and manly Justice" (lines 222, 224). And she warns severely against hypocrisies of sensibility: soft language substituting for benevolent action, concern for dying fawns and for flies entrapped by spiders rather than for real people, sympathy for the sufferings of fiction but not of actuality. She associates true sensibility with domestic life because the family provides an appropriate realm for its operation, and she insists on the connection between sensibility and rationality. Sympathy may originate in sheer impulse, she acknowledges, but wisdom and reason must intervene to direct it properly. Moreover, only sensibility can "give immortal MIND its finest tone" (line 263).

More's choice of couplets as the verse form for her discussion of sensibility emphasizes her urgent association between feeling and reason. Her poem exemplifies both, displaying her own sensibility in her praise for friendship, her effusions about her friends, and her account of those friends' personal suffering, and insisting on "reason" in its careful construction of an extended, discriminating argument in support of the quality she celebrates. Her exposition suggests some reasons why the concept of sensibility generated so much poetry in the period. Sensibility provided a context for registering and discussing the experienced relation between self and others. It was connected with established virtues. It justified emotional expansiveness while permitting the claim of rationality. It made room for poetic experimentation.

A number of poems before More's had explicitly taken up the subject of sensibility. Best known among them was "A Prayer for Indifference," written in 1759 by Frances Greville (née Macartney), which Roger Lonsdale declares "the most celebrated poem by a woman in the period."[3] Although the poem claims to reject sensibility, it testifies paradoxically to the quality's imaginative power. The speaker prays for indifference as a remedy for the pain of tender feeling: "Take then this treacherous sense [i.e., sensibility] of mine, / Which dooms me still to smart" (lines 29–30). Begging for relief, she specifies the commitment to others implied by sensibility:

> The tears, which pity taught to flow,
> My eye shall then disown;
> The heart, that throbb'd at others' woe,
> Shall then scarce feel its own.   (lines 41–44)[4]

She imagines a life of "sober ease" (line 62), in which she will rest contented in a state of being only "Half-pleased" (line 63) and will satisfy herself with a capacity of only half-pleasing.

Several poets responded to this provocative utterance (indeed, More reacts to it in *Sensibility*), including William Cowper, who in 1762 produced a poem in the same verse form entitled "Addressed to Miss Macartney on Reading the Prayer for Indifference." He urges the poet to form a "better pray'r" (line 20) for a "fate" (line 26) the opposite of the one she seeks. He emphasizes the urgency of concern for others and argues strongly for the pleasure attending even the pain of "Sympathy":

> 'Tis woven in the world's great plan,
>   And fix'd by heav'n's decree,
> That all the true delights of man
>   Should spring from *Sympathy*.
>
> 'Tis nature bids, and whilst the laws
>   Of nature we retain,
> Our self-approving bosom draws
>   A pleasure from its pain.
>
> Thus grief itself has comforts dear,
>   The sordid never know;
> And ecstasy attends the tear,
>   When virtue bids it flow.   (lines 45–56)[5]

As the poet imagines a life devoid of indifference, he summons for his addressee the blessings of "all a tender heart can feel" (line 103). Such ambiguous blessings – ambiguous because the capacity for tender feeling implies pain as well as pleasure – provide the essential subject of the poetry of sensibility.

Despite the emphasis on feeling in all three of these explicit discussions, the dominant mode of the poetry of sensibility need not conform to the patterns of "lyric." Both the "Prayer for Indifference" and its response, like Hannah More's longer discussion, belong to a discursive, argumentative genre. On a larger scale, such poets as Cowper and Charlotte Smith after him incorporated the themes of sensibility in lengthy, diffuse, often polemical verse. *The Task*, one of the most admired works of the late century, provides the paradigmatic example. Ranging over six books, with a mock-epic preamble ("I sing the SOFA . . ." [Book 1, line 1]), the long poem allows its author to incorporate personal and public concerns into a single texture. He represents himself as a man of tender feelings, concerned for the welfare of birds and domestic animals, of poor country folk and of imagined slaves and South Sea Islanders, and, above all, of his country. Figuring himself as a wounded deer who lives in isolation from his kind, he nonetheless summons a voice of high authority in which to denounce social and political corruption. But it is crucial to his project that he claim an impulse of sensibility as the source of his denunciations:

I was born of woman, and drew milk,
As sweet as charity, from human breasts.
I think, articulate, I laugh and weep,
And exercise all functions of a man.
How then should I and any man that lives
Be strangers to each other?

(*The Task,* Book III, lines 196–201)

Because of his "sympathy," his sense of human community, he must criticize deviations from what he considers a divinely ordained norm. His declarations of affection for animals, his imagining of a prisoner in the Bastille, his panegyrics of tea-drinking before a fire, and his fierce attacks on the frivolity of social life or the injustice of tyrants – all belong to a single enterprise: that of sensibility.

Often, though, the poetry of sensibility limits itself to a single subject: variations on the theme of personal sorrow. As Jerome McGann points out, "tears are the proper emblem of the literatures of sensibility and sentiment."[6] In her first important poem, written at the age of twenty-four, Anna Letitia Aikin (later Barbauld) inquired rhetorically, "What pleasing sounds from sorrow's voice can flow?" ("On Mrs. Priestley's Leaving Warrington," line 11). She disingenuously appears to assume the negative answer: "None," but she and her contemporaries consistently strove to make pleasing sounds from sorrow. Converted to an exclamation rather than a question, her words might have supplied a literary credo for the second half of the eighteenth century, when contemplation and expression of distress provided a stock in trade for writers of verse and prose alike. The verse counterpart of Henry Mackenzie's novelistic tear jerker, *The Man of Feeling*, is perhaps Charlotte Smith's *Elegiac Sonnets*, which went through ten editions (some of which added new poems to the sequence) in her lifetime. In these poems, the writer made the mishaps of her personal experience – in particular, her uncomfortable financial dealings with the executors of her father-in-law's estate – into the substance of lyric.

Gray and Cowper, among the male poets of melancholy, offer particularly strong statements. Gray's tone is depressive, his grievance predominantly internal rather than, like Smith's, external. Unlike the many poets who claim their tender feelings for others, Gray's persona suffers from a sense of isolation and alienation. The thematic statement epitomizing the note of his personal verse comes from the painful "Sonnet on the Death of Richard West": "My lonely Anguish melts no Heart, but mine" (line 7). The morning smiles in vain at the sonnet's opening; the speaker weeps in vain at its end: community is a fantasy for happier men. But Gray figures the sense of community also as an obligation he cannot fulfill. His allegorical "Hymn to Adversity" represents the eponymous goddess as teaching the figure of Virtue through the experience of sorrow: "from her own she learn'd to melt at others' woe" (line 16). At the poem's end, the speaker begs the goddess to teach him too: "Teach me to love and to forgive, / . . . What others are, to feel, and know myself a Man" (lines 46, 48). Feeling for others, capacity for love: the voice of the poems often seems cut off from such qualities, articulating the sentiments of "A solitary fly," as the insects label the speaker in "Ode on the Spring" (line 44). Even the poems Gray chooses to adapt from Norse originals, whose rhetoric does not obviously declare them part of the literature of sensibility, typically evoke a world in which mortals are only victims of fate and mutual feeling hardly exists. Gray offers, in short, negative evocations of the idea of sympathy that declare the concept's importance perhaps even more powerfully than the more familiar assertions of emotional identification.

Cowper's poetry of personal suffering – a small proportion of his total production – claimed more intense and more permanent misery than Gray ever directly professed. When the speaker imagines himself metaphorically as drowning or literally as damned, he asserts metaphysical rather than only social isolation. Yet the fundamental definition of suffering remains the same. Anguish consists in separation from one's kind. Insistence on this point marks much of the poetry of sensibility and differentiates it from the Byronic stance that would become familiar in the next century. The Romantic version of isolation might allege the pain it entails, but as a poetic topic or stance solitude came to function more importantly as a sign of specialness, of the Romantic hero's superiority to his kind. The same sense of superiority may be latent in such poems as Cowper's account of the man lost in a stormy sea, which concludes,

> We perish'd, each alone:
> But I beneath a rougher sea,
> And whelm'd in deeper gulphs than he.
> ("The Castaway," lines 64–66)

Yet the stress is significantly different. Explicitly, the speaker proclaims not that he is higher than others but that he is lower. Being "alone" inaugurates and helps to define his pain.

The "social" orientation of the poetry of sensibility thus emerges, at least indirectly, in its most plangent and personal strains. Even Charlotte Smith, in her *Elegiac Sonnets* apparently obsessed with the wrongs she as an individual has suffered and the anguish she as an individual has endured, describes her personal situation with reference to "Humanity" at large. In a sonnet addressed "To Fortitude," she observes, "Strengthen'd by thee, this heart shall cease to melt / O'er ills that poor Humanity must bear" (lines 9–10).[7] Although she incessantly delineates exactly that melting that she claims to wish to surmount, her self-reminder that the ills she undergoes belong to the human condition enables her to avoid the appearance of narcissism.

Indeed, the rhetoric and structure of the poetry of sensibility characteristically evade narcissism. If late eighteenth-century poets fall upon the thorns of life and bleed, they do not proclaim the fact in Shelleyan fashion. "Remote, unfriended, melancholy, slow," begins the speaker in Goldsmith's long (and immensely popular) poem, *The Traveller, or a Prospect of Society* (1764). He is describing his own condition. As the poem's subtitle suggests, though, his ostensible focus is the state of society, not of his psyche.

From a twentieth-century viewpoint, description of individual depression combines oddly with magisterial reflection on the social order. For poets like Goldsmith, though, the two modes belong to a single coherent enterprise. Public distress provides the crucial correlative for personal melancholy:

> to my breast alternative passions rise,
> Pleas'd with each good that heaven to man supplies:
> Yet oft a sigh prevails, and sorrows fall,
> To see the hoard of human bliss so small.   (lines 55–58)

> Here let me sit in sorrow for mankind,
> Like yon neglected shrub, at random cast,
> That shades the steep, and sighs at every blast.   (lines 102–4)[8]

The poet makes no separation between the communal and the personal. His rhetoric of sighs and sorrows and neglect coexists comfortably with his concern for "mankind," for humanity at large. In his more familiar *Deserted Village* (1770), Goldsmith speaks vaguely of his unspecified "griefs" (line 84), conveying his sense of desolation most vividly by his nostalgic evocations of the vanished delights of the village.

Like other poetry of sensibility, Goldsmith's poems aspire to give readers the satisfaction of sympathetic imaginative participation in the pain of others, a satisfaction comparable to that experienced by such protagonists as Charlotte Smith's persona or the hero of *The Man of Feeling*, Henry Mackenzies's 1771 novel of sensibility. To read the poetry of sensibility, ideally, implies affiliation with an emotional community defined by sensitivity as well as more specifically by suffering. The poetry attempts to evoke the sympathy it celebrates. Its concern with the situation of humanity at large as well as with individuals helps to locate its preoccupations.

The concern with humanity need not, as in Goldsmith, emphasize social actualities. Edward Young, probably the century's most famous melancholy poet, employs the metaphysical rather than the social as corollary for depression. In *The Complaint, or Night Thoughts on Life, Death and Immortality* (1745), he speaks at the outset about his "wrecked desponding thought" (Book 1, line 10), only to move promptly to the nature of God and of man ("How poor, how rich, how abject, how August, / How complicate, how wonderful is man!" [1, lines 67–68]).[9] His poem constitutes an extended argument against suicide and an exploration of metaphysical possibilities. For Young as for Goldsmith, though, the stance of unhappiness and painful isolation provides not only a rhetorical starting point but a source of authority.

The authority derives from sensibility itself, demonstrated by the "capacity for refined emotion," "the quality of being easily and strongly affected by emotional influences." I have emphasized the sympathetic responsiveness to humankind at large hinted in many poems of sensibility, but in fact the community of sensibility is in some sense an exclusive one. Not everyone has the capacity to experience him (or her) self as "Remote, unfriended, melancholy, slow." Not everyone moves, like Young's speaker, beyond his own bad dreams and uneasy sleep to concern for the human situation in the universe. The ability both to suffer and to articulate one's suffering belongs only to the sensitive, and sensitivity defines the protagonists of sensibility, in poetry and prose alike.

The association between such sensitivity and poetic authority, though not self-evident to later readers, is vital to the effects generated by the poetry of sensibility. Sensibility's acts of self-differentiation imply superiority and consequent power. When the speaker of *The Deserted Village* claims, toward the end of the poem, to "see the rural virtues leave the land" (line 398), specifying a list of personified domestic traits and adding to the list "sweet Poetry, thou loveliest maid" (line 407), he earns his visionary extravagance by the loving specificity with which he has portrayed domestic virtue in action in his nostalgic evocation. Such specificity details the objects of his sensitivity and the mode of his sensitivity's operation. Because he has demonstrated the nature of "Contented toil, and hospitable care, / And kind connubial tenderness" (lines 403–4) and the rest, and dramatized his response to them, he can now imagine them in overtly fanciful ways. He consolidates his right to his fancies by making sympathetic feeling the substance of his poetry.

This matter of authority has particular importance for women writers. Men and women alike wrote the poetry (and the prose) of sensibility, but the sexes would necessarily differ in their relation to public performance. Sensibility in its most physical sense was thought to belong primarily to women. As G. J. Barker-Benfield puts it, "The view that women's nerves were normatively distinct from men's, normatively making them creatures of greater sensibility, became a central convention of eighteenth-century literature."[10] If women had more delicate nerves, it was thought, they also possessed less capacity for reason than did men. But as the idea of sensibility developed and acquired philosophic dignity, partly by association with the work of such important philosophers as Adam Smith and David Hume, it also connected itself with reason. When Anna Letitia Barbauld, taking "Dejection" as her subject, writes of griefs that "Too deeply wound the feeling mind" (line 29), she explicitly claims the mind rather than the heart as the locus of feeling. The griefs that inflict deep wounds are those of pity – griefs not for the self but for another. Such emotion belongs, the logic of sensibility would have it, specifically to the mind because it implies a kind of consciousness possessing a rational as well as an irrational component.

Women as well as men, then, began to claim on the page the powers of reason combined with those of feeling. Stuart Curran points out that what he calls "the cult of sensibility" implied emphasis on the fact "that men, too, can feel." He adds, "The obvious literary struggle on the part of women authors was to convince those men that women, too, can *think*."[11] Hannah More's versified account of sensibility supplies valuable evidence of how the combination of thought and emotion might work. Even as the ideal of sensibility as a primarily emotional manifestation lost force, toward the very end of the century, the notion of this merging of faculties retained ideological power. But women's most daring assertions of sensibility's authority ignored reason, to insist on emotion alone as an energy of perception and to demonstrate the rhetorical force of feeling anatomized. Thus women might convert an asserted weakness into an imaginative strength.

The relation of sensibility to authority becomes strikingly apparent in Charlotte Smith's poetry, which uses dejection and complaint for self-assertion. In an invocation to "Fancy," for instance ("To Fancy"), she claims an early acquaintance with a kind of fancy that "shew'd the beauteous rather than the true!" (line 4). Such imaginings, she continues, no longer belong to her; now fancy dresses "in darkest hues" (line 6) the record of sad experience. The final quatrain reads,

> And I, as from me all thy dreams depart,
> Be to my wayward destiny subdued:
> Nor seek perfection with a poet's eye,
> Nor suffer anguish with a poet's heart. (lines 11–14)

Ostensibly recording the loss of poetic power – the departure of fancy's dreams – the sonnet actually affirms the superiority of a new source of poetic energy: the seeking and suffering from which the speaker begs to be released. Her "anguish" marks her imaginative force. If fancy's dreams have left her, what remains, personal and painful truth, is better still.

This pattern of disclaimer disguising assertion characterizes much of Smith's verse. Her best-known sonnet, "Written in the church-yard at Middleton in Sussex," provides a particularly impressive instance. In it, the poet evokes a horrifying scene of disruptive storm that "breaks the silent sabbath of the grave" (line 7) by tearing bodies and skeletons from their tombs. Ten lines of the poem delineate the chaos of the storm. In the final quatrain, the poet observes that the dead cannot be disturbed by "the warring elements" (line 12) – "While I am doom'd – by life's long storm opprest, / To gaze with envy on their gloomy rest" (lines 13–14). Once more, the statement of inferiority (the speaker envies even the dead, though she understands their rest as "gloomy") implies its opposite. As in the poem about fancy, Smith demonstrates her emotional sensitivity: her capacity to suffer and to participate imaginatively in wider scenes of suffering. But she also reveals her ability to articulate chaos, to find commanding correlatives for personal emotion, to proclaim her own "doom" through images that assert the magnitude of her poetic power.

When Smith turns to poetry of broader reference, abandoning herself as primary subject, she continues to maintain sensibility's poetic authority. At the end of the first book of *The Emigrants*, her long poem about refugees from Revolutionary France, she simultaneously praises and instructs Britain about "acts of pure humanity" (1, line 368), declaring them "nobler far" (line 369) than the laurels won on battlefields. Such acts, she concludes,

> Far better justify the pride, that swells
> In British bosoms, than the deafening roar
> Of Victory from a thousand brazen throats,
> That tell with what success wide-wasting War
> Has by our brave Compatriots thinned the world.
>
> (1, lines 378–82)

Not only does she praise actions of sympathy and benevolence – she explicitly *dispraises* the accomplishments of war, emphasizing its destructive outcomes (the opposite consequences to those of "pure humanity") and using the conventional phrase "brave Compatriots" to ironic effect. Hers is the vantage point of sensibility, from which she can decisively rebuke the culture of conquest. Without explicit self-aggrandizement or even self-concern, she implicitly makes the large claim that she has the right to posit a national system of values in opposition to, and by her assertion superior to, the established one. And she demonstrates once more the way that an ethos of feeling operates, directing individual emotional capacity toward large social concerns.

In the second book of *The Emigrants*, Smith offers a set piece on the suffering of Marie Antoinette. English hearts, she says, disclaim the vengeance or fear that keeps the queen a prisoner. Then she introduces a personal note:

> – Ah! who knows,
> From sad experience, more than I, to feel
> For thy desponding spirit, as it sinks
> Beneath procrastinated fears for those
> More dear to thee than life! But eminence
> Of misery is thine, as once of joy.   (ii, lines 169–74)

She makes the French queen into a heroine of sensibility, dominated and debilitated by fears for her family rather than herself. More importantly, she identifies herself with the royal figure. If Marie Antoinette enjoys "eminence Of misery," so does the writer, whose "sad experience" enables for her the full exercise of sensibility in the capacity to feel for another woman who appears (but in fact is not) altogether different from herself. As she figures herself in her verse, Charlotte Smith exemplifies suffering and consequently compassion. Her authority to speak about personal and extra-personal matters derives from that pairing of suffering and compassion, both signs of sensibility.

So powerful was the rhetorical authority of sensibility that even poets writing about subjects apparently remote from sensibility's realm often inserted set pieces to demonstrate their participation in the logic and feeling of compassion. Thus James Thomson, as early as 1726, using a conventional vignette of "melancholy" in his *Winter*, adds to it a specific mission for "forming fancy," one strikingly similar to Smith's:

> Then forming fancy rouses to conceive
> What never mingled with the vulgar's dream:
> Then wake the tender pang, the pitying tear,
> The sigh for suffering worth, the wish preferred
> For humankind, the joy to see them blessed,
> And all the social offspring of the heart!   (lines 68–73)[12]

If the emotions and manifestations awakened by fancy seem rather perfunctory in evocation, their specification yet insists on sensibility's importance specifically as a "social" quality. The poet can justify the operations of his solitary imagination by declaring them ultimately concerned with the welfare of others. Indeed, he authorizes his imagination by emphasizing its common concerns. The imagination presides over a region of feeling, and the feelings it acknowledges are benevolent.

In a crucial paradox, though, Thomson here reveals that the socialized imagination also sets the poet apart. These lines from *Winter* adumbrate an aristocracy of sensibility, the consequence of the "exclusive" aspect of the quality mentioned above. What fancy can conceive differentiates its possessor from the "vulgar" – not the poor, necessarily, but those lesser beings who lack the capacity for the sighs and wishes and joy that the poet's fancy summons. In feeling for all humankind, the person whom sensibility controls separates himself or herself from the herd – as Charlotte Smith does by her supremacy of misery, as Thomson here does by his benevolent imagination. All claims of authority necessarily differentiate authoritative figures from those over whom they exercise power. Sensibility's claims are no exception to this rule.

In the poetic rhetoric of sensibility, detail plays an important part. The poetry of sensibility contributed new kinds of detail to the poet's repertoire. Often, the new specificity focused on suffering:

> Now, wild as winds, you from your offspring fly,
> Or fright them from you with distracted eye;
> Rove through the streets; or sing, devoid of care,
> With tattered garments and dishevelled hair;
> By hooting boys to higher frenzy fired,
> At length you sink, by cruel treatment tired,
> Sink into sleep, an emblem of the dead,
> A stone thy pillow, the cold earth thy bed.
> ("On seeing an Officer's Widow distracted," lines 11–18)[13]

The full title of this poem by Mary Barber is "On seeing an Officer's Widow distracted, who had been driven to Despair by a long and fruitless Solicitation for the Arrears of her Pension." The poem's meticulous evocation of madness corresponds to prose vignettes by such masters of sensibility as Laurence Sterne and Henry Mackenzie. The insane now could emblemize the helpless, those victimized by society. Barber's effort to specify the experience of insanity marks a significant eighteenth-century development. She dwells on the subject for the sake of its emotional power, but like Hannah More chooses for her effusion of sensibility the traditional couplet form associated with reason and wit. And she claims a public purpose: the poem's last stanza directly addresses "Britain," warning that pestilence and famine are likely consequences for mistreating the worthy. The "thankless state" (line 4) must learn to care for its own. The poem demonstrates once more that sensibility could concern itself with large subjects.

Like other aspects of the poetry of sensibility, the emphasis on detail of misery showed up in poems by men as well as women. The minor poet Thomas Moss, for instance, in 1769 published a poem called "The Beggar" that consisted almost entirely of physical, psychological, and narrative detail about an unfortunate man asking for help. The last stanza duplicates the first:

> Pity the sorrows of a poor old man!
> Whose trembling limbs have borne him to your door,
> Whose days are dwindled to the shortest span.
> Oh! give relief – and heaven will bless your store.
>
> (lines 1–4, – also lines 41–44)[14]

In other words, the poem consisting of data of sensibility is imagined as impetus for the concrete manifestation of sensibility through charity.

But the reminder of literal charity may call to mind the issue of what Robert Markley has called "the theatrics of virtue." In an important essay on sentimentality that concentrates on fiction, never mentioning poetry, Markley observes that "If sentimentality is not a dead end, it is a discrete moment that can provide the impetus only for reflection, not action."[15] He points out that the novels primarily involved in tugging heartstrings offer no serious criticism of fundamental social arrangements and that they serve to support the values and assumptions of the middle classes. The poetry of sensibility likewise provides no impetus to action; typically it does not appear to imagine action as a possibility. Such a poem as "The Beggar" rests on the assumption that the existing system – beggars begging, the prosperous bestowing alms – is capable of resolving economic problems. Like the prose of sensibility, its poetry seems to take the stimulation of feeling as an end in itself.

Yet if such poetry lacks what we would recognize as ideological sophistication, it does not therefore lack ideological awareness. Charlotte Smith rebuking a culture of war, Mary Barber warning a government that neglects obligations to its citizens – such writers, at the very least, aspire to heighten readers' consciousness of social inequity and of discrepancies between individually-held humanitarian values and public failures. The literature of sensibility provided a precursor to social transformations that would alter, if not the fundamental structures of capitalism, at least the arrangements of oppression.

Let me return to the first definition cited from the *OED*: "emotional consciousness; glad or sorrowful, grateful or resentful recognition . . ." The quotations from poetry provided thus far have stressed, directly or indirectly, the sorrowful, the kind of emotion most readily associated with sensibility. Gladness and gratitude also seem plausible enough. But what of resentment? That does not accord well with the ostentatious "softness" of sensibility, the "melting" quality of its most familiar poetry, the implicit dominance of tears in that poetry's emotional repertoire.

Even Cowper as wounded deer, Smith as persecuted female, and Gray as solitary fly, though, communicate not merely personal resentment but a kind of anger that comprises an essential – and usually ignored – component of sensibility. This anger does not necessarily bear on issues of obvious social import. The poetry of sensibility, as the label itself suggests, never deals *only* with other people: its initial subject is always individual feeling: feeling that often includes anger. Sensibility's anger has no immediate consequences. Frustration is its essence, whether it expresses itself in personal or in social terms. Gray in his "Sketch of His Own Character" describes himself as one who "Could love, and could hate, so was thought somewhat odd" (line 3). His capacity to "hate" emerges not only in his surprisingly fierce political satires but in the poems that appear to belong to the milder category of sensibility. Anger directs itself, in these poems, primarily toward what cannot be changed: the actualities of the human condition. "Ode on a Distant Prospect of Eton College" begins as an elaborate exercise in nostalgia, glorifying a childhood of "bliss" and "joy," suggesting the weariness of the adult speaker and his pleasure in witnessing schoolboys at play. The poem continues by generalizing about the nature of youth, which possesses, it alleges, hope, health, wit, cheer, and the capacity to sleep well. But four of the ode's ten stanzas focus on an assemblage of gruesome personifications – furies, vultures, monsters of unspecified form, "black Misfortune's baleful train" (line 57), a "murth'rous band" (line 59) waiting in ambush to seize its prey. Ostensibly, these figures, representing such powers as passions, unkindness, remorse, madness, death, and poverty, portray the evils that inevitably face human beings as they age. Their implications emphasize the relative innocence and freedom of youth, the ignorance finally asserted as equivalent to bliss. Yet there is an odd disproportion in the intensity of their evocation, a willful dwelling in ugliness and terror that suggests, at the very least, resentment of life's conditions.

This is not social protest, nor will it conceivably lead to social protest. "Poverty," in Gray's figuration, sounds as inevitable as illness. But the quality of the emotion is important: the powerful personal resentment subsisting as concomitant of more socially acceptable emotions. That resentment develops necessarily, perhaps, from the tension between "sympathetic" feeling and the experience of alienation. It expresses itself even in Gray's most socially concerned poem, the *Elegy Written in a Country Churchyard*, with its subtext of frustrated personal anger in the concluding epitaph.

Distant as anger may seem from the ethos of sympathy and compassion, the poetry it infuses makes the same claim as, say, Charlotte Smith's personal complaints for the reader's imaginative sympathy. Nothing more vividly suggests the poetic ambition of this verse than its acceptance of the vast range of possible feeling, its assumption that nothing human will be alien from human readers. When anger justifies itself as indignation over injustice, its potential appeal to the "sympathetic" reader seems clear enough. But even Gray's anger over his idiosyncratic personal experience commands assent in the honesty of its utterance. Adam Smith's notion that people can see themselves in others allows large scope for the rhetoric of sympathy.

The stress of the relation between benevolent concern for others – school children doomed to become men, country people living and dead – and inarticulate rage lends urgency to Gray's poetry. In other writers of sensibility, similar tensions translate into terms that offer intimations of an unjust social order, although no hope of changing it. Cowper, for instance, frequently returns to public concerns. The sense of isolation and alienation he conveys in his image of himself as wounded deer receives fuller expression in his explicit criticisms of his country – for the specific nature of its capitalism as well as of its military exploits. Valuing the association of human beings based on feeling, he deplores alliances of self-interest:

> Hence merchants, unimpeachable of sin
> Against the charities of domestic life,
> Incorporated, seem at once to lose
> Their nature; and, disclaiming all regard
> For mercy and the common rights of man,
> Build factories with blood, conducting trade
> At the sword's point, and dyeing the white robe
> Of innocent commercial justice red.
> Hence, too, the field of glory, as the world
> Misdeems it . . .
> Is but a school where thoughtlessness is taught
> On principle, where foppery atones
> For folly, gallantry for ev'ry vice.
>
> (*The Task*, IV, lines 676–85, 688–90)

The standard of judgment invoked is that of sympathy: "mercy," a sense of "the common rights of man," "the charities of domestic life." By that standard, the commercial activities of building and trade become bloodthirsty processes, as destructive as war. Indeed, war has turned into frivolity, according to the poet's argument, and soldiers encourage one another in superficiality and vice.

A fine sense of outrage controls such utterances, which abound in *The Task*, as Cowper inveighs against various forms of social triviality, public degradation, and political corruption. The poem concludes in a rare utterance of self-satisfaction, with the speaker describing himself as a quiet man, treading "the secret path of life" (Book VI, line 956), attracting no notice, yet doing good to others. First he claims the conventional virtues of "sympathy." He exerts his influence, he says,

> In soothing sorrow and in quenching strife,
> In aiding helpless indigence, in works
> From which at least a grateful few derive
> Some taste of comfort in a world of woe.
>
> (VI, lines 963–66)

Gradually he develops a tone of contempt toward the "sensual world" (line 978) that surrounds him, complaining about the superficiality of that world, which judges by the eye instead of, like him, by conscience and heart. His rage increases, until he suggests the prevalence throughout society of vice which,

> Though well perfum'd and elegantly dress'd,
> Like an unburied carcase trick'd with flow'rs,
> Is but a garnish'd nuisance.   (VI, lines 991–93)

The powerful image of the corpse adorned with flowers conveys the fury and scorn of the godly toward the ungodly. Finally the poet justifies his own anger and his utterance by the longed-for approval of God, in whose service he writes.

God, of course, is sometimes an angry God. The man formed in His image can explain and condone in himself an emotion that may make him uncomfortable by imagining it as a pale reflection of divine wrath, directed at objects of which God would disapprove. Cowper as a poet of sensibility reflects about his own anger as well as his own benevolence and claims to consider both forms of service – to his country, his fellow human beings, and finally his God.

Writing without explicit invocation of divine sanction – a kind of invocation both unsettling (because God may not, after all, approve) and reassuring (because He may) – Oliver Goldsmith provides particularly compelling instances of a kind of poetry often verging on sentimental excess yet energized by an anger that directs itself explicitly toward actualities of contemporary social organization. His two longest poems, *The Traveller* and *The Deserted Village*, both describe existing social realities. And both openly express intense anger at what the speaker sees.

In *The Traveller*, the speaker explicitly calls attention to his own rage:

> Calm is my soul, nor apt to rise in arms,
> Except when fast approaching danger warms:
> But when contending chiefs blockade the throne,
> Contracting regal power to stretch their own,

. . . .

Fear, pity, justice, indignation start,
Tear off reserve, and bare my swelling heart.

(lines 379–82, 389–90)

The fact of "indignation" itself provides evidence for the extremity of the political situation here deplored. And the conjunction of indignation with pity condenses the poem's emotional pattern. Sympathy and sensibility provide the impetus for the traveler's observations: he wanders around Europe thinking about the situation of the people he meets and judging governments by their effects on the populace. And sympathy is imagined as reciprocal. As in *The Deserted Village*, the speaker fancies the consequences of depopulation, matrons and maids, sons and sires exiled from their homes to America, endangered by storms and by Indians. The "pensive exile" (line 419), the indignant speaker observes, "Casts a long look where England's glories shine, / And bids his bosom sympathize with mine" (lines 421–22). Presumably the exile sympathizes with the poet's anger at the decline of British freedom and justice: he, after all, is himself the victim of this decline. But exile and traveler alike find themselves helpless to alleviate a destructive political situation. The poem resolves itself in a way familiar in poems of sensibility, by rejecting the final relevance of the political and insisting that "Our own felicity we make or find" (line 432), quite independent of governments. Anger might, but need not, provide the impetus for reform. The presence of anger in the account of political realities reminds the reader that the potential energies of sensibility include the aggressive, but the textual deployment of anger reveals that the aggression here means only self- expression.

The Deserted Village, despite its repeated references to the narrator's emotional state, does not make his anger a personal matter. Instead, the poem conveys anger through fierce imagery: the nation as prostitute, decked out "In all the glaring impotence of dress" (line 294); the kingdom inflated by luxury, grown "to sickly greatness" (line 389) and converted by intemperance into "A bloated mass of rank unwieldy woe" (line 392). Such images convey the disgust and outrage appropriate in a patriot's response to his country's decline. As a man of feeling, he experiences the horror of what has happened. He perceives political actuality in concrete and specific terms and relates the fates of individual people to the situation of the country at large. Thus a few lines after elaborating the metaphor of the nation as prostitute, he describes a country girl in a situation of sexual degradation, huddling in cold and rain at her betrayer's gate. Her sexual corruption appears a direct consequence of the country's decline, the harsh reality that lies beneath apparent prosperity and luxury.

Frye, Northrop. "Towards Defining an Age of Sensibility," in James L. Clifford (ed.), *Eighteenth-Century English Literature: Modern Essays in Criticism*. New York: Oxford University Press, 1959.

Markley, Robert. "Sentimentality as Performance: Shaftesbury, Sterne, and the Theatrics of Virtue," in Felicity Nussbaum and Laura Brown (eds.), *The New Eighteenth Century: Theory, Politics, English Literature*. New York: Methuen, 1987.

McGann, Jerome. *The Poetics of Sensibility: a Revolution in Literary Style*. Oxford: Clarendon Press, 1996.

Mullan, John. *Sentiment and Sociability: the Language of Feeling in the Eighteenth Century*. Oxford: Clarendon Press, 1988.

13

JENNIFER KEITH

"Pre-Romanticism" and the ends of eighteenth-century poetry

Finding satisfactory labels for the poetry of the last decades of the eighteenth century has proven particularly difficult because most existing labels carry certain value judgments that diminish the worth or specificity of this poetry. Poetry from Pope's death in 1744 to the early publications of the first generation of Romantic poets in the 1790s has occasionally been defined according to its immediate past, by calling it "post-Augustan," but more often according to the future, by calling it "pre-Romantic." In an important essay first published in 1956, Northrop Frye suggested that we call this period an "Age of Sensibility" rather than define it transitionally "as a period of reaction against Pope and anticipation of Wordsworth."[1] While the label "Poetry of Sensibility" has gained some currency among specialists, "pre-Romanticism" continues to be used for this poetry, especially by non-specialists. Unfortunately, the label "pre-Romanticism" is seriously misleading to characterize the ends – the last poems as well as the objectives – of late eighteenth-century poetry.

To see later-eighteenth-century poetry as "pre-Romantic" has often meant to see it as not Romantic enough. Many critics of the term "pre-Romanticism" have found the label absurd in that it anticipates a future that the "pre-Romantic" writers could not have known. Though largely in disrepute today, "pre-Romanticism" has been resuscitated by Marshall Brown, who has redefined it with an emphasis on the "pre" "in its differentiating sense": not to define an inchoate romanticism but to show its difference from Romanticism.[2] For Brown, this difference lies in the failure of "pre-Romantic" poets to establish new goals though they were searching for something new.[3] The powerlessness that he associates with these writers appears in less sympathetic critiques of the period where aligning late-eighteenth-century poets with the Romantics is considered more interesting or significant than aligning late-eighteenth-century poets either with the Augustans or with the culture of sensibility. In this evolutionary narrative that favors the "pre-Romantic" label, poetry reaches the aesthetic heights of pure poetry with the Romantics after a miniature dark ages – what T. B. Macaulay called the "most deplorable part of our literary history" – in the decades that precede the Romantics.[4] Such an age begot, in the words of Harold Bloom: "doomed poets . . . , victims of circumstance of their own false dawn of sensibility."[5]

Anxieties about the place and capacity of the poet after Pope's death appear in the dream that mid-century poet William Collins reportedly told his schoolmate William Smith, a dream that had left the poet "particularly depressed and melancholy." According to Smith, Collins dreamt he had climbed a "lofty tree" and nearing the top, "a great branch, upon which he had got, failed with him, and let him fall to the ground." Devastated, Collins explained to Smith that "The Tree was the Tree of Poetry."[6] This dream serves as a paradigm of several features of mid- and late-eighteenth-century poetry: (1) the poet is isolated and, at least psychologically, wounded or debilitated; (2) the poetic faculty has been compromised by its loss of connection with Nature, seen here to no longer provide a system or place for the poet (in earlier-eighteenth-century poetry, the poetic faculty would consist in the imitation of Nature, seen as an ordering system); (3) the poet's fall from near the top of the tree suggests a failure at sublimity, one of the dominant aesthetic values in mid- and later-eighteenth-century poetry; and (4) the Tree of Poetry reflects anxieties that the poet himself will vanish from a place in literary history.

Such an alienated self-consciousness not only questions the ties to poetic history but also questions the self's relation to social, political, and religious orders that had anchored it in previous periods.[7] Late-eighteenth-century poets are well aware of the world they have lost, a world to which their predecessors the Augustan poets saw themselves very much connected. Far from either an Augustan world order or the egotistical sublime that Wordsworth would claim for the self, the late-eighteenth-century self is terra incognita to these poets who explore a poetic vision where social, poetic, and metaphysical comforts drop away. Much of the poetry of the end of the eighteenth century gives us back an image of our minds that we would rather not see.[8]

While "pre-Romanticism" as a label often includes mid-century poetry, such as Edward Young's *Night Thoughts* and poems by Mark Akenside, Thomas Gray, William Collins, and the Wartons, it can, impressionistically, include works even earlier in the century, such as James Thomson's *The Seasons*, with its sensitivity to the details of nature, and Pope's *Eloisa to Abelard*, with its sensitivity to feeling. This chapter, however, will focus chronologically on poems from the 1770s, 80s, and 90s, at the historical edges of Romanticism, to distinguish the conclusion of the eighteenth century from the beginnings of what is conventionally identified as the Romantic period. We will begin with the perceived failures of these poets and poems in order to see how the grounds on which late eighteenth-century poets have been condemned may provide a different foundation for understanding them.

The poet's failure and suffering are common thematic features of late-eighteenth-century poetry, but this failure ought not to be interpreted as the failure of the poems themselves. Critics often associate the sufferings of one of the better-known poets of this era, William Cowper, with his particular burden of self. A Calvinist, Cowper believed he faced eternal damnation, convinced that "he was the unique case of a creature whom God had at first elected for salvation and subsequently doomed to perdition."[9] Writing for Cowper was a temporary therapy for driving away this crushing consciousness of irrevocable damnation.[10] His wounds, which often appear in even his most light-hearted poetry, are everlasting and metaphysical; painfully, Cowper repeats his allegiance to a God that has forsaken him. His best-known poem, *The Task* (1785), is an epic-length meditation on themes including the merits of the sofa, the cultivation of cucumbers, Great Britain's avaricious imperialism, man's place in society, the poet's withdrawal from the world, and the beauty of nature. One of the most arresting passages from *The Task* shows the poet as wounded deer:

> I was a stricken deer that left the herd
> Long since; with many an arrow deep infixt
> My panting side was charg'd when I withdrew
> To seek a tranquil death in distant shades.
> There was I found by one who had himself
> Been hurt by th'archers. In his side he bore
> And in his hands and feet the cruel scars.
> With gentle force soliciting the darts
> He drew them forth, and heal'd and bade me live.
> Since then, with few associates, in remote
> And silent woods I wander, far from those
> My former partners of the peopled scene,
> With few associates, and not wishing more.
>
> (III, lines 108–20)[11]

The poet's wounds lead him to Christ's, but instead of attaining a joyful salvation, the poet is healed only to retreat in a posture of submission. Cowper's humility seems imitated by his seamless, unobtrusive, blank verse.

Abject spiritual submission is the basis of Cowper's art, as he indicates in the closing lines of *The Task*:

> But all is in his hand whose praise I seek.
> In vain the poet sings, and the world hears,
> If he regard not, though divine the theme.

'Tis not in artful measures, in the chime
And idle tinkling of a minstrel's lyre
To charm his ear, whose eye is on the heart.
Whose frown can disappoint the proudest strain,
Whose approbation – prosper even mine.   (VI, lines 1017–24)

For Cowper a relation to Nature is always subsumed by a relation to God: he instructs the reader to "Acquaint thyself with God if thou would'st taste / His works" (V, lines 779–80). Such an acquaintance, however, remains extratextual, not to be justified, as the Romantics would do, through representing transcendence. As foundations for poetic values and authority, Cowper's Christian humility and wounds do not correspond to either Augustan or Romantic notions of poetic competence. Milton knew the problem of basing poetic authority on Christian humility when he composed the complex and contradictory gambits for power in his invocations to *Paradise Lost*. Donne knew this in "Batter my heart," where his bold imperative to God and his imagery counter a pleading, masochistic persona. But Cowper's humility is such that spiritual and poetic approval remain suspended outside of the text and outside of this world, leaving the test of poetic worth to divine eyes.

Cowper's wounds are keen because of his sensibility; alive to wounds that never heal, the poet of sensibility fails to master himself. The exercise of sensibility informs this period's awkward place in literary history and its representation of the self. Whereas among the Romantic poets, sensibility may be featured in many poems, it is contained by or subordinated to other values, such as the imagination or the sublime. In late-eighteenth-century poetry, the fragility of sensibility is not salvaged by some other bid for poetic power: Cowper remains at the mercy of external forces. In his sensibility Cowper participates in a cultural phenomenon of the second half of the eighteenth century, where the cult of sensibility reflected the "cultural prestige of feminine feeling," and what many critics have identified as a feminization of poetry, with more women reading and writing it.[12] Charlotte Smith in *Elegiac Sonnets* (1784) was to establish her poetic standards on the basis of feminine sensibility which she linked not to her spiritual torments, as Cowper did, but to her legal problems. Both Cowper and Smith self-consciously express intense emotion. While Cowper's poetry is often seen as including the tone of self-pity, Smith's poetry has been seen as even more self-indulgent in bewailing the poet's torments, producing poems that Anna Seward unsympathetically called "everlasting lamentables . . . [and] hackneyed scraps of dismality."[13]

In *Elegiac Sonnets* Smith's speakers generally mourn their past or present sufferings, with the speaker serving as both subject and object of sensibility.

Smith bases her poetic authority on the authenticity and intensity of her feelings in the poem that begins *Elegiac Sonnets*:

> The partial Muse has from my earliest hours
>   Smiled on the rugged path I'm doom'd to tread,
> And still with sportive hand has snatch'd wild flowers,
>   To weave fantastic garlands for my head.   (lines 1–4)[14]

The speaker may seem self-aggrandizing in citing the muse's partiality towards her and in describing herself crowned by the muse, but she uses this classical source of poetic authority to establish non-classical standards for poetic merit based on the contemporary standard of sensibility and on her gender: hers is a garland of flowers rather than of laurel leaves, flowers that associate her with a tradition of female beauties described by male poets.[15] Bedecked by *wild* flowers, the poet marks herself as natural, another poetic value dominating the last half of the century, while her crown, although of roses rather than of laurel, shows she is not the object of description in a sonnet but herself a writer of sonnets. This "dear delusive art," "while it decks the head with many a rose, / Reserves the thorn to fester in the heart" (lines 6–8). Thus Smith identifies herself with the wounded nightingale, who, in the words of the earlier-eighteenth-century poet Anne Finch, sings best when its breast is "plac'd against a Thorn" (line 13).[16] Smith relates this poetics of feeling to Pope's final line of *Eloisa to Abelard* (1717), adapting the last line of his poem to her concluding couplet: "Ah! then, how dear the Muse's favours cost, / *If those paint sorrow best – who feel it most!*" (lines 13–14). But where Pope was to include this personal note only at the end of his poem, Smith makes it the core of hers. Referring to Pope and to the nightingale, Smith's wounds identify her connection to the poetic tradition.[17] Cursed by her sensibility, the speaker's Pity "Points every pang, and deepens every sigh" (line 11).

Despite Smith's real tribulations, mostly legal and marital, the poem is as much concerned with Smith's relating her work as a woman poet to a revered poetic tradition as it is with Smith's own pain. Smith both asserts the authority of feminine sensibility on autobiographical terms and consistently modifies the work of other poets to convey her own achievement, creating in her poetry a hybrid of earlier-eighteenth-century uses of the poetic tradition and late-eighteenth-century self-expressiveness.[18] Critiques of Smith's poetic self that have seen it as either too self-absorbed or too derivative lead us to reexamine our expectations of the poetic faculty: in what ways does or should the poetic faculty transform "the real"?

The poetry of Cowper and Smith presents us with different functions of the poetic faculty that are less familiar to readers of the twenty-first century, especially because of the poetry's situation between two different notions of representation: an earlier notion of representation as the imitation of Nature, seen, for example, in the poetry of Pope, and a later notion of representation as the expression of an individual's imagination and feelings, where the poet creates as much as imitates Nature, as seen in much of Wordsworth's poetry. Trying to negotiate between an increasing attention to originality as a poetic value and a continuing desire to see art as the imitation of Nature, many late-eighteenth-century poets would be criticized for representing the real too literally or too artificially. In the case of Robert Burns, the poet's use of Scottish oral traditions has led some critics to underestimate his artistry, assuming that he represents the real too literally or relies on Scottish oral tradition too heavily.[19] Thus some have aligned his poetry with "pre-Romanticism" as an index of aesthetic failure, but Burns may be aligned with late-eighteenth-century rather than Romantic poetry on other accounts, in particular, his erasure of the poetic self through a communitarian voice as well as his focus on the human in a framework that is more familiar and concrete than the conceptual frameworks of Romantic transcendence.

Burns presented himself as a "natural poet," particularly in his 1786 Preface to the Kilmarnock edition of his poems; he also fulfilled the ideal of a "bardic persona" who expressed the culture's view of itself rather than himself.[20] In his "Song – For a' that and a' that – " (1795–96), Burns's proletarian and Scottish perspective eclipses the individual poetic self. This communal poetic self designated as "we" combines with Burns's incorporation of Scots to speak for a community of the worthy, *Scottish* poor:

> Is there, for honest Poverty
>   That hings his head, and a' that;
> The coward-slave, we pass him by,
>   We dare be poor for a' that!
> For a' that, and a' that,
>   Our toils obscure, and a' that,
> The rank is but the guinea's stamp,
>   The Man's the gowd for a' that. –
>
> What though on hamely fare we dine,
>   Wear hoddin grey, and a' that.
> Gie fools their silks, and knaves their wine,
>   A Man's a Man for a' that.
> For a' that, and a' that,
>   Their tinsel show, and a' that;
> The honest man, though e'er sae poor,
>   Is king o' men for a' that. –　　　　　　(lines 1–16)[21]

Through his inclusive "we," Burns combines his voice with that of the poor and individualizes them through the personification of "honest Poverty / That hings his head." Just as humane details such as "hamely fare" and "hoddin grey" animate what might have been the empty personification of Poverty, so do context and iteration give life to what might have been a throwaway phrase: "all that." Through the accumulation of material circumstances and intangible worth the phrase becomes a plenteous "all" that expresses the noble spirits of the individual poor. No extensive conceptualizing aggrandizes Burns's poetic function here, and unlike its function in the poetics of the sublime, this infinite "all" is revealed to be a social rather than transcendental category. The more the poet gives his voice to the disenfranchised, the less the poet appears.

Like Burns, George Crabbe has been criticized for failing to transform "the real." In Crabbe, announced Coleridge unequivocally, "there is an absolute defect of the high imagination."[22] Wordsworth condemned Crabbe's poetry for failing to create as much as record reality: "if the Picture were true to nature, what claim would it have to be called Poetry? . . . The sum of all is, that nineteen [sic] out of twenty of Crabbe's Pictures are mere matters of fact."[23] Crabbe's "inadequate" poetic faculty is based on a mimesis in which the objects of representation seem to eclipse poetic control and self-aggrandizement; the poetic faculty represents many human and social truths rather than a unified transcendental Truth that demonstrated the canonical Romantic poet's triumph over his material.[24] In *The Village* (1783), the poet's wanderings in barren fields rob him of an idealized Nature that could have given a self-affirming position to either the Augustan or Romantic poet:

> Here wandering long amid these frowning fields,
> I sought the simple life that Nature yields;
> Rapine and Wrong and Fear usurped her place,
> And a bold, artful, surly, savage race.   (1, lines 109–12)[25]

Instead of a prospect of ordered nature, the speaker discovers the brutal abstractions of Rapine, Wrong, and Fear. Not only do these negative personifications and their "bold, artful, savage race" threaten to overrun the poet, but they also show how human agency is more responsible than Nature for social ills. Rather than a terrifying sublime in a natural setting, Crabbe's poem shows terrifying humanity. As an anti-pastoral, *The Village* attempts to give the "real picture of the poor" (1, line 5). Nature is not the occasion for sublime epiphanies but for reflections on the hardships of the laborer's landscape, where "Rank weeds, that every art and care defy, / Reign o'er the land and rob the blighted rye" and "thistles stretch their prickly arms afar, /

And to the ragged infant threaten war" (I, lines 67–70). The triumphant phrasing of topographical poems, such as Pope's *Windsor-Forest*, that show the power and promise of the land is here used by Crabbe to reveal the distance between the ideal and the real. Nature is a betrayer rather than an ordering foundation for man and art.

Unlike the wounded selves of Cowper and Smith, among others, used to authorize the poetic speaker, both Burns's and Crabbe's notions of the poetic function tend to conceal the self. By the second half of the eighteenth century, not only Nature has changed, but so has the past, with poets looking to earlier eras of English poetry for native traditions that would revivify their own work as well as satisfy Britain's increasing nationalism. Ironically, these antiquarian interests and searches for authenticity in the past also inspired forgeries, such as Macpherson's *Fragments of Ancient Poetry* (1760), which claimed to be the prose translations and transcriptions of the Highland bard Ossian of the third century, and Chatterton's Rowley poems.[26] Chatterton claimed to have transcribed the works of Rowley which he found in the muniment room of the old Bristol cathedral, where he had spent much time as a child; but in fact he forged the manuscripts, preferring to mask his role as poet with that of a transcriber of the past. His contemporaries debated whether Chatterton was an antiquarian recovering lost texts from a fifteenth-century secular priest, Thomas Rowley, or a forger. Clearly Chatterton expected a better reception of his work posing as a modern-day copyist of a fifteenth-century genius than as a patronless, poor teenager distributing these antique visions under his own name. Paradoxically, the more these works were forgeries, the more original they were. As outright deceptions, Chatterton's forgeries of the past strain the limits on how an author may transform reality.

One of the strengths of Chatterton's Rowley poems is their conjunction of vivid action and emotion made strange through the distant setting and language. His "Bristowe Tragedie or the Dethe of Syr Charles Bawdin" (written before October 1768, published 1772) reinvents an episode from Bristol's past. In this speech Sir Charles bravely accepts his death sentence ordered by the king:

> "How oft ynne battaile have I stoode
>   "When thousands dy'd around;
> "Whan smokynge streemes of crimson bloode
>   "Imbrew'd the fatten'd grounde;
>
> "How dydd I know thatt ev'ry darte
>   "That cutte the airie waie
> "Myghte notte fynde passage toe my harte
>   "And close myne eyes for aie?   (lines 129–36)[27]

The passage's emphasis on keen visual detail – "ev'ry darte / 'That cutte the airie waie" leads to the seat of sensibility, the heart. In its focus on the line of the arrow that separates life from death, the passage points to the power of imagination to see these possibilities. Romantic poet William Blake was to use this image in his unorthodox manifesto, *The Marriage of Heaven and Hell* (1790), to enlarge the reader's perception of the universe, asking, "How do you know but ev'ry Bird that cuts the airy way, / Is an immense world of delight, clos'd by your senses five?"[28] The simplicity and focus in Chatterton's lines, corresponding to his choice of the ballad stanza, work in counterpoint with the complexity of the unfamiliar language and peculiarities of imagery. In this early example of his use of Rowleyan language, Chatterton is just beginning to introduce a reorientation to "earlier" English and with it a reorientation of the work of poetry. The difficulty of his language increases in his later Rowleyan works such as the "Chorus" fragment from his drama *Goddwyn* (written about May 1769, published 1777). The atmosphere is dense and alien as we wade through the unfamiliar language that leads us to Freedom and Death, familiar personifications to eighteenth-century readers:

> Whan Freedom dreste, yn blodde steyned Veste,
>   To everie Knyghte her Warre Songe sunge;
> Uponne her hedde, wylde Wedes were spredde,
>   A gorie Anlace bye her honge.
>   She daunced onne the Heathe,
>   She hearde the Voice of Deathe;
> Pale-eyned Affryghte hys harte of Sylver hue,
> In vayne assayled [endeavored] her bosomme to acale [freeze]. . .
>   (lines 196–203)[29]

In earlier-eighteenth-century poetry such personifications would have the effect of including the reader in a shared iconographical and literary community; but here personifications appear forbidding and exclusive in a language that expresses the obscurity of primeval, Titanic forces.

The work's increased use of Rowleyan language makes the act of reading unavoidably self-conscious as we can no longer rely on our usual ways of making sense of poetry. Language reveals itself as matter with an obstructing consistency: language is no longer the dress of thought, as the Augustans saw it, but a quasi-opaque body. Chatterton's language is singularly isolated and isolating. Unlike conventional eighteenth-century poetic diction which uses a vocabulary shared by a readership, albeit an elite one, versed especially in the classics, Chatterton's Rowleyan diction has no existing community that shares its language. That Chatterton understood the "principle" of fifteenth-century language to be "lawlessness" makes its implications for poetry and the poet's relation to the reader especially intriguing.[30] Based on lawlessness, the language cannot be wholly shared. With its possibilities for variation virtually endless, Rowleyan language grants the poet an extreme authority over the reader that nevertheless reaffirms the poet's isolation. Just as Chatterton effaced his role as author, the linguistic strangeness of the poems risks estranging the reader as well. Using language to push the reader into a Nature or reality made strange, Chatterton's Rowley poetry is at once supremely elitist and democratic: its community must be made, with every reader entering into Chatterton's language on an equal footing, humbly guided by his "editorial" glosses.

Underlying the contested categories of the authentic and the real is the problem of what constitutes Nature in these decades. As the century wore on, like the self, Nature is understood less as a universal system and more as a series of individuated particulars – the consequences of an empirical view of Nature where particular perceptions erode a unifying organization. What constitutes Nature and the self, and how these two categories pertain to "the real" can be seen in late-eighteenth-century uses of the sublime. Although the sublime is an aesthetic criterion valued throughout the eighteenth century, it is a feature often associated with the Romantic project. While there are as many versions of the sublime as there are poems and theories of it, in a typical scenario, the human subject is awed or terrified by the sublime in nature. Although the effect of the sublime is to render the person experiencing it powerless, the encounter simultaneously expands and raises the mind, allowing it to repossess itself in a dynamic of transcendence.[31] The sublime requires a self that is stable enough to confront and survive the abyss. There is "nothing sublime," wrote Edmund Burke in his *Philosophical Enquiry into the Origin of Our Ideas of the Sublime and the Beautiful* (1759), "which is not some modification of power."[32] In late-eighteenth-century poetry we find many elements of the sublime but it is often a sublime manqué. Not unlike Samuel Johnson's satire manqué, the sublime manqué is foiled or bent by the pressure of the human, preferring human sentiment and strength over the power of a non-human Nature. [33]

A lover's passion and courage impinge on the sublime of nature in Burns's poem "Oh wert thou in the cauld blast." Written in 1796 for the woman who helped nurse him shortly before his death at the age of thirty-seven, this was one of the last poems Burns wrote:

> Oh wert thou in the cauld blast,
> > On yonder lea, on yonder lea;

> My plaidie to the angry airt,
>   I'd shelter thee, I'd shelter thee:
> Or did misfortune's bitter storms
>   Around thee blaw, around thee blaw,
> Thy bield [shield] should be my bosom,
>   To share it a', to share it a'.   (lines 1–8)

The poem's emphasis on emotion combines the conventions of the sentimental movement with the conventions of the sublime, where the harsh elements of the Scottish landscape show a native sublime.[34] But powerful Nature is subordinated to the heroic self-sacrifice of the lover, who possesses a Scottish courage, defying the "angry airt" with his plaid. Human emotion is presented as such instead of expanded into a transcendental system normally associated with the sublime. While heroic, this self is not what we expect from Romantic poetry: Burns's lover does not expand to contain the sublime. Unlike the Romantic poet who relates to the sublime through an isolation that is transcended during the sublime experience, Burns's speaker counters the sublime through love of another human, creating a community of two that is both powerful and earthbound.

The human sublime was a variety of the sublime that Hugh Blair described in his *Lectures on Rhetoric and Belles Lettres* (1783) as the "moral or sentimental sublime; arising from certain exertions of the human mind; from certain affections, and actions, of our fellow-creatures." This sublime is a kind of "heroism" of "high virtue" whenever "we behold a man uncommonly intrepid, and resting upon himself; . . . animated by some great principle to the contempt of popular opinion, of selfish interest, of dangers, or of death."[35] In an era commonly associated with poetic failure, we find much heroism, but it is a heroism that defines itself in small communities, often of only two. Anna Letitia Barbauld places the "moral or sentimental sublime" in the context of maternity in "To a little invisible Being who is expected soon to become visible" (w.c. 1795). The pregnant woman

>   only asks to lay her burden down,
> That her glad arms that burden may resume;
> And nature's sharpest pangs her wishes crown,
> That free thee living from thy living tomb.   (lines 17–20)[36]

Here the agony and danger of "nature's sharpest pangs" are too real to correspond to the conventional luxury of the sublime subject that can delight in terror precisely because he is in a position of safety: the material reality of dying in childbirth would have resonated for contemporary readers, a possibility glanced at in the figure of the "living tomb." Barbauld locates the marvelously real in a human sublime founded in the marvel of reproduction as the "invisible being" is imagined in his or her potential:

> Germ of new life, whose powers expanding slow
> For many a moon their full perfection wait, –
> Haste, precious pledge of happy love, to go
> Auspicious borne through life's mysterious gate.   (lines 1–4)

A wondrous potential of human capacity, the "invisible being" cannot yet guess "thy lofty claim / To grasp at all the worlds the Almighty wrought!" (lines 7–8). Securely stationed in a Christian worldview, the unborn child embryonically grasps the infinite without the unappeasable yearning of the Romantic poet. Mother and baby are heroes in a Nature that possesses much of the unity and harmony of a Christian worldview associated with the earlier eighteenth century, although this view is seen in the unfamiliar light of maternity and reproduction. This is a sublime founded on community and love rather than isolation and terror.

In "Yardley Oak" (w. 1792?), Cowper invokes the natural sublime to arrive at a prelapsarian community where Adamic language makes poetic language unnecessary. The poem is a sustained apostrophe to an ancient tree reputed to have existed since the time of William the Conqueror. Although the apostrophe to the tree may suggest an animation and elevation of nature akin to the Romantics, Cowper rejects pantheism in favor of a human spirituality. The tree is an object of the speaker's sensibility and a mirror of the speaker's self. Like the poet it is isolated, forgotten, and old: "Thou, like myself, hast stage by stage attain'd / Life's wintry bourn" (lines 144–45). The oak is

> Embowell'd now, and of they antient self
> Possessing naught but the scoop'd rind, that seems
> An huge throat calling to the clouds for drink.   (lines 110–12)

This powerful, mute voice on the verge of articulation figures the poet's concern with a language that will reach the divine. Recalling the ancient oracular trees of Dodona that could speak, the speaker responds to the mute oak: "I will perform / Myself the oracle" (lines 141–42).

Although an oracle, the speaker eschews the self-aggrandizing role of the poet-prophet, turning instead to the past. There he returns to the moment when Adam, naming the creatures,

> At once, unstood intelligent, survey'd
> All creatures, with precision understood
> Their purport, uses, properties, assign'd
> To each his name significant, and, fill'd

> With Love and Wisdom, render'd back to heav'n
> In praise harmonious the first air he drew.   (lines 173–78)

Prelapsarian man and language literally arrest the poem in its last lines:

> History, not wanted yet,
> Lean'd on her elbow, watching Time, whose course
> Eventful should supply her with a theme . . .   (lines 182–84)

Although a sublime object, the great oak is eclipsed by Adam's language, which arrests fallen representation and its worldly tropes of History and Time. Cowper's encounter with the sublime surrenders poetry up to the greater authority of the human divine. Unlike Collins's Tree of Poetry, this tree makes sublime Nature and the poetic tradition vanish in the presence of an unfallen humanity. Cowper does not fall from the tree, but through identifying with its decay he imagines his way back to a prelapsarian condition that needs no poet. Time, history, and poetry come with the Fall; with a return to spiritual wholeness, poetry as therapy comes to an end.

The assertion of a human sublime is countered in this period by a frequent poetic linking of the self with insubstantiality, fragility, ephemerality, and emptiness. This tendency, which increases during the eighteenth century, to scrutinize and question substance itself is an outgrowth of empiricism that reaches its skeptical extreme in Hume.[37] In showing what disappears, these poems present the void without filling it with a Romantic self. In Book v of Cowper's *The Task*, the poet's careful observations of his surroundings reveal a succession of details that eventually empty the self. Observing "a length of shadow o'er the field" that stretches "From ev'ry herb and ev'ry spiry blade," the speaker sees his own shadow "spindling into longitude immense" (v, lines 9–11). "In spite of gravity and sage remark / That I myself am but a fleeting shade," this spectre of himself, "Provokes me to a smile" (v, lines 12–14):

> With eye askance
> I view the muscular proportion'd limb
> Transform'd to a lean shank. The shapeless pair
> As they design'd to mock me, at my side
> Take step for step, and, as I near approach
> The cottage, walk along the plaister'd wall,
> Prepost'rous sight! the legs without the man.   (v, lines 14–20)

Such disappearances describe the speaker's relation to his social surroundings throughout *The Task*. Even though he insists on some connections with society, as in his sanguine outburst "Society for me!" (I, line 249), the social self in Cowper is often a withdrawing self that seeks "blest seclusion from a jarring world" (III, line 675).

The precariousness of the poet represented in many late-eighteenth-century works unfortunately mirrors their disappearance from literary history. In Charlotte Smith's "To the insect of the gossamer," the poet is perpetually on the verge of destruction by external forces. Smith's botanical eye compares the fragility of the poetic character to a minute spider in one of Nature's most fragile frames: [38]

> Small, viewless Aeronaut, that by the line
> > Of Gossamer suspended, in mid air
> > Float'st on a sun beam – Living Atom, where
> Ends thy breeze-guided voyage; – with what design
> > In Aether dost thou launch thy form minute,
> Mocking the eye? – Alas! before the veil
> > Of denser clouds shall hide thee, the pursuit
> Of the keen Swift may end thy fairy sail! –   (lines 1–8)

The poet's "gossamer" is woven by Fancy, which temporarily suspends the "young and visionary Poet" from mundane reality "while sevenfold wreaths / Of rainbow-light around his head revolve" (lines 12–13). This quasi-divine image of the poet suspended by a "golden thread" of fancy may suggest still more glorious images of the poet such as Coleridge's poet-magus in "Kubla Khan":

> Weave a circle round him thrice,
> And close your eyes with holy dread,
> For he on honey-dew hath fed,
> And drunk the milk of Paradise.   (lines 51–54)

Whereas Coleridge's poet inspires awe, Smith's inspires pity: "at Sorrow's touch" her poet's "radiant dreams dissolve!" (line 14) as the poet and his "golden threads" are abruptly destroyed.

The differences between Smith's "eighteenth-century" poem and Coleridge's "Romantic" poem (both of them published in the 1790s) may be further explored. Coleridge's poet is imbued with a potential that indicates an imminent triumph; he envisions his powers as surmounting nature, reviving the song of the Abyssinian maid to build in the future "that dome in air" (line 46). Instead of looking to the future, insofar as Smith's poet resembles the insect of the gossamer, the poet looks behind. In a footnote to the poem, Smith quotes the naturalist Dr. Lister's observation of this "minute species of spider": "to the purpose of rowing themselves along in the air, it is observable that they ever take their flight backward, that is, their head looking a contrary way like a sculler upon the Thames." In Coleridge's poem the poet

has a future unimpeded by external forces since the poet makes his own society, which is himself. Smith's poet is vulnerable precisely because he erects a dome in air – the gossamer web. Smith's poet soars, although, like the insects of the gossamer, as Dr. Lister explains, to "fly they cannot strictly be said, they being carried into the air by external force; but they can, in case the wind suffer them, steer their course, perhaps mount and descend at pleasure." Buoyed and restricted by nature, Smith's poet sings in his chains. For most readers today, such a loss of autonomy where the authorial subject even disappears may look less like a dim precursor of Romanticism and more like a paradigm of postmodernism.

There is a beauty in these fragile ends of eighteenth-century poetry, and poet and poetry appear together in marvelous fragility in Barbauld's "Washing-Day."[39] Barbauld's poetry rarely gives the sense of doom or despair often assigned to late-eighteenth-century poetry; rather, it investigates poetic alternatives with an elusive blend of the serio-comic. "Washing-Day" uses precise, realistic details to reveal the mysteries of the quotidian, where poetry and the world have both the substance and the ephemerality of a bubble. In adopting the bubble of soap used during the onerous "washing-day," Barbauld attends to alternative sources of poetry, women's labor, which she combines with alternative language. Thus she announces that "The Muses are turned gossips; they have lost / The buskin'd step, and clear high-sounding phrase, / Language of gods" (lines 1–3). The "domestic Muse, / In slip-shod measure loosely prattling on" (lines 3–4) will by the end of the poem explore no less than ontological questions through the image of the bubble. In the poem's conclusion, the speaker recalls sitting down as a child to "ponder much / Why washings were":

> Sometimes thro' hollow bole
> Of pipe amused we blew, and sent aloft
> The floating bubbles, little dreaming then
> To see, Montgolfier, thy silken ball
> Ride buoyant thro' the clouds – so near approach
> The sports of children and the toils of men.
> Earth, air, and sky, and ocean, hath its bubbles,
> And verse is one of them – this most of all.   (lines 78–86)

Barbauld's use of caesura, a figure of pause, and the suspending dash underscore the poem's concern with what is empty and open as well as what it connects and contains, where the unifying sphere connotes its imminent dissolution. Barbauld's question – "Why washings were" – turns an epistemological inquiry into an ontological one, where perceptions and analogies

predominate. Using the avowedly humble language of the domestic muse and the insights of the child, the poem transports the reader from domestic labor to the utmost boundaries of the world, boundaries that, depending on our perspective, may form or burst the imaginative bubble.

The shift in eighteenth-century poetry towards sensibility, social realism, and evanescence has been explained by some critics as a consequence of the ongoing inquiries of the Enlightenment itself, whose effects also led to the French Revolution – an event that although usually associated with Romantic literature can be seen as a culmination of Enlightenment thinking. Others have attributed the "crisis" in poetry of the last decades of the eighteenth century to the increasing commodification of art and artist, leaving the poet in an alienated condition to negotiate or defy the vagaries of the literary marketplace. (When Chatterton created his fictional poet Rowley, he added a telling detail to his antiquarian findings: he gave Rowley a magnanimous patron, Chatterton's response to his detachment from the patronage that he associated with England's past.) Still other critics associate late-eighteenth-century, as opposed to Augustan or Romantic, poetry with a culture of the feminine that placed a high value on stereotypically feminine qualities such as sensibility and that saw increasing numbers of women reading and writing poetry. These were the qualities that canonical Romantic poets would appropriate through metaphors of conquest to make poetry appear manly again.[40]

In understanding the ends of eighteenth-century poetry it is important to free them from merely anticipating the Romantics as well as to understand what the Romantics learned from them. The twentieth century has seen increasing attempts to understand the Romantics outside of the terms of Romantic ideology itself, with its claims to imagination, originality, and radicalism. In recent years, the Romantic chronological boundaries have been moved to include more of the eighteenth century. But despite the fact that Romantic ideology was available well before 1789, there are substantive differences between poets of the Romantic canon and those of the late eighteenth century. Attempts to pre-date Romanticism accurately acknowledge the elements shared by late-eighteenth-century and Romantic poetry but fail to acknowledge some of the aesthetic and psychological challenges specific to mid- and late-eighteenth-century poetry. Romantic poets would transform the notions of the poet and poetic faculties while standing on the shoulders of late-eighteenth-century writers: most Romantics learned that they had to create systems that would elevate or ironize the self in order to keep at bay the anguished or complicated psychological and social uncertainties explored by their predecessors. Wordsworth, for example, would transfigure

Nature as an order for defining a transcendent ego; Blake would reject Nature and the self altogether, locating his notion of "vision" in the discrimination of minute particulars by a human form divine. But before the Romantics, poets such as Cowper and Smith had inherited a vestigial notion of the self as "partly constituted by social context," which, like the phantom pain of an amputated member, continued to haunt their exploration of the self alone.[41] The radicalism and rebelliousness associated with the Romantics can be discerned in poets of the end of the eighteenth century whose sensibility informed many of the poems they wrote to defend the oppressed, including slaves, the poor, and children. But there is also a subtler radicalism in these poets betrayed by Nature though alive to its particulars. Whether suspended by, at best, an indifferent Nature or with feet firmly planted on the ground wearing their "hoddin gray," the radicalism of late-eighteenth-century poets is to investigate the precariousness and the strength of humanity often denied the consolation of transcendence that a large system could offer. As a result they question the self's relation to others, including how that relation might be best represented.

NOTES

1 See Northrop Frye, "Towards Defining an Age of Sensibility," in *Fables of Identity: Studies in Poetic Mythology* (New York: Harcourt, Brace & World, 1963), pp. 130–37 (first published in *ELH* 23: 2 [1956]).

2 Marshall Brown, *Preromanticism* (Stanford: Stanford University Press, 1991), p. 2.

3 *Ibid.*, p. 3.

4 Quoted in René Wellek, "The Concept of Romanticism in Literary History," in Robert F. Gleckner and Gerald E. Enscoe (eds.), *Romanticism: Points of View* (Englewood Cliffs, NJ: Prentice-Hall, 1970), p. 189 (first published in *Comparative Literature* 1 [1940]).

5 Quoted in Robert J. Griffin, *Wordsworth's Pope: a Study in Literary Historiography* (Cambridge: Cambridge University Press, 1995), p. 20.

6 Quoted in Richard Wendorf, *William Collins and Eighteenth-Century English Poetry* (Minneapolis: University of Minnesota Press, 1981), p. 9, from *The Poems of William Collins*, ed. William Crowe (Bath, 1828), pp. ix–xi. The story, notes Wendorf, may be apocryphal (p. 201*n*).

7 For an account of mid- and late-eighteenth-century poets as aliens, rebels, or religious pilgrims, see T. E. Blom, "Eighteenth-Century Reflexive Process Poetry," *Eighteenth-Century Studies* 10:1 (1976), 54–55.

8 See Blom's discussion in "Eighteenth-Century Reflexive Process Poetry" of the so-called inadequacy of later-eighteenth-century poetry as the inadequacy of the reader, p. 53.

9 See James Sambrook, "Introduction," *William Cowper: The Task and Selected Other Poems* (London and New York: Longman, 1994), p. 10.

10 See Deborah Heller, "Cowper's *Task* and the Writing of a Poet's Salvation," *Studies in English Literature* 35:3 (1995), 575–98.

11 William Cowper, *The Task and Selected Other Poems*, ed. James Sambrook (London and New York: Longman, 1994), pp. 114–15; all citations are from this edition.

12 Adela Pinch, *Strange Fits of Passion: Epistemologies of Emotion, Hume to Austen* (Stanford: Stanford University Press, 1996), pp. 55–58.

13 Quoted in Loraine Fletcher, *Charlotte Smith: a Critical Biography* (Basingstoke and London: Macmillan, 1998; New York: St. Martin's Press, 1998), p. 101.

14 *The Poems of Charlotte Smith*, ed. Stuart Curran (New York and Oxford: Oxford University Press, 1993), p. 13; all citations are from this edition.

15 On Smith's use of Petrarchan elements, see Stuart Curran, "Introduction," *The Poems of Charlotte Smith*, p xxv.

16 *The Poems of Anne Countess of Winchilsea*, ed. Myra Reynolds (Chicago: The University of Chicago Press, 1903), p. 268. See Deborah Kennedy, "Thorns and Roses: the Sonnets of Charlotte Smith," *Women's Writing* 2: 1 (1995), pp. 43–53.

17 See Pinch, *Strange Fits of Passion*, p 62.

18 In *Strange Fits of Passion*, Pinch analyzes the relation of Smith's quotations to the literary tradition, p 69.

19 For a discussion of the variety of ways in which Burns's art has been seen as lacking, see Carol McGuirk, *Robert Burns and the Sentimental Era* (Athens and London: University of Georgia Press, 1985), especially pp xxii and xxvi.

20 *Ibid.*, p. 106.

21 *Burns: Poems and Songs*, ed. James Kinsley (Oxford and New York: Oxford University Press, 1988), p. 602; all citations are from this edition.

22 Quoted by Jerome J. McGann, "The Anachronism of George Crabbe," *ELH* 48: 3 (1981), 555, from Coleridge's *Table-Talk* and *Omniana*, ed. T. Ashe (London, 1884), p. 276.

23 Quoted by McGann, "The Anachronism of George Crabbe," from Wordsworth's letter to Samuel Rogers, 29 September 1808, in *The Letters of William and Dorothy Wordsworth*, ed. Ernest de Selincourt, 2nd. edn., rev. by Mary Moorman (Oxford, 1969), p. 268.

24 McGann, "The Anachronism of George Crabbe," pp. 557 and 562.

25 *George Crabbe: Selected Poems*, ed. Gavin Edwards (London and New York: Penguin Books, 1991), p. 6; all citations are from this edition.

26 On the era's concern with antiquarian sources, see Nick Groom, "Forgery or Plagiarism?: Unravelling Chatterton's Rowley," *Angelaki* 1: 2 (1993–94), 41–54.

27 *The Complete Works of Thomas Chatterton: a Bicentenary Edition*, ed. Donald Taylor, 2 vols. (Oxford: Clarendon Press, 1971), p. 11; all citations are from this edition.

28 *The Complete Poetry and Prose of William Blake*, Newly Revised Edition, ed. David V. Erdman (Berkeley and Los Angeles: University of California Press, 1982), p. 35.

29 Chatterton, *Complete Works*, pp. 304–5.

30 Donald S. Taylor, *Thomas Chatterton's Art: Experiments in Imagined History* (Princeton, NJ: Princeton University Press, 1978), p. 49.

31 On the Romantic sublime, see Thomas Weiskel, *The Romantic Sublime: Studies in the Structure and Psychology of Transcendence* (Baltimore and London: Johns Hopkins University Press, 1976).

32 *A Philosophical Enquiry into the Origin of our Ideas of the Sublime and*

Beautiful, ed. and introd. Adam Phillips (Oxford and New York: Oxford University Press, 1990), p. 59.

33 W. Jackson Bate, "Johnson and Satire Manque," in W. H. Bond (ed.), *Eighteenth-Century Studies in Honor of Donald F. Hyde* (New York: Grolier Club, 1970), pp. 145–60.

34 On Burns's poetry in the context of Sentimentalism, see McGuirk, *Robert Burns and the Sentimental Era.*

35 Hugh Blair, from *Lectures on Rhetoric and Belles Lettres* (1783) in Andrew Ashfield and Peter de Bolla (eds.), *The Sublime: a Reader in British Eighteenth-Century Aesthetic Theory* (Cambridge: Cambridge University Press, 1996), p. 215.

36 *The Poems of Anna Letitia Barbauld,* ed. William McCarthy and Elizabeth Kraft (Athens and London: University of Georgia Press), p. 131; all citations are from this edition.

37 See Fredric V. Bogel, *Literature and Insubstantiality in Later Eighteenth-Century England* (Princeton, NJ: Princeton University Press, 1984).

38 See Judith Pascoe, "Female Botanists and the Poetry of Charlotte Smith," in Carol Shiner Wilson and Joel Haefner (eds.), *Re-Visioning Romanticism: British Women Writers, 1776–1837* (Philadelphia: University of Pennsylvania Press, 1994), pp. 193–209.

39 Published in 1797, although Elizabeth Kraft suggests it "may have been composed in the 1780s"; see her "Anna Letitia Barbauld's 'Washing-Day' and the Montgolfier Balloon," *Literature and History* 4: 2 (1995), 30.

40 Marlon B. Ross, *The Contours of Masculine Desire: Romanticism and the Rise of Women's Poetry* (New York and Oxford: Oxford University Press, 1989), especially p. 22. Women poets in the last decades of the eighteenth century will continue to play an interesting part in periodizing eighteenth-century as opposed to Romantic poetry. Of the poets discussed here, Chatterton, Cowper, Burns, and Crabbe are typically considered a part of the canon, and yet, like Barbauld and Smith, they rarely appear in surveys of the literature. With the increased interest in women writers, Barbauld and Smith may appear on more syllabuses than their male contemporaries as readers look for new ways to understand the relationship between eighteenth-century and Romantic poetry.

41 See Patricia Meyer Spacks, "'The Bonds of Nature': Mid-Century Poetry," in Christopher Fox (ed.), *Teaching Eighteenth-Century Poetry* (New York: AMS Press, 1990), pp. 61–73; p. 70.

FURTHER READING

Bate, W. Jackson. *The Burden of the Past and the English Poet.* New York: W. W. Norton, 1970.

Blom, T. E. "Eighteenth-Century Reflexive Process Poetry," *Eighteenth-Century Studies* 10, 1 (1976), 52–72.

Bogel, Fredric V. *Literature and Insubstantiality in Later Eighteenth-Century England.* Princeton, NJ: Princeton University Press, 1984.

Brown, Marshall. *Preromanticism.* Stanford: Stanford University Press, 1991.

Butler, Marilyn. *Romantics, Rebels, and Reactionaries: English Literature and Its Background 1760–1830.* Oxford and New York: Oxford University Press, 1981.

Crawford, Robert (ed.). *Robert Burns and Cultural Authority*. Iowa City: University of Iowa Press, 1997.

Davie, Donald. *The Eighteenth-Century Hymn in England*. Cambridge: Cambridge University Press, 1993.

Day, Aidan. *Romanticism*. London and New York: Routledge, 1996.

Doody, Margaret Anne. *The Daring Muse: Augustan Poetry Reconsidered*. Cambridge: Cambridge University Press, 1985.

Frye, Northrop. "Towards Defining an Age of Sensibility," in *Fables of Identity: Studies in Poetic Mythology*. New York: Harcourt, Brace & World, 1963. 130–37.

Griffin, Robert J. *Wordsworth's Pope: a Study in Literary Historiography*. Cambridge: Cambridge University Press, 1995.

Kraft, Elizabeth. "Anna Letitia Barbauld's 'Washing-Day' and the Montgolfier Balloon," *Literature and History* 4: 2 (1995), 25–41.

McGann, Jerome J. "The Anachronism of George Crabbe," *ELH* 48: 3 (1981), 555–72.

McGuirk, Carol. *Robert Burns and the Sentimental Era*. Athens: University of Georgia Press, 1985.

Priestman, Martin. *Cowper's Task: Structure and Influence*. Cambridge: Cambridge University Press, 1983.

Ross, Marlon B. *The Contours of Masculine Desire: Romanticism and the Rise of Women's Poetry*. New York and Oxford: Oxford University Press, 1989.

Taylor, Donald S. *Thomas Chatterton's Art: Experiments in Imagined History*. Princeton, NJ: Princeton University Press, 1978.

Whitehead, Frank. *George Crabbe: a Reappraisal*. Selinsgrove: Susquehanna University Press, 1995; London: Associated University Presses, 1995.

Woodman, Thomas (ed.). *Early Romantics: Perspectives in British Poetry from Pope to Wordsworth*. Basingstoke and London: Macmillan, 1998; New York: St. Martin's Press, 1998.

INDEX

Abrams, M. H., 148
Act of Union, 98
Addison, Joseph, 12, 137, 162; "Account of the Greatest English Poets," 180; *The Campaign*, 1, 41; *Cato*, 38, 162; *Spectator*, 76, 103, 142–45, 185, 211, 238, 244; on ballad of Chevy Chase, 211; as critic, 142–45; on dreams, 238; on Milton, 143–44, 185, 228; periodicals, 84–85; the Pleasures of the Imagination, 103, 140, 142–45, 185, 244; politeness as ideology, 87; Whig circles, 37–38; wit, true and false, 139–40
"Age of Sensibility," 271
Akenside, Mark, 52, 210–11, 217; *Epistle to Curio*, 51; "On Lyric Poetry," 204; *Odes on Several Subjects*, 203–4; *Pleasures of the Imagination*, 70, 137, 142, 146, 188, 244; *The Voice of Liberty: a British Phillipic*, 49, 187; business with publisher Robert Dodsley, 70; and English native tradition, 179; Greek lyric as influence, 204, 208; as Newcastle poet, 96; poetry and philosophy reconnected, 137, 142; as "pre-Romantic," 272; condemnation of Walpole, 45
Anne, Queen, 38, 40, 42, 158–59
Anstey, Christopher, 97–98, 122
Antoinette, Marie, 260
Arbuthnot, John, 38, 87
Ariès, Philippe, 235
Arnold, Richard, 214
Aristotle, 149
Armstrong, John, 190
Astell, Mary, 158, 159
Atterbury, Francis, 44
Atwood, William, 41
Auden, W. H., 232
Austen, Jane, 249

Bacon, Sir Francis, 136
Baillie, Joanna, 103–4, 171
ballad, 211, 213
Ballard, George, 169
Barbauld, Anna Letitia, "Dejection," 258; "On Mrs. Priestley's Leaving Warrington," 254; "To a little invisible Being who is expected soon to become visible," 281–82; "Washing-Day," 285–86
Barber, Mary, 163–64, 168, 262; "On seeing an Officer's Widow distracted," 261; in *Poems by Eminent Ladies*, 74, 169
Barker-Benfield, G. J., 257–58
Bath, literary representations of, 96–98
Bathurst, Lord, 46, 227
Baxter, Andrew, 242
Beattie, James, 149–50, 197; *The Minstrel*, 52, 118, 183–84
Bedingfield, Robert, 184
Behn, Aphra, 12, 63, 74, 160, 169
Bell, John, 75
Berkeley, Bishop George, 112, 242
Blackmore, Richard, 12, 37, 49
Blackwell, Anthony, 134, 150
Blair, Hugh, 147, 149, 281
Blair, Robert, 231, 235
Blake, William, 8, 173, 287; "The Human Abstract," 237; "London," 83, 85–87; illustration for Gray's "Ode on a Distant Prospect of Eton College," 242–43
blank verse, 24–25, 120–21, 186–90, 196–97
Bloom, Harold, 272
Blount, Martha, 6
Bluestocking Circle, 168–69
Blunt, John, 43, 46
Boileau-Despreaux, Nicolas, 187
Bolingbroke, Henry St. John, Viscount, 6, 27, 38, 42, 45, 46, 50, 57, 167

Index

Dennis, John, 141–42, 143, 149, 150, 228

desire in eighteenth-century poetry, 226–32

Dissanayake, Ellen, 153

Dixon, Sarah, 168

Dodsley, Robert, 70, 72, 73, 75, 78, 217, 218

Dollimore, Jonathan, 232

Donaldson, Alexander, 70–71, 75

Donne, John, 6, 227, 274

dreams in eighteenth-century poetry, 237–46

Dryden, John, 12, 63, 75, 160, 168, 206; *Absalom and Achitophel*, 39; *Annus Mirabilis*, 85; *MacFlecknoe*, 70, 233; "To Congreve," 22; on the "fairy way of writing," 144; influence on women poets, 162; odes to music, 203; on the progressive development of English poetry, 178–80; his refinement of English style, 151, 196; on "the rules," 135; Anna Seward's praise of his verse, 171–72; translation of Virgil, 114

Duck, Stephen, 123–24, 165, 212

Duncomb, John, 170

Dunton, John, 76, 77

Dyer, John, The Fleece, 2, 54–55, 114–15, 190; *Grongar Hill*, 117–18; *The Ruins of Rome*, 225; blank verse, 190; on British dominance, 2, 54–55, 114–15

Edinburgh, literary representations of, 98–100

Edwards, Thomas, 217

Egerton, Sarah Fye, 12, 22, 158, 159

elegy, 191–92, 210–11, 232–33

Elizabeth I, Queen, 41, 91

epitaph, 22, 232–34

Eusden, Lawrence, 42

Feldman, Paula R., 216

Fergusson, Robert, 99–100

Fielding, Henry, 45, 69

Finch, Anne, Countess of Winchilsea, 12, 159–62; "The Introduction," 160; "A Nocturnal Reverie," 159; in *Poems by Eminent Ladies*, 74, 169; influence on Charlotte Smith, 275; response to Pope, 160

Frederick, Prince of Wales, 48–49, 50

Freemantle, Bridget, 165

Freeth, John, 96

Freud, Sigmund, 136, 244

Frye, Northrop, 250, 271

Fuseli, Henry, 244, 245 (illustration)

future, as imagined in eighteenth-century poetry, 1–9

Garrick, David, 172

Gay, John, 46, 161; "Panegyrical Epistle to Mr. Thomas Snow," 43–44; *The Shepherd's Week*, 42, 116–17; *Trivia: or, the Art of Walking the Streets of London*, 86, 87–90, 99; burlesque of Ambrose Philips, 42, 116–17; use of the couplet, 22; critic of Walpole, 45; own epitaph, 22, 233–34; friend to Pope and Scriblerians, 38, 42, 161

Gentleman's Magazine, 77, 167–68

George II, King, 47

George III, King, 55, 57

georgic, 114–16, 188–90

Gerard, Alexander, 142

Gildon, Charles, 137, 138, 140–41

Gloucester, Duke of, 42

Glover, Richard, 48, 49

Godolphin, Sidney, 39

Goethe, 171

Goldsmith, Oliver, 197; *The Deserted Village*, 4, 57–58, 99, 122–23, 237, 257, 266; "Elegy on the Death of a Mad Dog," 233; *The Traveller, or a Prospect of Society*, 256, 265–66; contributions to Tory *Critical Review*, 77, member of Johnson's "Club," 74; as poet of sensibility, 257, 265–67; taken to task by George Crabbe, 123

Grainger, James, 115–16

Granville, George, Lord Lansdowne, 40

Graves, Richard, 72

Gray, Thomas, 52, 72–73, 250, 272; "The Bard," 52, 73, 99, 125–26, 195, 207; *Elegy Written in a Country Churchyard*, 3, 57, 73, 118, 210–11, 235, 237, 263; "Hymn to Adversity," 254–55; "Ode on the Death of a Favorite Cat, Drowned in a Tub of Gold Fishes," 233; "Ode on a Distant Prospect of Eton College," 241–42, 263; "The Progress of Poesy," 195, 207; "Sketch of His Own Character," 263; "Sonnet on the Death of Richard West," 217, 254; influence on Charlotte Smith, 171; on the language of the age, 151; odes, 79, 204, 207, 213; as poet of sensibility, 263–64, 267; Wordsworth's attack on, 216

Grenville, Richard, 48